GREAT
JEWISH
WOMEN

GREAT JEWISH WOMEN

Elinor Slater
and
Robert Slater

Jonathan David Publishers, Inc.
Middle Village, New York 11379

GREAT JEWISH WOMEN

Jonathan David Publishers, Inc.
68-22 Eliot Avenue
Middle Village, New York 11379

6 8 10 9 7 5

Library of Congress Cataloging-in-Publication Data

Slater, Robert, 1943 – and Slater, Elinor, 1944 –
    Great Jewish women/by Robert Slater & Elinor Slater
        p.   cm.
    Includes index.
    ISBN 0-8246-0370-2
    1. Jewish women—Biography.   I. Title
DS115.2.S59   1994
920.72'089924—dc20

93-43345
CIP

Book design by Jennifer Vignone
Printed in the United States of America

In Loving Memory
Dorothy Nachman Resnik
An Extraordinary Jewish Woman

ACKNOWLEDGEMENTS

When we began the research for *Great Jewish Women,* we quickly discovered, to our delight, that nearly everyone to whom we mentioned our book project offered helpful advice. However, this makes the task of acknowledging those who contributed to this book especially challenging.

A casual conversation with a friend or relative frequently began with, "What's going on in your life?" and moved quickly to a heated, but friendly, exchange over who we should and should not include on our list of the one hundred most prominent Jewish women in history. Moreover, we were amused—and bemused—by some evening get-togethers with friends at which the main topic of discussion became who our guests thought should be on our list.

We were also heartened to find that when we asked one relative or friend via electronic mail for his or her thoughts on our list, each person took the request seriously, and even asked others for their comments. One relative sent this message via electronic mail: "The subject became the main agenda at some of the finest Thanksgiving feasts from coast to coast."

Trying to thank individually the hundreds of people who took part in these "debates" is futile, but we hope that they understand how much we appreciate their interest and their input. While they may have felt that all they were doing was taking part in an interesting discussion, for us it was part of our research. We listened carefully to all of our friends and relatives, and gained a good deal of insight into what others thought about the kind of book we were trying to shape. Of course, the final decisions were ours.

Based on all of those spirited conversations, we are quite sure that our list will not please everyone fully. To do that, we learned early on, was an impossible mission. It will not surprise us that some will take exception to some of our choices. Readers will evaluate our list from their own points of view. We, however, began the project with a whole set of objectives that we thought would allow us to produce the most interesting and most relevant book possible.

To all of you whose names are not mentioned specifically here, please be assured that your recommendations did help us produce *Great Jewish Women.*

One of our greatest joys was in contacting a number of the women who appear in this book and asking them to answer some questions for our profiles. We wish to thank those whom we interviewed or with whom we corresponded: Bella Abzug, Amy Alcott, Yael Arad, Barbara Boxer, Dianne Feinstein, Ruth Bader Ginsburg, Leah Gottlieb, Rose Heilbron, Carolyn Heilbrun, Agnes Keleti, Ann Landers, Gertrude Michelson, Rita Levi-Montalcini, Bess Myerson, Ida Nudel, Sally Priesand, Miriam Rothschild, Angelica Rozeanu, Naomi Shemer, Helen Suzman, Simone Veil, Linda Wachner, Barbara Walters, Wendy Wasserstein, Ruth Westheimer, and Rosalyn S. Yalow.

A number of associates of the people on our list helped provide background information and sometimes paved the way for interviews with our subjects. We also wish to thank them: Alan Eichorn, Jenny Lyn Bader, Doug Beck, Josh Cohen, Marcella Consolini, Andrew Friedman, Judith Gottlieb, Verna Hunt, Claudette Josephson, Lucy LePage, Shulamit Levi, Lisa Mansoorian, Linda Marson, Rebecca C. McGreevy, Ron Melamed, Kathy Mitchell, Scott Monahan, Christine Montis, Juliet Myers, Linda O'Donnell, Wayne Osborne, Seth Oster, Scott Paulen, Larry Rand, Doug Stokke, and Edgar Vincent.

We thank those people and organizations that provided us with photographs. They are: Mary Ison, Library of Congress, Washington, D.C.; Yehoshua Gafni, Jerusalem Publishing House, Jerusalem, Israel; *The Jewish Forward*, New York, New York; Kevin Proffitt, American Jewish Archives, Cincinnati, Ohio; Moshe Shalvi; Geoffrey Wigoder; Central Zionist Archives, Jerusalem, Israel; Schwadron Collection, Hebrew University, Jerusalem, Israel; Steven Schloss, Managing Editor/Operations, *The Jewish Week*, New York, New York; Mark Solomon, *Time* magazine photo syndication, New York; Israel Government Press Office, Jerusalem, Israel; Amy Kronish, Israel Film Archive, Jerusalem, Israel; Irene Levite; and Amalyah Keshet, Director, Photographic Service, Israel Museum, Jerusalem, Israel.

We wish to thank Toby Atlas, Alice Cooper, Jennifer Frazer, Laura Geller, Shoshana Glatzer, Judith Green, Linda Greenlick, Esther Hecht, Judy Labensohn, Jean Max, Sharon Rosenfelder, Fiona Singer, Ned Temko, Beth Uval, Ruth Weisberg, and Carol Wolff.

We especially want to express our gratitude to Tresa Chambers, a reporter at *Time* magazine, who gave us crucial editorial assistance, helping us to obtain information about a number of the people on our list. We thank her very much. Robert Hughes, the art critic for *Time* magazine, offered us valuable advice. We thank him too.

We are also indebted to Shirley J. Longshore for her fine editing of the manuscript and to Fiorella deLima of Jonathan David Publishers, Inc., for her able assistance in preparing the manuscript for publication.

A special word about our family. Many of our relatives did not simply share their thoughts with us. They served as unofficial advisers to our project, taking a keen interest in our endeavors. We wish to mention specifically our children: Miriam, Shimi, Adam, and Rachel. There were many evenings when we missed a television program or put off doing the dishes in order to update one another on the progress of *Great Jewish Women*.

We also want to thank Judith Resnik, Elinor's sister. A professor of law at the University of Southern California, she gave us the benefit of her wide-ranging knowledge on the subject of Jewish women, especially pertaining to the law. She, for instance, urged us at a very early stage to include Ruth Bader Ginsburg, long before Justice Ginsburg's Supreme Court appointment.

Ruth Fein, a long-time activist for Jewish affairs in Boston, provided much valuable insight and we thank her as well.

We also thank Judd and Roslyn Winick, Jack and Bea Slater, and Michael and Bobbi Winick for taking us under their wings and into their homes during the summer of 1993. This allowed us to establish a foothold in New York, so that we could meet with some of the individuals profiled in these pages.

We conclude with a tribute, a sad one for both of us. Elinor's mother, Dorothy Resnik, who lived near us in Jerusalem, became ill and died while we were in the midst of our research on this book. Before she became ill, she played an active role in its shaping. She took great pleasure in the fact that the two of us were engaged in what she considered such a worthwhile project. Enriching us throughout her years, she led a life that was filled with love and dedication to us, and to all of her children and grandchildren, male and female. That is why we have chosen to dedicate *Great Jewish Women* to her.

In 1950, while in her seventh month of pregnancy, she defended, on appeal, a black man named Willie McGee, who had been sentenced to death for raping a white woman in segregated Mississippi. As his lawyer, Bella challenged the injustice of excluding blacks from juries and of applying the death sentence for rape largely to blacks. The case drew worldwide attention and some Southern newspaper editorial writers attacked her, calling her McGee's "white lady lawyer." However, despite her best efforts McGee was executed in 1951.

During the McCarthy period, when investigations were conducted against people for belonging to Communist groups, many attorneys were not eager to defend the targets of these "witch hunts." Bella Abzug offered her services to a number of civil-service employees who found themselves under such attacks by Senator Joseph McCarthy and his allies.

In the 1960s, during Lyndon B. Johnson's presidency, Bella Abzug helped write the legislation that eventually became the Civil Rights Act of 1964 and the Voting Rights Act of 1965. Later in the decade, when protests began to mount against the war in Vietnam, she was a dominant figure in the "Dump Johnson" movement, which led to President Johnson's decision to not to seek re-election in 1968.

Between 1961 and 1970, Abzug was the director of an anti-war group, Women Strike for Peace. The organization was founded after the United States and the former Soviet Union resumed nuclear testing. In October of 1970, columnist Jimmy Breslin put it well when he remarked that when it came to participation in the peace movement, "Some came early, others came late. Bella has been there forever."

A founder of the reformist New York City political organization called the New Democratic Coalition, Abzug first tried for public office when she ran for Congress as a representative from New York City's 19th district. Though predominantly Jewish, the district encompassed the Lower East Side, Chinatown, Little Italy, Greenwich Village and much of the Upper West Side, a diverse constituency that was attracted to Abzug's ideas and vigor as a candidate.

On the campaign trail, Bella Abzug was relentless. Broad-shouldered and solid in build, wearing one of her trademark wide-brimmed hats, she shook hands firmly and in her distinctive Bronx accent, talked earnestly to voters while gesturing with swift jabs of her fist to make her points. A dynamic speaker, she was direct, firm, and not at all restrained in her manner. Reporters coined various descriptive names for her, such as "Battling Bella," "Hurricane Bella," and "Mother Courage."

In the Democratic primary, Abzug defeated a seven-term Congressman, Leonard Farbstein. In the November election, she handily defeated the Republican-Liberal candidate, Barry Farber, popular host of a local radio talk show, when her 47,128 votes outnumbered Farber's 38,438. She became one of twelve women in the House of Representatives and the first Jewish woman to serve on Capitol Hill.

Bella Abzug was bound to have an impact in Congress, if only because she was impassioned about so many subjects. She noted then that, "I was lonely and an oddity, a woman, a Jew, a New York lawyer, a feminist, a Nixon opponent from way back, a peace activist who passionately opposed American involvement in Indochina and just as strongly favored aid to democratic Israel."

On her first day in Congress, January 21, 1971, Abzug introduced a resolution call-

Bella with one of her trademark hats.

ing for the withdrawal of all troops from Indochina by July 4 of that same year. she was known as an early critic of the war in Vietnam, and Bella spoke out about it despite the fears of some constituents that the administration might retaliate by cutting aid to Israel.

In her years as congresswoman, Abzug backed improvements in mass transit, peace efforts on many fronts, women's rights, environmental protection issues, and programs for the elderly.

In 1972, Bella introduced formal impeachment charges against President Nixon. A few months later, when Vice-President Spiro Agnew said, on the floor of the Senate, that before long Bella Abzug would be wearing hot pants in Congress, she retorted, "Hopefully, by 1972, hot pants and President Nixon *and* Vice-President Agnew will [all] be out of style."

After the United Nations adopted its "Zionism equals racism" resolution, Abzug made her views known in various forums. "Judaism," she asserted, "has had a very profound affect on me. Jews believe you can't have justice for yourself unless other people have justice as well. That has motivated much of what I've done."

In the late seventies, she suffered a string of political losses—a senatorial primary in 1976, a mayoral primary in 1977 and a bid for a House comeback in early 1978. Her public service continued to flourish even with these losses. In 1979, she served with a White House women's advisory group. However, President Jimmy Carter dismissed her when her outspoken criticism of his allegedly negative attitude toward feminism offended him.

By 1986, now sixty-six years old, Abzug again ran for office, as a candidate for Congress in Westchester County's 20th district. In the midst of the primary campaign, her husband of forty-two years died of a heart attack. Despite this great loss and although she did not campaign for some weeks afterward, she won the primary in September. But she lost the November election. In her concession speech, she said, "Martin was always with me, all through this." To the campaigners, who had worked so hard on her behalf, she sought to be encouraging, saying, "Be of good heart. We shall prevail."

This is characteristic of a woman who is strong-willed and dedicated to what she believes in, yet is a person with many sides. Explaining how she combined her public and private lives, Bella once said, "You try to adjust the family situation to the realities of your life. You don't put one ahead of the other. There is a balance, and you strive to keep that balance. The family grows with it. And the kids also know that the mother is a woman, wife, and lawyer. A total person. It makes them better people."

In 1993, while continuing to practice law, Bella Abzug served as co-chair of the Women's Environment & Development Organization, which combines two of her long-standing interests: women and the environment. She also chaired New York City's Commission on the Status of Women.

$\mathcal{S}$TELLA $\mathcal{A}$DLER

Queen of the Method

Born February 10, 1902, in New York, New York; died December 21, 1992. Acting Coach. Founder of the conservatory of acting named for her, in Manhattan, Stella Adler is considered the leading American teacher of Method acting. She first appeared in Yiddish theater productions, but she later made the transition to the English-speaking theater. Adler made her stage debut in 1906. She appeared in almost two hundred productions in the United States and abroad, mainly as a member of the Group Theater. For forty years she taught acting, shaping the film careers of thousands of performers who studied at the Stella Adler Conservatory of Acting, including Marlon Brando, Warren Beatty, Robert De Niro, and Eddie Albert.

$\mathcal{S}$tella Adler was born into a celebrated family of actors with roots in the Yiddish theater. Her parents were Jacob and Sara Adler, leading players on the Yiddish stage. Stella debuted on the stage in 1906 at the age of four in her father's production of *Broken Hearts* at the Grand Street Theater in New York City.

For the next decade she played girls' and boys' roles for her parents' Yiddish-speaking theater group and for other theatrical companies. Her brothers, Luther Adler and Jay Adler, also became well-known actors. Her famous parents were leaders of the Yiddish Art Company and ranked as the leading Yiddish stage tragedians in America.

"In my family, immediately—you could barely walk—you were put on the stage," Stella Adler once observed. "All the children!" With so much time spent on rehearsing and performing, formal education was minimal for Adler.

She was introduced to Russian director and teacher Konstantin Stanislavski's revolutionary acting technique, called the Method, at the American Laboratory Theater school where she studied in the mid-1920s.

In the 1930s, Stella Adler rose to prominence as a member of the experi-

The Jewish Week, New York

mental, Depression-era Group Theater. Stanislavski's acting theories heavily influenced the Group Theater.

Adler appeared in several of their productions: *The House of Connelly, Big Night,* and Clifford Odets' *Awake and Sing.* She took a leave of absence from the Group Theater in 1934 and went to Europe. There she studied under Stanislavski himself. Stanislavski instructed Stella Adler and others in the "inner technique" whereby the actor learns to control his sensations, emotions, purposes, and ultimately his creative imagination in order to recreate the chracters and situations of drama. He taught her, she said, that "the source of acting is imagination and that the key to its problems is truth, truth in the circumstances of the play."

Adler returned to the Group Theater in August 1934, shared what she had learned, and from then on the Group adopted many of Stanislavski's principles. In December 1935, she made an appearance with the Group Theater as an indomitable Clara in *Paradise Lost,* by Clifford Odets. At this point, Adler began to give acting classes. Her approach differed from that of Lee Strasberg, one of the three founders of the Group Theater, in that Strasberg trained his actors to call upon their own experiences in order to create the emotion of the character, whereas Adler taught her actors to think of a character's experiences as apart from their own and to create the character's experience through their imaginations.

Strasberg's unorthodox rehearsal methods urged actors to improvise, to do extemporaneous scenes based on situations that were like those in the play—exercises in "affective memory" or the memory of an emotion that the actor had felt at an earlier time.

Stella Adler disliked Strasberg's interpretation of Stanislavski's method, and was especially annoyed with his use of affective memory exercises. "The emphasis was a sick one," she said later. "You couldn't be on the stage thinking of your own personal life. It was just schizophrenic."

She left for Hollywood in January 1937 and acted under the name Stella Ardler. She appeared in a few films, including *Love on Toast* in 1938 and *Shadow of the Thin Man* four years later. She returned occasionally to perform with the Group Theater until it was dissolved in 1941. She once complained about the Group Theater's dearth of good roles for women, calling it "a man's theater…aimed at plays for men."

In the early 1940s, Adler started to teach acting at the Dramatic Workshop at the New School for Social Research in New York City. She left there in 1949 to establish the Stella Adler Conservatory of Acting.

In her acting classes, Adler taught her students to build characters through the evidence provided in the text, which could be embellished by their own imaginations as well as their awareness of the historical period. They were not to draw from their personal experience. "You must get away from the real thing because the real thing will limit your acting and cripple you," she told one beginning class of student actors. "Don't use your conscious past. Use your creative imagination to create a past that belongs to your character. I don't want you to be stuck with your own life. It's too little."

"The ultimate aim of the training," she explained in the school's syllabus, "is to create an actor who can be responsible for his artistic development and achievement." Students took a two-year program of classes in acting, speech, voice production, Shakespeare, make-up, movement, and sight-reading, and they participated in workshops in play analysis, characterization, scene preparation, and acting styles.

In later years, courses in rehearsal technique, mime, stage direction, playwriting, and theater history were added. Stella Adler taught principles of acting characterization and script analysis for many years.

She demanded maximum effort from her students. She encouraged, scolded, sometimes exploded. "I'm rough, but that's my way of being kind. My ability to bring out [the students' talent] is somewhere deep inside me, and I must do whatever I need to pull it out." "The teacher has to inspire. The teacher has to agitate," Adler said in an interview in *The New York Times.*

"The theater—acting, creating, interpreting—means total involvement, the totality of heart, mind, and spirit." She equated the craft of acting with life itself. In a 1968 interview she said that acting is: "the total development of a human being into the most he can be and in as many directions as he can possibly take."

Shelley Winters called Adler "a great theater teacher." Winters remembered how she had been especially helped with one difficult role.

"As Stella coached me," Winters said, "I got a firmer hold on the character and was no longer exhausted at the end of an emotional scene...Stella rehearsed me through the whole play...and did not leave until she felt I was secure in the role."

One member of the Group Theater was Harold Clurman, whom Stella Adler married, then divorced. She also married (and divorced) Horace Eleascheff. Her third husband, Mitchell Wilson, a physicist and novelist, died in 1973.

In 1966-1967, she served as adjunct professor for acting at Yale University's School of Drama and she headed the undergraduate drama department at New York University.

Adler was tall, well-proportioned, with honey-blonde hair and large gray-green eyes. She had one daughter, Ellen, from her first marriage. She wore lavish and dramatic clothes and layers of greasepaint, and was always accompanied by attendants. When she walked into class, the students would rise. When she left, they applauded as if they had watched her perform.

Although she appeared in over two hundred productions—and also directed some of them—her greatest influence was in the training that she provided to several generations of stage and film actors.

GRACE AGUILAR

Literary Champion of Jewish Women

Born June 2, 1816, in Hackney, outside London, England; died September 16, 1847. British novelist and historian. She wrote a number of novels on Jewish themes as well as religious works targeted largely to Jewish women. Seven of her books were not published until after she died. *The Value of Colors,* published in 1850, was her best-known Jewish novel; it was a romantic, highly-idealized portrait of the Spanish Marranos, medieval Jews forced to convert to Christianity who secretly continued to practice their Judaism to escape the persecutions of the Inquisition. Her writings helped English and American women attain a better sense of their Jewish heritage. She died at the age of thirty-one.

Grace Aguilar's ancestors were merchants who had lived in Spain, but were forced to flee to England. Grace's parents were descended from the Marranos. Her father, keeping the family tradition, was a merchant and her mother ran a small private school for boys in Hackney, a town outside London.

Because Grace was in delicate health, her parents educated her at home, teaching her the classics, history, Judaism and Hebrew. In 1828, because of her parents' poor health, the family moved from London to Devon in order to enjoy the better climate.

A voracious reader, Grace, who also exhibited musical talent, took up writing at an early age. When she was seven years old, she began a diary, keeping a precise, full record of her experiences and reactions to events and people. She had written a complete play before the age of twelve.

In 1835, she worked on a series of poems which were published anonymously in book form under the title *The Magic Wreath*. She was only nineteen years old and was not paid for her effort.

That same year she contracted measles, which left her in permanently ill health. She experienced great personal sorrow when her father later died of consumption. She turned to her writing talent in order to earn some money to support herself.

Grace Aguilar's most creative period started in 1842. Over the next five years—until her

Schwadron Collection. Hebrew University, Jerusalem

17

death—she wrote an extraordinary amount, especially considering the state of her health and the fact that she was helping her mother run the boys' school in Hackney.

Her first paid work, *The Spirit of Judaism,* was published in the United States in 1842 after it had been printed for private circulation in England. In the book's introduction, unpretentious and modest Aguilar, who never married, wrote that she hoped "that it may be permitted to find some response in the gentle minds of [my] own sex, to awaken one lethargic spirit to a consciousness of its own powers, its own duties.

"When, therefore, the author looks to her own sex for the support and countenance of her labours…her aim is to aid, not to dictate; to point to the Fountain of Life, not presumptuously to lead; to waken the spirit to its healing influence, to rouse it to a sense of its own deep responsibilities, not to censure and judge."

Grace Aguilar assailed what she observed to be the excessive interest in ritual and tradition of modern Jewish communities. She asserted that the spiritualism of Judaism and its moral code as presented in the Old Testament were of more importance.

American critics lavished praise on *The Spirit of Judaism,* which sought to prove that Judaism was superior to other religions. The book was regarded by Jewish women as one of the most influential theological works they had ever read.

Another book by Aguilar, *Women of Israel,* published in 1845, was considered to be her most important work. It included biographical sketches of biblical characters and was meant to arouse young Jews to take pride in their heritage and to document the role of women in Jewish tradition.

In the book, Aguilar railed against the part that Christianity had played in establishing ideals of womanhood. She argued that Christian writers had unjustly made feminine virtue identical with Christian virtue. "Education and nationality compel them to believe that 'Christianity is the sole source of female excellence.'" She wrote, "…that the value and dignity of woman's character would never have been recognized but for the religion of Jesus [Judaism]."

She rebutted accusations that Mosaic law oppressed women and insisted that within Judaism women, "have a station to uphold and a 'mission' to perform, not alone as daughters, wives and mothers, but as witnesses of that faith which first raised, cherished and defended them."

Still, Aguilar's attitude toward the key question of Eve's transgression was ambivalent. Although she boldly asked, "If He permitted, ordained, why did He punish?" she accepted that, "The very first consequence of woman's sin was to render her, in physical and mental strength, inferior to man."

Aguilar struggled with these questions of a woman's place in the world in fiction also. *Home Influence* was a novel that she published in 1847. She described it as "a story illustrative of a mother's solemn responsibilities, intense anxiety to fulfill them, and deep sense of the influence of home."

Aguilar was one of the first English Jews to write a history of the Jews in England; it appeared in 1847. Her novels sought to illustrate a certain moral theme, occasionally suggested in the title.

In *Woman's Friendship,* published in 1853, she showed the potential strength of women's friendships and their ability at times to go beyond class barriers. One character in the novel, Florence's "mother," who is later discovered not to be Florence's real mother, warns her daughter that the daughter's friendship with a certain Lady Ida Villiers can never amount to anything. Such was the case, according to Florence's "mother" "because friendship, even more than love, demands equality of station." However, mother and daughter are still devoted friends at the close of the novel even though they had been apart for a long time and had discovered Florence's true parentage. In a final chapter called "A Providence in All," Grace Aguilar comments on "how much female friendship—in general so scorned and scoffed at—may be the invisible means of strengthening in virtue."

Most (seven in all) of Grace Aguilar's books were not published until after she died. Two of these, *Home Influence* (1847) and its sequel, *Mother's Recompense* (1851), sold well.

The best known of Aguilar's Jewish novels was *The Vale of Cedars*, published in 1850. It was a romantic, highly idealized portrait of the Marranos in Spain. The novel was translated into German and Hebrew and has remained popular.

But it was the publication of *The Days of Bruce,* a romance set in fourteenth century Scotland, which was published in 1852, that made her famous.

In 1847, Grace Aguilar's mother took her to Frankfurt, Germany, in the hope of obtaining medical help. While there, they received a letter, written by one hundred women who wished to express their appreciation to Aguilar for raising their Jewish consciousness through her writing. "Until you," they wrote, "it has, in modern times, never been the case that a woman in Israel should stand forth as the public advocate of the faith of Israel."

As Grace Aguilar lay on her death bed, unable to speak, she spelled out with her fingers this biblical quotation: "Though He slay me, yet will I trust in him" (Job 13-15).

She died at the age of thirty-one.

Grace Aguilar's collected works, in eight volumes, appeared in 1861. Her life is commemorated by the Aguilar Free Library, which was begun in New York in 1886. When thousands of Jewish immigrants arrived in the United States in the years after that, this service institution provided books to aid them in understanding American culture.

AMY ALCOTT

Greatest Jewish Woman Golfer

Born February 22, 1956, in Kansas City, Missouri. American golfer. Turning pro at eighteen, she won the 1975 Orange Blossom Classic, only her third tournament. No other woman pro golfer had accomplished that feat so quickly. By March 1991, Amy Alcott had won twenty-nine tournaments, only one short of the total needed for automatic entry into the Women's Golf Hall of Fame. As of February 1993, she had earned $2,850,188.

*A*my has lived in the metropolitan Los Angeles area since she was six months old. She was a tomboy with skinned knees and dirty toenails who watched television on Saturdays with a bowl of ice cream by her side. She learned to love golf at an early age.

While her girlfriends were learning how to dress fashionably and apply make-up, Amy pretended that she was playing in the Masters or the U.S. Open. "I loved the click of the [golf] ball going into the hole. I marveled at the golf swing." She wondered if women played golf professionally.

At the age of nine, Amy vacillated between her interest in both tennis and golf, but soon she chose golf as her favorite sport. She began taking lessons from a well-known Los Angeles golf teacher named Walter Keller who owned a golf equipment shop. Zealous and intense, Amy hit golf balls into a net in the back of Keller's shop four hours a day. She also studied her swing in front a mirror.

Turning her backyard at home into a miniature golf course, Amy hit golf balls six hours a day. She put soup cans in the ground for holes and cut the grass short enough so she could putt. She chipped over the hedges to the cups. She had a truckload of sand dumped under her bedroom window so that she could practice hitting out of sand.

Amy Alcott started playing on municipal golf courses but soon switched to the renowned Riviera Country Club in Los Angeles where she went every day after school. Thanks to Riviera's small greens and deep bunkers, Alcott's short game improved. She was an average 220 to 230 yards off the tee and seldom got into serious trouble with sandtraps or other hazards. Her chipping and putting were accurate.

Freckled-faced, brown-haired, possessing a powerful torso and strong arms, Alcott sensed

Amy Alcott: Golf star of the 1980s.

that her athletic prowess made her seem different. "Boys were more or less in awe of me," she recalled.

The highlight of her amateur career came with her victory in the 1973 USGA Junior Girls tournament at the age of seventeen. During her junior career, Alcott won 150 golf tournaments.

Before turning professional, Amy Alcott won the Los Angeles Girls' title three times, the L.A. Women's championship and the California Women's Amateur title.

When she graduated from Pacific Palisades High School, Alcott chose a full-time golf career over college. She joined the Ladies Professional Golf Association in January 1975.

Amy finished twenty-second in her first tournament, winning only $350. But six months later her official earnings stood at $18,466, twelfth on the money list, $2,000 more than anyone had ever won in a year.

She won her first LPGA tournament at the 1975 Orange Blossom Classic. It was only her third tournament as a professional and she came in with a record nine-under-par 207 (68-68-71). Amy Alcott celebrated her nineteenth birthday on February 22 of that year by firing a second-round 68. For this win, she picked up a $55,000 prize check.

Amy Alcott was the best new player on the tour in years. She averaged 73.52 strokes that first year.

By the summer of 1980, Alcott had won twelve tournaments. She won the U.S. Women's Open in early July by nine strokes. "I'm as good as anyone out there," she boasted afterward. She overcame 105 degree temperatures to set an Open record of a four-under-par 280. That year, she averaged 71.51, the best score of her career. She credited her victories to losing weight a few months earlier. *Golf* magazine named her 1980 Player of the Year.

With success came popularity. "These Jewish parents keep calling me up and telling me they want me to meet their sons. They say, 'You'll like him. He'll walk the course with you'," she said. "I guess I should be out trying to meet a doctor or a lawyer, but I'm having too much fun."

In 1983, Amy Alcott became the sixth LPGA player to win $1,000,000 a year, attaining that figure at the Chrysler-Plymouth Classic when she collected $8,750. During three seasons (1979, 1980 and 1984) she has won four tournaments per season. In 1985, Alcott averaged 71.78 on the tour. The next year, 1986, she averaged 71.99.

Never lacking in self-confidence, she observed in early 1986: "I know in my heart I'm one of the best women golfers ever, not because I'm the biggest money winner, but because I've managed for eleven years to be consistent."

The year 1988 was Alcott's most successful season. She earned $292,349 and captured the first major tournament of the year, the Nabisco Dinah Shore, snaring the $80,000 first place prize. She thus became the third LPGA member to surpass the two-million-dollar mark in career earnings. In 1988 she had fifteen top-ten finishes. Her average on the 1988 tour was 71.71.

The year 1989 was the eleventh consecutive season in which Alcott earned over $100,000; she had a 72.16 average. In 1990, she earned $99,208, marking the first time in her career that she was ranked outside the top twenty on the prizewinnings list; her 1990 average was 73.12.

In 1991, she won the Nabisco Dinah Shore tournament for the third time, bringing her within one tournament victory of qualifying for the LPGA's Hall of Fame, one of sport's most formidable goals. That year she earned $258,269 and averaged 72.43.

Known for her consistent game, she uses a short backswing, which she compares to Arnold Palmer's; she is one of the longest hitters among the women's pros.

The secret of her success? Amy Alcott believes that "Learning to keep yourself totally under control is what separates the winners from the also-rans in golf. You don't shout out that bad word, no matter how much you want to. You have to save your frustrations for later, go home and bite a tree or something."

Alcott has her own annual charity golf tournament to benefit the Multiple Sclerosis Society, called the Amy Alcott Pro-Am for MS. She also works part-time as a short order cook at Westwood's Butterfly Bakery in Los Angeles, finding it good therapy to relieve the pressures of playing on the golf tour.

She has been working with Robert Trent Jones, Jr., and Cornish & Silva as a design consultant on golf courses in Kauai, Hawaii; Virginia; Kentucky; and Palm Springs, California. She has also prepared her own golf instruction video for adults and juniors. And she has a thoroughbred horse named after her, which started racing as a two year-old in 1989.

As of the close of 1993, the thirtieth tournament victory, which would place her in the Hall of Fame, still eluded her. "The number looms over me," she said forlornly. "I must be asked about it two hundred times a day. People don't realize what you've done to win twenty-nine...I've done everything I've done in golf for me. This thirtieth win seems to be more for everybody else. For me, it will be more of a relief."

$\mathcal{S}$HULAMIT $\mathcal{A}$LONI

Israeli Gadfly

Born in 1929 in Tel Aviv, Israel. Israeli politician. Longtime maverick and outspoken champion of citizens' rights in Israel, Shulamit Aloni began in politics in the 1960s within the ruling Mapai Party. Her independent views led her to establish her own Citizens' Rights Movement in the early 1970s. Since 1965, she has been a Knesset member for all but four years. She served as Minister without Portfolio in the mid-1970s; and as Education Minister from July 1992 until June 1993 when she was named Minister for Communications, Science and Technology. Next to Golda Meir, she has been the most outspoken politician in Israeli history.

$\mathcal{B}$orn in 1929 to Socialist-Zionist parents who emigrated from Poland (she does not divulge her exact date of birth), Aloni aspired to live in a kibbutz, but her parents urged her to become a teacher.

As a teenager, she served in the Palmach, the commando arm of the Haganah, prior to the formation of the state of Israel in 1948.

After Shulamit graduated from the Teachers Seminary in Jerusalem, she decided to study law, graduating from the Hebrew University Law School.

Politics appealed to her, and in 1959, she joined the ruling Mapai Party. Shulamit Aloni made her mark between 1961 and 1965 by producing several radio programs dealing with legislation and legal procedures. As a result of one of these programs, the Office of the Ombudsman was established in 1965.

It was only when Israel's founding father and former Prime Minister David Ben-Gurion left the ruling Labor Party in 1965 to form the Rafi Party that Shulamit Aloni came to the attention of the nation's leaders when she wrote an article attacking Ben-Gurion for defecting. Prime Minister Levi Eshkol was impressed with the article and asked her to join Labor's Knesset list of candidates for the next election. One condition: She had to cease her radio program.

She did so, but found the experience less than satisfying. As a political novice, she was expected to adopt a low profile. She did just the opposite. After being elected a Knesset member in 1965, she appeared at the swearing-in ceremo-

State of Israel Government Press Office

State of Israel Government Press Office

ny in the Knesset in a low-cut dress, antagonizing and exasperating Orthodox Jewish politicians. At other times she wore miniskirts, plunging necklines, bows in her hair, and sandals that accentuated her shapely legs. Touring the country, Aloni usually wore tight-fitting jeans and wool turtleneck sweaters.

Aloni asserted in 1966 that "solutions to the nation's problems should not be cooked in the kitchen of one woman," a reference to the high-level meetings occurring in the kitchen of Mrs. Meir, then Labor Party secretary-general. Aloni's remark infuriated Golda and was a source of great distress to government leaders.

Despite this discord, during her first four years as a Knesset member, Aloni managed to establish the Consumers' Council and serve as its chairperson.

One serious breach of political etiquette occurred prior to the 1969 elections when Israel barred the press from mentioning a Zionist uprising in the Soviet Union. Aloni protested, and when she leaked word of the ban, she was called on the carpet by Golda Meir who called her a "demagogue". Labor Party leaders, continually frustrated with Aloni's independent behavior, relegated her to a spot too low on the Labor list to win a seat in the 1969 Knesset elections.

Aloni pressed on with the fight for civil rights, becoming the foremost champion of liberal causes in Israel. She became incredibly popular because she took on many of the country's sacred cows, especially the religious establishment. For example, she assailed the practice of permitting Orthodox Jewish laws to determine the rules for marriage and divorce as well as all other aspects of personal status.

She has long fought Sabbath blue laws and was the inventor of the "Shulamit Aloni marriage," a contractual accord signed by a consenting male and female in front of a lawyer that bypassed the rabbinical court's monopoly on nuptials.

Through newspaper articles and her revived, twice-weekly radio program called "After Office Hours," on which she offered legal advice to listeners, she conveyed her unconventional views to the public. Those views did not include support for feminism. "I am not a 'women's libber,'" she insisted. "I am for the liberation of men and women. I am a 'human libber.' I put human rights above women's rights. I hate classifications and labeling."

Along with the praise came threats on her life, poison pen letters and anonymous phone calls in the night. The culprits appeared to come from the Orthodox Jewish community. "Only religious Jews want to kill me," Shulamit Aloni said matter-of-factly at the time. "Only the extremists are after me. The others treat me with respect."

In September 1973, Aloni formed her own political party, and called it the Citizens' Rights Movement. Winning three seats (considered an incredible feat at the time), Aloni's party succeeded because she had denounced government red tape and senseless bureaucracy. Other than the ailing Mrs. Meir, Aloni was now the most prominent female politician in Israel.

In 1974, Aloni joined Yitzhak Rabin's government as Minister without Portfolio, only the second woman in Israel's history to hold a cabinet post. She resigned when the National Religious Party joined the government later that year.

For a brief time in 1975 and 1976, Aloni formed a political party called Ya'ad. Between 1981 and 1984, she associated herself with the Labor Alignment.

Her greatest electoral success came in the June 1992 election after she successfully merged the three left-wing parties (her own Citizens Rights Movement, Shinui, and Mapam) just prior to the election campaign. As the head of this newly-formed group, named the Meretz Party, she campaigned on the theme of humanity.

"We have not entirely lost our feeling for the moral and humane Zionist ethos," she told audiences. "The people want it back." Returning to the Zionist ethos meant, in her view, abandoning the nationalist and religious values of the right-wing parties.

Meretz won twelve Knesset seats on June 23, 1992, making it the third largest party (after Labor and Likud) in the Knesset. The new prime minister, Yitzhak Rabin, made Aloni his Education Minister, a move which infuriated his other coalition partner, the ultra-Orthodox Shas Party. The outspoken Aloni frequently irritated Shas and other Orthodox Jews with her controversial anti-religious comments. Consequently, she became Rabin's largest domestic problem.

Aloni suggested the name of God be omitted from the text of the Yizkor memorial prayer at state ceremonies. She asserted that "man has already gone to the moon while here we still tell our children the world was created in six days," which was an affront to Orthodox Jewish beliefs. Rabin was annoyed, but was unable to curb Aloni's acerbic tongue. "Because of the six days of creation," quipped one of Rabin's ministers, "we'll end up destroying our government."

In May 1993, Aloni's acid tongue became the focus of yet another government crisis when Interior Minister Aryeh De'eri of the Shas Party demanded that she be removed as Education Minister. Rabin at first refused, leading De'eri to announce his resignation from the government. Aloni argued that the Interior Minister "has no right to claim guardianship over Jewish heritage. Women were also present at Mount Sinai."

Rabin convinced Aloni that she had to give up the education position. Otherwise, his government would fall, and the opportunity to achieve new peace agreements with the Arabs, considered improved since Rabin became Prime Minister, would disappear. Agreeing, Aloni gave up the education ministry for a much less powerful position, Minister for Communications, Science and Technology.

MARY ANTIN

Learning to Live in The Promised Land

Born in 1881 in Plotzk, Russia; died May 15, 1949. American author. One of the first American Jews to write a best-selling book. Her 1912 memoir, *The Promised Land*, was one of the earliest and best accounts of how immigrant Jews became Americanized. It was her conviction that immigrant Jews like herself had to throw off their past Jewish beliefs and mores in order to integrate themselves into their new land, America. Thousands of new immigrants, Jewish and otherwise, took her advice.

The Russia of the early 1880s, a dangerous, unpleasant place for Jews, held no special importance to Mary Antin. She had been born there in 1881 to Orthodox Jewish parents and when her father sailed to America, she sensed that her own rescue was imminent. It came in 1894 when her father sent for the family. Mary arrived in Boston, Massachusetts at the age of thirteen.

From the start, Mary's father labored feverishly to Americanize his family. When they left the pier in a rickety cab, Mr. Antin told his family not to lean out of the windows for fear that they would be branded as "greenhorns". That first day her father introduced Mary to bananas and rocking chairs and street lamps.

"The streets," Mary Antin wrote later, "were as bright as a synagogue on a holy day." To her, America was different, but delightful— "bewilderingly strange" was the way she put it fifteen years after setting foot in her new country. She also called it "unimaginably complex, delightfully unexplored." So much was free in America, she discovered—including education. How wonderful!

Mary was only fifteen years old when her first poem, *Snow*, was published in the *Boston Herald*. Three years later she wrote her first book, a record of her journey from her native town in Russia to America. *From Plotzk to Boston* was in the form of a collection of letters to her uncle, who was still in Russia. It was first published in Yiddish.

Educated in public schools in the Chelsea section of Boston, Mary Antin studied in 1901 and 1902 at Teachers' College, part of Columbia

Mary Antin: An early portrait.

University. While there, she met and married a non-Jewish professor of paleontology, Amadeus V. Grabau. She attended Barnard College in 1903 and 1904.

Mary Antin's best-known work was published when she was thirty-one years old. Her autobiography, *The Promised Land,* the first book by an American Jew to become a bestseller, had thirty-four printings and sold 85,000 copies. It was one of the earliest literary efforts that captured what it meant for new immigrants to confront and adjust to the strange, dizzying American culture. Originally serialized in the *Atlantic Monthly,* the book garnered numerous honors, turning Mary Antin into what she described with disappointment as an "unwilling celebrity."

Justifying the writing of an autobiography at such a young age, she noted that her life was similar to that of many others. "I am only one of many whose fate it has been to live in a page of modern history," she said. "We are the strands of the cable that binds the Old World to the New."

She wrote honestly about how difficult it had been to move from one country to another. Her readers easily empathized—having gone through the same experience. "Having made such good time across the ocean," she wrote, "I ought to be able to proceed no less rapidly on terra firma, where, after all, I am more at home. And yet here is where I falter. Not that I hesitated, even for the space of a breath, in my first steps in America. There was no time to hesitate. The most ignorant immigrant, on landing, proceeds to give and receive greetings, to eat, sleep, and rise, after the manner of his own country; wherein he is corrected, admonished, and laughed at, whether by interested friends or the most indifferent strangers; and his American experience is thus begun."

To Antin, full integration into American society could only come about by discarding all that one had clung to in the past, in her case, the family's Jewish beliefs and customs. Accordingly, *The Promised Land* recounted the often painful tale of a small girl who left Russia and its oppressive Tsarist regime, who put aside what were once strong convictions about Judaism, and acclimated herself to America. In the introduction to her memoir, Antin wrote of the past, trying desperately to discard all that she once held dear, while evidently not totally at peace with herself for having done so.

"All the processes of uprooting, transportation, replanting, acclimatization, and development took place in my own soul," she wrote. "I felt the pang, the fear, the wonder, and the joy of it. I can never forget, for I bear the scars. But I want to forget—sometimes I long to forget. I think I have thoroughly assimilated my past—I have done its bidding —I want now to be of today. It is painful to be consciously of two worlds, the Wandering Jew in me seeks forgetfulness. I am not afraid to live on and on, if only I do not have to remember too much. A long past vividly remembered is like a heavy garment that clings to your limbs when you would run."

Learning to become American was no bed of roses for the new immigrant, a point Antin stressed by relating the pitfalls that had befallen her father. He had experienced a number of false starts in business before the family joined him in the United States. "His history for that period is the history of thousands who come to America, like him, with pockets empty, hands untrained to the use of tools, minds stamped by centuries of repression in their native land. Dozens of these men pass under your eyes every day, my American friend, too absorbed in their honest affairs to notice the looks of suspicion which you cast at them, the repugnance with which you shrink from their touch." She berated native Americans for treating these new immigrants shabbily, for overlooking what they might offer. "Think," she urged them, "every time you pass the greasy alien on the street, that he was born thousands of years before the oldest native American; and he may have something to communicate to you, when you two shall have learned a common language." On balance, however, she loved America, and was thrilled with what it had given her. "It was good to get out of Dover Street," she wrote of those first few days as a new immigrant. "But I must never forget that I came away from Dover Street with my hands full of riches. I must not fail to testify that in America a child of the slums owns the land and all that is good in it. All the beautiful things I saw belonged to me...I had only to be worthy, and it came to me, even on Dover Street..."

In 1913, several of her short stories appeared in the *Atlantic Monthly*. A year later, she wrote her third book, *They Who Knock at Our Gates*. Her theme was similar to the one she espoused in *The Promised Land*, that "what we get in the steerage is not the refuse, but the sinew and bone of all the nations."

Antin's later years brought personal hardship. Her popularity declined. In 1920, her husband left her to settle in China. She then moved frequently, working at times as a social worker. She died in 1949.

Yael Arad

First Olympic Medalist for Israel

Born May 1, 1967 in Tel Aviv, Israel. Israeli women's judo champion. When she won the silver medal at the Barcelona Olympics on July 30, 1992, Yael Arad became the first Israeli to win an Olympic medal. She also took a gold medal in the women's 61-kilogram division at the French Open judo championships in February 1992. In July 1991, she placed third in the 61-kilogram division at the World Championships in Barcelona. Her dream is "to be the best in the world."

Although judo was not a popular sport for most Israeli eight-year-olds, it captured the imagination of Yael Arad. "People thought I was crazy, a young girl getting up early to train," she says. Bemused by a girl engaging in judo, boys challenged her to fights. "They weren't used to seeing muscular women," Yael Arad says with a laugh. "But look at me, I hardly look like a gorilla."

She does look strong, and compact—and is quite capable of pulling an opponent off her feet at a second's notice. And yet she has a grace that is her legacy from the hours she spent at ballet and swimming classes as a youngster. She found judo more exciting than swimming. When her brother Yuval, then eleven, took judo lessons in north Tel Aviv, eight year-old Yael tagged along. "I loved it," she says. "Judo is a very intelligent sport. If you're good at it, you sense it right away. And there's nothing more enjoyable for a child than to throw another child down."

She began by training twice a week; then four and six times a week; then every day.

At first Yael upended boys, not girls, though she found nothing unusual in that. She grew up with three older brothers and a sister ten years younger. Her parents are journalists.

One early competitive experience in judo was almost Yael's last. She took "only" second place in an Israeli judo championship at the age of nine. She was crushed. "I cried for three straight days and wouldn't leave home—all because I didn't win."

A year later, at age ten, she won

Yael (right) with her mother, Nurit, upon Yael's return from becoming Israel's first Olympic medal winner at the 1992 Barcelona Olympics.

Israel Government Press Office

29

the Israel judo championship in the 31-kilogram weight class, competing against children up to age fourteen. She remained Israeli champion for the next six years.

Her first coach, Moni Isaac, proved the greatest influence on Yael. He coached her from the time she was eight until she was eighteen. He taught her self-discipline, to honor her rival, to shake hands before each match, and that she must want to win.

When she was sixteen, Yael Arad was the runner-up in the 56-kilogram weight class for women in the German Open for Cadets which was held near the city of Hamburg. Once again she was shocked at being second. Becoming world champion seemed a remote dream, yet Yael's trips abroad instilled new self-confidence in her. "I saw that everyone was a human being like me and there was no reason why I couldn't win," she says. Yael decided to increase her training schedule.

Frustration set in when she was able to obtain funds sufficient only to travel to the world and European Championships. Arad wrote letters to the Knesset (Parliament) Sports Committee and to national sports officials to drum up support for her sport.

Arad's own international accomplishments in judo forced the authorities to take notice of Israeli judokas. She began participating in national championships in western Europe. When she was eighteen-and-a-half, six months after she began her two-year stint in the Israel Defense Forces, Arad traveled to the English Championships and stayed on to train with world judo champion Karen Briks of England.

After completing her time in the Israeli army, Yael Arad was uncertain about continuing her judo career. "There was no money to help sports people. All my friends, just out of the army, were going abroad. I felt I was missing something. I had invested all this effort. But nobody was helping me." She drew encouragement from Olympic judo champion Peter Seisenbacher of Austria.

In 1988, she took second place in the German Open. In 1989, Arad was third in her weight class at the European championships. In 1990 she defeated the world's top two champions at a tournament in France, before losing in the final. She also took the silver medal at a tournament in Germany.

To compete in the 1992 Barcelona Olympics, Yael Arad needed more financial support. Again she engaged in a letterwriting campaign directed at the Israeli authorities. As a result, the Israeli Olympic Committee selected her for the special pre-Olympics program that entitled her to a monthly income of 1,500 Israeli shekels ($625 dollars) a month. She also obtained sponsorship from the Israeli magazine *La'isha* (*For The Woman,* translated from Hebrew).

Her greatest advances came in the twelve months before the Barcelona Olympics. In July 1991, she placed third in the 61-kilogram division at the World Championships in Barcelona. At home she was hailed as a heroine but the attention only put more pressure on her.

She prepared for the French Open, the third most-prestigious judo tournament, set for February 1992. While at a training camp in Austria the week before, she became ill, and spent four days fighting a high temperature. On the fifth day she traveled to Paris to join the other twenty-one contestants in her weight class. Among them were Germany's Frauke Eichoff and France's Catherine Fleury.

Yael Arad and Fleury met in the semifinals before 6,000 fans. The Israeli judoka won on points in an evenly matched contest.

Arad vowed to herself there would be no crying session in the dressing room after the competition. She was determined to take the gold medal. "I have always been a bridesmaid and never a bride....Maybe I had secretly doubted my own ability and had stopped trying after I had attained a place in the semifinals."

Not this time. Her triumph over Czechoslovakia's Marika Januksa was never in doubt. A knee injury, suffered during the tournament, did not mar Arad's performance. This dazzling success placed even more pressure on her to do well in Barcelona. When her knee problem got worse, Arad underwent surgery in March 1992.

Watching a videotape of her triumphant final match at the French Open, Yael Arad noted that she has a whole battery of techniques to overcome an opponent. "Some have only one or two. I have five. A lot of judo is technique. But without strength you can't do the technique today, because judo is very sophisticated. Everyone today is strong. If you have enough strength, you can combine strength and technique. I'm considered very strong and fast—and dynamic. Others are considered static. I work a lot on tactics."

Having proven herself often in international competition, Arad no longer has to worry about getting adequate financial support. She travels to Japan once a year and to Europe several times a year for training. She is coached by a former Israel judo champion, Daniel Leopold.

She came close to realizing her dream of being the best in the world when she won the silver medal at the 1992 Olympic games in Barcelona. Her only loss was to France's Catherine Fluery in the finals.

On May 1, 1993, Arad captured the European under-61-kilogram class judo title at the European Championships in Athens, Greece. She beat Belgium's Gella Van de Caveye, and won the gold medal. In October of that year, she won a silver medal in the World Judo Championships in Hamilton, Ontario in the 61-kilogram class; the gold medal went to Van de Caveye.

Yael Arad dedicated her Olympic medal to the Israeli athletes murdered at the 1972 Olympic Games.

DIANE ARBUS

The Wizard of Odds

Born May 14, 1923, in New York, New York; died July 27, 1971. American photographer. She was renowned for her photos of dwarfs, twins, transvestites, and freaks. After she committed suicide in 1971, she became a cult figure. She altered the standards of what was permitted in photography by extending the range of acceptable subject matter.

She was born Diane Nemerov on May 14, 1923 and grew up in a New York City apartment. She had the closest relationship with her older brother, the poet Howard Nemerov. The Nemerov family was the owner of Russeks department store on Fifth Avenue.

At school, Diane displayed creativity, especially in art class where she sketched, painted in oils, sculpted, and made collages. One of Diane's art teachers, Victor D'Amico, said, "Her talent—her imagination—compelled her to live in a state of internal crisis, of excitement."

Diane attended the Fieldston School in the Bronx from seventh to twelfth grades. As a child she was often depressed without knowing why.

Once, she and a friend were swimming in an outdoor pool on an estate at Oyster Bay, Long Island. Suddenly Diane told the friend, as if she had forgotten, "I'm Jewish." Indeed, as a child, she had never been aware that she was Jewish. "I didn't know it was an unfortunate thing to be!" she observed later. "Because I grew up in a Jewish city in a Jewish family, and my father was a rich Jew and I went to a Jewish school, I was confirmed in a sense of unreality. All I could feel was my sense of unreality."

It was that sense of unreality that drove her to states of uneasiness. "It's irrational to be born in a certain place and time and of a certain sex," she said in 1967. "It's irrational how much you can change circumstances and how much you can't. The whole idea of me being born rich and Jewish is part of that irrationality. But if you're born one thing, you can dare—venture—be ten thousand other things."

Diane Nemerov was married at the age of eighteen to Allan Arbus, an actor and fashion photographer. Four years later, on April 3, 1945, they had a daughter, Doon.

A year later, Arbus acquired her first camera, a Speed Graphic, which she found difficult to use. The art of photography, however, fascinated her. She thought of photography as an adventure. A photograph, she once said, was "a secret about a secret; the more it tells you, the less you know."

During the 1950s Diane and Allan Arbus combined their talents to become successful fashion photographers for *Vogue* and *Glamour* magazines. Viewing herself more as a devoted wife and mother than a photographer, Arbus curbed her artistic impulses. In 1958, her mentor, Lisette Model, encouraged her to pursue "the forbidden" with her camera. Arbus's childhood depression, from which she still suffered, gave way to a new

32

sense of optimism about life.

She and Allan had a second daughter, Amy, who was born on April 16, 1954.

Perhaps because she thought of herself as different, Diane Arbus was drawn to the eccentric and odd.

"Do you know any streetwalkers?" she asked Lisette Model. Puzzled, her mentor replied, "Darling, those women work for a living, too; leave them alone." Arbus could not. Prowling New York City's streets during the early morning hours, unafraid, she talked to the prostitutes and the homeless.

During the summer of 1959, the Arbuses became estranged and they eventually divorced ten years later. But Arbus's nightly prowls continued. She haunted circus sideshows and looked for portraits of strange people. Among her earliest photographic efforts were portraits of twin fetuses bobbing in a bottle of formaldehyde and the "headless man" clad in a business suit.

By the end of 1962, she added to her freakish subjects another subject matter: nudists.

Her greatest triumph came in March 1967 when the Museum of Modern Art in New York exhibited her *New Documents* show. The exhibit introduced her work to a wider audience and legitimized her unusual kind of photography. Proud of the exhibit, Diane Arbus sent out hundreds of announcements to past and present acquaintances.

On the opening night of the show Andy Warhol, Richard Avedon, and other luminaries of the art and photography worlds attended. Arbus wore a white silk dress and, according to actress/photographer Roz Kelly, "looked like an angel in the midst of a huge crowd."

A book of eighty of her photographs was published and sold more than 100,000 copies. Her biographer, Patricia Bosworth, wrote that the book's "overriding themes—sexual role-playing and people's irrevocable isolation from each other—seemed to express the rebelliousness, alienation, and disillusionment that surfaced in the sixties and flowed into the seventies."

One critic called Diane Arbus "The Wizard of Odds." Another declared: "She caters to the peeping Tom in all of us."

Other critics noted that the exhibit marked the end of one era of documentary photography and began another. Before, the photographer had distanced himself or herself from the subject. But, in Arbus's photographs the subject and photographer collaborate, revealing themselves both to the camera and to each another. The Arbus photographs set a new standard in the field: By attempting to capture ambiguity in people as well as the eccentrics of society, Arbus extended the range of the acceptable in documentary photography.

Marion Magid wrote in *Arts* magazine: "Once having looked [at Arbus's work], and not looked away, we are implicated. When we have met the gaze of a midget or a female impersonator, a transaction takes place between the photograph and the viewer. In a kind of healing process, we are cured of our criminal urgency by having dared to look. The picture forgives us, as it were, for looking. In the end the great humanity of Diane Arbus's art is to sanctify that privacy which she seemed at first to have violated."

Soon after the exhibit opened, *Newsweek* reporter Ann Ray walked around the display and with Arbus by her side, listened to the photographer say that "...I'm not virtuous...I can't do anything I want. In fact, I can't seem to do anything that I want. Except be a spy...I'm clever...I don't mean I can match wits with people 'cuz I can't. But I can figure myself into any situation. I choose photography projects that are somehow Mata Harish. I'll not risk my life but I'll risk my reputation or my virtue—but I don't have so much left." Ironically, the success of the exhibit made her feel more pressured—to be productive.

Diane Arbus said she wanted to photograph beautiful people in addition to freaks because "beauty is itself an aberration—a burden, a mystery." To prove her point, she shot a remarkable portrait of Gloria Vanderbilt's sleeping baby son, Anderson Hays Cooper, for a *Harper's Bazaar* Valentine's Day issue. Biographer Bosworth wrote: "...The infant resembles a flat white death's head—eyes sealed shut, mouth pursed and moist with saliva."

In 1971, unable to cope with the severe depression that was always a part of her life, Diane Arbus committed suicide.

A year after her death, the Venice Biennale exhibited ten large blowups of Arbus's photographs of human oddities including midgets, transvestites, and nudists. *New York Times* art critic Hilton Kramer wrote that they were "the overwhelming sensation of the American Pavilion."

HANNAH ARENDT

Model of Jewish Intellectualism

Born October 14, 1906, in Hanover, Germany; died December 4, 1975. German-born political theorist, editor, writer and teacher. She was known for her philosophical books and for her analysis of contemporary political movements. Her books include *The Origins of Totalitarianism,* published in 1951, *The Human Condition* (1958), and *Eichmann in Jerusalem* (1963). Editor-in-Chief of Schocken Books in the late 1940s, Arendt also taught at Princeton, Columbia, the University of Chicago, and the New School for Social Research over the next two decades.

Hannah Arendt was born in Germany. Her family, upper middle-class and highly-assimilated, lived in the city of Hanover.

She earned her doctorate in philosophy at the University of Heidelberg in 1920. Working under the noted German philosopher Martin Heidegger, she wrote a thesis entitled "The Concept of Love in St. Augustine," an exploration of existential elements in the Christian concept of love. It was a preamble for her later writings on human freedom and politics.

In 1933, with the rise of Nazism, and Hitler's ascent to power, Arendt fled to Paris. There she worked with Youth Aliyah, the Zionist group that sought to transport young European Jewish refugees to Palestine. She served as its director in France between 1935 and 1938, accompanying groups of young Jewish refugees to Palestine.

In 1940, Arendt was interned in the Gurs concentration camp in France. In 1941, U.S. President Franklin Roosevelt intervened on behalf of one hundred intellectuals and their families. Arendt and her husband, Henrich Blücher, reached New York, along with her widowed mother. After settling in America, Arendt wrote articles for the refugee newspaper *Aufbau.*

In 1942, she wrote an essay called *From Dreyfus to France Today,* which helped her win the post of research director of the Conference on Jewish Relations, a position she held from 1944 to 1948. She also served as Editor-in-Chief of Schocken Books.

Hannah Arendt published some review-essays in *The Nation* on philosophy and politics. To the writer Alfred Kazin, she was a "blazing Jew," an "intense, dominating woman with a gruff voice" whose "thought dominated her life."

From 1948 to 1952, she taught at the University of Chicago and the New School for Social Research in New York. She became an American citizen in 1951.

In 1952, Arendt wrote one of her best-known works, *The Origins of Totalitarianism,* one of the first books to point out the similarities between Nazism and Soviet Communism. In the book, she argued that the Jewish experience was central to understanding modern European history. She asserted that anti-Semitism and other such dehumanizing and depoliticizing attitudes, had to be looked at as causes of totalitarianism and the decline of the nation-state. Angry and analytical, based on her rich background in philosophy and history, the book was regarded as original and erudite.

The book made Hannah Arendt a major intellectual figure. She was now sought after to write articles for important journals and to lecture at universities. She became a visiting professor at Princeton, Berkeley, Columbia, and then took on her most permanent post at the University of Chicago.

In 1958 she wrote *The Human Condition,* which was a caustic rebuttal of Marxist social thought. Conservative thinkers loved it.

Arendt covered the Adolf Eichmann trial for *The New Yorker* magazine in 1961 and wrote a five-part series about it which was published in 1962 and 1963 issues of the magazine. Her reports evolved into a book that was published two years later, *Eichmann in Jerusalem: A Report on the Banality of Evil.* The state of Israel had hoped to turn the Eichmann trial into a reminder of the horrors of the Holocaust. But Hannah Arendt debunked the idea that Eichmann and the Germans were solely responsible for what happened to the Jews. She asserted that the Jews, themselves, by not putting up a strong enough resistance, were in part responsible. Seemingly sympathetic to Eichmann, she wrote that "Adolf Eichmann went to the gallows with great dignity."

Arendt argued that the trial was a legal and public-relations failure since the prosecutors ignored evidence that Eichmann's bosses were more responsible than he was for Holocaust crimes, and that Eichmann, rather than representing evil incarnate, was nothing more than a cog in the larger Nazi machine. She minimized Eichmann's crimes by claiming that each individual has the same capacity for evil as Eichmann. In fact, her theory was that Eichmann, rather than symbolizing the worst possible traits in all mankind, represented merely the "banality of evil."

She concluded that Israel had no right to try the former Nazi war criminal. She contended that the trial should have been conducted under the aegis of an international tribunal. Then, touching a sensitive nerve in the Jewish community, she blamed the European Jewish leadership for having failed to save its people from Nazi destruction. She argued that the "disastrous role" of the *Judenraten,* the Jewish councils, formed "the darkest chapter of the whole dark story."

As a result of these contentious views, a bitter feud arose between her and world Jewry which very quickly sought to discredit her accusations. The feud gave Hannah Arendt a notoriety within Jewish circles that lasted for years. Exploding in anger, Norman Podhoretz, the editor of *Commentary* magazine, recoiled at her description of Eichmann as but a "small cog," arguing that Hannah Arendt had made "inordinate demands...on the Jews to be better than other people, to be braver, wiser, nobler, more dignified—or be damned." Alfred Kazin noted that "the banality of evil" was a "dangerous and glib concept...Hannah was the prisoner of German philosophy, which traditionally trivialized evil people as lacking the mentality of German philosophers." To Arendt's charge of Jewish aloofness, the writer Irving Howe retorted that "hundreds of thousands of good middle-class Americans will have learned from [Arendt]...that the Jewish leadership was cowardly, inept and even collaborationist. You will forgive some of us if we react strongly to this charge." The board of the New York-based Leo Baeck Institute, which did research on German Jewish history and culture, expelled her from its organization.

Gershom Scholem, the scholar of Jewish mysticism, called her work "heartless...sneering and malicious." Such views contributed to Arendt's alienation from the Jewish community.

Moshe Kohn, reviewing the book for the *Jerusalem Post,* accused Arendt of portraying Eichmann and most of his superiors and henchmen as "idealists doing their duty." In contrast, Kohn argued, Arendt painted the Jews as Zionist knaves or "silly sheep" who permitted themselves to be slaughtered.

Arendt replied to Scholem's accusation that she lacked a love of the Jewish people. "You are quite right...I have never in my life loved any people or collective....Indeed I love 'only' my friends and the only kind of love I know of and believe in is the love of persons."

Some Arendt sympathizers argued that, despite this feud with her Jewish detractors, she felt a deep emotional attachment to Jews and Judaism. One example: Until just before her death, she kept up an active membership on the board of directors of the Conference on Jewish Social Studies. There were respected people who took a stand in her favor during this time. Hans Morgenthau, the political philosopher, defended her in public.

Her other publications include: *Between Past and Future* (1961); *On Revolution* (1963); *Men in Dark Times* (1969); and *Rachel Varnhagen—The Life of a Jewish Woman* (1974).

Hannah Arendt was an impressive intellectual and scholar whose work stirred great controversy.

ℒAUREN ℬACALL

"The Look"

> **Born September 16, 1924, in New York, New York.** American actress. Sultry, husky-voiced, known as "Bogie's baby" after her romance with Humphrey Bogart. Bacall debuted on screen with him in *To Have and Have Not,* followed by another twenty of her own movies. Moving on to the stage, she captured two Tony awards, one for the 1970 play *Applause,* the other for the 1981 musical *Woman of the Year.*

She was born Betty Joan Perske in New York City on September 16, 1924. Her father William, born in Alsace, France, was a salesman. Her mother Natalie (Weinstein) Perske, a native New Yorker and medical-supply salesperson, was of German-Romanian background.

Natalie Perske was a stage mother who sent her precocious daughter to dance school at the age of three. Seven years later, Betty's parents divorced. Her father moved out of their lives completely. "It was me and my mother against the world," Lauren Bacall recalled.

To separate herself further from her husband, Natalie resumed her maiden name of Weinstein, but made an interesting alteration. She translated Weinstein ("wine glass" in German) to Bacal, taken from *bokal,* the Russian word for wine glass. (In later years, after others kept rhyming it with "cackle", Betty added an "l", becoming Bacall).

While her mother worked as a secretary, Betty was sent to a private boarding school, Highland Manor, in Tarrytown, New York. At age twelve, she began attending the Julia Richman High School for Girls in Manhattan. A year later, cutting classes, she and a girlfriend sat through *Marked Woman* with Bette Davis and Humphrey Bogart. "I'm crazy about that man," Betty told her companion. "I love Davis, but *I* should play opposite him." The fantasies of a thirteen-year-old?

Evidently not. After graduating from high school, she enrolled at the American Academy of Dramatic Arts. Ushering at a Broadway theater brought in some pocket money; it also encouraged her to dream of seeing her name in lights. Taking the initiative, Bacall made the rounds of producers' offices while modeling to earn lunch money.

In 1943, just nineteen years old, she debuted on Broadway in a walk-on part. Fashion magazine editor Diana Vreeland spotted her and turned her into a successful model. In March of that year, Betty Bacall's face appeared on the cover of *Harper's Bazaar.* Mrs. Howard Hawks, wife of the great director, told her husband of the young model, whose lowered head and smoldering eyes formed what Hollywood publicists later dubbed "The Look."

Although tall, gawky, and skinny, she impressed the director enough for him to sign her to play opposite Bogart in the 1944 film *To Have and Have Not.* After she was given a new first name, Lauren, press releases were circulated promoting Bacall's lusty "come-on" expression. One reporter described her as "a leggy blond huntress."

It was in that film that Lauren Bacall delivered her now-famous line, "If you want anything, just whistle."

Humphrey Bogart whistled. While shooting the film, Bacall and Bogart, who was married to his third wife at the time, fell in love off-screen. Bogart, forty-five, divorced his wife and married the twenty-one year-old Bacall on May 21, 1945.

It turned into one of Hollywood's more enduring marriages. "Bogie was a very complicated, fascinating man," Bacall said later. "Trouble for a nineteen year-old because I didn't know anything, but totally solid and totally dependable. Character just oozed out of his pores."

On screen, Bacall usually played the smart-alecky, witty, cynical woman, often opposite husband Bogie. (*The Big Sleep* [1946] and *Key Largo* [1948], are two of their more famous films). They had two children and lived in California. During 1956 and 1957, for ten months, Bacall stayed by Bogie's side when he was dying of cancer.

"She's my wife—so she stays home and takes care of me," he said admiringly. "Maybe that's the way you tell the ladies from the broads in this town." Bogie died in 1957. In her memoirs, Bacall called Bogart too old for her. "He drank, he was an actor, and he was *goyim*," she wrote. She also said, however "No one has ever written a romance better than we lived it."

Bacall had other romances, a brief one with Frank Sinatra, and a marriage to Jason Robards from 1961 to 1969, but to her, it seems, Bogart was her greatest love.

Other notable Bacall films included *Confidential Agent* (1945); *Dark Passage* (1947); *Bright*

An early portrait of Lauren Bacall, known as "Bogie's Baby."

Leaf (1950); and *How to Marry a Millionaire* with Marilyn Monroe, (1953).

After a long absence from the screen, Bacall returned in 1974 as part of an all-star cast for the film version of Agatha Christie's *Murder on the Orient Express.*

One critic noted that "Bacall's deep, sexy voice, warm personality and air of sophisticated toughness were assets in film *noirs* and melodramas, and also carried her through more conventional romances and occasional comedies."

Bacall won the most respect from critics for her Broadway roles: *Goodbye Charlie* (1959); *Cactus Flower* (1965); *Applause* (1970); and *Woman of the Year* (1981). She won Tony Awards for her roles in *Applause* and *Woman of the Year.*

"This show," she said, speaking of *Applause* on April 25, 1970, "has begun a whole new cycle in my life. No, it's more than a cycle. It's as though the last twenty-five years never happened."

When fans refer to her as "Bogie's Baby," she bridles. "Is it ever going to stop?" she asks. "Bogart's been dead for years. And being a widow is not exactly a profession, you know. It's time I was allowed a life of my own, to be judged and thought of as a person, as me."

Bacall won an American Academy of Dramatic Arts Award for Achievement in 1963. Three years later she was cited by the woman's division of the Anti-Defamation League of B'nai B'rith for her efforts to "strengthen democracy." In 1967, she won the Hasty Pudding Woman of the Year award. Six years later Bacall won an Emmy nomination for the television version of *Applause.*

She wrote her bestselling memoirs, *Lauren Bacall by Herself,* in 1979, noting in it that she was "just a nice Jewish girl from New York." She wrote of being Jewish: "Going back through my life now, the Jewish family feeling stands proud and strong, and at least I can say I am glad I sprang from that. I would not trade those roots—that identity."

In 1988, upon completion of her twentieth film, *Mr. North,* she talked about being an actress. "I have a reputation for being difficult and I suppose in a way I'm like [Barbra] Streisand in that I'm a perfectionist," she said. "If that's difficult, then I'm difficult."

Bacall found it hard to fathom why people asked her, at age sixty-four, why she was still working. "I've worked all my life," she answered. "Why would I stop now? What else would I do?" In 1994, approaching her seventieth brithday, she was at work filming director Robert Altman's movie *Prêt à Porter.*

Bacall's son Sam Robards is the only one of her children to have followed her into the entertainment business.

Asked in 1988 which man she found sexy, Bacall replied surprisingly, "Gorbachev. I think he's really attractive. He has a real attitude. He knows who he is, he knows what he wants. I think he's very sexy. I love smart, you see." Bacall also put dancer Mikhail Baryshnikov and actor Robert Redford high on her list.

THEDA BARA

"I Live Cleopatra, I Breathe Cleopatra, I *Am* Cleopatra"

> **Born in 1890 in Cincinnati, Ohio; died in 1955.** American actress. Born Theodosia Goodman, a tailor's daughter from Cincinnati, she was catapulted into stardom when Hollywood publicists turned her into the mysterious, exotic vamp called Theda Bara. She became an overnight smash in the 1915 movie, *A Fool There Was,* which established the role of the vamp as a permanent Hollywood fixture in the 1920s. Her famous on-screen line "Kiss me, my fool," became a popular phrase of the time.

*G*etting at the truth behind Theda Bara is not easy. So much of her life was fiction, a Hollywood invention designed to woo the masses.

The ploy worked. The public loved Theda Bara, the on-screen seductress whose real life story appeared even more adventurous and wild than what audiences saw in the movie theater.

Yet the question remains: Who was Theda Bara?

Other than the fact that she was born Theodosia Goodman in 1890 in Cincinnati, Ohio, very little else is known about Theda Bara's pre-Hollywood years—with good reason. Hollywood wanted it that way.

Starting with an anagrammatical name, Theda Bara was Hollywood's creation. She became a movie star whose past and present were molded out of the inventive minds of publicists seeking to surround her with as much mystery and exotica as possible.

It all started with the making of a movie in 1914 called *A Fool There Was,* based on a Rudyard Kipling poem, "The Vampire". Bara had been appearing in stock companies, working from time to time as a Hollywood extra with no one paying much attention to her. Then William Fox purchased a stage play called *A Fool There Was.* The play's director, Frank Powell, then chose Theodosia Goodman to play the role of a ruthless *femme fatale,* or vamp (short for vampire). The publicists called her, "the woman who did not care."

Until then Hollywood had not cared much about the characters in its films. Movie actors—no one called them stars in those days—were anonymous, faceless figures. Film production companies sold movies, not their leading players, to the public.

Once it became apparent that the public wanted to know more about the actors and

actresses, however, it was not long before the Hollywood publicity departments of film production companies were born. Many of the movie makers actually had boring, uninteresting lives. To arouse interest, an ounce of inventiveness did not seem out of line.

In addition to promoting the actors, Hollywood began to take a new look at sex on the screen. Hollywood's screen heroines had been virginal up to this point. Few seemed interested in or were permitted to take sex seriously while performing in front of the camera. Theda Bara changed all that.

She was not the first screen vamp, but she was the most successful. Little footage remains of Bara's screen performances, yet so powerful is the legend surrounding her that her reputation as a sultry siren of the screen has remained intact for years.

A Fool There Was enjoyed such box-office popularity that William Fox was encouraged to form his own company. He was also encouraged to launch the first major promotional publicity for a Hollywood star.

A whole new identity, based upon what one critic called her "dithery sultriness" was created for Miss Bara, making her the first Hollywood star to be featured commercially as an object of sexual fantasy.

The shy, nearsighted Bara, the tailor's daughter from Cincinnati, was transformed seemingly magically, into a lusty, seductive siren. The publicists insisted that this "Arabian beauty" had been born in the Sahara desert and that she had been the love child of a French artist and his Egyptian mistress. Or perhaps her father was an Italian artist or a desert sheik who had mated with an Egyptian mistress. Or was it a French actress?

It would add to the mystery and excitement, the publicists thought, if Theodosia had a new name. How about one that conjured up her exotic background? How about the anagrammatic Theda Bara (Arab Death)? To add to the image, Theda Bara wore only black. And when the press was permitted near her, she made sure that she was seen stroking a serpent in a room that was filled with incense. If anyone asked, a publicist insisted that the blood of the Ptolemies flowed in her veins and that her astrological signs were the same as Cleopatra's.

There was more fiction from the publicists: Bara had been weaned on serpents' blood, given in mystic marriage to the Sphinx and fought over by wild, nomadic tribesmen. She wore Arabian robes, pretended not to speak English, and was driven in a white limousine attended by Nubian footmen. Prompted by her publicists, she insisted that she had been alive in a previous existence as the serpent of the Nile. She said frequently, in all seriousness: "I live Cleopatra, I breathe Cleopatra, I *am* Cleopatra."

Dark-haired, Theda Bara had large eyes that seemed to stare. Her films left the impression that she was what one writer called, "a depraved, merciless enslaver of men." Another film analyst argued that she "survived less on oxygen and victuals than by wrecking homes and devouring men. She was a mystic semisorceress." To stress her pallor, she wore indigo makeup; to live up to her bio, she surrounded herself with the symbols of death such as human skulls and ravens.

In one interview, Theda Bara exonerated her vampire-inspired actions as part of the duel between the sexes: "…Believe me, for every woman vamp, there are ten men of the same…men who take everything from women—love, devotion, beauty, youth, and give nothing in return! 'V' stands for vampire and it stands for vengeance, too. The vampire that I play is the vengeance of my sex upon its exploiters. You see...I have the face of a vampire, perhaps, but the heart of a 'feministe.'"

The public loved all this fabricated information. Hollywood movie publicists were quick to sense how to market other Theda Baras, how to give the public what it wanted.

Between 1914 and 1919, Theda Bara appeared in over forty films. She played such vamp roles as Carmen, Madame Du Barry, Salome, and Cleopatra. She also played some non-vamp parts, including Juliet to Harry Hilliard's Romeo and the kindhearted gypsy Esmeralda in *The Darling of Paris,* based on the book, *The Hunchback of Notre Dame.*

Israel Film Archive, Jerusalem, Museum of Modern Art Film Library

Ironically, it appears that the great exposure given Theda Bara ultimately led to her downfall. Moreover, in the years following World War I, film audiences became more sophisticated, no longer appreciating her exotica.

Along the way, Theda Bara had married director Charles Brabin. In 1919, she left Hollywood to seek a career on the Broadway stage, but she was unsuccessful. Though her own career did not flourish during the 1920s, the vamp remained a stock female character since female stars had strong box-office appeal.

Bara tried a movie comeback in the mid-1920s but it was short-lived. She made her final screen appearance in 1926 in a comedy short that was co-directed by comedian Stan Laurel and called *Madame Mystery.* It was a parody of her former screen image.

Bara faded into obscurity and died in 1955.

In January 1993, a musical comedy called *Theda Bara and the Frontier Rabbi* ran at New York's off-Broadway Jewish Repertory Theater. It concerned the exotic silent-screen vamp and a nice, young rabbi, proving that Theda Bara's reputation lives on.

MIRIAM BEN-PORAT

Israel's first female Supreme Court Justice

Born April 26, 1918, in Vitebsk, Lithuania. Israeli state comptroller and retired deputy president of the Supreme Court of Israel. In 1976, she became the first woman appointed to Israel's Supreme Court. As Israel's state comptroller since July 4, 1988, she has proved to be the most aggressive and provocative person ever in that job, taking on government ministries. She has been called "the public official Israeli politicians most love to hate." In 1991, she won the Israel Prize, the country's top honor, for her special contributions to society and state.

*M*iriam Ben-Porat was born in 1918 in Lithuania and graduated from the Hebrew Gymnasium in Kovno, Lithuania (the equivalent of a junior college). As a teenager in 1936, she immigrated to Palestine. In her family, education was valued; six of her seven brothers and sisters received higher educations. "Mother used to bake our bread and we all wore hand-me-down clothes so that there would be enough money for tuition fees," Miriam Ben-Porat recalled.

Ben-Porat began practicing law after earning her law degree from the British Mandatory School of Law in 1945. She served in the state attorney's office from 1948 to 1958, the latter five years as deputy state attorney. In 1958, she was appointed a judge of the District Court of Jerusalem and, in 1975, became the president of the court.

Of her first moments on the bench, she remarked, "I was unsure, even a little shy, but I was determined to do my best. Gradually I began to develop the self-confidence that a judge must possess, plus, of course, the stamina to prepare myself for each and every case with as much care as possible."

One of Ben-Porat's more celebrated cases occurred in 1976 involving a group of extremist Israeli Jewish youths who had tried to conduct a religious service on Jerusalem's Temple Mount, site of the ancient Jewish Temple, but revered as holy by Muslims as well. Overruling a lower court's decision that exonerated the defendants, she explained that "in view of the sensitive and dangerous situation prevailing against the intercommunal background, the exercise of the Jewish right of prayer on the Temple Mount is charged with grave dangers to public order as long as no regulations are adopted."

Ben-Porat taught law at the Hebrew University in Jerusalem from 1964 until 1978, becoming associate professor of law.

Ben-Porat, who is married and has one daughter, believes that laws governing the minimum marriage age and tax exemptions for working mothers are essential. "We need protective legislation for them, since many elements of our population groups still bear a tradition of discrimination against women. After all, women comprise at least half of the population and discriminatory practices against them would only result in delaying the

State of Israel Government Press Office

building up of our country." Named to the Israeli Supreme Court in 1976, she was the first Israeli woman to serve on the high court. She served for twelve years, becoming vice president of the court.

It has been, however, in the role of state comptroller, a post she assumed on June 14, 1988, that Miriam Ben-Porat has had the greatest impact on Israel. She was elected by the Knesset in a secret ballot for a five-year term and was permitted to serve one further five-year term.

The state comptroller's task has been to audit the government bureaucracies, selecting those agencies for exposure that deserve public attention. In the past, state comptrollers had not levelled criticism at senior politicians, but had confined their findings to the agencies of lower-ranking bureaucrats. Hence, their annual reports were hardly read and hastily forgotten.

That was not the case with Miriam Ben-Porat's reports. She has acted with greater zeal than any prior Israeli state comptroller, causing huge controversy. As Rochelle Furstenberg, writing in *Hadassah* magazine, noted in 1990, two years after Mrs. Ben-Porat became state comptroller: "The seemingly humorless seventy-two year-old, her hair pulled back in an upsweep, appears at times to be a stern school principal rebuking the wayward children of the government for their waste, inefficiency and even at times their criminality."

In November 1990, Ben-Porat appeared before a Knesset committee and assailed what she termed the government's lack of preparedness in absorbing Soviet immigrants. "The heart aches over the shortsightedness, inactivity and failures of the government," she said. That led Prime Minister Yitzhak Shamir to excoriate her for "exceeding her authority." She refused to debate Shamir in the press.

In December of 1990 she accused the Shas Party, which comprised Sephardi Orthodox Jews, of keeping double books and failing to account for hundreds of thousands of Israeli shekels in government funds. In response, Shas' Knesset members accused her of being "anti-Sephardi" and a "publicity-seeker." Ben-Porat replied: "I am responsible to the people, not to those who defame me."

In January 1991, Ben-Porat issued a blistering report, accusing successive governments of mismanaging Israel's water system. "There's nothing easier than writing a report," snarled Knesset member Pesach Grupper, a former agriculture minister.

That same month, *The Jerusalem Report* published the line that has become famous: "Miriam Ben-Porat has become the public official Israeli politicians most love to hate."

David Libai, then the chairman of the Knesset's public audit committee, which reviewed the comptroller's reports, said: "She deals with our central issues—immigration, political corruption, the water crisis. No state comptroller before her ever examined party finances so closely and that helps explain the intensity of the reaction against her. She is a strong and courageous woman. No one can intimidate her."

Following the 1991 Gulf War, Ben-Porat issued a report on the ineffectiveness of some of the gas masks used. Her report spawned a great controversy and resulted in the army providing new, improved gas masks to the public.

When Ben-Porat was awarded the Israel Prize on April 18, 1991, for her special contribution to society and state, she received a standing ovation. It was clear that the public was cheering her work as state comptroller.

"I do not seek out controversy," she told *The Jerusalem Post* in April 1992, "but the public interest is the keystone in my decisions. I choose to deal with what I consider important, and I don't pay the slightest attention to sacred cows."

Ben-Porat was mentioned as a candidate for the Israeli presidency before Ezer Weizman was elected early in 1993.

Lawyers who have worked with Ben-Porat point to her ability to remain aloof and detached. A former clerk said, "She is thoroughly objective. If she is uncertain about a matter, she will delve into it until she is convinced that she has found the truth. Miriam Ben-Porat is a classic representative of Israeli law."

She clearly found her work stimulating. Asked in April 1992, at the age of seventy-four, whether she had the strength for another term, Ben-Porat replied: "I work long hours every day and there is never a dull moment. As to the future—I'll have to consider it....In any case I do not think I will find myself unoccupied. I can be an arbitrator, write books, lecture at the universities. Time will tell."

In May 1993 Miriam Ben-Porat was re-elected to another five-year term as state comptroller.

GERTRUDE BERG

"Yoo-hoo, Mrs. Bloom"

Born in 1899 in New York, New York; died in 1966. American actress. She was creator, chief writer, producer and director as well as the star of the highly-popular radio program *The Goldbergs*. It was radio's longest running daytime serial, airing from 1929 to 1948. When it moved to television screens in 1949, it became one of that medium's earliest successes, running for six years until 1955. Many viewers acquired their first taste of authentic American Jewish life by watching the television program.

Gertrude Berg was born in 1899 in New York City. Her father, Jacob Edelstein, ran a resort in New York state's Catskill Mountains. Gertrude wrote and performed skits and monologues for the guests.

In 1918, Gertrude married Lewis Berg, a mechanical engineer. They had two children: a son, Cherney, born in 1922, and a daughter, Harriet, born in 1926.

Gertrude enrolled in writing courses at Columbia University. The only outlet for her theatrical impulse was the Jewish Art Theater. As for her writing, most of her articles were rejected by the magazines to which she submitted them.

When her husband's career began to slide, friends urged Gertrude to try to sell her skits to radio. She sold one script, *Effie and Laura,* a dialogue between two salesgirls, to CBS. Berg played one of the characters in the four half-hour episodes that were scheduled to run. After one broadcast, however, it was evident that the show flopped, and the other three shows never aired.

In 1929, she produced *The Rise of the Goldbergs,* which was a triumph and was broadcast over a national NBC radio network until 1935. Berg was paid $75 for producing the weekly series, from which the salaries of the rest of the cast had to be paid. But as the show became an enormous success, her salary rose to $7500 a week.

In the series, Gertrude Berg portrayed a sympathetic and sentimental character living out the adventures of a Jewish family trying to adjust to life on the East Side of New York City. She was a short, plump, homey Jewish mother, a character Berg modeled after her own mother and grandmother. The show had humor and appealed to all kinds of audiences.

Gertrude Berg's *Molly Goldberg* became one of the fixtures of radio in the late 1940s. Her trademark, trying to get her upstairs neighbor's attention by shout-

Cleveland Press, Reference Department

Molly Goldberg of The Goldbergs.

ing out her window, "Yoo-hoo, Mrs. Bloom!" delighted millions of listeners.

Berg wrote, produced and directed the program. It became one of several notable "ethnic" comedies during the 1930s and 1940s (joining *Lum and Abner* [Arkansas hillbillies], *Amos 'n' Andy* [blacks in Harlem] and *Life with Luigi* [Italians in Chicago]. The Berg series was radio's longest-running daytime serial, airing from 1929 to 1948.

In 1938, Gertrude Berg branched out to the movies, writing the film, *Make a Wish*.

When the radio program left the air in 1948, Berg sensed that there might be a chance to get into television, then a fledgling medium.

That year, she wrote and starred in a Broadway production of *Me and Molly*. The play was successful and helped create interest in the television program.

Premiering on January 10, 1949, *The Goldbergs* became one of television's earliest successes. The CBS network's first major situation-comedy, it soon became one of the most popular and lucrative programs on television. For many viewers, it marked the first time that they came into contact with an authentic representation of American Jewish life.

Phillip Loeb was cast as Jake, Molly's husband, the role he had played on the radio version from 1945 to 1948. Their interaction was crucial to the success of the show. Loeb played Jake Goldberg on television from 1949 to 1951.

Molly managed the household; Jake ran a small clothing business. Molly was both peacemaker and family gossip. She was always looking for the "perfect match" for their teenage son or daughter.

In the early scripts, the characters used heavy Yiddish accents. In time, Berg altered the dialogue, hoping to create humor not from her accent, but from her malapropisms (known as Mollypropisms).

The program appealed to both Jews and non-Jews. Once a mother superior from a Philadelphia convent wrote to Berg asking for a synopsis of six weeks of programs. The nuns, regular Goldberg fans, had given up the program for Lent and wanted to be filled in on what they had missed.

The Girls' Club of America honored Gertrude Berg as the Radio and TV Mother of the Year in 1950.

Misfortune struck in the spring of 1951. It was the time of the McCarthy "witch hunts" and Phillip Loeb was a target. His name had been put on a blacklist along with other performers and writers suspected of being Communists.

General Foods, the show's sponsor, came under heavy pressure to have Loeb dropped from the show, eventually telling Berg that it would pull out of the show unless Loeb was dismissed.

For Gertrude Berg, it was an agonizing choice. To support her co-star and lose a sponsor seemed foolish, however laudatory. To support the sponsor and jettison her co-star appeared sensible, but heartless. She consulted with Phillip Loeb, certain that he was innocent of the charges against him.

She chose to resist the pressure from General Foods and hope that the storm would pass. When it did not, General Foods withdrew its advertising from the program. The corporation claimed it was "dissatisfied with the show's ratings," which was odd because millions of viewers were watching it.

The network got into the act. Feeling the pressure, CBS dropped *The Goldbergs*. NBC picked up the show at once. No sponsor, however, would touch the show as long as Phillip Loeb remained in the cast.

Gertrude Berg would not budge, knowing all too well that unless *The Goldbergs* returned to TV soon, it would disappear from its viewers' minds. Another factor weighed heavily on her mind: If she retained Loeb, she would force the forty other members of the cast and crew to lose work.

Grudgingly she decided in December 1951 to offer Loeb an $85,000 cash settlement if he would quit the show. "I certainly have tried," she said forlornly. "I think everybody in the business knows it pretty well."

Loeb turned her down, continuing with his struggle to stay on the show, winning little support. Finally he accepted Gertrude Berg's offer. By waiting as long as he did, he received less money. The settlement had dropped to $40,000. Loeb praised Gertrude Berg for her behavior throughout the ordeal. *The Goldbergs* found a new sponsor, The Vitamin Corporation of America, and, without Phillip Loeb, returned to television in February 1952, this time with Harold J. Stone in the role of Jake.

In the fall of 1955, with ratings dropping, the Goldberg television family moved to suburbia. But the show's folksy immigrant humor was wearing thin. The show left television after that season.

Gertrude Berg went on to other triumphs. In 1959, she played Mrs. Jacoby, who falls in love with a rich Japanese man, in the Broadway play *A Majority of One*.

In 1961 and 1962, she starred in her own television series, called *The Gertrude Berg Show*. Playing an older version of Molly Goldberg, she was Sarah Green, a widow who in late middle age enrolls in college to earn her degree. The humor in the show came from the interplay of Mrs. Green's Yiddish-accented dialogue with her English teacher, Professor Crayton, played by Sir Cedric Hardwicke. His character was on exchange from Cambridge University, and very British in manner and speech.

In 1963, at the age of sixty-four, she played Libby Hirsch, who employs psychoanalysis to help her family with their problems, in the Broadway musical, *Dear Me, The Sky is Falling*, capping a rich theatrical career before her death in 1966.

SARAH BERNHARDT

"The Divine Sarah"

Born October 25, 1844 in Paris, France; died in 1923. French actress. She was the outstanding actress of her time, known both for her great artistic performances and her eccentricities. Except on rare occasions, especially in her later years, she always performed in French. Her most notable roles on the stage were the lead in *Magda* and that of the Duc de Reichstadt (Napoleon II) in *L'Aiglon*.

She was born Sarah Henriette Rosine Bernard and was the eldest of three illegitimate daughters born to Judith van Hard, a Dutch Jewish courtesan and music teacher. Her father was Edouard Bernard, a French student of law.

Sarah's mother, who thought that her daughter interfered with her lifestyle, enrolled the child, at age ten, in the convent of Versailles. Sarah, a frail and sickly child, was baptized at Versailles at age twelve. Although Sarah was proud of her Jewish heritage, she did, however, consider becoming a nun. As a child she was described as "a frail little girl with great almond-shaped eyes and a rebellious mass of wavy chestnut hair."

She was talked out of a religious life by the half-brother of Napoleon III, one of her mother's lovers. He convinced her to become an actress and even arranged for her to attend the *Conservatoire Français,* a state dramatic school associated with the *Théâtre Français.* Sarah disliked her instructors and, in turn, her teachers thought she had little chance of becoming an actress.

Nonetheless she made her acting debut at the *Comédie Française* in 1862 as Iphigenie in Racine's *Iphigenie en Aulide.* Sarah Bernhardt was not beautiful. Critics at the time pointed to her frizzy red-gold hair and her thin, pale face combined with sharp eyes and a slim, frail body as the sources of her attractiveness.

At times, her temper got in her way. On one occasion she slapped the face of another actress and was fired from the company. She had doubts about continuing as an actress. During this period, she gave birth to a son, fathered by Henri, Prince de Ligne.

Bernhardt continued in the theater. From 1866 to 1872, she performed in plays at the Odeon Theater, achieving her first true success, in *Le Passant,* in which she played a page named Zanetto, her first male role. She gave a command performance before Napoleon III. Her voice was described as similar to a "golden bell" and the "silver sound of running water."

In 1870, during the siege of Paris, Sarah Bernhardt turned the Odeon theater quite literally into a military hospital to treat the wounded. Later, she performed in Victor Hugo's *Ruy.* Hugo called her "golden-voiced" dubbing her "the divine Sarah."

Bernhardt returned to the *Comédie Française* and became one of the most outstanding interpreters of the French dramatist Jean Racine's plays, portraying the lead roles in *Adromaque* in 1873 and *Phèdre* in 1874. She ended her career at the *Comédie* because of her mercurial temperament and an impatience with those in authority. Her departure from the company was front-page news and was said to have cost her 100,000 francs, apparently for not fulfilling her contract.

Sarah's then embarked on a career as an independent star not affiliated with a company, making her American debut at Booth's Theater on November 8, 1880. This was the first of nine American tours that she would undertake, the last one in 1916. For her first appearance, she wisely chose the role her American critics considered her best part, playing the doomed actress in the title role in *Adrienne Lecouvreur*.

So famous was Sarah Bernhardt that her sellout tour earned her over $156,000. She was paid $1,000 a performance plus traveling expenses, an enormous sum in those days.

Sarah's fans worshipped her, kneeling and kissing the

hems of her dresses; royal ladies laid bouquets at her feet; kings kissed her hand. In the midst of anti-Semitic difficulties in Tsarist Russia, aristocrats took time to give her a beautiful coat and muff of hand-picked furs. The tributes paid to her were so overdone that Bernhardt once remarked casually to a friend, "Yes, I attract all the lunatics of the world!" When anyone happened to make an anti-Semitic remark in her presence, she retorted proudly, "I, too, am a daughter of the great Jewish people!"

In 1882, she married the actor Jacques Damala. He died seven years later.

Her American critics thought she was best in emotional roles and weaker in truly tragic parts. *The New York Herald* observed, "In depicting human suffering she seems to absolutely control every organ of her body—her cheek blanches, tears come at her bidding...but where her lines call for the grand and imposing effects of concentrated passion...Mademoiselle Bernhardt lacked breadth, force and passion."

Sarah Bernhardt was the greatest example of the French classic school of acting, which was characterized by acting with plenty of emotional nuances and tears.

Beyond this, Bernhardt had a fire of her own. Critics thought this fire came from her

Jewish ancestry. Her influence over the drama of her day was immense. Her world tours made her an ambassador of French culture to the rest of the world.

Bernhardt had a sporadic love-hate affair with early cinema. In 1900, Sarah Bernhardt made her film debut in *Hamlet's Duel*. She remarked afterward that she hated the new medium. However, she agreed to appear in a second film, *Tosca* in 1908. After witnessing the first rushes, she insisted that the negatives be destroyed. Nonetheless, she appeared in a third film, *La Dame aux Camelias,* in 1911, which was considered a critical and popular success. Indeed, her appearance in the film helped to boost the new medium of the cinema.

In 1912, Sarah Bernhardt made the British film *Queen Elizabeth.* Using the profit from this film, Adolph Zukor founded the Paramount movie studio.

Bernhardt embarked on a series of tours abroad, drawing crowds wherever she went. She acted during the London theater season virtually every year until 1922. She also acted in Germany, although not until 1911 to demonstrate her patriotic sentiments, Russia, Latin America, and Australia.

Bernhardt liked to live well, spending more money than she earned. She earned 20,000 francs a year, but she often spent 50,000. Her furs came from Russia, her velvets from Italy, her silks were woven to order in Lyons, France. She earned a huge $6,000,000 from her American tours alone.

She founded her own theater company in 1899, naming it the Theatre Sarah Bernhardt. She served as its director until her death in 1923.

Playing the title role in Sardou's *Tosca* in Latin America in 1905, Sarah Bernhardt jumped off a cliff in the final act, injuring her knee. For ten years she neglected the injury and, as a result, complications arose. She had to have her right leg amputated in 1914. She continued to appear in roles that permitted her to lie on a sofa.

During World War I, Bernhardt appeared before French troops, and was carried around to entertain them for eighteen months. She wrote her autobiography, *Ma Double Vie,* and published it in 1907. She was sixty-three years old.

In 1923, at the age of seventy-nine, Bernhardt began making a film called *La Voyante* largely because she was badly in need of money. In seriously failing health by then, she had to remain in her Paris hotel room. To enable her to appear in the movie, the filmmakers turned her quarters into a movie studio. She died before the film was completed.

Glenda Jackson portrayed Sarah Bernhardt on the screen in *The Incredible Sarah* in 1976. Bernhardt's legend survives.

BERURIAH

Talmudic Scholar

Born in the first quarter of the second century in Palestine; date of death unknown. Talmudic scholar. One of the most remarkable women in Jewish history and literature, she is the only woman recognized in the Talmud as a scholar in her own right. She is also the only woman whose views on Halachic (the body of Jewish law and tradition) matters were taken into account by the scholars of her time.

The story of the second-century Talmudic scholar Beruriah is unusual. At that time it was hard to find a woman who could understand the Talmud since Jewish girls were not permitted to study the subject. Beruriah, who was born in the second century B.C.E., challenged tradition when she set out to become an authority on these works of Jewish law.

She was the daughter of Rabbi Hananiah ben Teradion, one of the greatest sages of his time and one of the "ten martyrs" about whom Jews read on Yom Kippur. She was also the wife of Rabbi Meir, the prize student of Rabbi Akiva. Rabbi Meir was regarded as one of the greatest Rabbinic scholars in Jewish history.

Beruriah lived most of her life in Tiberias on the eastern shore of the Sea of Galilee in northern Palestine. Through reading and studying, she acquired an incredible amount of knowledge and engaged in discussions with the scholars of the academy. Several times, she convinced them of a point she wanted to make.

Beruriah was highly respected for her scholarly pursuits and became a model, a yardstick for students of Jewish law. From the Talmud one learns that Rabbi Simlai asked Rabbi Johanan to teach him the complex Book of Genealogies in three months. Rabbi Johanan grew angry and said, "If Beruriah, who was able to learn three hundred laws from three hundred teachers in one day, nevertheless took three years to learn the Book of Genealogies, where did you get the absurd idea that you could do it in three months?"

Her life, however, was filled with hardship. One after another, members of her immediate family encountered tragedy. Because of his devotion to the Torah, her father was killed by the Romans. So, too, was her mother. Both Beruriah's children died on the same day. A younger sister of Beruriah's was carried off to a foreign city by the ruling Romans, and placed in a house of prostitution. Fortunately, Rabbi Meir, Beruriah's husband, managed to extricate his sister-in-law.

Both Beruriah and her brother, who was close to her in age, were considered brilliant students. While very young, they became authorities on complex questions of Jewish law. Once, when Beruriah and her brother were questioned on a difficult point of Jewish law, Judah ben Baba, a Mishnaic scholar, hearing that the brother and sister disagreed, remarked, "Rabbi Hananiah's daughter teaches better than his son."

Perhaps because his exceptional sister outshone him in his studies, Beruriah's brother fell in with a band of robbers. Betraying his fellow conspirators to the authorities, he was killed in revenge, his mouth filled with dust and pebbles. Beruriah was not harmed, most likely because she was married to Rabbi Meir, known to be apolitical and to have been friendly with an influential Roman.

The personal tragedies of Beruriah's family were part of the larger misfortunes occurring to the Jewish people at this time. When the new Roman emperor, Hadrian, restricted the observance of such Jewish religious practices as circumcision, Jews became furious. Simon Bar Kochba, a Jewish military leader, led an insurrection that kept the Romans on the defensive for two years. Bar Kochba was eventually subdued and Jerusalem was rebuilt as a pagan city where Jews were prohibited from entering. The teaching of the Torah was proscribed along with the ordination of rabbis.

Surviving teachers of Jewish law, including Beruriah's father, ruled that to avoid death and torture all laws except the most important (those prohibiting murder, adultery and idolatry) could be broken. Rabbi Teradion and other rabbis, however, adopted a more rigid stance. Beruriah's father was burned to death by the Romans and he was later considered a martyred.

Part of Beruriah's brilliance lay in her ability to fire off incisive barbs. When Rabbi Yose the Galilean met her at some unidentified point on a journey, he asked, "By which road should we travel in order to reach Lydda?"

"Galilean fool," she replied. "Did not the rabbis say, 'Talk not overmuch with women?' You should have asked: 'How to Lydda?'"

Beruriah was a woman of unflagging fortitude. Her strength of character and complete commitment to God was exemplified best in the way she broke the news to her husband that their two sons had died on a Sabbath. To prevent her husband from grieving on the Sabbath, Beruriah kept the news from him upon his return from the academy on that Sabbath morning. Nonetheless, all day long her husband asked where the children were.

She kept her silence. The Sabbath finally over, she posed this question to him: "Some time ago a valuable object was entrusted to my safekeeping. Now the owner demands that I return it. Am I obliged to do so?"

Rabbi Meir replied without hesitation, "How can you doubt it?"

"Very well," Beruriah said, and then led her husband to the room where their dead sons were lying. He began to weep. She asked him: "Did you not tell me that we must give back what is given on trust?"

Beruriah then quoted Job: "The Lord hath given and the Lord hath taken away; blessed be the name of the Lord." The Talmud declared that Rabbi Meir was comforted by his wife's wisdom and piety.

Some evidence exists that Beruriah resented the restrictions placed upon women as well as the contempt held by some men for women's intellectual powers.

According to a legend mentioned by Rashi, the great medieval Jewish commentator on the Talmud, Beruriah made fun of a saying of the Rabbinical sages that "Women are lightheaded." Her husband Rabbi Meir, hoping to prove that Beruriah was wrong, and that indeed women *were* lightheaded, sought to test her virtue. In his mind apparently, one example of lightheadedness was being of easy virtue.

Rabbi Meir ordered one of his students to try to seduce his wife. She eventually yielded, after which she was so ashamed that, some contend that, she committed suicide.

Scholars have cast doubt on the veracity of this incident, for it seems preposterous that Beruriah would have committed the immoral act of adultery.

Her canon in biblical interpretation, "Look to the end of the verse" (Beruriah 10a) became an axiom for later authorities. The Talmud related the example of the non-believer who said to Beruriah, "It is written (Isaiah 54:1): 'Sing, O barren, thou that did not hear.' Because she did not have children is she to sing?"

Beruriah replied: "You fool! Look at the end of the verse where it is written, 'For the children of the desolate shall be more than the children of the married wife, saith the Lord.' The point is that at present she is barren but in the future, as related by the end of the passage, she shall have many children."

Beruriah explained that by "the desolate," Isaiah meant Jerusalem and by the "married wife" he meant Rome, so that eventually Judea and Jerusalem would be more populated than Rome.

Beruriah assured her place in history through her thoughtful interpretations of the religious writings of her time. Her ideas influence scholars to this day.

RAHEL BLUWSTEIN

Modern Hebrew Poet

> **Born in 1890, in Saratov, Russia; died in 1931 in Palestine.**
> Hebrew poet. Known simply as Rahel, she was one of the first
> authentic voices of the modern Jewish community in Palestine. Her
> writings helped shape the culture of the modern state of Israel. She
> emigrated from Russia, becoming a farmhand from 1908 to 1913.
> She left Palestine before World War I, returning after the fighting.
> She wrote some of the most memorable poetry in modern Hebrew
> and was one of the first Hebrew language poets to write in a conver-
> sational style.

"Rahel" was the way Rahel Bluwstein wanted to be known. She never used her surname. She was born in 1890 in Saratov, a town on the Volga River in northern Russia. She was raised in the Russian town of Poltava and began to write poetry in her native language at the age of fifteen. She also studied painting.

Emigrating to Palestine in 1909, Rahel settled in Rehovot when she was nineteen years old. Within her first year there, she was working at Kinneret, an agricultural settlement on the southern tip of the Sea of Galilee.

Once in Palestine, Rahel abandoned her native Russian language and learned Hebrew. Feeling the strong influence of the Zionist pioneer Hanna Maisel Shochat, Rahel became one of the first trainees at the young women's training farm at Kinneret. At Kinneret she met Aaron David Gordon, a philosopher who studied Zionist agrarianism. She hoped, as she told those at the time, "to make music with the hoe and to draw upon the earth." In 1920, she wrote her first poem in Hebrew and dedicated it to Gordon. It was called *Halokh Nefesh (Mood)*.

Bluwstein left Palestine before World War I but because she was unable to return there as the fighting raged on, she traveled back to Russia where she taught Jewish refugee children.

Rahel returned to Palestine after the war and settled in Degania, a kibbutz on the southern shore of Lake Kinneret. Degania had been organized in 1909 and was the first kibbutz of the Yishuv, the Jewish community in Palestine.

Bluwstein proved to be the voice of the Degania settlers both in her poetry and prose. In 1919, she expressed the feelings of those settlers when she wrote: "We trod ground which preserves the footsteps of our father Abraham; we heard the echo of the ancient word of the Lord 'and I will make thy name great.'"

She wrote lovingly of Lake Kinneret: "Its waters are said to be blessed with wondrous properties; whoever drinks therefrom, albeit only once, will return again and again. Is it not that our sons in strange lands yearn for the quiet shores of the Sea of Galilee for here their forefathers broke their thirst?"

Referring to those early days of settlement near the River Jordan, Rahel wrote: "The more meager the meal, the more joyous were our youthful voices. We shunned material comfort as an abhorrence, and welcomed hardship, sacrifice, privation. Through them we would sanctify the name of the homeland. The Sea of Galilee is not merely a scenic gem, a fragment of geography. It is interlocked with the destiny of a nation. From its depths our past gazes upon us with innumerable eyes, and with innumerable lips speaks to our hearts."

In his book, *Living With the Bible,* Moshe Dayan wrote movingly of Rahel Bluwstein, who in the early 1920s had taken care of him when he was only five years old: "...The sight of her countenance, noble, pallid, remains fresh in my mind to this day."

Bluwstein developed tuberculosis at that time and had to give up looking after the infants and young children of the kibbutz. She was given other work while undergoing treatment, but did not respond to the medication; she grew steadily weaker. The kibbutz physicians advised her to leave Degania for a healthier climate.

What Rahel knew of Hebrew came both from the developing spoken idiom and the Bible. She wrote in a modern conversational style. Critics have noted that her poetry contained clear, simple lyrical lines which sounded almost musical—a rarity in Hebrew poetry.

Her poems were short. One critic called her tone elegiac and nostalgic, reflecting the poetess's pessimism, undoubtedly forced on her by her illness. She became immensely popular.

She has become one of the major Hebrew-language poets and is considered a national poet of the modern state of Israel. Much of her poetry has been put to music, adding to her popularity for many decades. She also translated Russian, French, and Yiddish poetry into Hebrew.

Two volumes of her verse appeared while she was alive. *Safi'ah (Aftergrowth)* was published in 1927, and the other was *Mi-Neged (From the Opposite)* appeared in 1930. A third, *Nevo,* was published posthumously in 1932. In 1935, her poetry was collected in *Shirat Rahel (The Poetry of Rahel).*

Moshe Dayan, a great admirer of Rahel Bluwstein's poetry, wrote: "There was a depth of meaning to Rahel's poetry which I could grasp only in later years, when I had come to know something of life's struggles. But even as a child I was much moved by the poem entitled after her matriarchal namesake, Rahel." Dayan added that it read "like a Bible story. I loved its content, its rhythm, its

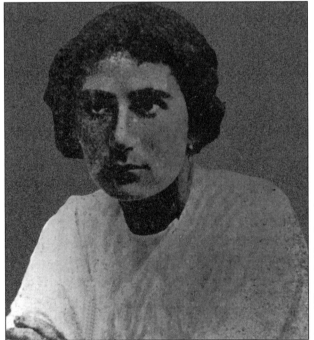

An early portrait taken April 16, 1931.

Central Zionist Archives, Jerusalem

short lyrical lines, its fantasy and its longings. I took in the words at their face value, and I believed them. I knew that they were the truth."

Rahel Bluwstein often laced her poetry with references to biblical events and characters, thus connecting the past with the present.

Her poem called *Barren* has been quite popular. She wrote:

> If only I had a child,
> a child of my own.
> Curly-haired, clever, and dark.
> To hold by the hand as we slowly
> strolled through the park.
> A child.
> Of my own.
>
> Uri, I'd call him, Uri my own.
> Gentle his name and clear,
> a droplet of a stream.
> To the dark child of my dream,
>
> 'Uri,'
> I'd call.
>
> Like Rahel our Mother I am bitter still.
> Still pray as Hannah prayed, her womb a stone.
> Still, still I await
> my own.

Israelis read Rahel's poetry and learned what moved their pioneering forbearers at the turn of the century, especially their growing attachment to the land as they settled it.

In *My Country* Rahel wrote:

> I haven't sung thy praise
> Nor glorified thy name
> In tales of valor
> And in wars.
> Only a tree I plant
> On Jordan's bank.
> Only a path my feet have tracked
> Across the fields.

In his book, *The Israelis,* Amos Elon writes that these lines "reflect the original ethos of this entire enterprise, the extraordinary craving to plant and to build that was such a powerful force in the early days of settlement."

One of Rahel Bluwstein's most popular poems was *Perhaps,* which described her "golden moments" on the shores of Kinneret:

And perhaps it was only a dream after all?
And perhaps
I never really went forth with the dawn
to toil with the sweat of my brow?

Can it be on those flaming and endless days
when we reaped,
that I never gave voice to a song as I rode
on a cartful of sheaves high-heaped?

That I never did bathe in the perfect and placid
blue gleam
of Kinneret, my sea, ah Kinneret, my own,
were you real, then, or only a dream?

BARBARA BOXER

A Liberal Politician from California

Born November 11, 1940, in Brooklyn, New York. American politician. Drawn to politics by the civil rights movement and the Vietnam War, Barbara Boxer served in Congress as a U.S. Representative for five terms before capturing one of the two United States Senate seats from California in November 1992. (The other Senate winner in that state was Dianne Feinstein.) When Boxer and Feinstein won their Senate races, it marked the first time that the state was represented in the Senate by two Jews.

Barbara Levy was born in 1940 to Ira and Sophie Levy and grew up in a lower middle-class neighborhood in Brooklyn. The Levy home followed kosher dietary rules, but Barbara's parents did not consider themselves overly religious. "My father was against the organized aspects of religion," Senator Boxer remarked. Still, she retains fond memories of seders and Jewish holiday celebrations at home. "It was another time," she says. "I grew up in the last generation of warmth and that oldtime [Russian Jewish], immigrant family of love."

She was a student at Brooklyn College in 1962 when she married Stewart Boxer. As newlyweds that year, Barbara and Stewart lived in a Brooklyn apartment which they enjoyed, but the musty carpet in the lobby seemed jarring. A promise came from the landlord to replace it. Nothing happened, and a few months later Barbara Boxer organized the tenants of the building into a protest group. The landlord promptly conceded and the rug was changed. It was Barbara Boxer's first "political" victory.

Her hope was to become a stockbroker but she grew frustrated when she found that getting the kind of job she wanted was nearly impossible. Though she had passed her qualifying exams, she says, "I was told, 'Women don't do this.'" That frustration led her into the world of politics.

Courtesy of Barbara Boxer/U.S. Senate

Visiting relatives in northern California, Boxer convinced her husband it was time to move. They settled in Marin County where they raised their two children, Doug and Nicole.

While her husband pursued his legal career, Boxer searched for ways to become active in public affairs. This was the era of Vietnam and the civil rights movement, and she knew she wanted to get involved in something worthwhile outside her home. She looked around for a worthy local pro-

Barbara Boxer (right) and Dianne Feinstein raise their hands in victory after the 1992 California primary.

RNS Photo/Reuters

ject with which to start. Inviting a group of neighborhood women to her backyard one day, Boxer helped to organize a program to counsel high school dropouts. It was successful enough eventually to be taken over by the county school system.

From 1974 to 1976, Barbara Boxer worked at the weekly newspaper, the *Pacific Sun*. She also served as a district aide to Representative John Burton, a Democrat. By now she called herself a "tough, unapologetic Democrat."

From 1976 to 1982 she served on the Marin County Board of Supervisors and from 1980 to 1982 was its first woman president. Barbara Boxer has not lost an election since 1976.

In 1982, Boxer won a seat in Congress, her first of five terms in the House of Representatives. She began her career in Congress with a highly publicized attack on Pentagon coffeepots which she discovered cost $7,622 each. She continuously rattled the Pentagon for condoning waste in the military. She fought in Congress against the AMX tank, the B-2 jet bomber and other expensive armaments that her male colleagues were constantly supporting.

Later, when she ran for the Senate, Boxer promised that her first move toward reducing the deficit would be to end the $150 billion subsidy of U.S. defense of Europe and Japan. "Bring that money home," she insisted.

Boxer was considered one of the most liberal voices in the House. She focused on women's rights, gay rights, the environment, health care and AIDS research.

In 1989, Boxer won support from most female members of Congress when she challenged Illinois' Henry Hyde, who was against her campaign to restore Medicaid funds in order to pay for abortions for victims of rape or incest. What was ultimately named the Boxer Amendment, passed both houses of Congress before President George Bush vetoed it. An unsuccessful attempt was then made to override the veto. Seventy percent of the female Congressional Representatives voted to override the veto, in contrast to just fifty-four percent of the men.

In the fall of 1992, Boxer ran for a full six-year term to become the successor to retiring Democrat Alan Cranston. She ran against Republican Bruce Herschensohn, an archconservative Jewish television commentator, for the U.S. Senate. She argued that male Senators could not be trusted to promote womens' issues; only a woman would do.

No other Senate race offered such a clear ideological choice with Barbara Boxer stressing her liberal agenda of abortion rights, environmental coastal protection and heavy military cuts. She promised that, if elected, she would "become [conservative North Carolina Senator] Jesse Helms's worst nightmare." Herschensohn, for his part, argued for a flat tax, against abortion, and for an end to environmental regulation.

It was a tough race. Herschensohn cut Boxer's comfortable twenty-point lead in half by late October due to an effective series of television ads criticizing Boxer. He branded her a Washington insider who wrote overdrafts on the House bank.

Both Boxer and Herschensohn were considered pro Israel; the Republican, however, scored some points by accusing his opponent of voting against foreign aid and military assistance bills that included aid for Israel. Those votes made Boxer somewhat suspect among the Jewish community. She rarely mentioned Israel during her Senate campaign. Early in the race she spoke at a Jewish rally in San Francisco and failed to mention the words "Jewish" or "Israel." Later, at a similar event in Los Angeles she did mention Israel but only briefly; she concentrated more on domestic and gender issues.

At a late October rally in Santa Monica, Boxer did say that Israel was "our best friend in the Middle East." She also favored moving the American Embassy from Tel Aviv to Jerusalem, something Israeli leaders have also pushed for over the years.

Many voters, it was believed, did not realize that Boxer, or Herschensohn for that matter, were Jewish, another reason why Judaism played such a small role in the campaign. Boxer turned up at an Hadassah rally and was surprised to learn that so many people in the audience did not realize she was Jewish.

On Election Day, the race was too close to call. Barbara Boxer won by a narrow margin, receiving 4,856,103 votes to Herschensohn's 4,288,284 votes. She became one of ten Jewish senators. Thirty-three fellow members of Congress were Jewish.

When Barbara Boxer and Dianne Feinstein won their Senate races in that 1992 election, it marked the first time any state had sent two women to the upper house. It also marked the first time a state was represented in the Senate by two Jews. Boxer and Feinstein were also the first Jewish women to make it into the Senate.

Appearing on NBC television the day after the election, Boxer said she felt that the women who had won in the elections had a shared vision of the future. "New priorities, [a new] domestic agenda, really having a pro-family America," she said.

FANNY BRICE

Funny Girl

Born October 29, 1891, in New York, New York; died May 29, 1951. American comedienne and singer. One of the early great Jewish show-business performers. Her career began in 1916, when Fanny Brice appeared in the Ziegfeld Follies and introduced the song that made her famous, "My Man." Her motion picture credits include *My Man, The Great Ziegfeld,* and *Everyone Sing.* In 1936, she created one of radio's most famous characters, Baby Snooks. She played the seven year-old imp over the radio almost continuously until her death in 1951.

Fannie Borach was Fanny Brice's name at birth. Her mother, Rosie Stern, born in a village near Budapest, Hungary, struggled to eke out a living by working in the garment industry in New York City. In later years, Fannie sang a song called "The Song of the Sewing Machine," which described the plight of her mother and many other women like her.

Rosie Stern had met and married a bartender named Charlie Borach. Their daughter Fannie was born in 1891 on the Lower East Side. Later, her parents separated. Rosie took the four Borach children—an older sister and two brothers—to Brooklyn.

Burlesque was big business in New York City, the entertainment capital of America. Many of the thousands of Jewish immigrants were bound to try their luck in this new musical comedy genre. From an early age, Fannie Brice talked of breaking into burlesque.

As a teenager, Fannie demonstrated a budding talent in show business. She could mimic different accents and intonations, she was funny, and she could sing. She was fourteen years old when she debuted on the stage of Brooklyn's Keeney Theater. The audience threw coins to her on stage. Owner Frank Keeney was impressed enough to ask her to perform at his two other theaters. The money was not bad; she earned $60 a week.

The next step was burlesque in Manhattan. Fannie wore clothes that were too tight, did a lot of wiggling to get the customers' attention, and sang some of her songs twice, once straight, but the next time in her own, comedy-laced style.

This was the era of the "coon song," a song sung by white entertainers in blackface who mimicked a Negro dialect. Fannie Brice sang such songs. She put on blackface and sang one of them

American Jewish Archives, Cincinnati Campus, Hebrew Union College, Jewish Institute of Religion

63

called "Lovely Joe," while appearing in the 1909 show *College Girls*. A year later, the famous Florenz Ziegfeld spotted her in a burlesque show and selected her for his *Ziegfeld Follies*. He admired her extraordinary timing, humor, and ability to strike a variety of poses. He was also intrigued by a theme that ran through many of her songs—the innocent woman as victim.

For her first number, Brice put on an Indian costume, adopted a Yiddish accent, and belted out, "I'm an Indian." As a performer, she was multifaceted: She also played a clutzy ballet dancer, an innocent ingenue who has become pregnant, and a sweet girl whom men misused.

Her singing-comedy routines contained social commentary. In "Becky is Back in the Ballet," which she recorded in 1922, told of a possessive mother who commanded her daughter to show off now that she was back dancing in the ballet. (Brice pronounced it "belly.") Fannie's targets were those first-generation Jewish Americans who saw ballet and other similar cultural pursuits as the best way to assimilate themselves.

Fannie Brice sang about "Mrs. Cohen at the Beach," supervising her children's bathing, gossiping with an old woman friend, telling her husband what to do. "Brice's carping," wrote one sympathetic critic, "her overzealousness, and her general bossiness made Mrs. Cohen an infuriating but funny Jewish busybody."

She justified her Jewish routines this way: "In anything Jewish I ever did, I wasn't standing apart, making fun of the race. What happened to me on stage is what could happen to them. They identified with me, and then it was all right to get a laugh, because they were laughing at me as well as at themselves."

During the early 1920s Fannie Brice became romantically involved with the Jewish gangster, Nicky Arnstein. They were married in February 1920, but the path of their marriage was bumpy. In 1921, when Fannie sang "My Man" on the stage of the *Ziegfeld Follies* professing love for her faithless lover, audiences sympathized with her. In 1924, Arnstein spent a year in jail. Fannie remained loyal—for a while. They were divorced in 1927.

Brice had a son and daughter with Arnstein. "I always hoped I'd have a boy and a girl, and I had them. I always hoped the boy would have talent, and not the girl, and it worked out that way. Because, as I realize it, I didn't want my daughter to have a career. Because if a woman has a career, she misses an awful lot."

She left the *Ziegfeld Follies* in 1923. During the 1920s and 1930s Brice performed in musical shows. Some were written and produced by Billy Rose, whom she married in 1929. (She was married three times and divorced three times.) Her best-known songs included "Second-Hand Rose" and "My Man." Audiences requested them frequently. She also made "Oy, How I Hate that Fellow Nathan" famous.

Her first movie performance came in 1929, with the Warner "talkie" called *My Man*. Though the film was a hit, Fannie Brice preferred live stage appearances. She returned to Broadway. In 1934, she appeared in the *Shubert Follies*.

With the rise of radio in the 1920s and 1930s, Brice appeared more frequently on the new mass medium. In 1929, she was often a guest on *The Rudy Vallee Show*. It was not until 1936 that she became a fixture on radio.

On February 29, 1936, on the *Ziegfeld Follies Show of the Air*, she introduced Baby Snooks, a character she created, an impish seven year-old who outwitted adults. The audiences loved her portrayal of Baby Snooks. The popular character provided Brice with a public outlet, financial security, and a less taxing format for her talent. Fanny Brice and Baby Snooks seemed interchangeable; Brice often gave interviews using the seven year-old's voice.

Fannie Brice will always be remembered for Baby Snooks. The naughty, smart-aleck child formed the basis of one of Brice's most memorable musical comedy acts.

In December 1937, Brice joined NBC in a musical comedy called *Good News of 1938;* her Baby Snooks character was a regular feature of the sixty-minute show. In March 1940, the program was renamed *The Maxwell House Coffee Time* but was cut to thirty minutes. (Fifteen minutes for Baby Snooks; fifteen minutes for comedian Frank Morgan.).

In 1944, *The Baby Snooks Show* became a thirty-minute program on CBS. The following year Brice suffered a mild heart attack. By 1949, *The Baby Snooks Show* was back on NBC. Right up to the time she died in 1951, Brice was performing as Baby Snooks on the air.

In 1964, a musical called *Funny Girl,* based on the life of Fanny Brice, was produced on Broadway. Four years later a movie by the same name was released. In that movie, Barbra Streisand, playing the starring role, displayed her great singing talent. A sequel, *Funny Lady,* was made in 1975. Fanny Brice was gone, but not forgotten.

ANITA BROOKNER

Outstanding British Novelist

Born July 16, 1928, in London, England. British art historian and novelist. After a long career as an art historian, Brookner developed into one of Great Britain's most important novelists. Before turning to fiction, she lectured in art history at London's Courtauld Institute of Art for more than twenty years and wrote books on artists and art criticism. In 1984, her novel *Hotel du Lac* won the National Book League's Booker Prize, Great Britain's most lucrative and prestigious literary award.

Integrating into England proved a challenge for Anita Brookner. She has described herself as "a sort of Jewish exile." Her maternal grandfather came from Poland, as did her father who brought a successful business with him when he immigrated to England.

Perhaps because of her parents', Newton and Maude (Schiska) Brookner, inability to adjust to their new country, Anita felt like an outsider growing up in England. "I have never learned the custom of the country," she said in a 1985 interview. "We were aliens. Jews. Tribal....I loved my parents painfully, but they were hopeless as guides."

To aid Anita in fighting off that sense of estrangement, when she was seven years old, Newton Brookner suggested she read Charles Dickens. From that great novelist Anita learned that the good and decent people triumph over bad ones, an idea she disputed in her own novels.

From Maude Brookner, who had abandoned a career in singing for marriage, Anita gained an appreciation of how wide the gap can be between expectations and reality. "She wanted me to be another kind of person altogether," Anita Brookner said. "I should have...been more popular, socially more graceful, one of those small, coy, kittenish women who get their way. If my novels contain a certain amount of grief it is to do with my not being what I would wish to be."

For that reason, she acknowledged that she had inherited from her parents "a very great residual sadness."

Anita attended James Allen's Girl's School. She also studied history at King's College, London, from which she received her bachelor of arts degree. During her King's College days, she attended lectures in art history at the National Gallery. That experience encouraged her to study the subject of art further, which she did, at the Courtauld Institute of Art from which she earned her doctorate degree.

After three years in Paris, she completed her thesis on the literary sources of some genre pictures of the pre-Revolutionary French painter Jean Baptiste Greuze.

From 1959 to 1964, Brookner was a visiting lecturer in art history at the University of Reading in Berkshire; then a lecturer at the Courtauld Institute. The director who appointed her was Anthony Blunt, later revealed to be a key figure in a spy scandal that also involved Guy Burgess.

Brookner became an authority on eighteenth- and nineteenth-century French art; she authored four studies in that field.

In 1967 and 1968, she was the Slade Professor of Fine Arts at Cambridge, the first woman to hold the post. In 1977, she became a reader in the history of art at the Courtauld with the rank of professor. She has also been a fellow of New Hall, Cambridge.

In the early 1980s, Anita Brookner began writing novels. She

Courtesy of *The Jewish Chronicle*

Anita Brookner (right) with fellow novelist Melvyn Bragg at a reception in London organized by the Friends of the Jewish National and University Library in Jerusalem. June 6, 1986.

started her first during a long summer vacation in 1980, calling the effort "a little exercise in self-analysis." Each year, since 1981, she has written a short novel. Possessing little action, her novels are instead studies of character. Writing of bourgeois manners and morals, she describes the tensions and agitations that her characters experience. Her protagonists are women—lonely, intellectual, well-groomed, possessing the kind of moral code that keeps them from going after or getting the kind of man they eagerly seek. Is honesty the best policy in pursuing romantic love? Brookner asks that question often in her novels.

Her first novel, *A Start in Life,* published in 1981, was called *The Debut* when it appeared in the United States. It told the story of Dr. Ruth Weiss, a quiet scholar who was devoted to the study of Balzac. She decided at the age of forty that literature had destroyed her life and that those who were virtuous were doomed to become passive victims with no choice but to live unsatisfying lives.

Brookner's second novel, *Providence,* was published in 1982. It was followed by *Look at Me* (1983); and *Hotel du Lac* (1984), which won the Booker Prize.

The hero of *Hotel du Lac* is a writer of romantic fiction who is sent to Switzerland after an "unfortunate lapse" (jilting her bridegroom on their wedding day), she is recuperating there, pining away for a man whom she loves, but who is married and will not leave his wife and children.

In 1985, Brookner wrote *Family and Friends,* departing from her previous works in order to respond to critics who felt that her fiction, by being largely autobiographical, had been too restrictive. The novel chronicled the affairs of a wealthy Jewish family during the 1930s and 1940s.

A year later, Brookner wrote *The Misalliance,* which returned to her theme of women living on their own. In this novel, Blanche, newly divorced, seemed eccentric to others; she accused herself of being too genteel and caring, thus resulting in her sense of isolation.

Other Brookner novels are *A Friend from England* (1987); *Latecomers* (1988); *Lewis Percy* (1989); and *Brief Lives* (1990).

The Brookner protagonist is typically a lonely women of early middle age, sometimes exiled, or orphaned, frequently clinging to traditions. Inhibited and solitary, these women tentatively take on love affairs that often lead to disappointment. Turning to artistic creation of one sort or another, the protagonist becomes only more lonely. Critics have said that no woman writer since Charlotte Bronte has pursued these themes with as much aggressiveness as Anita Brookner.

Critic Lyn Pykett noted: "Brookner's own element is time, and life in her novels is viewed as a long, slow, process of attrition, more or less passively endured."

A recurring concern of Brookner novels has been the choice between marriage and a single life. Though her characters yearned for marriage and domesticity at times, her novels have been filled with examples of how inadequate, frustrating and difficult marriages can be.

In *Brief Lives,* the character Fan Langdon says it well: "There must be several things a woman can do other than think of love and marriage. The young, of course, know this or they seem to nowadays. My generation was less realistic. It seems to me now that my own youth was passed in a dream, and that I only came to see the world as it was when it was already too late."

Critic Gerda Charles noted that Brookner has "an almost magical gift for making important what can only be described, with the pleasure of recognition, as the trivia of day to day living."

In her reviews and interviews, Anita Brookner has spoken out against feminists and feminism, though her novels explored the contradictions of marriage and romantic love in ways that feminists might approve.

In 1990, Brookner, who has never married and lives in an unassuming apartment in London, was named a Commander, Order of the British Empire.

DEBORAH

Judge and Prophet of Ancient Israel

> **Born and died 12th century B.C.E.** Biblical figure. The only female biblical judge, Deborah was a charismatic figure who was a judge and prophet, uncommonly prominent roles for women of her era. She was a warrior who unified Israel and became a political leader as well. *The Song of Deborah* is considered one of the oldest extant examples of Hebrew literature.

The great heroines of the Bible—Sarah, Rebecca, Leah and Rachel—were revered as mothers and wives, and as women who carried out God's will. Miriam, a leader and prophet, as was Deborah, led only the women of Israel. Esther saved the Jews, but under her cousin Mordechai's direction. Only Deborah acted on her own as judge, leader, prophetess, warrior.

According to the Bible, Deborah is the only judge who actually judged. It was her habit to dispense justice while seated in the hill country of Ephraim, between Beth-El and Ramah under the "palm-tree of Deborah." It was an unidentified site sacred to the people and possibly identified by popular tradition with Allon-Bachuth, the burial site of Deborah, Rebeccah's nurse. Commentators have suggested that Deborah passed judgment in the open air because it was not proper for men to visit a woman in her own house.

Deborah's tribal affiliation is uncertain. Yet her place of residence indicates she was an Ephraimite or may have been related to Issachar. Both in the narration of the events and in *The Song of Deborah,* she appears to be a national leader who earned the title "mother in Israel." It is known that Deborah was married, but nothing is known about her husband other than that his name was Lappidoth.

Some see in Deborah's image the *kahin* (or *kahina*), known among the nomadic Arab tribes as a judge in a sanctified place, a magician, and fortune-teller who aroused the warriors to battle with a song.

During Deborah's life, early in the twelfth century B.C.E., the Israelites found themselves in serious trouble. It was only a few generations after Joshua's conquest and there had been a Canaanite revival. Jabin, the Canaanite king of Hazor, who was presumed to be a descendant of the Jabin, whom Joshua had defeated soundly, was in control of northern Canaan.

Deborah became the first leader after Joshua to take up arms against the Canaanites. To lead a war of liberation against Jabin, Deborah selected the tribal leader Barak, ordering him to bring together 10,000 soldiers. She commanded Barak to fight Sisera, Jabin's general. The battlefield was not considered a suitable place for women in biblical tales.

Deborah broke that mold. Barak would not enter battle without Deborah accompanying him. Her role was to draw Sisera, commander of King Jabin's forces, to the valley of the River Kishon to the west. This would give Barak the opportunity to attack from the rear.

Deborah went with Barak to Kedesh-Naphtali, where he enlisted "ten thousand men from the tribe of Naphtali and the tribe of Zebulun." The biblical account is not clear about Deborah's precise battlefield role; though she was present, at least for some time, it seems that she remained aloof from the fighting, yet very much in charge. Mobilizing a powerful coalition of northern and central tribes at Mount Tabor in northern Israel to his side, Sisera gathered nine hundred iron chariots. His enemy had none.

Promising her troops victory, Deborah commanded Barak to exploit the fortuitous flooding of the valley of the Kishon Brook. When he did, Sisera's chariots sank in the mud and were disabled. Sisera's army was wiped out.

Sisera fled the battlefield by foot, taking refuge in the tent of Jael, wife of Heber the Kenite. Jael greeted him pleasantly enough, then offered him milk and agreed to stand guard at the tent door while Sisera slept. Once her guest was asleep, Jael split Sisera's skull open with a tent peg. This fulfilled Deborah's prophecy that Sisera would "fall into the hands of a woman."

With Deborah's victory, the strength of the Canaanites in the north was broken. While not entirely destroyed, they disappeared as a political force from that area of the country. Deborah's victory started a forty-two-year period of peace for Israel—until the Philistines arose to challenge their hegemony over the Promised Land.

On that day of victory Deborah and Barak sang *The Song of Deborah*—one of the oldest passages in the Bible—to celebrate their triumph.

Deborah's war is the only one described in the *Book of Judges*. It might have been Israel's final campaign against the Canaanites.

Some biblical commentators have expressed surprise that Deborah initiated a war, living as far from the Canaanite kingdom as she did. It has also surprised some that she summoned Barak, who also lived a great distance from the Canaanite kingdom.

These events are related in two separate accounts in the Bible. One is in prose form in Judges 4; the other, in Judges 5, is in verse, and is called *The Song of Deborah*. It is one of the earliest examples of poetry in the Bible. Deborah is considered the author of this triumphant song of victory that spells out, among other things, in precise detail how Jael kills Sisera in his sleep. "With the hammer she struck Sisera, she crushed his head; she struck and his brains ebbed out."

The song praises God, who brought "the stars in their courses" in order to beat back Sisera. It congratulates those forces who participated in the battle. Scorning those who did not, it heaps blessings on Jael, winding up with a plea for the destruction of all of God's enemies. "Champions there were none," goes the song, "none left in Israel, until I, Deborah, arose, arose, a mother in Israel...."

Among the most magnificent and, according to biblical scholars, the earliest of Hebrew heroic poems, Deborah's song was apparently sung antiphonally. The presence of numerous feminine images reinforces the view that the author was a woman. The poem opens with an invitation to kings and princes to listen and a prologue describing nature's ecstatic response to the revelation at Sinai, as well as to Deborah's war.

Efforts to determine the precise time and place of Deborah's war or to date the song have repeatedly failed. The best guess among scholars, however, puts the period of its writing at about 1200-1125 B.C.E.

The story of Deborah and the associated episode of Jael and Sisera have given rise to very few literary works. They were the subjects of illustrations in thirteenth- and fourteenth-century manuscripts; the Psalter of St. Louis (French, thirteenth-century) contains a work of art showing Deborah going forth with Barak and his men to make war on Sisera.

In Germany's Ulm Cathedral, Deborah, sword in hand, figures in the row of female prophets on the hand-carved, fifteenth-century choir stall. She also appears occasionally in baroque paintings. Her image is one of courage and strength—a woman who paved the way for many others through the centuries.

GERTRUDE B. ELION

1988 Nobel Prize Winner

Born January 23, 1918 in New York, New York. American biochemist. In 1988, she won the Nobel prize for demonstrating the differences in nucleic acid metabolism among normal cells and disease-causing cancer cells, protozoa, bacteria, and viruses. Her research in new drug creation and medicine has been revolutionary. Because of her research into various compounds, childhood leukemia went from a disease that was fatal to one in which eighty percent of its victims survive. She also developed treatments for gout and herpes as well as the first drug to attack viruses. Her research set the stage for AZT; for years AZT was the only drug approved by the Food and Drug Administration for treatment of AIDS patients.

Gertrude—whom everyone called Trudy—was born in New York City in 1918. Her father, Robert Elion, was the descendant of many generations of rabbis. At the age of twelve, he came to the United States from Lithuania. Trudy's mother, Bertha Cohen, had arrived from Russia on her own when she was fourteen. A music lover, Robert Elion frequently took Trudy to the Metropolitan Opera.

Bertha urged Trudy to find a career so that she would be free to decide what she wished to buy rather than have to ask her husband's approval.

After her grandfather, a watchmaker and biblical scholar, arrived from Russia, the family began to speak Yiddish to one another.

When Trudy was six, her brother Herbert was born and the family moved to the Bronx. Shy, fond of books, Trudy eagerly sought knowledge. "It didn't matter if it was history, languages, or science. I was just like a sponge." Her childhood idols were Louis Pasteur and Marie Curie, because they had made scientific discoveries.

When her father went bankrupt during the 1929 stock-market crash, Trudy's prospects of attending college dimmed. However, her high grades won her admission to Hunter College, which charged no tuition. She chose her career goal after visiting her grandfather in the hospital; he was dying slowly, painfully, from stomach cancer. His illness was an incentive to her to help conquer the disease. She chose chemistry as her field, rather than biology, since she was unhappy at the thought of dissecting animals.

In 1937, Elion graduated from Hunter with high honors. Though she was a Phi Beta Kappa scholar, she was unable to obtain financial aid or an assistantship to pursue her doctorate. She blamed it on discrimination against women. At one job interview, she was told that she was qualified, but "we think you'd be a distracting influence."

Frustrated, she enrolled in secretarial school. About that time, she fell in love with a brilliant statistics major at City College. They decided to marry, but he became desperately ill and died. Elion never totally recovered.

For the next seven years she worked at uninteresting jobs and, by living at home, saved what was then the large sum of $450. Attending graduate school in chemistry at New York University, Elion held down a part-time job as a doctor's receptionist and was a substitute teacher in New York City high schools.

In 1942, as World War II had caused the supply of male chemists to dwindle, she began working in research labs. Two years later, she was working at Burroughs Wellcome, a British pharmaceutical firm which had its American headquarters in Tuckahoe, New York.

By virtue of her altering the way drugs are discovered and her discoveries of various crucial drugs, Elion has had a revolutionary effect upon medicine.

Discarding the usual trial-and-error method, she and George Hitchings, her collaborator, did research on the small differences between how normal and abnormal cells reproduce. They then developed drugs to interrupt the life cycle of abnormal cells, leaving the healthy cells unharmed.

Courtesy of Burroughs Wellcome

After work each evening Elion traveled by subway to the Brooklyn Polytechnic Institute where she pursued her doctorate. After two years the dean insisted that she quit her job and work on her doctorate full-time. She refused and was subsequently dropped as a doctoral candidate.

In 1950, only thirty-two years old, Elion achieved major breakthroughs in medical research, synthesizing two effective cancer treatments.

The first drug she discovered was a purine compound that interfered with the formation of leukemia cells.

Half of all children with acute leukemia died within three or four months; fewer than a third lived a year. When the drug, called Diaminopurine, was tested on animals at the Sloan-Kettering Memorial Hospital in New York City, it appeared so effective that it was immediately tested on two terminally-ill leukemia patients. The compound proved, however, to be too toxic.

Elion did not give up. She substituted a sulfur atom for the oxygen atom on a purine molecule, giving her a new compound that was called 6-mercaptopurine, 6-MP for short.

Though not a cure for leukemia, the drug sent the disease into temporary remission. Yet children who were given the compound still suffered relapses and eventually died.

In 1950, Elion also synthesized thioguanine, a close relative of 6-MP. Once doctors learned to combine 6-MP or thioguanine with other drugs, they were able to treat childhood leukemia effectively, completely curing some eighty percent of its victims.

By the late 1950s, researchers were trying to cure other illnesses using 6-MP. In 1961, a kidney transplant worked, because of a drug called Imuran, a highly sophisticated version of 6-MP that Elion had synthesized. Imuran is still used to prevent kidney rejection and to treat autoimmune lupus, anemias, hepatitis, and severe rheumatoid arthritis.

Another compound called allopurinol, developed in the laboratories of Burroughs Wellcome, had the effect of reducing the body's production of uric acid, which, when too much is made, causes gout. This same drug was also useful in treating leishmaniasis, a disease which had been prevalent in South America and Asia.

In 1967, when George Hitchings retired from active research, Elion became head of the Department of Experimental Therapy at Burroughs Wellcome.

The next year, she began a decade-long search, frequently in secret, for a drug that would work effectively against viruses. After years of work, she helped achieve a breakthrough, working out the mechanism of action for Zovirax. This was a drug that was Burrough Wellcome's biggest-selling product with $1.1 billion in sales in 1992. The drug combats shingles, genital herpes, chicken pox and herpes encephalitis.

In 1983, Elion retired and became a consultant to Burroughs Wellcome. A year later, her old unit, which had relied on her approach, produced Azidothymidine, or AZT. Until late 1991, AZT was the only drug licensed to treat the AIDS virus in the United States. Though she is frequently given credit for developing AZT, Elion claims she did not play a direct role in the advent of the drug.

Elion heard about winning the Nobel prize at 6:30 A.M. on October 17, 1988. She was a co-recipient along with George Hitchings, and Sir James W. Black of the University of London. The three winners shared the $390,000 in prize money. It was the first Nobel prize awarded for drug research in thirty-one years and one of only a few to be given for cancer treatment. Elion won the prize for demonstrating the differences in nucleic acid metabolism between normal cells and disease-causing cancer cells, protozoa, bacteria, and viruses. Elion was one of the few people ever to win a Nobel prize in the sciences without obtaining a Ph.D.

However thrilled she was at getting the big prize, she always placed it second in importance to saving lives. "It's very nice," she said of winning the prize, "but that's not what it's all about. I'm not belittling the prize. The prize has done a lot for me, but if it hadn't happened, it wouldn't have made that much difference."

In 1991, she won the National Medal of Science, the nation's highest science honor.

Thomas Krenitsky, research vice president at Burroughs Wellcome, said, "In fifty years, Trudy Elion will have done more cumulatively for the human condition than Mother Theresa." High praise for a dedicated and hard-working female Jewish scientist, who has devoted her life to finding cures.

ESTHER

Biblical Heroine

Exact place and time of birth and death unknown. One of the most beloved women in Jewish history, Esther is the heroine of the biblical Book of Esther. She is considered one of the most beautiful women who ever lived. She was first called Hadassah, but later assumed the name of Esther, which is the Persian name of Hadassah. It was Esther who saved the Jews of Persia when they faced extinction at the hands of the king and the wicked Haman.

Her father died prior to her birth; her mother died giving birth to her. She was a descendant of the tribe of Benjamin, an orphan who had been brought into the house of her cousin Mordechai. Esther's Hebrew name was Hadassah (myrtle); the rabbis explained that just as the myrtle spreads fragrance, so Esther spread good deeds throughout the land.

She grew into an attractive Jewish maiden, and some have called her one of the most beautiful women who ever lived. Mordechai may have married her. He had an office in the household of Ahasuerus, the king of Persia (who some believe to be the Xerxes of history). The king dwelt in the capital city of Shushan.

Haman, the prime minister, encouraged the king to believe that the Jews, who were scattered throughout his empire, were a pernicious people. The king, accepting what Haman had told him, gave his vizier authority to kill all of the Jews who dwelt within the realm.

The Book of Esther tells how Esther averted this great calamity. The story is told in two forms: one, a shorter form, consists of 167 verses in the Hebrew Bible; the longer form, 270 verses, appears in the Septuagint, the Greek translation.

The story of the Book of Esther relates that Ahasuerus (Xerxes), the Persian king, arranged a banquet for the nobles of his 127 provinces. His queen, Vashti, refused to come to the men's feast. The king sent her away and issued a decree that all wives should obey their husbands.

Some time later, obviously distressed by his wife's behavior, he summoned all the beautiful maidens of the kingdom so that he could choose a new queen.

Israel Museum

Esther: detail from The Rothschild Miscellany, *illuminated manuscript, Italy, 1470-1480.*

The king chose Esther, Mordechai's ward, because of her beauty. He did not know her race or parentage. Esther has been described as gifted, charming, modest, obedient, and loyal. Esther became queen but told no one that she was a Jew.

Haman the Agagite became prime minister. When Mordechai refused to bow down to him, Haman became so furious that he resolved to kill all the Jews, including Mordechai.

Haman therefore cast lots (purim) to determine which month was favorable for his plan. The lot fell on the month of Adar. He then declared to the king that there was a people (he did not mention the Jews by name), who were scattered and dispersed in the kingdom, who had laws of their own, and did not obey the king's laws. He made it clear that he thought these people should not be permitted to live in the kingdom anymore. The king backed him up and letters were sent out to slay the Jews on the thirteenth of Adar.

Upon learning of the decree, the Jews grew extremely worried; they started to fast and mourn. Mordechai sent a messenger to Esther, urging her to appeal to the king. She feared that if she went to the king uninvited, he would slay her. Mordechai pressed her further, and she gave in, deciding that it was worth the risk.

Fortunately for Esther, the king decided to spare her despite her unexpected appearance at his side. She invited him and Haman to a banquet. When the king, suspicious about the invitation, asked what she wanted, she urged the king and Haman to attend the banquet on the following night. At the banquet, Haman met Mordechai, who again did not bow to him. Angered, Haman built a gallows fifty cubits high and asked the king to have Mordechai hanged from it.

Unable to sleep that night, the king asked that royal records be read to him. From them he learned that Mordechai had uncovered a conspiracy against him. The next day the king instructed Haman to reward Mordechai even though Haman had wanted him hanged.

At a second banquet, the king asked Esther what she wished from him. She revealed that both she and her people faced the threat of destruction. Angered, the king asked who was to blame. Esther pointed to Haman.

Ahasuerus departed the feast in anger. When he came back, Haman was lying on Esther's couch. That led the king to suspect that he was about to assault the queen. The king immediately ordered Haman to be executed from the gallows that Haman had prepared for Mordechai.

Even though Haman was dead, the Jews worried that they would be destroyed. Thanks to Esther's appeal, Ahasuerus issued new decrees, permitting the Jews to defend themselves against any attackers.

Esther and Mordechai declared that the anniversary of this deliverance should become the feast of Purim. Jews still commemorate this deliverance in the yearly festival of Purim, on the 14th and 15th of Adar (February, March). The previous day is observed as the Fast of Esther in Jewish tradition. This came into being much later in history. It has no connection with Esther's request that the Jews of Shushan observe a fast while she made preparations for her appearance before Ahasuerus to plead for her people.

On Purim, the Scroll of Esther is read in the synagogues. Children dress up in colorful costumes, girls particularly enjoy masquerading as Queen Esther.

Evaluating Esther's character, Adin Steinsaltz, the noted Jewish scholar, wrote, "There is the danger she underwent for the sake of the nation, and her declaration that a day of celebration and feasting be initiated to commemorate the events. This was the act of a woman who had carried out a dangerous mission and felt a need to perpetuate that mission, not only in the deepest social and national sense but also as something of profound significance in her own life. She felt her deed had value as a sacrifice and epitomized the many tasks fulfilled for national or ideological reasons."

Steinsaltz argued that Esther was not a totally pure soul. "The moment when Esther was required to go to Ahasuerus, and use every means of seduction and temptation at her disposal in order to lift the sentence of death that had fallen on the Jews, was not just a moment of personal danger. She was required to pass from a passive state to an active one, to become the temptress. Previously, Esther could claim that, to some extent, she was in a situation in which she was held under duress. From the moment when she took the initiative in approaching the king to seduce him, she lost her last shreds of innocence.

"Where previously she could feel pure, at least in spirit, she was now to some extent sullied...consciously she now decided to endanger not only her life but her soul; and from this moment onward, she becomes the savior of the Jewish people."

Ahasuerus and Esther enthroned, receive a report of the numbers slain in Shushan. Wall painting from the synagogue of Dura—Europos. Third century A.D.

The Jerusalem Publishing House

DIANNE FEINSTEIN

The Mayor Who Became a U.S. Senator

Born June 22, 1933 in San Francisco, California. American politician. Dianne Feinstein's career in politics dates back to the 1960s. She served as a member of the Board of Supervisors for San Francisco in the 1970s and was president of the board for five of those years. She was appointed mayor of San Francisco in 1978, filling out the unexpired term of an assassinated mayor. She was elected mayor in 1979 and 1983, ran unsuccessfully for governor of California in 1990. In November 1992, she and Barbara Boxer were elected as California's two U.S. Senators. It marked the first time that any state had sent two women to the upper house.

Dianne Feinstein was born in San Francisco on June 22, 1933. Her father, Leon Goldman, was a professor of surgery at the University of California Medical Center. He was one of eleven children of Polish Jewish immigrants. Feinstein's mother, Betty Rosenburg, is a former model. Like her parents who fled St. Petersburg in 1917, Feinstein's mother belonged to the Russian Orthodox Church.

Dianne's father insisted that she go to Hebrew school after her day classes at the Convent of the Sacred Heart in San Francisco. "I was the first Jew at Sacred Heart," she said in October 1990, "and it turned out to be a pretty good recipe. In Judaism you believe in a code of morality and ethics to live as the one God would have you live. In Catholicism, it is more a day-to-day code, and I eventually found a lot of solace in the Catholic Church."

Though given a Catholic religious education, she was confirmed in the Jewish faith at the age of thirteen. (The Bat Mitzvah ceremony was not yet performed in the 1940s.) Dianne chose her father's faith and has lived as a Jew. All three of her husbands have been Jews. "I have always considered myself Jewish," she told the authors of this book in an interview.

When Dianne Feinstein was twenty-six, she decided to take up government service as a career. She had sometimes modeled new clothing lines for an uncle in the garment business. He sometimes took her to meetings of the Board of Supervisors. He called it the "Board of Stupidvisors." "Dianne," he told her, "you get an education and do a better job."

Feinstein received her undergraduate degree from Stanford University, where she had been student-body president her junior year, in 1954. She married and later divorced Jack Berman, who became a Superior Court judge. They had a daughter Katherine.

Convinced that to be effective in political life, women had to become experts in one particular field, she specialized in criminal justice after college. In 1955 and 1956, she was a public-affairs intern with the San Francisco-based Coro Foundation. In 1956 and 1957, she was assistant to the California Industrial Welfare Committee in both Los Angeles and

San Francisco.

Her marriage to neurosurgeon Bertram Feinstein in 1962 ended with his death in 1978.

From 1962 to 1966, she served as vice chairwoman of the California Women's Board of Terms and Parole. From 1967 to 1969, she was chairwoman of the San Francisco City and County Advisory Committee for Adult Detention.

She was a member of the Board of Supervisors for the city and county of San Francisco from 1970 to 1978; she served as board president from 1970 to 1972, 1974 to 1976, and in 1978.

Competing in the 1971 mayoralty election, she challenged Democratic Mayor Joseph

Courtesy of Dianne Feinstein

Alioto, but finished third. She lost her bid to be mayor again four years later.

Dianne Feinstein jumped into the national spotlight on November 27, 1978, with the assassination of Mayor George Moscone and Supervisor Harvey Milk by a disgruntled city employee. Feinstein immediately became acting mayor of San Francisco. A week later, the Board of Supervisors selected her to complete Moscone's term through 1979. She was the first woman mayor of San Francisco.

Feinstein steered her city through that tragedy and through the aftermath of the Jonestown massacre (whose victims had been members of a San Francisco-based cult) which preceded the double assassination by nine days. In an attempt to calm the city, she quickly chose a homosexual, Harvey Britt, to replace the murdered Milk—also gay. She won the mayor's race in 1979, receiving solid backing from the city's large homosexual community.

Feinstein's efforts to ban handguns got her into trouble. In 1983, a radical pro-gun group, the White Panther Party, began a referendum to unseat her, but she defeated it with an eighty-four percent vote in her favor.

In November 1983, she was re-elected mayor with an eighty-two percent majority.

Seeking to become governor of California in 1990, she defeated state Attorney General John Van De Kamp for the Democratic nomination in the June 1990 primary. She ran even in the polls against Republican Pete Wilson after that. For the first time in her political career, she stressed her Jewish background.

"I've had many people tell me that they get a real sense of pride, that here is a Jewish woman who can win, who can bring honor to everybody," she told a campaign gathering.

Wilson assailed Feinstein for promising to appoint women and minorities to state jobs in proportion to their share of the state's population. She replied that she opposed quotas "as one who knows that quotas can be used to keep people like us locked out. That's what happened to me as a woman, and it's also happened to me as one whose religion is Jewish."

She was aided in her race by the assets of her third husband, Richard C. Blum, an investment banker whom she married in 1980. It was said that he had arranged more than $3,000,000 in campaign loans.

She narrowly lost the race for governor to Wilson. She felt the loss bitterly. Eager to remain in politics, she kept up a nonstop schedule on the hustings for the next few years.

In 1992, Feinstein ran for the United States Senate. During the primary, she reminded voters that her paternal grandfather, Sam Goldman, had fled Poland for San Francisco, where he helped found three synagogues and the Hebrew Free Loan Association.

When we asked her how Judaism had affected her career, she replied that: "It increased my sensitivity with respect to issues of discrimination and human rights in general."

She campaigned in the 1992 election on the theme that "two percent is not enough," a reference to the fact that only two women were in the one hundred-member United States Senate prior to the November 1992 election.

By late October, Dianne Feinstein maintained a seventeen-point lead over Republican John Seymour, the appointed senatorial incumbent. A lawsuit charging Feinstein with misreporting $8,000,000 in campaign contributions in her unsuccessful gubernatorial race two years earlier apparently had not cut into her popularity.

In the senate election she defeated John Seymour, the Republican candidate, 5,493,418 to 3,777,635 votes.

This short-term Senate race was to fill the remainder of the term of Governor Pete Wilson who was elected a Senator in 1988 but had left the Senate in 1990 to run for Governor. John Seymour was appointed interim Senator in January 1991. The winner of this race would serve as Senator until 1994.

Feinstein became one of ten Jewish U.S. Senators. (In 1994 there were thirty-three Jewish members of Congress.)

Appearing on NBC television the day after the election, Senator-elect Feinstein predicted that the new group of women senators would "work together and work for change in a way which is unparalleled."

EDNA FERBER

A Giant of an Author

Born August 15, 1887 in Kalamazoo, Michigan; died April 16, 1968. American novelist and playwright. Edna Ferber ranks as one of the most popular women writers of the twentieth century. She was a noted playwright, though most of her eight plays were collaborations with George S. Kaufman. In over twenty novels, she dealt with the life of ordinary Americans. Often the central character in Ferber's books is a woman. Historian William Allen White said of her: "The historian will find no better picture of America in the first three decades of this century than Edna Ferber has drawn."

Edna Ferber's mother was American-born. Her father, who came to America from Hungary, was a successful shopkeeper in Kalamazoo, Michigan. Abandoning that job, he moved his family to Chicago, then a year later in 1890, when Edna was three years old, he moved them to Ottumwa, Iowa.

For the next seven years, the Ferbers lived in that coal-mining district, which had a rough element in its population. Edna found the townspeople hostile, but she enjoyed the stock theater companies that passed through the town. The real-life people of Ottumwa appeared as characters in her later writing.

In 1897, when Edna was ten years old, the family moved to Appleton, Wisconsin. There, Edna found the people friendlier. She read incessantly, but gave no thought to becoming a writer, though she did write articles for the high-school newspaper.

As Edna's high school graduation approached, she won the state declamatory contest.

Ferber hoped to attend a school of declamation and become an actress. Her father, however, was going blind, forcing her mother to work in the family store. Edna had no money for further education.

As the state's declamatory champion, the seventeen-year old achieved sufficient celebrity status to land a job as a local reporter with the *Appleton Daily Courant.*

Ferber was doubly pleased—she wanted to write and she wanted to help bolster the family's dwindling income.

Eighteen months later, she moved to the *Milwaukee Journal* where her beat became her hometown of Appleton. Shortly thereafter, she was reassigned to Milwaukee where she worked

for the next three-and-a-half years.

The long hours and hard work took their toll and she became ill. She had to return to live with her family in Appleton while she underwent a long convalescence. With time on her hands, she used the recovery period to begin writing fiction on a used typewriter she had purchased.

It was only fitting that Ferber's first novel, *Dawn O'Hara,* should deal with a newspaperwoman in Milwaukee. But she was unable to get it published. Distraught, she tossed the manuscript out. However, in November 1910, *Everybody's* magazine published her first short story, "The Homely Heroine."

After her father's death, Ferber moved to Chicago, along with her mother and sister. Seeking to become a reporter with the *Chicago Tribune,* she was not hired because she was a woman.

Unbeknownst to Ferber, her mother had retrieved *Dawn O'Hara* from the garbage and sent it to a publisher. When it was published in 1911, it sold over 10,000 copies and was considered a great work.

Following that surprise success, Edna Ferber began writing short stories, selling almost all of them. Though the happy ending was practically obligatory in popular American literature, she bent the rules, offering less-than-joyous finales. Her readers did not complain.

One of Ferber's earliest fictional creations was Emma McChesney, a delightful, witty, independent woman who supported her family as a "traveling salesman" of petticoats. Though it is only natural to see in this attractive example of the American businesswoman an early prototype of the modern, liberated woman, Ferber had no such conscious feminist drive lurking within her writing.

The Emma McChesney stories, thirty in all, were highly popular and provided Ferber with her first steady paycheck from fiction writing. In 1915, the Emma series was turned into a book—called *Emma McChesney & Co.*—giving Ferber her first recognition as a professional writer.

In 1912, the budding author moved to New York City where she mixed with other writers and artists, and covered the Democratic and Republican national conventions. She also sold the drama rights for the McChesney stories. *Our Mrs. McChesney,* with Ethel Barrymore as Emma McChesney, enjoyed a long Broadway run.

By 1915, Ferber returned to writing novels. As background for *Fanny Herself,* she chose her own school days in Appleton, including an industrious, self-sacrificing Jewish mother, who was modeled after Ferber's mother. *Fanny Herself* is the story of a Jewish girl and her relationship with other people.

Ferber's next novel, *The Girls,* dealt with life in Chicago from the Civil War to World War I.

A third novel, *So Big,* was published in 1924 and earned Ferber the Pulitzer prize for fiction. It was the story of a middle-aged woman who spent her life working in a truck farm outside of Chicago. It was also the story of a woman's struggle for independence. *So Big,* which sold more than 300,000 copies, spawned two motion pictures, one silent, one with sound.

Two years later came one of Ferber's most widely-read novels, *Show Boat.* The idea came to Ferber after she saw a "floating palace" off the coast of North Carolina. She had never been on the Mississippi or in the deep south, the locale of the novel. Her only preparation for the writing of this best-selling novel were a trip to North Carolina and numerous visits to the New York Public Library. Jerome Kern and Oscar Hammerstein turned *Show Boat* into a lavish Broadway musical.

Other best-selling novels followed: *Cimmaron* (1930), *Saratoga Trunk* (1941) and *Giant* (1952). All three were made into motion pictures.

Ferber's characters are average people such as store owners and housekeepers whom she thought of as the hardworking people of America. Those who led idle lives held little interest for her. She sought to describe those who had been given seemingly unfair burdens in life, whether it was the homely girl or the lowly immigrant, or the elderly parent, unable to work, forced to live with children. "I found creative satisfaction in writing only about the people and the land I knew and, in a measure, understood," Ferber said.

A playwright as well, Ferber is best known in that field for *Dinner at Eight* (1932) and *Stage Door* (1936). Both were written in collaboration with George S. Kaufman.

Ferber wrote relatively little about Jews and Judaism. In 1939 she published an autobiography, *A Peculiar Treasure* (the title is from Exodus 19: 5-6). It told of her American Jewish family, and contained stinging criticism of anti-Semitic feelings she thought were prevailing in Europe. Ferber voiced concern that an unaware America might fall prey to such ideas.

In 1965, the New York World's Fair featured a Women's Hall of Fame honoring twenty outstanding women of the twentieth century. Edna Ferber was one of them. Edna Ferber never married, calling her books, "my children."

Because of her twenty novels and eight plays, especially her novel *Show Boat,* which is an American classic, Edna Ferber counts as one of the great women writers of the twentieth century.

ROSALIND E. FRANKLIN

Contributed to the Discovery of DNA

Born July 25, 1920 in London; died in April 1958. British scientist. It was Rosalind Franklin's description of the probable structure of DNA, a class of nucleic acids containing deoxyribonucleic acid, which is the key to heredity, that paved the way for James D. Watson and Francis H. Crick's discovery of DNA. Without Franklin's magnificent X-ray photographs of DNA, Crick and Watson's efforts to unravel DNA's secrets could not have been confirmed as soon as they were—and the Nobel prize might have gone to others. She died too prematurely to know if she might have won the Nobel prize herself.

Rosalind Elise Franklin was born to a prominent English-Jewish family in 1920. One relative, on her mother's side, was Sir Moses Montefiore, the most important Jewish philanthropist of the nineteenth century. Rosalind's father, Ellis Franklin, belonged to a well-known Jewish banking family. Rosalind Franklin was distantly related to some of the most distinguished families of English Jewry.

She was the second of five children, three boys and two girls. Because her parents had been heavily involved in Anglo-Jewish affairs, it was assumed that Rosalind would show an interest in community service.

For a number of years, she was the only girl in the family—her sister was eight years younger. Not a strong child, Rosalind felt disadvantaged compared to her three brothers who were robust and active; she considered being a female more of a minus than a plus.

She was sent to St. Paul's Girls' School, one of the finest schools in London. It was assumed that graduates would attend universities even though it was unusual for English girls of that era.

Rosalind's father suggested that she take up charitable work. She countered that she wished to become a scientist. At age fifteen, Rosalind decided to specialize in science. At seventeen, she chose chemistry as her field of concentration.

In 1938, at age eighteen, Franklin entered Newnham College, Cambridge, where she studied physical chemistry. She overcame her father's objections to her becoming a scientist by winning an exhibition, a reward for scholastic excellence.

Franklin graduated from Newnham in 1941 and won a research scholarship as the student of Ronald G. W. Norrish, the Nobel prize winner for chemistry in 1967. She studied gas-phase chromatography. However, she fought a great deal with Norrish. Seeking the same recognition that her male colleagues were given, Franklin was frustrated to see herself viewed by Norrish as a mere women's liberationist and not the brilliant scientist she was becoming.

About this time, she met Adrienne Weil, a French refugee who had won a research fellowship. Weil had fled from Bordeaux, France with her young daughter before the Germans began to occupy the city. Weil, a charming French Jewess, taught Rosalind the

French language, and encouraged her to become an X-ray crystallographer.

Not happy with her work at Cambridge, Rosalind Franklin pursued another job and was hired a year later by the British Coal Utilization Research Association in London. She had joined some young physicists just out of college who were working on the structure of carbons. Though the uncertainties caused by World War II often disrupted her studies, Franklin continued to work independently, putting in long hours in her laboratory. She published five papers on the microstructure of coal over the next four years.

Not only did Franklin develop into a gifted scientist, she had courage and resolve. Once, she knelt accidentally on a sewing needle and, though in great pain, walked to a hospital to have the needle removed. An amazed physician could not understand how she walked with a needle angled across her knee joint.

At the British Coal Association, she worked on the physical structure of coals and carbonized coals. Years later her writings on coal still retain their significance. An Oxford professor noted that Rosalind Franklin's research "brought order into a field which had previously been in chaos."

Franklin wanted to branch out into different fields. Through Adrienne Weil, Franklin began working in 1947 for the *Laboratoire Central des Services Chimique de l'Etat*. There she learned X-ray diffraction techniques, a means of analyzing the spectra of crystalline substances and its application to the structure of coal.

Franklin used that method to study carbons and structural changes accompanying graphitization. She also worked on the crystallography of coal and graphite, groundbreaking work for what later became carbon-filter technology.

Rosalind Franklin became a recognized authority in industrial physical chemistry and her work had important applications to industry. Crystallography not only expanded the study of metals and minerals; it was applied to the study of molecular biology as well.

Franklin loved Paris and her French improved. However, the prospects for advancement for a foreign researcher in Paris were not good; there was no possibility of further advancement at the Central Laboratory. She reluctantly returned to London.

In 1950 John Randall's Medical Research Council unit at King's College, London, offered Franklin the chance to set up a new X-ray diffraction laboratory and to apply the technique to the study of dioxyribonucleic acid (DNA). She jumped at the opportunity.

Utilizing her X-ray diffraction photographs, Franklin found two forms of DNA: form A, a crystalline form, and form B, a wet form. Using the Patterson synthesis, a complex mathematical technique, she began studying the A form. Franklin believed at first that the A form did not have a helical structure. She hypothesized a figure-eight structure. Further investigation showed that the A and B forms had to have double helixes—two coaxial helical chains running in opposite directions.

Franklin correctly postulated that the main sugar phosphate chain of nucleic acid lay on the outside of the spiral. A colleague studied her laboratory notes years later and realized that Rosalind Franklin was two steps away from deciphering the entire DNA structure.

Though successful at King's College, she found little happiness there. Not only was she the only woman in her department, she was also the only Jew. The common room was for men only. Because this was where fruitful scientific discussion often occurred, being excluded affected her work and isolated her from her colleagues.

In 1953, Franklin moved to Birkbeck College, London. She remained there until her death in 1958. At Birkbeck, she pursued pioneering research on tobacco mosaic virus (TMV), one of the most thoroughly studied plant viruses. Relying upon her knowledge of X-ray diffraction, she discovered the infective element of the virus particle, which was its ribose nucleic acid (RNA). Her model of the TMV molecule was the first of its kind; it was the central feature of the virus exhibit at the Brussels World's Fair.

Franklin developed cancer in 1956 at the age of 36, but told few people of her illness so that she could continue with her work at Birkbeck. Despite several operations, she eventually succumbed to the disease two years later.

During her last year, she started to study poliomyelitis, a dangerously infectious virus—against the wishes of her colleagues. At the time of her death, the head of the laboratory at Birkbeck wrote: "As a scientist, Miss Franklin was distinguished by extreme clarity and perfection in everything she undertook. Her photographs are among the most beautiful X-ray photographs of any substance ever taken. She was an admirable director of a research team and inspired those who worked with her to reach the same high standards."

ANNE FRANK

Teen-aged Diarist of the Holocaust

Born June 12, 1929 in Frankfurt, Germany; died 1945. Dutch victim of the Holocaust. While she and her family hid from the Nazis, Anne Frank composed her famous diary. Through the words of this diary of a teen-age girl, she became a symbol of all of the victims of the Holocaust and particularly of the persecuted Jewish children. By reading the diary and watching the play and film based on it, millions of people around the world were introduced to the Nazi persecution of the Jews. Anne Frank's diary is considered one of the most poignant documents of World War II.

Anne was born in Frankfurt, Germany in 1929. Ten years later, when the Nazis assumed power, she and her family moved to Amsterdam, Holland, where Anne was educated. She was bright and perceptive, and dreamt of becoming a writer. In Europe, however, storm clouds were gathering. Hitler's Nazis were conquering Western Europe, turning against the Jews, and before long Anne and her family would be caught up in that storm.

Beginning in the summer of 1940, Anne's father, Otto Frank, prepared for the eventuality of having to hide from the Nazis in the event that they took over Holland. In the summer of the following year, when public schools were closed to Jews because of the German occupation of their country, Anne transferred to the Jewish High School.

On July 5, 1942, Anne's sixteen-year-old sister Margot received a letter from the Central Office for Jewish Emigration that ordered her to appear for forced labor. That letter sent the Frank family into hiding.

Four days after the letter arrived, the Franks chose rooms at the back of the offices of Otto Frank's business premises on the *Prinsengracht* for their hiding place. The day after, the family moved into this vacant annex of Otto's office. Four of his employees (Victor Kugler, Johannes Kleiman, Elli Voskuijl and Miep Gies, helped them to hide. A few days later the family was joined by the Van Daan family, including their son Peter.

On November 16, 1942, a dentist named Albert Dussel became the eighth person to hide in the annex. The small space grew crowded; food and clothing were difficult to obtain. Otto's employees, managed, however, to supply what was needed.

From July 10, 1942, until August 4, 1944, the Frank family remained in their hiding place.

For her thirteenth birthday, in 1942, Anne

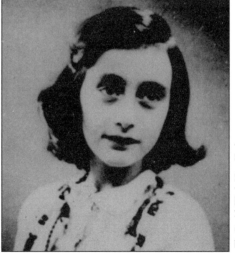

Israel Film Archive, Jerusalem

Scene from the movie The Diary of Anne Frank, *Twentieth Century Fox.*

was given a diary. She began at once to make entries and addressed them to an imaginary friend she named Kitty. She wrote about all sorts of things: what it was like to hide; each day's events; family relationships; her wish to be a writer; her passage from puberty and adolescence to young womanhood; and the efforts made by others to protect all of the annex residents from the Nazis.

In addition to filling up her diary, Anne wrote stories and a *Book of Beautiful Phrases,* filled with quotations she liked. There seems little doubt that she knew what fate awaited her and her family. In October 1942, she wrote in her diary: "If it is as bad as this in Holland, whatever will it be like in the distant and barbarous regions [the Jews] are sent to? We assume that most of them are murdered. The English radio speaks of their being gassed." Despite suspecting her fate, she did not dwell on her fear of being murdered.

Here is a diary entry from April 11, 1944: "We have been pointedly reminded that we are in hiding, that we are Jews in chains....We Jews mustn't show our feelings, must be brave and strong, must accept all inconveniences and not grumble.... Sometime this terrible war will be over. Surely the time will come when we are people again, and not just Jews.

"Who has inflicted this upon us? Who has made us Jews different from all other people? Who has allowed us to suffer so terribly up till now? It is God that has made us as we are, but it will be God, too, who will raise us up again. If we bear all this suffering and if there are still Jews left, when it is over, then Jews, instead of being doomed, will be held up as an example. Who knows, it might even be our religion from which the world and all peoples learn good, and for that reason and that reason only do we have to suffer now. We can never become just Netherlanders, or just English, or representatives of any country

88

for that matter, we will always remain Jews, but we want to, too....

"During that night I really felt that I had to die...but now, now I've been saved again, now my first wish after the war is that I may become Dutch! "

Elsewhere in the diary, she wrote: "I don't believe that the big men, the politicians and the capitalists alone are guilty of the war. Oh, no, the little man is just as keen....There is an urge and rage in the people to destroy, to kill, to murder, and until all mankind, without exception, undergoes a great change, wars will be waged."

Anne Frank was forever an optimist, and that is what made her situation so poignant. As she wrote: "I hear the ever approaching thunder, which will destroy us, too. I can feel the sufferings of millions and yet, if I look up into the heavens, I think that it will all come [out all] right, that this cruelty too will end, and that peace and tranquility will return again." An act of betrayal resulted in the discovery of the group in hiding by the German police. On August 4, 1944, the SD (the security and intelligence service of the SS, the Nazi elite) in Amsterdam was told that Jews were hiding in the annex at *Prinsengracht* 263. The eight Jews, including Anne and her family, were found, arrested and sent to the Westerbork prison camp. Kleiman and Kugler, who had helped them throughout their confinement, were also arrested and interned in Holland.

On September 2, 1944, the Franks were sent from Westerbrook to Auschwitz. They arrived on the last transport to leave the Dutch camp. In December, Anne Frank arrived in Bergen-Belsen with her sister Margot. There, Anne fell ill with typhus and she died in March 1945. Otto Frank survived Auschwitz. He was liberated by the Soviets on January 27, 1945.

In the wake of the arrest of the eight Jews, Miep Gies took Anne Frank's diary and other papers she found in the annex. She returned them to Otto Frank after the war who, in turn, had Anne's diary published.

The first edition appeared in 1947. It was titled *The Annex* and became an instant success. Later titled *Anne Frank: The Diary of a Young Girl*, it was followed by numerous other editions, and has become a classic. The book was translated into many languages and Anne Frank became the symbol of the persecuted Jewish children, in particular, and the victims of the Holocaust in general. Since the diary's publication, it has appeared in more than fifty languages and has sold more than twenty million copies. A book of Anne Frank's stories, *Tales From the Secret Annex,* was published in English in 1950.

A stage play based on Anne's diary opened on Broadway on October 5, 1955. It won the Pulitzer prize for best play of the year. In 1959, a film version was released as well.

In 1960, the annex on *Prinsengracht* 263 was turned into a museum representing the struggle against the anti-Semitism and racism endured by its wartime occupants. The original diary is on display there.

On June 12, 1979, the 50th anniversary of Anne Frank's birth, Queen Juliana of the Netherlands dedicated an exhibition room in the Anne Frank House in Amsterdam. Anne's elderly father Otto was present for the ceremonies, which honored his courageous and memorable daughter whose words continue to say so much.

Anna Freud

Pioneer in Child Analysis

Born December 3, 1895 in Vienna, Austria; died October 9, 1982. Austrian psychoanalyst. Freud virtually invented the systematic study of the emotional and mental life of the child. She was a proponent, defender and the definitive interpreter of the theories of her father, Sigmund Freud. In 1947, she founded the London-based Hampstead Child Therapy Clinic as a research facility and training ground for analysts, directing it until her death. She was called the leading psychoanalyst of her day. The youngest of his six children and the third daughter of Sigmund Freud, Anna Freud was the only one to follow in his footsteps as a psychoanalyst.

Anna was born in Vienna, Austria on December 3, 1895. She was named after Anna Lichtein whose father had been a teacher of Freud's and later a personal friend. Her father made no secret of the fact that he would have preferred Anna to be a boy, even telling a friend that he would have communicated the news of her birth by telegram rather than letter had she been a male.

Anna attended the Cottage Lyceum in Vienna while growing up at Freud's famous address, *Berggasse* 19. She remained there until the Nazi occupation forced the family to flee in 1938.

In 1900, while Anna was still a child, her father used one of Anna's dreams to illustrate his theory of wish-fulfillment. Freud's comments appeared in *The Interpretation of Dreams* and related to a time when Anna was nineteen months old. The infant Anna had had a vomiting attack and was subsequently put to bed hungry. That night, apparently dreaming, she cried out in her sleep, asking for wild strawberries and other delicacies to eat.

As a young child, Anna was interested only in stories and tales that "might be true. In the face of any unrealistic or supernatural element—my attention flagged and disappeared." She retained that quality throughout her life, she later wrote.

Her father wrote her, when she was an adolescent, that her plans for school could wait. In fact, Anna left school early, ending her formal education without completing the Gymnasium, or secondary school.

In 1913, when Anna was eighteen and her father fifty-seven he wrote to a colleague: "My closest companion will be my little daughter, who is developing very well at the moment."

For several years Anna taught elementary school. Her devotion to her father, however, brought her into increasing contact with the practice of psychoanalysis and she grew interested in child psychology. None of Sigmund Freud's other children showed interest in their father's field, clearing the path for Anna to have unhindered access to her father.

Anna Freud never married. She cared for her father, particularly during his later years when he was fighting cancer. Becoming her father's companion, secretary and student, she began to attend meetings of the Vienna Psycho-Analytical Society in November, 1918.

In the mid-1920s psychoanalysts took their first systematic steps to observe normal childhood behavior and study it in relation to detailed scrutiny of all forms of behavior. Young neurotic children would benefit from this study as they were treated in this context.

Anna Freud became very interested in this field of study. She became a psychoanalyst although she had no medical degree, which was highly unusual.

In 1922, Anna Freud published her first paper, *Beating Phantasies and Day Dreams.* That was enough for her colleagues to take her seriously.

Freud's father psychoanalyzed her. This was very out of the ordinary considering that a therapist was supposed to be neutral and objective. Many wondered how he could be either one, given that the field of psychoanalysis included the theory that the sexual longing of a child for the parent of the opposite sex was a normal occurrence.

Anna Freud began to practice psychotherapy in 1923, a period when Sigmund Freud's theories were still provoking bitter opposition from medical specialists and more academically-oriented psychologists. In 1925, Anna Freud became secretary of the newly established Vienna Training Institute, headed by Helene Deutsch.

Anna Freud's notable work was *The Ego and the Mechanism of Defense,* published in 1937. This book shifted the focus within psychoanalysis from unconscious conflicts to research into the ego or "seat of observation," which mediates between instinctual drives and reality. Anna Freud elaborated upon a variety of defense mechanisms, including repression, projection, and sublimation by which the ego wards off anxiety and permits someone to function psychologically.

This book was a pioneer contribution to the field of ego psychology and became very useful in understanding the adolescent more fully.

In 1938, Anna Freud persuaded the Gestapo to talk only with her, rather than interrogate both her and her father, as the organization had planned. She was able to keep them both out of harm's way.

That year, she escaped from Austria, traveling to London, and taking her elderly father with her. There she started to work as a children's analyst in the Hampstead Nurseries. Only a year later, on September 23, 1939, her father died at age 83.

During World War II Anna Freud and her colleague, Dorothy Bulingham, wrote three books based on their work at the Hampstead Nurseries, which they regarded as a laboratory for child development. It was in fact a residential center for eighty children, many of whom had been separated from their parents and had lost their homes in

Courtesy of *The Jewish Chronicle*

the Nazi bombings. These books were: *Young Children in Wartime* (1942); *Infants without Families* (1943); and *War and Children* (1943).

Freud and Bulingham described the treatment of children separated from their families and subjected to the stressful conditions of war.

In 1943, Anna Freud founded the famous Hampstead Clinics in Great Britain. She planned to study the effect of war upon children, especially those who had been separated from their parents by war. In her work at the clinic, she pioneered a diagnostic system that stressed the child's level of psychological development and organization instead of looking only at symptoms out of context.

The Hampstead Nurseries closed in 1945. Two years later Anna Freud founded the Child Therapy Course.

Despite the lack of formal psychiatric training, Anna Freud exerted much influence in the psychiatric field. Many colleagues considered her to be her father's successor. Later in her career, American psychiatrists and psychoanalysts rated her the foremost practitioner of her day.

Anna Freud is presented with a certificate of honour by ther Hebrew University of Jerusalem at Befdford College on July 14, 1976.

In 1951, Freud became director of the Hampstead Child-Therapy Clinic, an outgrowth of the Hampstead Nurseries, which became the largest center in the world for the treatment and analysis of children. It has changed—and perhaps saved—the lives of countless youngsters.

Anna Freud and her disciples questioned old assumptions that had been based on the notion that healthy child development depended upon firm discipline. Instead, she used the tool of psychoanalysis to treat children's neuroses by interpreting their dreams and play.

Her book *Normality and Pathology in Childhood* (1965) is a comprehensive summation of her thought.

Anna Freud's contribution to child analytic therapy and child psychology was immense. She showed that her father's reconstructions of child development and pathology through his analysis of adults were valid. She also added much more to what was already known through her methods of direct observation of children.

Though her work related to the reactions of young children, especially institutionalized ones, who are separated from their parents and deprived of emotional ties, Anna Freud had a major impact on social policies and influenced the future of child care.

Anna Freud resisted personal publicity, refusing hundreds of requests over the years for interviews. She worried that personal appearances and interviews might affect her patients and interfere with treatment. Her work came first and her dedication to it was awe-inspiring.

$\mathscr{B}$ETTY $\mathscr{F}$RIEDAN

Senior Stateswoman of Feminism

Born February 4, 1921 in Peoria, Illinois. American author and feminist activist. The modern American feminist movement traces its start to Betty Friedan's 1963 book, *The Feminine Mystique*. In this controversial best seller, Friedan debunked the widely held myth that a woman could only fulfill herself only by being a wife, mother, and consumer. Friedan dubbed the myth the "feminine mystique." When *Life* magazine chose the one hundred most important Americans of the twentieth century in its fall 1990 edition, Betty Friedan was the only Jewish woman on the list. *Life* called her "the housewife who liberated every woman."

$\mathscr{B}$etty Friedan was born Betty Naomi Goldstein on February 4, 1921 in Peoria, Illinois. She was the first of Harry and Miriam (Horwitz) Goldstein's three children.

Betty's father went from selling buttons on street corners to owning a jewelry store. Mrs. Goldstein had her own confrontation with the feminine mystique that left a lasting mark on Betty: Miriam had been forced to quit her job as editor of the women's page of a Peoria newspaper when she married her husband.

Anti-Semitism during Betty Friedan's childhood in Peoria played its part in opening her eyes to social injustices. Jews were barred from the high school sororities and the country club. "When you're a Jewish girl who grew up on the right side of the tracks in the Midwest, you're marginal," she said in 1966. "You're in, but you're not, and you grew up an observer."

Friedan was class valedictorian and publisher of a literary magazine in high school. While at Smith College in Northampton, Massachusetts, she founded and edited the college newspaper and studied under the well-known Gestalt psychologist Kurt Koffka. In 1942, she graduated summa cum laude with a B.A. degree in psychology. The next year she studied psychology on a research fellowship at the University of California at Berkeley.

A highly independent young woman, it has been said that if a young man tried to open a door for her, she would kick his foot.

In June, 1947 she married Carl Friedan, a producer of summer theater in New Jersey. They had three children: Daniel, Emily, and Jonathan. (They were divorced in 1969.) When her first

Betty Friedan: A portrait.

Susan Wood

child was born in 1949, Friedan took maternity leave, then returned to work as a reporter. In 1952, when her second child was born, and she requested a maternity leave, she was promptly dismissed and a man was hired to replace her.

Carl Friedan entered the advertising business and achieved great success. In 1957, the Friedans bought a home overlooking the Hudson River. Betty Friedan had become the typical suburban wife and mother.

Friedan wrote articles that glorified the American housewife, "I had begun to feel so guilty working," she wrote, "and I really wasn't getting anywhere in that job. I was more than ready to embrace the feminine mystique." Her findings led her to write a book.

The Feminine Mystique, published in 1963, became a best seller, with over two million copies sold.

In her book, Friedan wrote: "The feminine mystique says that the highest value and the only commitment for women is the fulfillment of their own femininity. It says that the great mistake of Western culture, throughout most of its history, has been the undervaluation of this femininity. It says this femininity is so mysterious and intuitive and close to the creation and origin of life that man-made science may never be able to understand it....The mistake, says the mystique, the root of women's troubles in the past, is that women envied men, women tried to be like men, instead of accepting their own nature, which can find fulfillment only in sexual passivity, male domination and nurturing maternal love."

Friedan charged in the book that American women had been seduced back into their "doll's house," living through their husbands and children instead of finding their own individual identities. Some women readers were outraged, cursing her and suggesting she get psychiatric help. They accused her of being more of a threat to America than the Soviets. After dinner party invitations stopped coming and her children were eliminated from car pools, Friedan was moved to return to New York City with her family. During the late 1960s, she taught nonfiction writing at New York University and at the New School for Social Research.

The Feminine Mystique had a major impact on society, in effect launching the modern women's liberation movement in America. "I am still awed by the revolution that book helped spark," Betty Friedan wrote two decades later. "Even now, women—and men—stop me on the street to reminisce about where they were when they read it."

Friedan abandoned research on a second book, in which she hoped to talk about women who had met the demands of marriage, motherhood and career. She had found "only women with problems." As a result of this realization, she decided to pursue political action as the best way to help the burgeoning women's liberation movement in America.

The road was rocky. Friedan tried to get legislation passed such as the Equal Rights Amendment (ERA) to the Constitution, intended to ensure women's equality, but could not get it enacted. Frustrated at her inability to get Congress to enforce the ban on sex discrimination in employment, she and several others formed NOW, the National Organization for Women. In 1966, she served as NOW's first president. NOW's original aim was to encourage women to fight discriminatory laws and practices. Radical feminists, however, pushed their own agendas of lesbianism and class warfare against men. This angered Friedan who felt that most women would not identify with these issues.

By 1971, Friedan had joined with Shirley Chisholm, Gloria Steinem, and Bella Abzug to found the National Women's Political Caucus (NWPC) in order to encourage women to seek public office. Disillusioned, when so many of her efforts were shortcircuited, Friedan abandoned political activism in favor of writing and lecturing in the late 1970s.

Friedan's 1981 book *The Second Stage* outlined the issues that she felt feminists should address in the coming decade: flexible work schedules, parental leave, child care, and new housing arrangements. She found good things to say about the notion of family. She argued that women could help men appreciate the benefits of restructuring the workplace and the home only if feminists "confront anew their own needs for love and comfort and caring support" by reclaiming the family as the "new feminist frontier."

In 1988, Betty Friedan served as a distinguished visiting professor at the University of Southern California's journalism school and at its Institute for the Study of Women and Men.

As for the meaning of feminism for Jewish women, Freidan is aware that some people are threatened by the strength of women, "but this strength is not a threat to the Jewish family. Feminism is not a threat to the Jewish family. Family is basic to the survival of Jews. The liberation of women to full personhood will only help in the strengthening and evolution of the family."

On October 18, 1984, she wrote in *The New York Times Magazine*, "I had never considered myself religious. I am a daughter of the secular city. For me, as for other Jewish feminists, religion perpetuated the patriarchal tradition that denied women access to Judaism's most sacred rituals and enshrined them within the strict confines of their biological role. But when women like me broke through to our authentic personhood as women, we also found the strength to dig deep into ourselves on other levels."

On May 5, 1993 Friedan underwent surgery to replace her aortic heart valve. "I am in fighting shape," she said after the operation. Indeed, she was.

In the fall of that year her new book, *The Fountains of Age* was published and became a best seller. Again, she deals with a mystique—what she calls the "mystique of age." She asks in her book: "What did the image of the 'plight' or 'problem' of age leave out? What explained the absence of any image of older people leading active and productive lives? The image of age as inevitable decline and deterioration, I realized, was also a mystique of sorts...." Betty Friedan continues to utilize her life experiences, at each of the stages we all encounter, to inform and help the rest of us understand the wider implications and universality of it all. Exploding the myths, she deals with the realities of life as she sees them in her own life.

RUTH BADER GINSBURG

American Supreme Court Justice

Born March 15, 1933 in Brooklyn, New York. U.S. Supreme Court Justice. Ruth Bader Ginsburg was appointed to the high court on June 14, 1993, the second woman (the first was Justice Sandra Day O'Connor) to serve there. The first Jew to serve on the high court since Abe Fortas resigned in 1969, Justice Ginsburg served as a United States circuit judge for the United States Court of Appeals for the District of Columbia Circuit between 1980 and June 1993. Prior to that, she was a law professor at Columbia and Rutgers Universities.

Ruth Bader was born in 1933 in the Flatbush section of Brooklyn. Her father Nathan was a furrier and worked in clothing stores. Her mother Celia stressed to Ruth the importance of achievement and independence. Celia Bader encouraged her daughter to read by taking her to a public library atop a Chinese restaurant off King's Highway in Brooklyn. Ever since, Ruth has associated the aroma of Chinese food with the pleasure of reading.

Ruth was the second daughter; her older sister, Marilyn, who nicknamed her Kiki, died of meningitis at the age of six.

At Public School 238 in Brooklyn, Ruth edited *The Highway Herald* and editorialized on the meaning of the Magna Charta and the Bill of Rights. She graduated from James Madison High School.

Ginsburg grew up with the Holocaust always in the background. As she wrote to the authors of this book in January of 1993: "World War II raged on during my grade school years. Jews fortunate enough to be in the United States during those years could hardly avoid identifying themselves with the cause of the Jewish people."

In high school, Ruth twirled batons and belonged to the "Go-Getters," wearing a black satin jacket with gold letters while selling tickets for football games. She ran for student government but lost.

Her mother died at the age of forty-seven of cervical cancer. It happened on the day before Ruth's high-school graduation in June 1950. Ruth, scheduled to speak, missed the ceremony.

In 1954, Ginsburg graduated from Cornell University, where she had the reputation of being very beautiful, popular and exceptionally smart. At Cornell, she met Martin D. Ginsburg, a fellow pre-law student; they were married in June 1954.

She attended Harvard Law School from 1956 to 1958, part of which time she took care of her new daughter, Jane.

One of nine women in a class of over 500 students, Ginsburg attended a dinner in honor of women students that was a major turning point for her. She was aghast at the words of the dean, who was host, as he asked each woman to explain what she was doing at the law school occupying a seat that could have been filled by a man. "When my turn came," recalled Justice Ginsburg, "I wished I could have pushed a button and vanished through a trap door."

When her husband obtained a job at a law firm in New York, Ginsburg transferred to Columbia Law School. She was named to the law reviews at both Harvard and Columbia. Her husband became one of the pre-eminent tax attorneys in the country. Ross Perot was one of his clients.

In 1959, Ginsburg graduated from the Columbia Law School. She was tied for first place in her class.

President Clinton listens to his new Supreme Court appointee at the White House announcement.

Ginsburg, upon discovering that women were not welcome in New York City's major law firms, clerked for Federal Judge Edmund L. Palmieri of the U.S. District Court Southern District of New York from 1959 to 1961. "Not a single law firm in the entire city of New York bid for my employment," she said in 1993.

In 1960, the dean of the Harvard Law School, Albert Sachs, proposed that Ruth Ginsburg, whom he considered one of his star pupils, work as a law clerk to Supreme Court Justice Felix Frankfurter. Saying that he was not yet prepared to hire a woman, Frankfurter declined to employ Ruth Ginsburg.

Ginsburg became an assistant professor of law at Rutgers Law School. Pregnant with her second child, she feared her teaching contract would be terminated. "I got through the spring semester without detection, with the help of a wardrobe one size larger than mine, borrowed from my mother-in-law," she noted. Her son James arrived that fall, just before classes resumed.

In 1963, Ginsburg found herself irked that her salary was smaller than that of her male colleagues at Rutgers. She helped in the effort to make the legal case that led to the large increase she and other women faculty members received.

When complaints of unequal treatment were referred to her by the New Jersey affiliate of the American Civil Liberties Union, she began to take an interest in cases dealing with sex discrimination.

Ginsburg had not entered the law, she insisted, to strike a blow for women's rights, but, "for personal, selfish reasons. I thought I could do a lawyer's job better than any other. I have no talent in the arts, but I do write fairly well and analyze problems clearly."

Ginsburg became a full professor at Rutgers in 1969. Three years later, she became the first tenured female professor at Columbia. Her daughter Jane, an authority on copyright law, is now on the faculty there.

In 1972, Justice Ginsburg became a founder of the American Civil Liberties Union Women's Rights Project through which she sought to demonstrate that the law discriminated between males and females and often was unconstitutional in doing so.

Later in 1972, in *Struck v. Secretary of Defense*, Ginsburg successfully challenged the discharge of a pregnant officer in the Air Force before the U.S. Supreme Court. From 1973 to 1976 she argued six women's rights cases before the Supreme Court, and won five, thus greatly changing the law as it affected women.

Susan Deller Ross, a Georgetown University Law School professor who worked for the Women's Rights Project during the 1970s, put it this way: "She made the equal protection clause a meaningful vehicle for the analysis of sex discrimination laws."

Constitutional scholar Erwin Griswold once singled out two lawyers in modern times who had altered the nation's course—Thurgood Marshall and Ruth Bader Ginsburg.

Ginsburg drew criticism from the Jewish community in 1992 when she was part of a three-judge appellate panel that rejected jailed spy Jonathan Pollard's appeal of his life sentence. The panel held that the district court did not exceed the large discretion it had over sentencing.

The culmination of her already impressive career came on June 14, 1993 when President Clinton selected Ginsburg to take the Supreme Court seat vacated by Byron R. White.

In announcing his choice, and with Ginsburg standing by his side in the Rose Garden at the White House, Clinton said he believed that "she will be able to be a force for consensus-building on the Supreme Court."

Tears rolled down the President's face when Judge Ginsburg paid tribute to her late mother. "I pray that I may be all that she would have been had she lived to an age when women could aspire and achieve and daughters are cherished as much as sons."

The day after Ginsburg's appointment, the media focused on her seemingly ambiguous views on abortion, noting that she had ruled in favor of abortion rights, but had also criticized the 1973 Supreme Court decision that made abortion a Constitutional right, saying it went too far, too fast.

Justice Ginsburg is an opera fan, reads the mysteries of Amanda Cross and Dorothy L. Sayers, loves old movies, and likes horseback riding, water skiing and golfing.

In preparation for her Senate confirmation hearing in late July 1993, Justice Ginsburg was scrutinized by the media thoroughly. That was the big change in her life. When the authors of this book asked her on August 8, 1993 what had changed most for her, she said unhesitantly, "All this publicity."

She passed the Senate hearings with flying colors and was sworn in as a Supreme Court Justice on August 10, 1993. The Supreme Court had always seemed beyond her reach. "I never thought of the possibility of being a judge," she said, "when I got out of law school and began to teach, women were only three percent of my students." Soft-spoken, smiling frequently, clearly pleased at what was happening to her, Justice Ginsburg said happily: "This is a great time in my life."

Having two women on the Supreme Court, she believed, would make a difference "because it will seem natural. If you are the only woman, eyes are on you all the time."

In January 1994, Justice Ginsburg experienced the dream of many opera buffs: Along with Supreme Court Justice Antonin Scalia, another opera lover, she donned a white-powdered wig and played an extra in the Washington Opera's initial performance of Richard Strauss's *Ariadne auf Naxos,* about eighteenth-century high-society Vienna. On stage for eighty-five minutes, Justice Ginsburg neither spoke nor sang for this one-time performance.

GLUECKEL OF HAMELN

Early Yiddish Memoirist

Born in 1646 in Hamburg, Germany; died in 1724. Yiddish memoirist. Glueckel of Hameln was the most famous Jewess of the late seventeenth and early eighteenth century. She was a memoirist and chronicler of central European life. Her main work, *Glueckel of Hameln,* is a portrait of the eighteenth-century immigrant woman prior to reaching America. Glueckel's memoirs, covering the years 1645 to 1719, are a key source for Central European Jewish history and culture and for the linguistic and literary studies of early Yiddish. Her writings constitute the only full-length memoir written by a Jewish woman before the nineteenth century that was accessible to the public.

Glueckel, the daughter of Beila and Leib Pinkerle, was born in Hamburg, Germany, two years before the end of the Thirty Years' War, a time of immense tragedy for Central European Jews.

When Glueckel was three years old, the Jews of Hamburg were expelled from their city, taking refuge nearby in the then-Danish town of Altona. By special permission, they still did business in Hamburg.

Glueckel's father, a dealer in jewels and other wares, was the second richest Jew in Altona and served for many years as the Parnas or president of the community. In 1657, he obtained approval to resettle in Hamburg. However, returning Hamburg Jews had no right of residence and could not attend a synagogue.

Glueckel's maternal grandmother lived with the family. As a child, Glueckel found it fascinating to listen to her grandmother tell about the Thirty Years' War—the epidemics, the hardships. Most of the other children in the community were undereducated, but not Glueckel. Her father insisted on both a secular and religious education for her. At school, Glueckel learned how to pray, read and write.

By age twelve, though the two had never met, Glueckel was betrothed to thirteen-year-old Chaim Goldschmidt. He was from Hameln (the same Hameln of "Pied Piper" fame).

Two years later Glueckel set off with her parents to meet and marry her future husband. The marriage was a success. When Chaim died thirty years later, Glueckel wrote: "I truly believe I shall never cease from mourning my dear friend."

However, Glueckel and Chaim differed over Hameln. Though it had only two Jewish families, Glueckel adjusted easily. Chaim disliked the place intensely. Chaim won out, and for the next two years, because Chaim believed his business prospects were better in Hamburg, they lived with Glueckel's parents there. Chaim bought up old gold and sold it to jewelers and merchants. Glueckel gave birth to her first child a few years later.

Chaim Goldschmidt was right: His business prospered. He was aided by Glueckel,

A painting of Glueckel of Hameln by Polish painter Leopold Pilichowski c. 1925.

who looked after the business when Chaim went on out-of-town trips. Chaim sought Glueckel's advice before entering into any business deal.

None of this led Glueckel to overlook her children at home. Ultimately, she bore thirteen children, one of whom died in childhood. Glueckel was energetic and had a strong character. In fact, after her husband died in 1689, she continued to manage his business though she had to cope with large debts and six children still to marry off. To clear outstanding debts, she sold the remaining merchandise and began buying and selling pearls.

Glueckel endured many hardships. Jews, Glueckel wrote in her diary, were considered no better than "chalk, cheese, charcoal...." Taking in all that she saw and heard, and suffering from sleepless nights, Glueckel had an urge to put her thoughts down on paper. She turned out to be a gifted writer.

She began writing her famed memoirs in 1690 at the age of forty-six, in part to dispel the melancholy that had overcome her following her husband's death. The memoirs were not meant for publication, but only for Glueckel's children and grandchildren. Her purpose was to acquaint them with the family background. Glueckel's memoirs consisted of seven short books, five of which she had finished by 1699. Then, after a break of sixteen years, she resumed her writing and completed the last two sections. These last two portions were written after her second husband had first entered into bankruptcy and later died.

Ten years a widow from her first marriage, Glueckel had married a second time at age fifty-four to the president of the Metz community, Reb Hirsch Levy. A year after the marriage, Hirsch Levy lost all of his money and most of Glueckel's. Glueckel lived alone for a while, but after a severe illness during one winter, she moved in with her daughter Esther in Esther's magnificent new home. Glueckel lived with Esther for about nine years.

Glueckel's memoirs tell of Jewish life in cities such as Hameln, Hanover, Hamburg, Altona, Metz, Berlin, and Amsterdam. Glueckel's memory was superb; she had a gift for poetic expression, and a pious outlook. She was intimately familiar with Talmudic lore and often turned to parables and fables to illustrate a moral. Her book is filled with vivid anecdotes describing the precarious life of the Jews of that time. She often dwelt on dowries; how she felt during her pregnancies; her memories of when her children were born.

Glueckel's language was Judeo-German, written in Hebrew letters. This language, largely German but with Hebrew making up about fifteen percent of the total vocabulary, was the precursor of modern Yiddish.

Glueckel's world was filled with wars, insecurity, infant mortality, pogroms, military conscription of small children, kidnapping, forced conversion, perpetual flight. However, she never wavered in her firm faith.

It was hard for a Jew to survive during this period, and Glueckel tried to suggest that the only solution was to have a deep and abiding faith in God. "This, dear children," she wrote, "will be no book of morals....We have our holy Torah....The best thing for you, my children, is to serve God from your heart, without falsehood or sham, not giving out to people that you are one thing while, God forbid, in your heart you are another." Here is more from her memoirs:

> Before I was twelve years old I was betrothed and the betrothal lasted two years. My wedding was celebrated in Hameln. My parents, accompanied by a party of twenty people, drove there with me. When we reached Hanover, we wrote to Hameln for carriages to be sent to us. My mother imagined it to be a town like Hamburg and that, at the very least, a carriage would be sent for the bride and her parents. On the third day, three or four farm wagons arrived, driven by such old horses that they looked as if they themselves should have been given a lift in the wagons. My mother was greatly offended, but as she could not change it, entrusting ourselves to the God of Israel, we seated ourselves in the carts and arrived in Hameln....

Glueckel died in 1724, at age seventy-eight, five years after she had completed her memoirs. Her original manuscript is lost but copies made by her descendants have been preserved.

On the basis of a copy of her manuscript prepared by her son, Rabbi Moses Hameln of Baiersdorf, Glueckel's memoirs were first published in their original Judeo-German in 1896. They were translated from the original Yiddish text by a descendant, Bertha Pappenheim.

EMMA GOLDMAN

"Red Emma"

Born June 27, 1869 in Kovno, Lithuania; died May 14, 1940. American anarchist propagandist. Emma Goldman embraced the political philosophy of anarchism, and became its most famous advocate in America. She was the outstanding female anarchist of this century. Goldman was among the first to speak out against the abuses of Communism and Fascism. Her effectiveness was mitigated in part by her apparent willingness to use violence to achieve her goals.

Emma was born in Kovno, Lithuania, in 1869 in the "Pale of Settlement," an area where Jews could live, but were not free to leave. She was the first child of the second marriage of Taube Bienovitch Zadekoff and Abraham Goldman. She acquired her revolutionary ideas in St. Petersburg, Russia, as a teen-ager.

Emma's relationship with her father was strained. Unable to earn a decent living, he vented his anger at Emma. When she was fifteen, her father found a husband for her. Emma objected. Furious, her father took the book she was reading and threw it into the fire. "Girls do not have to learn much," he snapped. "All a Jewish daughter needs to know is how to prepare gefilte fish, cut noodles fine, and give the man plenty of children." He then proceeded to beat Emma.

Emma Goldman had two half-sisters, Lena and Helena, from her mother's first marriage. In 1885, Lena had left for America and settled in Rochester, New York. Shortly thereafter, Emma and Helena joined their sister. There, Emma worked a sixty-hour week in a corset factory where she earned $2.50 an hour. She soon thereafter found work at $4.00 an hour.

Goldman was appalled by the living conditions of the poor and the working conditions of the lower classes. She concluded that the government was at fault, and that the world would be better if governments did not exist. She believed that people should be free and that freedom and justice for the individual could be obtained only by overthrowing all existing political and economic systems. The notion of anarchism, which she maintained was in conformity with man's basic nature and wish for freedom and would prove a workable, orderly, political and economic system.

In 1887, four anarchists were accused of exploding a bomb which killed seven policemen in Chicago's Haymarket Square. The four were convicted and executed. Angered at their executions, Emma Goldman decided to join the anarchist movement. The anarchists hoped to dispense with laws and governments, through acts of terror especially the assassination of eminent people.

During this time, Emma Goldman's personal life suffered through twists and turns. She married a card-playing Russian Jew named Jacob Kersner, divorcing him a year later after discovering that Kersner was impotent. Under pressure from her parents, who by now had joined her in the United States, and Kersner himself, who threatened suicide,

Goldman agreed to remarry him. She eventually left him permanently.

At age twenty, Goldman moved from Rochester to New York City. She was less than five feet tall and plump; she was filled with energy and had great oratorical and writing talent. Drawn into the company of other anarchists, she helped organize young girls to form unions and was elected to the board of the Anarchist Congress in 1890, when she was barely twenty-one years old. Her fellow anarchist Alexander Berkman became her lover.

A major turning point in Emma Goldman's life came with the Homestead Strike in 1892. During that strike, guards of the Carnegie Steel Corporation shot a number of striking steel workers. Goldman and Berkman believed that the company president, Henry Clay Frick, should pay for the strikers' death. They plotted to kill him. At first they tried to construct a bomb. However, Goldman feared that innocent lives would be lost. Berkman was unswayed. He shot Frick with a pistol, injuring but not killing him. Berkman was sentenced to twenty-two years in jail. Emma Goldman led the anarchist cause during those years. Within a year of Berkman's incarceration, Goldman was also jailed, for seven months for inciting to riot.

After her release, Goldman studied nursing and midwifery in Vienna, Austria. She then returned to New York in 1896, a fully qualified nurse-midwife.

Goldman continued to speak out on behalf of workers. In Yiddish, German, and English, she lectured on birth control and women's rights. She noted that "everything within a woman that craves assertion and activity should reach its fullest expression." She was a forceful presence to officials; sometimes the police intimidated landlords into not allowing her to use their halls for her speeches.

In 1901, when President McKinley was fatally shot by a disturbed anarchist named Leon Czolgosz, journalists accused Emma Goldman of incitement to murder the President. Because of Goldman, open accusations of the Jewish role in the assassination were voiced during the week between the shooting and the President's death.

Searching for a vehicle to express the ideas of anarchism in the press, Goldman founded a monthly magazine entitled *Mother Earth* in 1906. It was published for the next eleven years. After Alexander Berkman was released from prison, the couple co-edited *Mother Earth*.

At the start of World War I, Emma Goldman became a pacifist. During the fighting, she and Berkman were jailed for two years for opposing the draft. She was sent to the Federal House of Detention in Jefferson City, Missouri, where she used her nursing skills to help fellow female prisoners.

No sooner was Goldman released from prison in 1919, than she was forced to leave the country. Disenchanted with the new Communist regime in Russia, America fell victim to a "Red Scare;" anarchists like Emma Goldman were perceived to be dangerous to the nation because they were considered pro-Communist. As a result, Goldman acquired the nickname "Red Emma."

Conditions aboard the ship on which she sailed away from America were so grim that the crew nearly mutinied. When Goldman finally arrived in Russia, she was heartened by what she saw happening during the Russian Revolution and the rise of Bolshevism. She was convinced that Lenin would aid the Russian people.

What she found in Russia shocked her: starving and freezing masses of people forced to live in the streets; others marched off to be shot for opposing the Bolsheviks. Goldman, accompanied by Alexander Berkman, spent two years in Russia, but, appalled by the brutality of the Bolsheviks, they decided to leave. At first, Lenin tried to prevent the two from departing; he urged the Swedes and Germans to deny them visas. Sweden eventually permitted Goldman and Berkman to enter that country, but briefly. (Berkman contracted cancer in later years and committed suicide in 1936).

When she wrote about her feelings of disillusionment while in Russia, Emma Goldman ran afoul of the liberals and radicals in the United States and Western Europe who remained sympathetic to the Communists.

During the 1930s Goldman lectured throughout Europe on the rising Nazi menace in Germany and the regime of the Fascists in the Spanish Civil War. She reached England and married a Scottish widower in his late 60s, James Colton.

Goldman died while traveling in Canada in May 1940 and was buried in Chicago near the graves of the anarchists who were the casualties of the Haymarket riot. The obituary filed by the Associated Press described Emma Goldman as "an incorrigible revolutionist to the end."

Although she was part of the radical fringe of her day, many causes Emma Goldman espoused—the freedom of the individual, the right to form unions, birth control, and women's rights—eventually became part of the fabric of American life as we know it now.

NADINE GORDIMER

Nobel Prize Winner in Literature

Born November 20, 1923, in Springs, Transvaal, South Africa. South African writer. Nadine Gordimer's twenty works of fiction, including ten novels, have illustrated the strains of racial divisiveness and oppression on South Africa by examining their effect on the lives of her characters. As a private citizen, she has been even more outspoken against apartheid than in her books. She won the Nobel prize for literature in 1991, the first woman to win that award in twenty-five years and one of only seven women to win it in its ninety-year history.

Springs, Transvaal, Nadine Gordimer's birthplace and early home, is a small town thirty miles from Johannesburg, South Africa.

Gordimer was born there on November 20, 1923. Her father, Isidore Gordimer, was a watchmaker who had emigrated from Lithuania to South Africa at the age of thirteen. Nadine's mother, Nan (Myers) Gordimer, was descended from generations of English Jews. Nadine's father was Orthodox Jewish; her mother was not, which led to an unhappy marriage. Nadine's mother despised her husband's background. Nadine wrote: "We didn't ever go to synagogue; my father went on the high holidays on his own. We didn't keep kosher—we ate bacon. He was very much dominated by my mother, and proud of being married to someone who could speak [English] perfectly."

Nadine went to the Convent of Our Lady of Mercy in Springs, "but I must say the nuns didn't try to make a Catholic of me." As a student, Gordimer was indifferent, restless. It was only when she began studying comparative religions that Gordimer learned about Judaism.

Gordimer calls herself a natural writer, having begun to write at age nine.

Her first story, *Come Again Tomorrow*, appeared in *Forum*, a Johannesburg weekly in 1939 when she was only fifteen years old. Her first collection of short stories, *Face to Face*, was published ten years later by a Johannesburg firm, Silver Leaf Books.

Gordimer's political-mindedness came not from her parents, but from books. She found her middle-class colonial background dull, and she discovered that she did not share the prejudices of white South Africans against the blacks. "I lived with and among a variety of colors and kinds of

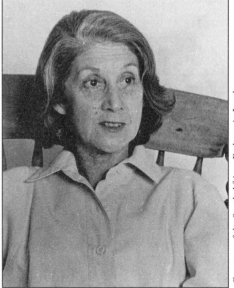

Courtesy of the South African Embassy in Israel

people," she wrote in 1975. "This discovery was a joyous personal one, not a political one, at first; but, of course, as time has gone by, it has hardened into a sense of political opposition to abusive white power."

In 1945, Gordimer entered the University of Witwatersrand in Johannesburg for a year's study. Four years later, she married Gerald Gavronsky and they had one daughter. In 1952, the marriage ended in divorce. Two years later, she married Reinhold Cassirer, an art dealer and the director of the Johannesberg branch of Sotheby Park Bernet. They have one son.

Many of the stories in *Face to Face* were among the twenty-one that appeared in her first book of short stories, *The Soft Voice of the Serpent,* published in 1952 in the United States. Her stories focused on exile and alienation and missed opportunities to understand and love.

In 1953, Nadine Gordimer wrote her first novel, *The Lying Days.* Autobiographical in form, it details the life, up to the age of twenty-four, of a character named Helen Shaw who lives in a mining suburb of Johannesburg.

In later novels, especially *Occasion for Loving,* published in 1963, Gordimer sought to describe the ways the color bar destroyed the integrity of relationships between decent people.

Her novel *A World of Strangers,* published in 1958, was banned by the South African government, the first of three Gordimer books to be likewise banned. The other two are: *The Late Bourgeois World* and *Burgher's Daughter.* (The ban on all three novels was eventually lifted.)

The Late Bourgeois World, which came out in 1966, was the most overt indictment of South Africa to date. The novella recounted twenty-four hours in the life of a character named Elizabeth Van Den Sandt. Learning that her former husband has just committed suicide, Elizabeth dwells on his ineffective revolutionary efforts and betrayal of African nationalism.

One critic, Ursula Laredo, noted that "Miss Gordimer evokes with considerable power the sterility and fear which increasingly makes the 'bourgeois world' of the middle-class whites irrelevant and, in a metaphysical sense, dead."

Though opposed to the South African government, Gordimer continued to live in her native land, hoping to use her writing talent and her growing influence to fight against apartheid. "But in my books I have never allowed myself to write propaganda," she told an interviewer for *The Guardian* on May 30, 1969. "...by that I mean, to see my characters in a distorted way...to make absolutely perfect the characters whose political ideas coincide with mine and to make villains for the others—because this offends me as an artist."

Among those influencing her writing were D.H. Lawrence, Ernest Hemingway and J.D. Salinger.

In 1971, Nadine Gordimer taught at Columbia University as an adjunct professor of writing. In 1975 she was a visiting professor at Barnard College.

When she appeared on the "The Dick Cavett Show" in 1979, one critic described her this way: "A tiny woman with the carefully cultivated fierceness of the fragile found in Joan Didion and Oriana Fallaci, she is a commanding, even a theatrical presence. Her features are sharp, her face is etched with lines of humor and indignation. She speaks crisply and with a cutting candor."

In 1976, thirty-one of Nadine Gordimer's short stories written over thirty years and chosen by her from her five earlier collections were published together. Then, in 1987, Gordimer published a novel called *A Sport of Nature,* a full-length work in which, for the first time in her novels, she dealt with the experience of being Jewish.

Critic Leon de Kock wrote that "Most of Gordimer's main characters are involved in the very serious business of finding suitable moral apparatus to cope with the excruciating mental difficulties of living white, with a conscience, in a minority within a greater South African minority."

Gordimer won the Nobel prize for literature in 1991. She was the first woman to win the literature prize in twenty-five years. Despite the ban on some of her books in South Africa, President F.W. de Klerk congratulated her for what he called "this exceptional achievement, which is also an honor to South Africa."

Gordimer prefers not to mix her Judaism with her political activities. "I don't think that my Jewishness is an influence," she said, "and I get rather annoyed when people say that my opposition to racism comes from being Jewish. It's a terrible deflection if you have self-interest in acting against racism. It distressed me that in my own country there have been such paradoxes among Jews...."

None of Gordimer's family died in the Holocaust, so the idea of Israel and what it meant to Jews was an abstraction for this renowned writer. She was troubled about going to Israel because of the cooperation in defense weapons that existed between Israel and South Africa. "I think for all Jews it was a sorrow, really, and a shame," she stated. "I can't accept all the explanations about 'what other friends does Israel have?' For Israel to have friends like [former president P.W.] Botha is a disgrace."

Asked in a 1991 *Time* magazine interview whether her books have had an impact on the public changes under way in South Africa, Gordimer replied that her books "have influenced the understanding of people outside South Africa. This can't be done in daily newscasts."

$\mathcal{L}$EAH $\mathcal{G}$OTTLIEB

From Raincoats to Bathing Suits

Born September 17, 1918 in Sajoszentpeter, Hungary. Israeli bathing suit designer. After manufacturing raincoats in Hungary and later in Israel, Leah Gottlieb realized that sun-drenched Israelis were more likely to buy bathing suits than apparel for wet weather. So, in 1956, she built the internationally-acclaimed bathing suit firm, Gottex, into a fifty-million-dollar a year enterprise that exports merchandise to seventy-five countries. Customers include England's Princess Diana, movie actresses Sophia Loren and Elizabeth Taylor, King Hussein's ex-wife Princess Muna of Jordan, and Henry Kissinger's wife Nancy. Gottex enjoys a major share of the designer bathing suit market in the United States.

$\mathcal{G}$ottex bathing suits are world-famous. The colors are splashy, the design is always exquisite, the rich and famous won't be seen in any other beach wear. Nearly half of the American market in designer bathing suits has been cornered by this incredible firm. It's all because of a diminutive, softspoken Hungarian native named Leah (Roth) Gottlieb.

Born in 1918, Leah was an outstanding chemistry student in high school in Budapest. She dreamed of going to the university and becoming a research chemist. Then, in 1939, Jews were forbidden from attending universities in Hungary. "I thought this was the end of my life," she recalled in June 1993.

Gottlieb's life, while not over, grew more complicated with the advent of World War II. In 1940, she married Armin Gottlieb, who was running a raincoat factory, and a year later they had their first child, Miriam. Three years later, their second daughter, Yehudit, was born. Armin Gottlieb was sent to a number of work camps near Budapest. Meanwhile, using fraudulent papers, Leah remained in Budapest and hid from the authorities. She retains sad memories of that period. A half-century later, recounting the tale of her hiding, she broke down in tears. "I never speak about this," she told an Israeli reporter.

After the war, Leah Gottlieb took a course in fashion design in Prague. Though neither she nor her husband were Zionists, they decided to travel to Israel. Armin Gottlieb would have preferred going to the United States, but the only destination possible was the new one-year-old Jewish state.

Courtesy of Gottex, Inc.

Courtesy of Gottex, Inc.

A few of the 950 worldwide employees of Gottex, Inc.

With eighty-eight dollars between them, Leah and Armin settled in a transit camp called Be'er Ya'acov near Tel Aviv. They eventually moved to Tel Aviv in 1950.

At first they sold children's clothes. Then, beginning in 1951, the Gottliebs revived their raincoat factory, at first producing raincoats for other firms, then selling their own brand. Working from their three-room apartment, Leah Gottlieb set one room aside for sewing. During the early 1950s, she and her husband made both raincoats and bathing suits.

The Gottliebs' transition from selling raincoats to bathing suits is part of Israeli business lore. The year 1956 brought the crucial turning point. "We looked up in the sky each October and November," remembered Leah, "to see if there was going to be rain. We knew that if there were no rain by then, we would not have a good season selling raincoats." That year, there were no early rains. Yehudit Gottlieb added: "My parents learned from experience that the sun was very certain here, but you had to pray for rain."

That same year, the Gottliebs launched Gottex (a slimmed-down version of Gottlieb Textiles). Leah concentrated on the design; Armin looked after the finances. Thanks to Leah Gottlieb's eye for splashy colors, and her ability to "feel" the best texture for bathing apparel, the firm acquired an outstanding reputation. Leah's idea was not merely to produce a bathing suit. (She was not thrilled at the idea of her models appearing at a fashion parade dressed "only" in bikinis.) She wanted her bathing suits to make a fashion statement. So she designed bathing suits with coordinated cover-ups and accessories, creating a whole new style in swimwear.

In 1958, Gottex launched its first swimsuits in cotton and Lastex. It was the first company in the world to adopt the Lycra blend fabrics that give Gottex bathing suits their sexy, tight fit. In that year, Gottex began exporting their suits to other countries. "We have always been export-minded," said Leah Gottlieb proudly.

Beginning in 1962, Gottlieb added more luster to the Gottex name by creating an annual theme for the new, yearly Gottex collection of swimwear.

By 1980, Gottex was selling ten-million dollars worth of exports to sixty-five countries, nearly half to the American market. The next year, Igedo, the international textile exhibition in Dusseldorf, honored Leah Gottlieb as one of its two "designers of the year."

From her days studying chemistry, Leah had learned the joy of creating something new. "I like to make something out of nothing," she said in 1964, "and I like 'fantasy.' Designing a bikini is like playing a game. That is probably why I never enjoyed raincoats, at least men's raincoats, very much. Also, from the first moment, I kept in mind the trends in dress styles. Swimsuits are fashion. That's something I never forget."

Over the years, Gottex developed into one of the world's leading swimwear firms, with fifty million dollars in sales in 1992, and exports to seventy-five countries.

The two Gottlieb daughters also work at Gottex: Miriam handles marketing and sales in the United States from the company's New York office; Yehudit does designing in Tel Aviv.

Leah Gottlieb says the secret of Gottex's success is that each year the company displays a new collection, one that differs from previous collections. "We always come up with surprises. Every year the world knows that each year Gottex is coming out with something new," she says. "I never look at what someone else is doing."

For her inspiration, she has searched flea markets around the world, especially in Paris and London. She also has sought what she calls the "historic moment" for inspiration. It might be the Olympics, or the 500th anniversary of the discovery of America, or the movie *Dances with Wolves.*

How does a basic idea or central theme come to her for a complete collection? "This year [1976] it happened this way. I was abroad, and I saw that the theme now is Arab dress. So I thought, *What does that mean? Here I am sitting in Israel and I'm not using that? Then I thought, Why don't I translate the Arabic line into an Israeli collection?* Thus Gottlieb created her 1977 line of ensembles, calling them "Jerusalem of Gold," "Jericho," "Magic Carpet," all based on Bedouin designs with Israeli motifs.

Other ideas come from a variety of places. Gottlieb designed one collection after visiting an exhibition of impressionist painting at the Grand Palais in Paris. One collection was inspired by a visit she made to the Matisse exhibit in 1990 in Paris and New York.

"I'm a perfectionist," she said. "I build the swimsuit collection like a building with a central idea and variations on our theme."

As Gottex's reputation grew, the great designers of the world waited to see the Gottex collection and only then decided on their own collections. Because of the company's reputation, so too was it able to lure such top supermodels as Claudia Schiffer and Naomi Campbell to model Gottex swimsuits.

Now, the "who's who of the world" wears Gottex. Princess Diana of England gets a catalogue sent to her each year, and chooses bikinis. When Muna, ex-wife of Jordanian King Hussein, shops for Gottex bathing suits, she asks (and gets) approval to shut down the entire swimsuit department at Harrod's department store in London.

During the spring of 1993, Leah, 74, and Armin, 82, were still running Gottex, still showing up each day along with the other 350 employees at Tel Aviv headquarters (Gottex worldwide has 950 employees).

REBECCA GRATZ

Ivanhoe's Heroine

Born March 4, 1781 in Philadelphia, Pennsylvania; died August 27, 1869. American social welfare activist. The most eminent American Jewish woman of antebellum America, Rebecca Gratz was the founder of the Jewish Sunday school as well as a number of other key institutions in Jewish life, including the first Jewish benevolent organization in the United States. She is believed to be the model for the heroine of Sir Walter Scott's novel *Ivanhoe*. She was a prototype for all those proficient upper-middle-class American Jewish women who labored for the general good before male professionals took over.

Rebecca Gratz was born in 1781 (a mere five years after the signing of the Declaration of Independence). Her German Jewish parents' marriage was a merger of prominent early American families in Pennsylvania. Rebecca's father, Michael Gratz, came from Langendorf, Germany. Her mother, Miriam Simon, was the daughter of Joseph Simon, a leading merchant from Lancaster, Pennsylvania.

Rebecca was the seventh of her mother's ten surviving children. Miriam had borne twelve infants in all. Rebecca lived with her family in Philadelphia. Her father owned a general store, traded in land and furs, and ran a kosher meat business. Her brother Hyman also prospered and left his fortune for the founding of a Philadelphia college that would educate the city's Jews. It was called Gratz College.

The Gratzes clung to their Orthodox Judaism fervently. Their home was strictly kosher. Moreover, when Miriam Gratz's sister married a non-Jew, Rebecca's mother ended her relationship with her sister. Rebecca grew devout and came to believe firmly in the superiority of Judaism.

Though she received little formal education, Rebecca Gratz had numerous advantages that accrued from being part of such an important family. She was always dressed neatly in plain black with a thin white collar and cuffs, and a close-fitting bonnet over her dark brown curls. Elegant, cultured, good-natured, she was no radical feminist, yet she clearly sought to develop her own identity.

She moved in social circles with prominent figures of the day—Washington Irving and Henry Clay were among her acquaintances. Famous artists, including Thomas Sully, painted portraits of the Gratzes. Well-read, Rebecca was also an ardent letter writer.

Gratz's parents died young and Rebecca took on the challenge of running the household, which included several unmarried brothers and her sister's nine children who were left motherless when her sister also died prematurely.

Caring for her many nieces and nephews drew Rebecca into the world of social work where one day she met a young lawyer named Samuel Ewing. One of the most promising up-and-coming attorneys in the city, he was the son of Dr. John Ewing, the noted clergyman and educator, and Provost of the University of Pennsylvania. The younger Ewing and Rebecca Gratz attended a number of public gatherings together and eventually fell in love. He proposed marriage to her.

Though she was desperately in love with him, Gratz refused him. He was not Jewish and Rebecca had strong memories of the pain her aunt's marriage had inflicted on her family. No matter how great her love for Samuel Ewing, she could not bring herself to cause the same suffering. Crestfallen, but picking up the pieces of his shattered life, the young attorney married someone else. He died at the relatively young age of 39. To demonstrate that she had not forgotten him, at the funeral, Gratz placed three white roses on his breast, inside his coffin, as well as setting a miniature portrait of herself next to his heart. Rebecca Gratz never married.

To overcome her distress at Ewing's early death, Rebecca Gratz sought the diversion of immersing herself in charitable works. In 1801, she served as the secretary of the Female Association for the Relief of Women and Children in Reduced Circumstances. Much later, in 1819, she founded the Female Hebrew Benevolent Society, which cared for the many Jewish immigrants flocking to the United States. The Society was the first full-fledged Jewish philanthropic institution in America. It served as the inspiration for all other American Jewish welfare agencies to come. Rebecca Gratz also founded the Philadelphia Orphan Asylum, which was the first Jewish orphan asylum in the United States. She was its secretary for forty years.

Rebecca Gratz became renowned for founding the first Jewish Sunday school system in America in 1838. Until that time, most American Jews grew up without receiving significant Jewish education. Impressed by the Christians teaching their children religion one day a week, Gratz drew up plans for the first Hebrew Sunday School in America. She was its president and supervisor for twenty-six years.

The first Jewish Sunday School was a community school that was not attached to a congregation. It was free and open to everyone, especially girls. It had, however, a decidedly Christian atmosphere at first. Some of the early textbooks were from Christian sources and the words "Jesus" and "Christ" appeared in them.

Because it was the only edition in print at the time, the English King James version of the Bible, published in 1611, was used as well. To make sure the students did not see certain passages, Gratz pasted small pieces of paper over some text. When the school opened, the only Jewish texts written in English were much older theological works.

For each class, Gratz composed prayer-hymns, prepared a reading from the Scripture, and put together interpretations of the Scripture to help the children understand them. These became the school's first curriculum.

Rebecca Gratz's efforts had a great effect. The Sunday School movement spread to Richmond, Charleston, Savannah, Baltimore, and New York. By the 1890s, no other type of Jewish educational effort was as important as the Sunday School.

Ironically it was in a non-Jewish context that Rebecca Gratz attained a certain historical significance. Often, she visited Saratoga Springs, New York, with her brother Joseph. She met the writer Washington Irving there and when she learned that his fiancee Matilda Hoffman was gravely ill, Gratz nursed Matilda through those difficult days. In addition to her beauty and charm, it was Rebecca Gratz's devotion to Matilda that especially impressed Irving. During a visit to England in 1847, he recounted the story of Rebecca Gratz's attention to his fiancee to his friend Sir Walter Scott. Scott was in the midst of writing *Ivanhoe*. He was so impressed with Irving's description of Rebecca Gratz that he modeled his fictional heroine after her. After *Ivanhoe's* publication, Scott wrote to Irving in 1819: "How do you like your Rebecca? Does the Rebecca I have pictured compare well with the pattern given?"

In 1844, an event occurred that strengthened Gratz's belief in the concept of freedom of worship. Tension between the established population of Philadelphia and Irish newcomers to the city resulted in riots. Catholic churches were burned; over one hundred people were killed or wounded. In a letter to her brother Ben, Rebecca Gratz wrote an indictment of the events: "The whole spirit of religion is to make men merciful, humble and just....Unless the strong arm of power is raised to sustain the provisions of the Constitution of the United States, securing to every citizen the privilege of worshipping God according to his own conscience, America will no longer be the happy asylum of the oppressed and the secure dwelling place of religion."

Rebecca Gratz, the earliest American Jewish woman activist, died at the age of eighty-eight.

Gratz's niece wrote that "My aunt was an old maid, at least in the common acceptance of the term. True she never married, but she was a mother to the orphan and the destitute, to the friendless and oppressed, to those in poverty and want, and to the sinner and contrite."

GOLDIE HAWN

Mistress of Malapropism

Born November 21, 1945 in Washington, D.C. American comedienne and actress. With her large bright eyes, highly mobile face, and infectious giggle, Goldie Hawn became the leading figure on comedians' Rowan and Martin's television series, *Laugh-In*, between 1967 and 1970. She played a kooky paramour in the movie, *Cactus Flower* in 1969, for which she won an Oscar for best supporting actress. In one of her best-known movies, *Private Benjamin* (1980), Hawn sought to show that women need not be merely "dumb blondes," but can pursue independent, fruitful lives.

Born Goldie Jeanne Hawn in Washington, D.C., on November 21, 1945, Hawn was raised in Takoma Park, Maryland. Her mother is Jewish; her father, Protestant. Her mother, Laura Hawn, was a jewelry wholesaler. Her father, Rutledge Hawn, was a professional musician who played violin, saxophone, and clarinet with society bands at White House and embassy affairs. He was a direct descendant of Edward Rutledge, one of the signers of the Declaration of Independence and later a governor of South Carolina. Goldie Hawn has an older sister, Patty.

Laura Hawn insisted that Goldie study tap dancing and ballet from the age of three, as well as jazz and modern dance from the age of eleven. Goldie's father gave her voice lessons. All of her childhood memories are pleasant, Goldie Hawn has said. There were no conflicts, no parental pressure, no competition within the family. "When I decided to go into show business, no one disagreed," she said in 1969.

Goldie was always uninhibited. She was not as pretty as her sister. "Boys didn't ask me out," she noted. "I didn't really want to go, but, uh, I wanted them to ask me."

As a teen-ager, Goldie participated in school and community dramatic productions. She made her professional acting debut at age sixteen playing Juliet in a production of Shakespeare's *Romeo and Juliet* performed by the Virginia Stage Company.

Hawn graduated from Montgomery Blair High School in Silver Spring, Maryland, then studied drama at American University while she taught dancing for the next year and a half. She paid her tuition by running a dance studio.

In 1964, Hawn dropped out of college, traveled to New York City, and landed her first job—a chorus

Israel Film Archive, Jerusalem/Universal Pictures

line can-can dancer at the Texas Pavilion of the New York World's Fair. She also appeared in summer stock musicals and was a go-go dancer at Dudes 'n' Dolls, a discotheque in Manhattan, as well as later at the Desert Inn in Las Vegas. She called her go-go dancing period "the saddest time" of her life. She felt "temperamentally and morally unsuited for Las Vegas and nightclubs."

In 1967, agent Art Simon "discovered" her when she was dancing in the chorus of an Andy Griffith television special. As her manager, he helped her win the supporting role of Sandy, the nutty neighbor in *Good Morning, World,* a situation-comedy about two disc jockeys. The television series had a short run on CBS Television that fall.

The great leap forward for Goldie Hawn came with the NBC Television hit *Laugh-In.* She was one of its stars from 1967 to 1970. Malapropisms flowed from her mouth. She was the dizzy blond who proved to be the engine of the greatest comedy show of the decade.

Stars of the show, including Goldie Hawn, did skits and offered puns, non sequiturs, and tongue twisters. Hawn displayed both innocence and sexiness in her character on the show, whom she described as "childlike. She's naive, gullible. I'm like her in many small ways."

It was her infectious, charming laugh that characterized Hawn; she had a natural and spontaneous reaction to whatever seemed embarrassing or bewildering on the show. It took time for Hawn's comedic talent to be obvious. "At first we hired her because she danced and she looked kinda cute," producer George Schlatter said in 1969. "Then we gave her an intro, and she blew it, and we broke up. Then we told her to do it again, and she blew it again, and then I thought, *wait a minute,* and then we started switching the cue cards on purpose. We do awful things to her now—hold up dirty words, pictures— the works."

Following her *Laugh-In* triumph, Goldie Hawn made her movie debut in *Cactus Flower* in 1969, an adaptation of the hit Broadway light comedy. Walter Matthau played a prosperous dentist who protects his bachelor status by making his mistress, played by Goldie Hawn, think he is already married to his secretary, played by Ingrid Bergman. Goldie Hawn was singled out as the movie's redeeming feature. *The New York Times's* critic Howard Thomson wrote: "It is mainly the emerging sweetness and perceptions of this girl's character, as an inquisitive Greenwich kook, that gives the picture its persuasive luster and substance."

Goldie Hawn won an Academy Award in the best supporting actress category for her performance. She also won the Female Star of the Year award of the National Association of Theater Owners.

There's a Girl in My Soup (1970), her second movie, gave Goldie Hawn her first starring role. Since 1969, she has appeared in such movies as *Butterflies are Free* (1972); *Shampoo* (1975); *Foul Play* (1978); and *Bird on a Wire* (1990).

Goldie Hawn's romantic life has had its ups and downs. In May 1969, she married Gus Trikonis, an actor and film producer whom she met when both did a road production of the musical, *Guys and Dolls.* The marriage lasted only a few years. She then married Bill Hudson, a member of the Hudson Brothers rock-comedy group, but they were later divorced. Hawn has had a long love affair with actor Kurt Russell, whom she met in 1983

Israel Film Archives, Jerusalem Universal Pictures

Goldie Hawn on the set of Sugarland Express *(1974).*

when the two co-starred in the World War II comedy-drama *Swing Shift*. She has three children, Oliver and Katie (with Hudson), and Wyatt (with Russell).

One of Hawn's best-known movies is *Private Benjamin* (1980). She was the movie's

State of Israel Government Press Office

Goldie Hawn chatting with then Prime Minister Yitzhak Shamir, November 9, 1986.

executive producer as well as its star. Until this movie, she had been typecast as a blonde with no brains. In *Private Benjamin* she plays Judy, a single woman whose life's goal is to marry. On her wedding night, however, her husband dies. She then enlists in the Army, and the movie records the half-comic, half-serious adventures of a young woman in a "man's army." The film earned over $100 million.

Hawn had decided by this time to produce movies, as well as to star in them because she felt it was important to "parlay what I had into something more."

In the spring of 1991, Goldie Hawn made a thirty-million-dollar, seven-picture deal with Disney Pictures. That prompted her to display some modesty. "My daddy said that if you think you're too big for your britches, just go stand in the ocean and feel how small you really are. I always remember that."

In 1992, she starred along with Bruce Willis and Meryl Streep in *Death Becomes Her,* a farce that focused on a magical potion that offers those who imbibed it youth and a body that would not die—whatever the abuse put to it. Hawn played a scheming villain. The point of the movie was to make fun of baby boomers who are obsessed with aging.

One of Hollywood's more successful actresses, Goldie Hawn has been a major movie personality for over two decades.

LILLIAN HELLMAN

Provocative American Dramatist

Born June 20, 1905 in New Orleans, Louisiana; died June 30, 1984. American playwright and screenwriter. Lillian Hellman is a renowned playwright and author whose major theatrical achievements were *The Children's Hour* (1934); *The Little Foxes* (1939); and *Toys in the Attic* (1960). Her plays dealt with troubling themes, including race, greed, hypocrisy, and sex. She twice won the New York Drama Critics Circle Award for best play of the year: for *Watch on the Rhine* and *Toys in the Attic*. She also received the National Book Award in 1970 for her autobiography, *An Unfinished Woman*.

Lillian was the only child of middle-class Jewish parents, Max Bernard, a businessman, and Julie (Newhouse) Hellman. She attended public schools in New York and studied at New York University from 1922 to 1924 but did not earn a degree. She did not have a good relationship with her mother, but admired her father very much.

In 1924, at age nineteen, Hellman worked as a manuscript reader for the book publishing firm of Horace Liveright. A year later she married playwright Arthur Kober. She was a book reviewer for the *New York Herald Tribune* from 1925 to 1928.

During her two-year marriage to Kober, she traveled to Paris and Bonn. She also spent time in Hollywood where she worked briefly as a play-reader at fifty dollars a week. She became interested in the labor unions, noting the bitterness their members felt toward the big studios. Through this exposure to the situation in Hollywood, she became radically left-wing in her politics. Hellman, by then divorced, returned to New York and began writing plays.

The most important event in her life, politically and emotionally, occurred in 1930 when she met mystery writer Dashiell Hammett, who was an alcoholic. When they met, he had published four novels and was about to become famous through the publication of *The Maltese Falcon,* his best and most famous novel. Hellman lived with him from the early 1930s until his death in 1961.

Lillian Hellman's first play, *The Children's Hour,* opened in 1934. Despite its controversial subject matter (the play was banned in London), it was a long-running hit. The play was based on a Glasgow Court case in which a student falsely accused two female teachers of lesbianism. Later, Hellman adapted it for the screen, and Audrey Hepburn and Shirley Maclaine played the key roles.

In 1936, Hellman visited Russia and France. She spent a month in Spain while the civil war raged there. Her next play, *The Little Foxes,* was produced in 1939. It was a study of a turn-of-the-century acquisitive, reactionary Southern family, trying to maintain its position in the face of social change and the rise of the industrial South. Tallulah Bankhead starred in the play, Bette Davis in the 1941 movie, and Elizabeth Taylor in the 1981 Broadway revival.

Watch on the Rhine, Hellman's 1941 play, became her most famous one. It was based on her strong anti-Fascist beliefs and depicted a German who risked everything to resist Hitler's new regime. In 1957, together with Richard Wilbur and Leonard Bernstein, Hellman wrote *Candide,* a comic opera based on Voltaire's satirical classic. Her next play, *Toys in the Attic,* in 1963, dealt with the problems of race and sex and was set in her native New Orleans.

Dealing with such anguishing themes as race, greed, sex and hypocrisy, Hellman's dramas were, however provocative, highly praised. Twice, she won the New York Drama Critics Circle Award for best play of the year: once, for *Watch on the Rhine,* and once for *Toys in the Attic.* Her 1969 memoir, *An Unfinished Woman,* won the National Book Award.

One analyst said that "Miss Hellman's best writing has been characterized by a superb sense of theater, taut construction, and acute personal observation of human behavior, often coupled with an attempt to probe major moral and political issues." Most of Hellman's plays were dominated by women; none of her characters was Jewish. Though she lived through perilous times for Jews, she exhibited almost no interest in the Jewish plight.

Her ambivalence about her Jewishness became apparent in an interview she gave in 1981: "I myself make very anti-Semitic remarks, but I get very upset if anybody else does. I wasn't brought up as a Jew. I know almost nothing about being one—I'm sorry to say—though not sorry enough to go to the trouble of learning....[I] decided a long time ago that I was very glad I was born a Jew. Whether brought up as one or not, somewhere in the background there was the gift of being born a Jew."

Paul Johnson, writing in his 1987 study, *A History of the Jews,* noted that Lillian Hellman "tortured her Jewish humanitarianism to fit the prevailing Stalinist mode (as did many thousands of Jewish intellectuals) so that her anti-Nazi play, *Watch on the Rhine* (1941), gives a weird view of the Jewish predicament in the light of later events. She would not allow her love of justice to find its natural expression in outraged protest at the fate of her race. So it was perverted into a hard-faced ideological orthodoxy defended with rabbinical tenacity. The need to avert the face from the Jewish facts led her to doctor truth with fiction. As late as 1955 she was associated with a dramatization of *The Diary of Anne Frank* that virtually eliminated the Jewish element in the tragedy."

Indeed, when Hellman worked on the play, *The Diary of Anne Frank,* she sought to sanitize the story by universalizing Anne's character and playing down the murder of six-million Jews. Ultimately the play was not produced because the family of Anne Frank blocked attempts to stage the Hellman version.

Hellman's romantic relationship with Hammett, a Communist party member since 1938, led to her being asked to testify before the House Un-American Activities Committee in May 1952. "I am not willing, now or in the future, to bring bad trouble to people who, in my past association with them, were completely innocent of any talk or any

Dean Martin (right) in a scene from Toys in the Attic, *Universal Pictures.*

Israel Film Archive, Jerusalem / Universal Pictures

action that was disloyal or subversive," she told the Committee. "I do not like subversion or disloyalty in any form and if I had ever seen any I would have considered it my duty to have reported it to the proper authorities. But to hurt innocent people whom I knew many years ago in order to save myself is, to me, inhuman and indecent and dishonorable. I cannot and will not cut my conscience to fit this year's fashion."

For saying this, Hellman was blacklisted throughout the 1950s. Unable to find work, she was forced to sell her house. Hammett went to jail for refusing to name donors to a fund set up to support Communist causes.

Hellman continued to write and publishers sought her books. She recounted her long relationship with Hammett in her 1969 memoir *An Unfinished Woman*. In her 1973 book, *Pentimento*, she wrote about a woman who sacrificed her life in the anti-Nazi underground in Germany. In another memoir, *Scoundrel Time*, published in 1976, Hellman told of her experiences as an uncooperative witness before the House committee.

Lillian Hellman was one of the most celebrated of America's writers, one of its most controversial, and one of its most courageous.

RUTH PRAWER JHABVALA

Oscar-winning Screenwriter

Born May 7, 1927 in Cologne, Germany. German-born novelist and playwright. Though Ruth Prawer Jhabvala arrived in India already an adult, she became, through her novels, a leading interpreter of the country to Western readers. She spent twenty-five years in India, writing novels, short stories, and screenplays, and later moved to New York where she wrote novels with settings in the United States and England. For the latter, she won an Oscar for the screen adaptation of *A Room With a View* which was based on the E.M. Forster novel. In 1993, she won a second Oscar for best screenplay based on material previously produced or published for adapting another E. M. Forster novel, *Howard's End*, for the big screen. Her most recent film effort, *The Remains of the Day*, won her an Oscar nomination for best screenplay.

Born in Cologne, Germany, in 1927, Ruth is the younger child and only daughter of Marcus Prawer, a Polish-Jewish lawyer, and of Leonora (Cohn) Prawer. Ruth's father was the cantor of Cologne's largest synagogue.

She and her older brother, Siegbert Salomon Prawer, attended segregated Jewish schools in Germany. As soon as she learned the alphabet at age six, Jhabvala began writing stories and essays in German, mostly on Jewish and religious topics.

Ruth's comfortable and secure childhood came apart in the early 1930s when the Nazis displayed hostility toward German Jews. By April 1939, when Ruth was twelve years old, her family emigrated to England where she quickly learned English.

During World War II, the Nazis murdered many of Ruth's relatives and friends. After the war, she studied at the Stoke Park Secondary School in Coventry. Then, from 1940 to 1945, the Hendon Grammar School, and later at Queen Mary College where she majored in English.

Jhabvala earned a master's degree in English from the University of London in 1951; her thesis was on the short story in England from 1700 to 1750. In 1948, she became a British subject. That same year her father committed suicide; he was overwhelmed with grief after hearing reports of how over forty of his relatives died in concentration camps. One of Ruth's early novels, *A Backward Place* (1965) recalled the tragedy.

In 1951, Ruth married a fellow London University student, Cyrus S. H. Jhabvala, a native of New Delhi and an architect. She returned with him to New Delhi. "I simply got married and went there," she said in 1975. "I knew nothing about it and I didn't ask. I had read *A Passage to India* but not *Kim*. I was enchanted. It was paradise on earth. Just to look at the place—the huge sky, the light, the colors. I loved the heat, going round with few clothes, the stone floors."

Between 1951 and 1960, the Jhabvalas had three daughters. Within that period, Ruth wrote four novels, all set in New Delhi. "I did this quite instinctively," she wrote in

1975. "...It never struck me at that time that there was anything strange in my writing in this way about Indians as if I were an Indian."

The first, *To Whom She Will*, (1955), republished in America under the title, *Amrita*, is a romantic comedy of Indian manners. *The Nature of Passion* (1956) is a satiric story of corruption in the worlds of business, government and the arts. *Esmond in India* (1958) referred to the continuing disillusionment with India felt by an English resident in Delhi. *The Householder* (1960) tells of the growth of love and maturity within an arranged marriage.

Jhabvala wrote mainly about the Hindu extended family, its households with their large numbers of in-laws and other relatives. The self-deprecating Hindu humor was but one aspect of Hindu domestic life that reminded Ruth of her own Jewish background.

Ruth Jhabvala with James Ivory (left) and Ismail Merchant.

Merchant Ivory Productions

Jhabvala wrote about being part of a dispossessed expatriate Jewish community in Britain in a story called "A Birthday in London" written in 1962.

Jhabvala's next novel, *Get Ready for Battle*, published in 1962, touched on the way in which India's wealthy classes exploited the country's poor. In the mid-1960s, Ruth's writings reflected her growing disenchantment with her adopted country. This disenchantment showed up in three collections of her short stories: *Like Birds, Like Fishes* (1963); *An Experience of India* (1966); and *A Stronger Climate* (1968).

Jhabvala examined westerners in India in her next three novels: *A Backward Place* (1965), which focused on the social interaction of western expatriates and English-educated Indians in Delhi; *A New Dominion* (1972); and *Heat and Dust* (1975). One critic noted that "in the best of her stories of India there appears, invariably, the misplaced European, a tragic wanderer of middle age and older, a person of no means and no occupation, without a place in his adopted society, living on sufferance."

Being both an outsider and an insider, Ruth Prawer Jhabvala was able to analyze India with great rigor and with a fresh perspective. One critic wrote that what was significant about her writing was "her precise, sometimes comic grasp of characters in social situations that could occur in other places and times."

Meanwhile, Ruth began pursuing a new career—scriptwriting. She concentrated on

Israel Film Archive, Jerusalem

Anthony Hopkins (left) and Emma Thompson in a scene from the movie Howard's End.

films set in India. Her first screenplay was written for a movie version of her own novel, *The Householder,* and was released by Merchant-Ivory Productions in 1963.

In the 1970s and 1980s she reworked for the movies the writings of authors she thought of as masters of the English novels: Jane Austen, Henry James—and E. M. Forster (*A Room With a View* (1986)). For the latter, she received an Oscar in 1986 for her adaptation of that novel to the screen.

In 1972, she wrote that "The central fact of all my work, as I see it, is that I am a European living permanently in India....I have quite a good view of both sides but am myself left stranded in the middle....My books may appear objective but really I think they are the opposite: for I describe the Indian scene not for its own sake but for mine."

Her eighth novel, *Heat and Dust* (1975), was awarded Great Britain's major literary prize, the Booker Award.

In 1975, Ruth and her husband moved to New York where she began spending nine months of each year, revisiting India in winter and Britain in early spring. She became an American citizen.

Jhabvala's ninth novel, *In Search of Love and Beauty* (1983), was set in New York; it presented a picture of European Jewish refugees in America.

"Two-way traffic" was the way Jhabvala described her double life writing fiction and screenplays, in which "what I have learned in films I put back into my books, and what I have learned about characterization, relationships, happenings, and everything else that goes into writing fiction, I've put to use in writing films."

In 1986, after living in the United States for over a decade, she wrote that she "cannot claim that India has disappeared out of—synonymously—myself and my work; even when not overtly figuring there, its influence is always present. But influence is too weak a word—it is more like a restructuring process of one's way of thinking and being. So I would say that, while I never became Indian, I didn't stay totally European either."

She also did screenplays for the films *Madame Sousatzka* in 1988; and *Mr. and Mrs. Bridge* in 1990.

Ruth Jhabvala received her second Oscar in 1993 for her adaptation of E.M. Forster's novel *Howard's End* to the screen. In 1994, her screenplay for *The Remains of the Day* received an Academy Award nomination.

Her eleventh novel, *Poet and Dancer,* was published by Doubleday in the spring of 1993. India as a setting is entirely absent from the book. Instead, the setting is Manhattan. Having acquired a reputation as the foremost Western writer on India, Jhabvala, has become one of the film world's most notable screenwriters.

IDA KAMINSKA

Queen of the Yiddish Theater

Born September 4, 1899 in Odessa, Ukraine; died May 21, 1980.
Character actress. After World War II, Ida Kaminska was considered
the reigning queen of Yiddish theater. In 1965, she won international
recognition for her performance as the aged Jewish shopkeeper in
the Czech film *The Shop on Main Street*.

Ida Kaminska was the daughter of a celebrated actor and actress of the Yiddish theater. Her father, Abraham Isaac Kaminski [sic], was a well-known playwright, director and
producer, as well as an actor. He was the founder of the Yiddish Theater in Moscow. Ida's
mother, Esther Rachel, known as "the mother of the Jewish stage," was considered the
leading Yiddish actress of her time until her death in 1925.

Ida was born on September 4, 1899 in Odessa, in the Ukraine, where her parents were
on tour. Her father had organized his own theatrical company in Warsaw. When the Russian ban on Yiddish theater was lifted in 1908, Abraham Kaminski also toured in Russia.

Ida was Abraham and Esther's sixth daughter; tragically, the only one who survived
childhood. They had one son, Joseph, who became a composer and the first violinist of
the Israel Philharmonic Symphony Orchestra.

Debuting on stage at the age of five, Ida appeared in a Shakespearean comedy produced by her father's company. Graduating from the Gymnasium Francke in Warsaw in
1916, she hoped to become a psychiatrist and had been admitted to a university to begin
her studies when her parents cast her in a leading role in an operetta. Kaminska was
blessed with a rich singing voice; once it became obvious to her that audiences loved her
acting and singing, she abandoned her plans for higher education and decided on a stage
career.

By age eighteen, Ida Kaminska was already directing plays, mostly from the company's European repertoire. She toured Russia with the company in 1918 and 1919, appearing in comedies and dramas. She became the leading figure in her father's company.

Ida Kaminska married Zygmun Turkow, a member of her parents' theatrical company, on June 16, 1918. In 1923, now twenty-four, she performed at Warsaw's Centralny
Theater. She and her husband organized the Warsaw Jewish Art Theater, which flourished
for another eight years.

After her divorce from Turkow in 1931, Kaminska organized her own company, the
Drama Theater of Ida Kaminska. She directed it until 1939. Between the mid-1920s and
mid-1930s, she appeared in several Polish films.

Ida Kaminska had blonde hair and blue eyes. Standing only five feet tall, she spoke
French, German, Yiddish, Polish, and Russian.

With the 1939 German invasion of Poland, the Kaminskas fled to the Soviet-occu-
pied zone. In 1940 and 1941, Kaminska served as managing director of the Jewish State

Theater of the Western Ukraine in Lvov. As the Nazis advanced further, the family fled to Frunze (today, Bishkek, capital of Krgyzia) in Soviet Central Asia where Kaminska appeared on stage from 1941 to 1944. She later reached the safety of Moscow where she did some radio propaganda work for the Soviet government.

American Jewish Archives, Cincinnati Campus, Hebrew Union College, Jewish Institute of Religion

After the war, the Polish Jewish community was less than one percent of its prewar population of three-and-a-half million. Nevertheless, Kaminska decided to reorganize the Jewish theater, working with her second husband, Meir Melman, whom she had married in July 1936. "There was no good reason to do it," she told a reporter in 1968, "for most of the Jews were gone. But we had the wish to make a monument to the murdered Jews and the government helped us." She described the reopening of the Yiddish theater in Warsaw to a full house in November 1946 as the most moving experience of her life.

In 1949, the Polish government designated Kaminska's theater the Jewish State Theater of Poland, granting it a full subsidy. Although it produced mainly classic Yiddish dramas, its seventy-play repertory included works by Ibsen, Shaw and Brecht. Some plays, produced on stage in Yiddish, were translated from English to Yiddish by Kaminska. She herself played Nora in Ibsen's *The Doll House*, as well as the title roles in Brecht's *Mother Courage* and Max Bauman's *Glikl Hameln Demands Justice*.

To remain in the good graces of the Polish Communist government, Kaminska was forced to present some plays with clear ideological content. Hence, she played the role of Ethel in Leon Kruczkowski's *Julius and Ethel*, a play about the Rosenberg atomic bomb spy case. Each year the Jewish State Theater of Poland gave 150 performances, half in Warsaw, half in the provinces, performing fifteen to twenty plays each year. It was the only permanent Yiddish language repertory theater in the world.

Kaminska received international recognition for her performance in the 1965 Czech film *The Shop on Main Street*. She was nominated for an Oscar for best actress. She also received a Cannes Film Festival acting award for that performance. In the movie, she played Rosalie Lautmann, an eighty-year-old widowed shopkeeper whose senility and deafness kept her from understanding what was happening to her and her fellow Jews during the Nazi occupation of Czechoslovakia. The film won the 1966 Oscar as the best foreign film of the year and the 1966 New York Film Critics Award.

Writing in *The New York Herald Tribune* on January 23, 1966, Jan Kadar, co-director of the film with Elmar Klos, wrote: "...I am sure that audiences will find it hard to forget the white-haired, hard-of-hearing and bewildered old lady with the innocent face. She is the most powerful reminder I know of fascism and its victims."

Frank Morris wrote in the *Toronto Globe and Mail* on March 22, 1967: "Not since the late Madam Maria Ouspenskaya have we had a character actress who can probe into the deepest facets of a role as does Miss Kaminska here. She gives an unforgettable portrait...and her final scenes are starkly convincing."

Ida Kaminska's emergence as an international star persuaded Polish officials to cover the expenses for the Jewish State Theater's eight week tour to New York. Twenty-five of the troupe's thirty-five members travelled to the United States, including Kaminska, her husband, her daughter Ruth and her son-in-law, Karol Latowicz.

For the tour, Ida Kaminska chose two plays about which she felt strongly: *Mirele Efros,* a comedy-drama written in 1898 about a long-suffering matriarch victimized by a greedy daughter-in-law (Kaminska's mother had starred in this play during her New York engagement in 1911); and Bertold Brecht's antiwar drama, *Mother Courage and her Children.* A *New York Times* critic commented about Kaminska's portrayal of *Mother Courage*: "Brecht's lines roll off her tongue witheringly. There is no quavering little old lady here. She dominates the stage."

In 1968, The State Theater came under pressure from the Polish Government to denounce what it regarded as the "worldwide Zionist campaign slandering Poland." Refusing to yield to this pressure, Ida Kaminska resigned as director and on August 23, 1968 she and members of her family flew to Vienna. A few months later they immigrated to the United States where Kaminska tried unsuccessfully to establish a permanent Yiddish repertory theater.

On January 1, 1969, 20,000 people paid tribute to Ida Kaminska at the Hanukkah Festival for Israel in Madison Square Garden. Three months later, the Kaminska troupe was due to embark on a ten-week tour of the United States and Canada to perform *Mirele Efros.* It was canceled when Kaminska suffered a heart attack.

Ida Kaminska died in New York City in 1980 at the age of eight-one.

AGNES KELETI

Hungarian Gymnast with Five Gold Medals

Born January 9, 1921, in Budapest, Hungary. Hungarian gymnast. Agnes Keleti is one of the world's greatest women gymnasts. She won five Olympic gold medals and a total of eleven Olympic medals during the 1940s and 1950s. In 1956, after the Melbourne Olympics, she remained in the West. At the Melbourne games, she won gold medals in the free-standing exercise, beam exercises, parallel bars, and combined exercise-team (portable apparatus). She also won silver medals in the combined exercise and combined exercise-team (nine exercises).

Agnes was born in 1921 in Budapest, Hungary. Her father loved sports and Agnes Keleti remembered fondly going skiing with him in the winter, and taking nature walks in the spring and fall.

When Agnes was four years old, doctors found a defect in her lung and told her to exercise. She took up gymnastics. Her sister, eight years older, also participated in gymnastics. Agnes also began swimming and playing tennis.

By age eight, Agnes was one of the best gymnasts in her school. She was fifteen years old when she joined the famous VAC (Fencing and Athletic) Sports Club, the only Jewish sports club in Hungary. She was determined to become a great gymnast, but she knew she had handicaps to overcome. "The only way to succeed was to fight, first of all because I was a woman." Second of all, because she was a Jew. She added tartly: "I never relied on the people at the top."

Keleti's parents were not particularly observant Jews. On Yom Kippur and other holidays, the family would gather at Agnes's grandparents house. Her parents would go to synagogue while she played outside.

World War II had a devastating influence on Agnes's gymnastics career. In 1942, the Nazis removed her from the Hungarian national team. Jews were not permitted to train in any sport in her native country. In March, 1944, when the Nazis moved into Hungary, Agnes's gymnastics career was brought to an abrupt halt. She was also separated from her parents.

Keleti's father and other close relatives were sent to the Auschwitz concentration camp in Poland where they died. Only Agnes Keleti, her mother and her sister survived. Her mother and sister were spared

Agnes Keleti in 1949 in Budapest on the uneven parallel bars.

129

Agnes Keleti (far left) with other athletes in Melbourne, 1956.

when the Swedish diplomat Raoul Wallenberg, well-known for saving many Jews from the grip of the Nazis in Hungary, obtained refuge for them in a "Swedish house" in Budapest. Keleti eluded the Nazis by purchasing Christian documents that enabled her to leave Budapest.

After World War II, Keleti returned to gymnastics. She found a place to train and studied physical education in Budapest. She captured her first Hungarian title in 1946 in the uneven bars competition. By 1947, she was the star of the Central European Gymnastics Championships.

From that year until 1956, she won the all-around Hungarian Championships ten times. At the same time, she kept up her studies and in 1952 she received the equivalent of a Master's degree in physical education. From 1950 to 1952, Keleti worked as an assistant in the gymnastics department at the university in Budapest.

Keleti is the recipient of many Olympic medals. In London, in 1948, she was awarded a silver medal for team-combined competition. She had been injured late in training and could not participate. However, she was awarded a medal because she was still considered a member of the team.

In the 1952 Helsinki Olympics, Keleti won a gold medal in the free-standing exercise, a silver medal in the combined team competition, and two bronze medals in hand apparatus-team and uneven parallel bars. Agnes Keleti became the 1954 world champion in uneven bars and that year was a team member of the squad that won the team exercises with portable apparatus.

"Hungary," she said later, "gave me everything. The Communists were very interested in sports for political reasons. It gave them, they thought, much prestige. They could win the population over. It didn't bother them that I was Jewish. There was no discrimination by the regime. I worked so hard so I could see the world. Sport was the best way to achieve that."

Two months before the Melbourne Olympics, the Hungarian revolt of October 1956 was squelched by the Soviets. It was a tense time, but Keleti and the team left for Melbourne in time to compete.

At the Olympics, Keleti won gold medals in the free-standing exercise, beam exercises, parallel bars, and combined exercise-team (portable apparatus). She also won silver medals in the combined exercise and combined exercise-team (nine exercises).

Once the Olympics were over, Keleti was caught in a dilemma: should she remain outside her native country or return? She had left her mother and sister in Hungary. She was concerned that the regime would seek revenge against her mother. When Keleti learned that her mother was planning to leave Hungary soon for Australia, Keleti decided to remain abroad. A number of her Hungarian colleagues from the Olympic delegation, as well as other Eastern block athletes who had competed in Melbourne, also remained in the West.

After spending eight months in Australia, Agnes Keleti went to Israel in June 1957. She may have been one of the few Jews who made *aliyah* without knowing that the state of Israel had been established. She knew about Palestine but had not seen or read about the new state in the Hungarian press. In 1960, she brought her mother to Israel as well. In 1959, Keleti married a fellow Hungarian who taught physical education. They had two sons, in 1963 and 1964.

Israel's gymnastics program was very inferior to what Agnes Keleti had known in Hungary. Her first coach told her to bring her own equipment. "'...he said to me, 'this is a difficult country in which to live.'"

Though she arrived in the Jewish state in time for the 1957 Maccabiah Games, she did not compete because gymnastics was not yet a competitive sport in Israel. Keleti was far superior to any of the other gymnasts, so she gave two special performances that demonstrated her amazing skills. She was then thirty-six years old, elderly for a gymnast.

Agnes Keleti was pleased with her life in Israel. In the summer of 1993, sipping coffee in her apartment in Herzylia, dressed in a track suit, she told the authors of this book what it was about living in the Jewish state that she particularly cherished: "I felt it was good to stay here. I had freedom. I didn't have to worry about anyone taking my documents away from me. I decided to stay here. I thought I would try to make these people healthy—by teaching gymnastics."

Keleti became an instructor in physical education in a Tel Aviv college which later became the Wingate Institute for Sport in Netanya. There she developed and trained a number of national gymnastic teams. She also taught coaches and was instrumental in creating a gymnastics school at Wingate.

In December 1991, Agnes Keleti was invited back to Hungary where she was inducted into the Hungarian Sports Hall of Fame. She is a member of the Jewish Sports Hall of Fame in Israel. She continues to coach children in gymnastics in the Israeli town of Ra'anana.

IRENA KIRSZENSTEIN-SZEWINSKA

World's Greatest Woman Track and Field Athlete

Born May 24, 1945 in the former Leningrad, Russia. Polish track and field star. Irena Kirszenstein-Szewinska is considered the greatest woman track and field athlete of all time. She won medals in each of the first four Olympics in which she competed, a feat never accomplished before by any runner, male or female. She has been recognized as one of Poland's greatest athletes. The Soviets named her the greatest woman athlete in the world.

Irena was born to Polish parents who had fled to Russia during World War II. She and her parents eventually settled in Warsaw. When Irena's athletic ability became apparent at school, her mother urged her to join a local sports club. Irena became a sprinter and long jumper.

When she was eighteen, Kirszenstein took everyone by surprise at the 1964 Tokyo Olympics when she won silver medals in the 200-meter relay and the long jump and a gold medal in the 400-meter relay. She established a national record of 21 feet, 7 1/2 inches in the long jump and in the 200-meter relay, she set a European record of 23.1 seconds. Kirszenstein ran on Poland's winning and world record-breaking 400-meter relay team.

The following year Irena studied economics at Warsaw University while continuing to pursue her athletic career. She started the season by tying the world record for 100 meters with a sprint of 11.1. In a meet in Warsaw against the United States that same year (1965), she triumphed over two American Olympic champions in the 100- and 200-meter races. She also raced a leg on the winning 400-meter relay team, as well as winning the long jump. In the 200-meter race she broke the world record with a 22.7 second time.

Irena's victories that year gained her recognition as a national heroine in her native Poland. Tens of thousands applauded her. Songs were sung in honor of her achievements. She was stopped on Warsaw streets, and stared at in awe; her autograph was in great demand. Some anti-Semitic Poles conveniently forgot that Kirszenstein was Jewish.

Kirszenstein was named Poland's Athlete of the Year in 1965. *Tass,* the official Russian news agency, voted her the outstanding woman athlete in the world. After she captured three gold medals (in the 200-meter race, long jump, and 400-meter relay) and a silver medal in the 100-meter race in the European championships in Budapest in 1966, the British magazine, *World Sport,* chose her as Sportswoman of the Year.

Irena Kirszenstein married Junusz Szewinska in 1967. Her husband, a photographer who was once a runner and also her coach, is not Jewish.

In 1968, in Mexico City, she captured a gold medal in the 200-meter Olympics race, establishing a new world record of 22.5 seconds. She also won a bronze medal in the 100-meter race.

After these triumphs, Kirszenstein-Szewinska was burned out and spent the year without competing in sports. The rest was beneficial both physically and mentally.

Kirszenstein-Szewinska gave birth to a son named Andrzej in February 1970. She believed having a child helped her performance in sports. She felt better, trained better and enjoyed running more. And her performance improved. She devoted all her time outside her family to her passion—track. Because she never tired of the sport she was still able to beat younger rivals.

Between 1971 and 1973, Irena Kirszenstein-Szewinska was still a great sprinter, although not number one in the world. She won two more bronze medals after her son's birth: in the 200-meter event at the 1971 European Championships and at the 1972 Munich Olympics.

Until 1972, Kirszenstein-Szewinska's principal events were the 100-meter and 200-meter sprint. After the Munich Olympics, she focused on the 400-meter race and

Courtesy of the Jewish Sports Hall of Fame

in 1974 she became the first woman to break 50 seconds at that distance, running it in 49.9 seconds.

She made a terrific comeback in 1974 after her place at the top had been taken by the younger sprinter Renate Stecher of East Germany. In that year Kirszenstein-Szewinska knocked a tenth of a second from her 200-meter world mark by running that distance in 22.0 seconds. And she recorded the second fastest time ever for a woman in the 100-meter race: a 10.9 second sprint.

Finally, Kirszenstein-Szewinska won the European 100-meter and 200-meter races, beating Olympic champion Stecher in both events. Kirszenstein-Szewinska clocked 11.13 in the 100-meter, the third fastest electronic time ever for a woman. She had an undefeated season at each distance. And she even ran an incredible 48.5 anchor for Poland's team in the 1,600-meter relay in the European championships held in Rome.

For her accomplishments, United Press International voted Kirszenstein-Szewinska Sportswoman of 1974. *Track and Field News* named her Woman Athlete of the Year. At the 1976 Montreal Olympics, she won the 400-meters race, establishing a world record at 49.29, and lowering her own world record by nearly half a second. For her, it was her most exciting victory. It provided her with a seventh Olympic medal. When asked if her triumph was a victory for the Communist system, she answered: "I know the people from Poland were very happy to see the Polish flag flying highest. But I run because it gives me great pleasure and satisfaction. I run for me."

Kirszenstein-Szewinska's total of seven Olympic (three of them gold) and ten European (five gold) medals is a record that has no rival in the history of women's track and field. However, Kirszenstein-Szewinska still maintained that no title gave her as much pleasure as the birth of her son. She insisted that she continued to compete for many years because she enjoyed the training and the competition, particularly the most challenging meets like the Olympics. She did not enjoy the easy meets where she knew she would win without exerting great effort. Her greatest achievements came in the major competitions where she had to fight to win.

The year 1977 was one of Kirszenstein-Szewinska's most successful years. She won the 400-meter race in the Dusseldorf World Championships, setting a new world record of 49.0. In 1978 and 1979, Kirszenstein-Szewinska worked toward the goal of trying to be the first person to win eight gold medals in the Olympic Games, bettering the record number of seven won by Mark Spitz at Munich in 1972. Age had caught up with her by the 1980 Moscow Games and she came home without a single medal.

In April 1987, Kirszenstein-Szewinska visited the United States on a goodwill tour for the Polish Track Federation. She was invited to run in a two-mile race in Central Park. Since she was forty years old, Kirszenstein-Szewinska was not sure she was up to it. Race officials told her that it was all right if she ran a little and walked a little. "So I began running. I saw no person walking, so I ran all the way," she said. Kirszenstein-Szewinska completed the run in twelve minutes, a little more than a minute off the 10:51 posted by the winner. She discouraged the idea that she would then start a new career as a distance runner. "My race was not bad for the first time," she said. "But it was the first and last time."

Irena Kirszenstein-Szewinska is a member of the Jewish Sports Hall of Fame in Israel. A graduate of Warsaw University, she is now an economist, working in the Transportation Research Center in Warsaw.

*L*EE *K*RASNER

Emerging from the Shadow of Jackson Pollock

Born October 27, 1908 in Brooklyn, New York; died in New York City on June 19, 1984. American painter. Lee Krasner was a leading Abstract Expressionist painter and the wife and artistic partner of Jackson Pollock. For thirty years, she was a force in the New York art world. She was one of the pioneers of the New York School of Abstract Art.

She was born Leonore Krasner in Brooklyn in 1908. Her parents, Jewish immigrants, came from Odessa, Ukraine. Of the seven Krasner children, Lee was second youngest and the first to be born in America.

Lee became an artist at age thirteen. At first she studied at the Women's Art School of Cooper Union. Then, from 1929 to 1932, she studied at the National Academy of Design.

In the 1930s, it was very difficult for women to break into the male-dominated art world. From 1936 to 1940, Krasner studied with Hans Hofmann, the Abstract Expressionist painter and teacher. Intending to complement her, Hofmann stood by Krasner's easel and offered her the first praise she had ever received as an artist: Her painting, he told her, was "so good you would never know it was done by a woman."

Krasner learned the fundamentals of Cubism in Hofmann's class. The most "valid thing" he supplied her with, she said, "was his enthusiasm for painting and his seriousness and commitment to it."

The great crossroads in her life came in 1938 when she met Jackson Pollock, the great but iconoclastic abstract painter. His work astounded her from the moment she first saw it. Krasner was already a proficient painter; Pollock was merely starting out. Becoming romantically involved, Krasner and Pollack lived together, bought a farm near East Hampton, Long Island for $5,000, and in 1945, they were married.

The couple lived in poverty, at that time thought to be a natural state of affairs. "Nobody had any money in those days," Krasner explained. "We were living on no money. Whenever we had some, we used it for physical comfort, like putting in heat or hot water." From the art patron Peggy Guggenheim, Pollock received $150 a month for whatever he painted.

Krasner painted in the living room; he painted in the bedroom. "Our studios were always separate," Krasner noted. "We entered by invitation only. Jackson would say, 'Would you care to see what I'm doing?' Although Pollock gave her advice to take out a spot or change a curve, she, never advised him.

Pollock had the paradoxical effect upon Krasner of boosting her career, yet overshadowing her, forcing her into an ill-deserved obscurity until after his death in August 1956.

Despite her far-ranging contacts in the art world and her obvious professional touch, Krasner found her male colleagues reluctant to admit her into the all-male "club" of painters—a group that included Matisse, Picasso and Mondrian. In the 1940s some of them, known as the Irascible Eighteen, engaged in a famous public protest against the lack of American art in New York's Metropolitan Museum. Barney Newman, a painter and protest organizer, was the one who phoned the Pollock home, getting Krasner on the line.

"Lee, get Jackson, it's very important. Go get him. I must speak with him."

She obeyed, but she was later furious that she had neither been informed about the protest, nor asked to sign the protesters' public statement.

In the late 1940s and early 1950s, while Pollock was producing the major portion of his work, especially his landmark "drip" paintings, Lee Krasner established herself as a painter in her own right.

In 1946, getting rid of Cubist strictures, she began a series of small paintings— among them "Noon" employing colors that are atomized into a completely abstract field, covering the entire picture surface.

In 1951, Krasner had her first one-person show at the Betty Parsons Gallery.

Lee Krasner's 1984 obituary in *The New York Times* noted that "she used her mastery of line and color to produce paintings that could be both elegiac and fierce, filled with ripe, bulbous shapes and almost demonic lines and images that haunt or cut into her animated and agitated pictorial fields. Although her work shares the gestural decisiveness of other Abstract Expressionists, it also has an inwardness and feeling for color that are close to European artists like Matisse and Bonnard."

Writing in *The New York Times* in 1984, Grace Glueck wrote that between 1956 and 1981, "her high-key floral abstractions of the late 1950s, such as 'Listen,' with its brilliant bursts of color arrestingly played off against 'open' areas of bare canvas, have a contagious exuberance. They are succeeded by a series of angry, large-scale canvases...'Charred Landscape' of 1960, a turbulent massing of peaky and ovoid forms that suggest cosmic catastrophe."

Krasner's first important retrospective was in London in 1965.

After Jackson Pollock's death at the age of 44, Krasner did her most important work. Nonetheless, Krasner continued to live in his artistic shadow. The art world heard of her largely as the "art widow" who had control over Pollock's works and their prices. At her funeral, *Time* magazine art critic Robert Hughes noted how difficult it must have been for her to play the role of the widow of a famous artist before her own talents were fully recognized by the art world. "She bore it with extreme grace," he said.

Only in the late 1970s and early 1980s did Lee Krasner obtain some acclaim on her own. This was attributed in part to the growing strength of the women's movement; but also in part because of exhibitions such as the 1981 New York show called "Krasner/Pollock: A Working Relationship."

After her retrospective at the Museum of Fine Arts in Boston in October 1983, Krasner finally was recognized as a painter of the first rank.

"She was a fabulous draftsman and had an incredible color sense," said Barbara Rose, an art critic and senior curator of twentieth-century art at the Houston Museum. "She did not follow any color rules, and she is one of the very few women who has really expressed violence and aggression in her work."

Another aspect of her work, said Rose, was "her rigor. Like Mondrian, she was a beacon of a certain kind of integrity. She had an absolute inability to compromise with anything."

Lee Krasner once explained her relationship to the canvas this way: "When I see a blank canvas, my preoccupation is with the entire surface of it. One goes between the curvilinear...and the horizontal and vertical there. But I'm not conscious of a conflict there. You try to make as live a contact as you can, to bring that two-dimensional surface into vibration and life. You work with shapes and colors. Instead of my directing it, I let it happen. I'm concerned primarily with the area I'm trying to decorate...occupy."

Krasner's work went in cycles. Between stages, she produced heavily overpainted, indecisively gray canvases, what she called "my mud periods." Then she would make a breakthrough, and achieve a new clarity on canvas. "If a painting doesn't quite sit with me I put it away, and sooner or later get hold of it and rework or collage it. I'm not interested in how long it takes. I might pick it up years later." For instance, one painting, called "Night Moses," is dated "1958-1982;" twenty-four years in the making.

The standard histories of the New York School of twentieth-century art ignored Lee Krasner, though, as Rose noted, "Krasner had contact with all of the major forces that shaped its evolution. She is one of the significant painters of the twentieth century, an artist whose importance is only now beginning to be seen."

ANN LANDERS

Grand Dame of Advice

Born July 4, 1918 in Sioux City, Iowa. American advice columnist. According to the 1992 *Guinness Book of World Records,* Ann Landers is the most widely syndicated columnist in the world, with an estimated ninety million readers in over 1,200 newspapers. Her daily column, "Ask Ann Landers," offers advice to readers who write to Landers to ask her how to solve their problems. A Gallup Poll taken in 1975 showed that she was one of the twenty most admired women in the nation.

Ann Landers, one of four sisters, was born Esther Pauline Friedman in Sioux City, Iowa, on July 4, 1918. Her twin sister Pauline Esther (also known as Abigail Van Buren, writer of the "Dear Abby" advice column) was born seventeen minutes after. That was the start of what became a bitter rivalry.

Ann is the daughter of Russian immigrants, Abraham and Rebecca (Rushall) Friedman. Her father owned a chain of movie theaters. Landers has described herself as "typically upper middle-class Midwestern Jewish."

She and her twin sister Abby are both five feet, two inches, and blue-eyed. As children, they dressed alike, double-dated, sometimes sat in for one another during high-school classes (depending on who had done the homework). At Central High School, Esther was "Eppie;" Pauline was "Po-Po." The two Friedman sisters even had a double wedding.

From 1936 to 1939, Ann Landers attended Morningside College. The two sisters became adversaries in 1955 when Ruth Crowley, the original Ann Landers, died. To find a successor for Crowley's advice column, the *Chicago Sun Times* ran a contest. The winner was "Eppie" who got some expert advice with her sample answers from Notre Dame President Theodore Hesburgh and Supreme Court Justice William O. Douglas.

Landers began writing her daily column "Ask Ann Landers" on October 16, 1955. Thousands of letters poured in to the *Sun Times.* Landers' sister Pauline offered to help answer the backlog of letters. Two months later, she launched her own column in the *San Francisco Chronicle.* She called herself Abigail Van Buren. Annoyed, Landers did not speak with Abigail for several years. Meanwhile, both of their respective columns were huge hits, winning readers on five continents. Later, the twins made up. Ann Landers said that "If anyone had written to me with the problem [of two sisters spatting], I would have said, 'Forgive and forget.'"

Ann Landers' column was syndicated in over 800 newspapers and became the most widely read column in the world, with some sixty million readers. Eight secretaries poured over the 1,000 letters a day that readers wrote to the columnist.

An interviewer once asked her how she learned to relate to people with problems. "You don't have to have lived through an immense amount of agony and pain in order to relate to people who are suffering," she told *Time* magazine in 1989.

"I really care about what happens to people, and when I first began to read those letters, it was an eyeopener. I came from a very solid Midwestern Jewish home. You see, I led a very sheltered life. I had never seen a man hit his wife. I had never seen any drunkenness. I had never seen any poverty. I knew these things were happening, but they never happened to me. The mail grew me up in a hurry."

Ann married Jules W. Lederer on July 2, 1939. Thirty-six years later, she announced in her July 1, 1975 column that she and Jules were divorcing. "The lady with all the answers does not know the answer to this one," she confessed in her column. "The sad, incredible fact is that after 36 years of marriage Jules and I are being divorced. As I write these words, it is as if I am referring to a letter from a reader. It seems unreal that I am writing about my own marriage." Some 30,000 readers wrote to express their sympathy.

Courtesy of Ann Landers

Providing no reason why she was divorcing, Ann Landers asked readers not to write or call for details. She called the divorce announcement "the most difficult column I ever have written, but also the shortest." Four inches of blank space followed the column "as a memorial to one of the world's best marriages that didn't make it to the finish line."

In 1975, a Gallup Poll ranked Ann Landers as one of the twenty most admired women in the nation.

In 1978, Landers published *The Ann Landers Encyclopedia,* which dealt with a wide variety of contemporary issues.

Most of the letters Landers receives are written by middle-aged people. While Landers' views have generally been conservative, she has loosened up in recent years on questions of sex and divorce. In 1981, she confessed that, while she still was not comfortable with teen-age sex, she no longer clung to the notion that "every girl must hang on to her virginity until marriage or death, whichever comes first."

Whatever Ann Landers' readers wish to discuss, she has blunt, common-sense answers for them.

Here are some examples:

> Dear Ann Landers: A man twelve years my junior talks of marriage, but his conversations all wind up with questions about my financial situation. If he is insincere...why does he swear he worships the ground I walk on? (Signed) Miss B.L.K.

Dear Miss B.L.K: He probably thinks there's oil under it.

A second example:

Dear Ann Landers: I'm a mail carrier and my job starts at eight a.m. This is time enough for women to get a dress on and run a comb through their hair. Most housewives look so terrible it's enough to spoil a man's day. (Signed) The Mailman

Dear Mailman: You ain't never been a woman at eight o'clock in the morning.

Yet, one more letter:

Dear Ann Landers: I am fifteen years old and my biggest problem is my mother. All she does is nag, nag, nag. From morning till night, it is, turn off the TV. Do your homework. Wash your neck. Stand up straight. Go clean up your room. How can I get her off my case? (Signed) Pick, Pick, Pick

Dear Picky: Turn off the TV. Do your homework. Wash your neck. Stand up straight. Go clean up your room.

In reply to a letter from the authors of this book, Ann Landers wrote on January 19, 1993 that she had a "limited" Jewish education. She was helped in feeling a positive and strong identification as a Jew by attending Shaare Zion Synagogue in Sioux City where she attended Junior Congregation on Saturday mornings. The most meaningful Jewish holiday to Landers is Yom Kippur. She attends services then.

While she "absolutely" publicly identifies herself as a Jew, Ann Landers wrote she does not feel that being Jewish influenced her choice of career or career path. As to whether Judaism influenced her outlook or attitudes about life in general, she replied: "I am inclined to support the underdog."

According to the 1992 *Guinness Book of World Records,* Ann Landers is the most widely syndicated columnist in the world, with an estimated readership of ninety million in over 1200 newspapers.

In 1980, President Jimmy Carter appointed her to serve on the Board of the National Cancer Institute for six years. In 1981, President Ronald Reagan appointed Landers to the board of the President's Commission on Drunk Driving. During her career of dispensing levelheaded and reasonable advice to people with problems of all kinds, Ann Landers has established herself as an expert on life's experiences. Her great credibility makes her someone whose opinions are sought in many realms.

Wanda Landowska

High Priestess of the Harspichord

Born July 5, 1879 in Warsaw, Poland; died August 16, 1959.
Pianist and harpsichordist. Although an excellent pianist, Wanda Landowska gained her greatest fame from playing the harpsichord. One of the first to revive harpsichord music in the twentieth century, she was considered the greatest performer of the harpsichord of her day. She was an authority on seventeenth- and eighteenth-century music. Her concerts and lectures reawakened interest in Baroque music. She lived in Paris until World War II, then settled in the United States.

Wanda was born in Warsaw, Poland, in 1879 and came from an urbane family. From the age of four, she began to study the piano. As she grew, Landowska demonstrated a definite preference for the Baroque masters. Recognizing her genius, her teachers urged her to study at the Warsaw Conservatory with Moritz Moszkowski and the well-known Chopin interpreter, Michaelowski. When she got there, Landowska found that the only Bach works in the curriculum were transcriptions by Liszt and other Romantics. She made sure to play some Bach as well as the set pieces proscribed by the course of study.

Landowska went to Berlin in 1895 to study counterpoint and composition. She was attracted to vocal music. Among her compositions were "Hebrew Poem for Orchestra," "Serenade for Strings," and numerous works for the piano and for the harpsichord as well as cadenzas for Mozart and Haydn concertos. Landowska also did transcriptions and arrangements of folk songs.

In 1900, living in Paris, she married Henry Lew, a man of many interests who wrote Hebrew folk music and specialized in Hebrew folklore. He was also an actor and journalist. They collaborated on a book entitled *Musique Ancienne,* which was published in 1909.

From 1900 to 1913 Landowska was a member of the faculty of the Schola Cantorum. Most musicians thought the modern piano was a perfectly suitable musical instrument for the music of Bach and his contemporaries. Wanda Lan-

dowska, however, disagreed. She preferred the harpsichord, which went against the conventional wisdom of the time. Indeed, she was practically alone in her belief.

In 1903, she played the harpsichord for the first time in public. Three years later, she began her career as a concert pianist. Although she was a capable pianist, it was the harpsichord that made her world-famous.

Beginning in 1909, she devoted herself to reviving the harpsichord. Her friends were annoyed that so gifted a pianist had abandoned the piano in favor of the harpsichord (they called it an old "tin-pan" instrument), but they encouraged her to play it anyway. Landowska's husband was her greatest supporter. He helped her in her research and in her campaign to, as she put it, "reconstitute a harpsichord approaching as closely as possible those of the middle eighteenth century."

Landowska disliked it when people distinguished between old and modern music, preferring the modern. "There's no such thing as 'ancient music'; it's simply 'music,' that of today, yesterday, and forever," she liked to say.

In 1910, Wanda Landowska toured Russia and gave concerts on the harpsichord. She was invited twice to stay with the world-renowned author Leo Tolstoy and his family at Yasnaya Polnaya, where she played the harpsichord for them. A lover of old music, Tolstoy became a fervent supporter of Wanda Landowska's effort to popularize the harpsichord.

Finally, in 1912, the piano maker Pleyel built her a special harpsichord. She had it constructed according to her personal specifications. The instrument was displayed for the first time at the Bach Festival in Breslau that year.

A year later, Landowska became professor of the harpsichord at the *Berlin Hochschule fur Musik,* a post created solely for her. She was chosen to direct a harpsichord class that was being offered only because she was there to teach it.

Landowska and her husband were confined to Germany as aliens throughout World War I. Landowska was allowed to teach. When her husband died in a car accident soon after the war, she left for Switzerland, and later settled in Paris. She resumed her concert tours and teaching.

In 1923, she debuted in the United States as pianist and harpsichordist with the Philadelphia Orchestra. She then toured the United States for several seasons and also recorded her music at this time. She traveled widely in Europe, Asia, Africa and both Americas, as well as teaching harpsichord at the Fontainbleau Conservatory.

One music analyst wrote that "...as pianist and harpsichordist, her style is characterized by extreme refinement, sensitivity, and grace. For this reason, she is at her best in the music of the distant past—in Bach and in Mozart. As a harpsichordist she has explored new resources for the instrument. She may be said to have been the greatest performer on that instrument of her day."

Landowska was also a recognized authority on seventeenth- and eighteenth-century music. In 1925, she founded the School for Ancient Music at the colorful Saint-Leu-la-Forêt near Paris. She had a concert hall built in the garden. Music lovers and pupils joined her there in the years leading up to World War II.

In 1933 Landowska was ready to give her first complete performance of Bach's "Goldberg Variations" on the harpsichord. She told her audience she had been practicing them for forty-five years.

Landowska inspired a number of composers to write music for the harpsichord. In 1926, she commissioned Manuel de Falla to compose a concerto. She premiered Francis Poulenc's *Concert Champetre* in Paris which he had dedicated to her.

In 1937, she received the Grand Prix of the Paris Exposition Jury for her concert of old Polish music.

When the Germans marched on Paris in 1940, Landowska had to leave her school, with its library and museum that housed her unique collection of musical instruments. The invading army looted the treasure. Landowska escaped to Banyuls-sur-Mer in the eastern Pyrenees, and then went on a concert tour of Switzerland.

She sailed for America in 1941, arriving on December 7, the day Pearl Harbor was struck. She lived in New York for a time, then settled permanently in Lakeville, Connecticut. She taught, composed, and made recordings. She also wrote a great deal about music. Her reappearance as a soloist was widely acclaimed by harpsichord lovers.

Many of the old classics that she played and popularized were ones she herself found first in libraries and music collections. She inspired such modern composers as Poulenc and Manuel de Falla to write music for the harpsichord.

Wanda Landowska liked to say: "A true artist always compares what he does with what he intended to do." In an apparent reference to the harpsichord: "A successful miniature is better than a bad fresco. But the one needs to be studied at close range, the other looked at from a distance."

The critic B. Gavoty said of her: "Exceptional instruments demand exceptional performers; and in the end they always obtain them."

SHERRY LANSING

One of Hollywood's Most Powerful Women

Born July 31, 1944 in Chicago, Illinois. American film producer. Sherry Lansing is one of the most powerful women in the film industry. Lansing is the first woman to be put in charge of production at a major Hollywood film studio. She is the producer of such films as *Fatal Attraction, The Accused,* and *Indecent Proposal.* She was named President of Production at Twentieth-Century Fox on January 2, 1980. On November 4, 1992, the former mathematics teacher, model, and actress was named studio chief of Paramount Communications. *Premiere* magazine, in its May 1993 issue, ranked her eleven (up from eighty-three the year before) on its list of the one hundred most powerful figures in Hollywood.

Sherry Lansing was born in Chicago, Illinois, on July 31, 1944. She is one of two daughters of Margo Heimann, who had fled to the United States from Nazi Germany. Her father died young and her mother later married Norton Lansing, a furniture manufacturer. They had two more children.

In 1962, Sherry graduated from the University of Chicago Laboratory High School, a special school for gifted children. Four years later, she earned a bachelor's degree graduating summa cum laude from Northwestern University's theater department. She was an outstanding student.

A year after the 1965 riots in Watts, Lansing went to that Los Angeles ghetto area to teach mathematics in a public high school. Four years later she quit, acknowledging that she had "lost passion" for teaching.

Lansing turned to modeling, appearing in television commercials between 1969 and 1970 for the Max Factor and Alberto-Culver companies.

Tall, with long, dark brown hair, wide-set blue eyes, and high cheekbones, Sherry Lansing has been compared to Sophia Loren, Rita Hayworth, and Jacqueline Onassis for her striking beauty.

Lansing had small parts in two films: as Susan, a "chic sexpot," in the 1970 movie *Loving,* and as the victimized and disfigured Amelita in *Rio Lobo,* also a 1970 release.

She also appeared with the national company of the 1970 Pulitzer-prize winning play, *No Place*

to be Somebody.

Lansing thought herself a "terrible actress." An inveterate moviegoer, she became fascinated by the production process, and so she enrolled in film courses at UCLA and USC.

In accordance with her parents' expectations, she married a doctor. The marriage ended in divorce in 1970.

By 1970, Sherry Lansing was reading scripts for five dollars an hour at Raymond Wagner's small production company, Wagner International.

Lansing discussing her movie School Ties *on the set.*

Courtesy of The Jewish Chronicle

Two years later she was working with writers to develop screenplays. In 1975 she became executive story editor at MGM, then the highest nonacting job a woman could attain at a major studio.

In March 1977, Sherry Lansing advanced to vice-president for creative affairs, the second-ranking production post and her first vice-presidency. Two months later Sherry joined Columbia Pictures as vice-president for production. In September 1978 she became senior vice-president.

In April 1979, Lansing told *Life* magazine that she doubted that "in [her] working lifetime, [she would] see a woman as a president of a movie company." Two months later, she told *Working Woman* magazine: "People were suspicious of me. A woman couldn't make a mistake without everyone's wondering how she got the job." At Columbia, Sherry Lansing oversaw the completion of the prestigious 1979 films *The China Syndrome* and *Kramer vs. Kramer.*

In *Kramer,* Lansing was concerned with "reordering sequences to increase the likability" of the male protagonist, whose wife walks out on him. She held out for Dustin Hoffman to play the husband, even after he had twice rejected the role (He won an Oscar for Best Actor for his performance.) She also fought for the casting of Meryl Streep, then a relative unknown. (She won Best Supporting Actress.)

Lansing's contract at Columbia expired in November 1979. On January 2, 1980, Lansing was appointed president of the company's feature-film division. Her three-year contract stipulated an annual salary of $300,000 plus bonuses. This made her one of the highest-salaried women executives in any industry. Her appointment—and her invasion of a male-dominated Hollywood—sent the news media into shock.

Sherry Lansing's goal was "to make movies that stir up your emotions; movies where you root for the people." She explained: "When I was growing up, I loved *The Pawnbroker, A Thousand Clowns, Petulia*—all movies that came out of somebody's passion."

Aware that she has had to overcome an image of not being aggressive, she distinguished between strength and toughness. "I would like to think of myself as being a strong woman. But I'm not a tough woman. I don't understand why human decency, kindness, respect for people, have to be mutually exclusive from strength."

Lansing's tenure at Fox included overseeing such hit films as *9 to 5, The Verdict, Quest for Fire,* and *Taps.* Her biggest thrill was in acquiring the rights to *Chariots of Fire.* Lansing resigned her position at Fox in 1983 to form her own production company.

Jaffe-Lansing Productions, which Sherry Lansing formed in partnership with Stanley Jaffe in 1983, made such films as *Black Rain, The Accused, Racing With the Moon,* and *Fatal Attraction.* Lansing was attracted to *Attraction* because it had the potential of delivering a feminist message.

In October 1987 she told Susan Faludi, author of *Backlash*: "I always wanted to do a movie that says you are responsible for your actions...I wanted the audience to feel great empathy for the woman." The film's box-office receipts made Lansing personally wealthy. Jaffe-Lansing also produced *School Ties,* the story of a Jewish quarterback at a fancy, mostly non-Jewish private board school in the 1950s.

For Lansing, being Jewish counted as something important. Although she never had a bat mitzvah, she explained that her parents had been secular Jews who grew up believing Judaism "was something always inside of you, something to be proud of, something that carried with it a certain responsibility." Accordingly, she too assumed responsibilities in Jewish life. In 1981, she took the post of chairman of the UJA entertainment division. "I have always liked being Jewish," she said.

Talking about her production company, Lansing said: "Each of our movies has had a common theme: that your actions have consequences. It all comes back. That's what Michael Douglas's character learns in *Fatal Attraction.*" She was once asked what makes a story work for her as a movie. "It's like falling in love. Who knows? I could give you a hundred reasons, but it usually comes down to something you can't put your finger on, something that you feel."

Lansing is honest about her own talents. "I'm no writer. I couldn't write a sentence if my life depended on it. Maybe that's why I [call] all those people back every night—so I wouldn't have to write memos. But I love to work development, to talk with the writers and try and get them to solve problems, and try and bring the whole thing along and get people to do their best work."

On November 4, 1992, Sherry Lansing was appointed studio chief of Paramount Communications. In the new post, she did not wield the same power held by her predecessor, Brandon Tartikoff. She was given the new title of chairman of the Motion Picture Group of Paramount Pictures. Unlike Tartikoff, she did not oversee Paramount's television division. Lansing reported to Stanley Jaffe, president of Paramount Communications and her former producing partner.

In 1991, Lansing married director William Friedkin whose movie credits include *The French Connection* and *The Exorcist.*

In 1993, Sherry Lansing produced the box-office hit *Indecent Proposal* starring Robert Redford and Demi Moore; it grossed $105 million. Her most recent films are *Intersection* and *Addams Family Values.*

From model to actress, from actress to studio chief, Sherry Lansing has moved up the ladder in Hollywood. She is not only one of the most powerful women in Hollywood, she ranks among the most influential female executives in the United States.

$\mathscr{E}$STÉE $\mathscr{L}$AUDER

Queen of the American Cosmetics Business

Born July 1, 1908 in New York, New York. American cosmetics giant. As she applied cosmetics for women customers, Estée Lauder dispensed advice, gave away free samples, and thus built Estée Lauder, Inc. into the world's largest family-owned beauty company. In June 1993, Lauder's personal wealth was estimated at $3.4 billion. She frequently appears on lists of the most admired businesswomen in America. When President Ronald Reagan entertained the Prince and Princess of Wales at the White House, Princess Diana asked for three guests: Robert Redford, Bruce Springsteen and Estée Lauder.

For years, Estée insisted that she had been born in a Hapsburg castle and grew up as a countess. In fact, she was born Josephine Esther Mentzer in Queens and had lived over a hardware store.

She was born on July 1, 1908 in Corona, a community in Queens, New York, the youngest child in the large family of Max and Rose (Schotz) Mentzer, which included Mrs. Mentzer's five sons and a daughter from a previous marriage.

As a child, Estée was ashamed of her immigrant parents' European-style, straight-laced manners and their heavily-accented English. She wanted to be "one hundred percent American." Her father, a custom tailor by profession, bought a neighborhood hardware store. Estée helped her father arrange merchandise and create attractive window displays.

Soon after World War I began, John Schotz, Mrs. Mentzer's brother, who was a chemist specializing in skin-care preparations, moved in with the family. In the tiny stable behind the house, he set up a makeshift laboratory. Estée was fascinated. "I watched as he created a secret formula," a cream potion filling vials and jars which smelled wonderful, and, "made your face feel like spun silk."

John showed her how to concoct a face cream. Estée, who dreamt of becoming a scientist, named it Super-Rich All Purpose Cream, and tried it out on her family and friends.

In January 1930, Estée married Joseph H. Lauter (soon changed to Lauder), a moderately successful garment-center businessman. Their first child, Leonard, was born three years later.

Over the next few years, Lauder refined and improved her uncle's creams. Among her first customers were Florence Morris, the owner, and clients of an Upper West Side beauty salon, House of Ash Blondes. When Florence opened a new salon on the Upper East Side, Estée ran the beauty concessions. Estée expanded her business to homes and hotels. She always gave a small free sample either a few teaspoonfuls of powder or some lipstick—with any purchase. Estée Lauder became a fixture on the guest lists of New York's most influential hostesses. Accordingly, her business grew.

In 1939, she divorced her husband. Working mostly in Miami now, she tried to sell her skin preparations to rich vacationers and retirees. In December 1942 Estée remarried

Library of Congress

A make-over with Estée Lauder (left).

Joseph Lauder. Their second child, Ronald, was born in February 1944.

Estée Lauder, Inc. began in 1946, with Estée in charge of marketing and Joseph handling the finances. They had four skin-care products: Creme Pack for blemished or problem skin; a cleaning oil; Super-Rich All Purpose Creme, and a light, nourishing lotion, plus a face powder, eye shadow and lipstick. Lauder's greenish blue packaging was distinctive, and "Lauder blue" became the Estée Lauder trademark.

To stimulate demand, Estée Lauder gave away thousands of samples at charity events in the New York region. She thought she could make department-store cosmetics buyers her customers. Lauder's "factory" was a converted restaurant on the Upper West Side. She and her husband did everything—from cooking the creams, mixing them, sterilizing the jars, to pouring and packaging.

Lauder's first big break came when Saks Fifth Avenue placed a large eight-hundred-dollar order and sold it all out two days later. Lauder insisted on selling her products only in the best stores. She trained saleswomen herself, spending half of each year on the road. The year 1953 was a big turning point. It was then that Lauder introduced her first fragrance, Youth Dew, a bath oil with a warm, sweet, scent that could be used as a perfume. Priced at $8.50, it was a huge hit. It became the best-selling perfume in the world.

By the early 1950s Estée Lauder counters were found around the country.

Lauder kept the company private. That enabled her to take risks associated with developing new products free of stockholder pressure for immediate profits. It also meant that sales figures would be unavailable to the public.

Lauder worked hard at overcoming buyer resistance. In Paris, she "accidentally" spilled some Youth Dew on the floor at Galleries Lafayette. Permeating the store was this new, heady scent. Customers quickly inquired about the perfume. By the 1970s, Estée Lauder products were sold in over seventy countries.

The two Lauder children have entered the business as have the two Lauder daughters-in-law. In January 1973 Leonard Lauder succeeded his mother as president of Estée Lauder, Inc. Estée Lauder's husband Joseph became executive chairman. Lauder herself assumed the title of chairman of the board, permitting her more time to cultivate her position in society. In 1982 Leonard Lauder became CEO and Ronald was named chairman of Lauder International, which accounted for half of the company's sales volume.

It has been Lauder, with her astute nose for fragrances who created the perfumes that made her name famous. Among these were the tangy Azurée, in 1969; Aliage, the first so-called "sport" fragrance, in 1972; Private Collection, in 1973; White Linen, in 1978; Cinnabar, in 1978; and Beautiful, in 1985. Only family members know the formula for each of these fragrances. Cut-rate manufacturers have no chance of duplicating the fragrances.

Lauder's husband died in January 1983.

When Estée Lauder's unauthorized biography, written by Lee Israel, was about to be published, she rushed to write her own autobiography—*Estée: A Success Story*—and get it into print in November 1985.

During the 1980s Estée Lauder owned more than one-third of department store counter space, featuring Estée Lauder, Clinique, Aramis, and Prescriptives cosmetics. While she sold only about one-tenth of all beauty products, more than one third of all the women's beauty aids sold in department stores were from her company. One-quarter of the men's cosmetics sold were also Estée Lauder products.

In the October 12, 1986 issue of *Fortune* magazine, it was reported that Estée Lauder's cosmetics empire was worth $1.6 billion.

Lauder knew how to promote her products—and herself. "Never say, 'May I help you?'" she advises. "Say, 'Madame, won't you please let me show you how this finest of creams, made from only pure ingredients, can make your complexion glow with youth and radiance?'"

When Estée Lauder handles the cosmetics counter, showing how it's done, she touches the woman's face, and gives her a free sample. This gimmick of giving a free gift to women who make a modest purchase has become a marketing tool that is now commonplace in the beauty business. To sell her products, Lauder handpicked her own saleswomen—numbering 7,500 by the late 1980s—and calling them beauty advisers.

By the end of 1990, Estée Lauder was number one in department-store makeup sales and department-store skin treatment sales. She ranked third among beauty-product companies and was also number three in overall makeup sales.

EMMA LAZARUS

"Give Me Your Tired, Your Poor"

Born July 22, 1849 in New York, New York; died on November 19, 1887. Poet for the masses. Emma Lazarus was thirty-four when she wrote "The New Colossus," the inscription for the Statue of Liberty. A line from that poem, "Give me your tired, your poor, Your huddled masses yearning to breathe free," is one of the most famous in the English language. The statue has become the symbol of American liberty and Lazarus' poem stands as one of the great testimonials to the American ideal of freedom. Because of that poem, she ranks as one of the major literary figures in American Jewry. She weaved into her poetry her strong interest in Russian Jewry and Zionism.

Not like the brazen giant of Greek fame,
With conquering limbs astride from land to land,
Here at our sea-washed, sunset gates shall stand
A mighty woman with a torch, whose flame
Is the imprisoned lightening, and her name
Mother of Exiles. From her beacon-hand
Gloves world-wide welcome; her mild eyes command
The air-bridged harbor that twin-cities frame.

"Keep, ancient lands, your storied pomp!"
Cries, she
With silent lips.
"Give me your tired, your poor,
Your huddled masses yearning to breathe free,
The wretched refuse of your teeming shore,
Send these, the homeless, tempest-tossed to me:
I lift my lamp beside the golden door."

Had she written *only* these words, Emma Lazarus would be remembered as one of the great literary figures of American Jewry.

Emma was born in 1849 in New York City and grew up in the comfortable home of her Sephardic parents. Her great grandfather, a descendant of those fortunate Jews who had fled the Inquisition, had arrived in America even before the American Revolution.

Attractive, small and dark-eyed, Emma, who never married, thought herself exceedingly plain. Her disposition was gloomy. A frail child, she tired

Schwadron Collection, Hebrew University, Jerusalem

easily. Forced to remain at home a great deal, she was educated by private tutors from whom she developed a love of classic literature and modern language. As a teenager, she consumed hours immersed in the novels and poetry of English authors and the more modern American writers. Although she jotted down her innermost thoughts, Emma Lazarus was too shy to share them with anyone. However, excited by the artistic and spiritual side of life, she began writing verse.

Lazarus' poetry was good enough to attract the attention of the foremost literary figure in America, Ralph Waldo Emerson, to whom she dedicated her second volume, *Admetus and Other Poems* (1871).

In their extended correspondence, Emerson encouraged Emma to continue writing. *Admetus* contained a poem on a Jewish theme, "In the Jewish Synagogue at Newport."

Lazarus' novel *Alide: an Episode of Goethe's Life,* was published in 1874. Two years later, Lazarus published *The Spagnoletto,* a historical novel with a tragic theme. In 1881 Lazarus translated Heinrich Heine's poems and wrote a biographical study of the poet.

The Statue of Liberty.

In the late 1870s, Rabbi Gustav Gottheil of New York City's Temple Emanu-El persuaded her to translate and write poetry for a new prayer book he was preparing. Until then Lazarus had not been very religious (her family observed only the holidays) nor had she identified with her Jewish background. She disliked "Jewish things," she once said.

As Emma Lazarus acquired celebrity, she felt that some great theme was missing from her writing. She found the theme she was looking for in the devastating news from Russia about the treatment of Jews there. Awakening her interest in her Russian brethren were the pogroms of 1881 and 1882 as well as George Eliot's novel, *Daniel Deronda,* with its call for a Jewish national survival. It portrayed a Jewish family's quest to return to Zion.

Lazarus began to envision a homeland where Jews could once again live under their own sovereignty. That same year she met Russian Jewish immigrants arriving at Ellis Island. She was as moved by their poverty and religious pride as she was enraged at assimilated American Jews who harangued against these "foreigners."

Lazarus stopped writing poetry temporarily, paying regular visits to Ward's Island where the immigrants were housed, giving them money from her own pocket, immersing herself fully in their plight.

"I am all Israel's now," she wrote. "Till this cloud passes—I have no thought, no passion, no desire, save for my own people." Her book of essays, *Songs of a Semite,* was the result of this new preoccupation. It included such passionate Jewish poems as the Zionist

"Banner of the Jew," with its memorable lines: "Wake, Israel, wake! Recall today the glorious Maccabean rage...Oh, deem not dead that martial fire, say not the mystic flame is spent! With Moses's law and David's lyre, your ancient strength remains unbent, Let but an Ezra rise anew, to lift the Banner of the Jew!"

Lazarus studied Hebrew and later translated the classic Hebrew poems of the great literary figures of Spain's golden age including Judah Halevi, Ibn Gibirol, and Ibn Ezra. Her translations found their way into standard prayer books.

In 1883, in "An Epistle to the Hebrews", she set forth ideas and plans for deepening Jewish life through a national and cultural revival in the United States and Palestine. Four years later she wrote the prose poem "By the Waters of Babylon." In "The New Ezekiel," a short poem, she advocated the idea that Palestine must be re-established as a Jewish homeland: "the Spirit is not dead, proclaim the word, Where lay dead bone, a host of armed men stand! I open your graves, my people, saith the Lord, And I shall place you in your promised land."

Emma Lazarus' best-known sonnet was written that same year. Funds were needed for the huge pedestal on which the Statue of Liberty, a gift of the French to the United States, would rest. The Statue of Liberty, which was to reach the United States in 1885, was to stand in New York Harbor where it would welcome immigrants to the New World.

To raise the necessary funds, Mrs. Constance Harrison planned to publish poetry and sketches by famous authors and artists including Henry Wadsworth Longfellow, Walt Whitman, Bret Harte, and Mark Twain. The poetry and sketches were to be sold for the benefit of the pedestal fund. Mrs. Harrison approached Emma Lazarus to enter the competition.

"I cannot write verse on order," Lazarus replied.

"Think of the Russian refugee," Mrs. Harrison retorted.

That was enough inspiration for Emma Lazarus. Obsessed with her own vision of the United States as a haven for the refugees of Europe and Russia, she wrote the poem.

Two days later Emma Lazarus handed the fund "The New Colossus," in which America was depicted as the hope of the oppressed. Its benefit sale brought the unheard-of amount of $21,500 for a short piece of poetry.

The poet James Russell Lowell read Emma Lazarus' verses, then wrote: "I liked your sonnet about the statue better than I liked the statue itself. But your sonnet gives its subject a *raison d'être* which it needed as much as it needed a pedestal." Emma Lazarus died in 1887, four years after composing the sonnet, after a lengthy illness during which she isolated herself from everyone. She was thirty-eight years old. Memorial services were held for her in all of the New York synagogues. She was buried in a Long Island cemetery.

Nehama Leibowitz

World's Greatest Bible Teacher

Born in 1905 in Riga, Latvia. Israeli Bible Scholar. Nehama Leibowitz is considered the world's greatest teacher of the Bible. For over sixty years, she has taught Biblical commentary to all sectors of Israeli society, and conducted correspondence courses with thousands around the world. She is a legend in the Jewish world and her books have become a valuable source for teachers and rabbis. Her popular studies and comprehensive study guides on the weekly Torah portion are in the homes of countless Jews.

By virtue of her incredible teaching skills, as well as the breadth of her knowledge of the Bible, and the immense literature of classical and modern commentary she has written, Nehama Leibowitz has become a role model for women in Torah learning. She is legendary among her students. Yet, in her own eyes, she deserves no celebrity. She wishes only to transmit to her students how valuable the Bible can be for their everyday lives.

Nehama's parents were religious Jews from Riga, Latvia, where she was born in 1905. Though it was not common for Hebrew to be spoken at home, it was the language Nehama's family spoke among themselves. Nehama's father taught her the Torah at home. She always wanted to become a Biblical scholar.

In 1914, Nehama moved with her parents and brother to Berlin. There, she graduated from high school. She pursued higher education, ultimately obtaining her doctorate in Bible Studies from the University of Berlin. She did her doctoral research on German-Jewish translations of the Bible. In 1930, she moved to Palestine with her husband, who was blind. They had no children.

That year she began teaching Bible at the Mizrachi Women Teachers' Seminar in Jerusalem and taught there until 1955. For the next sixty-three years, Nehama Leibowitz, with her trademark briefcase, simple brown suit, and brown beret tilted to the side, traveled throughout Israel to teach Biblical commentary to tens of thousands of students.

Leibowitz's aim in teaching the Bible is simply that by studying passage after passage, her students will discover the Bible's intrinsic merit. To her students who ask her, "Why are we studying chapter twelve this week?" she replies: "Because last week we studied chapter eleven."

One of Leibowitz's longtime students noted: "She is a pathfinder in her field, an enormous popularizer of the whole tradition of Biblical commentary. She was a pioneer of a literary approach to the Bible, and opened the door of Biblical commentary to the modern world in an intellectually exciting and personally transforming way."

Before Nehama Leibowitz, the traditional approach to learning the Bible had been to cite what Biblical commentators had written about the text. Leibowitz, however, has urged her students to ask why a given commentator had been motivated to make his comment. Thus, the student would be led to grapple with problematic sections of the text as

Scoop 80

Receiving her honorary doctorate from Bar Ilan University, Israel.

well as with the role of commentary.

Leibowitz also had students confront the differences among the commentators and the implications of those differences. She demanded that students extract the principle on which Rashi and Ramban disagree, thus exposing her pupils to the dynamics of discussion and debate among the commentators. As for the text itself, she developed literary comparison into a fine art.

For years Nehama Leibowitz gave a weekly Bible lesson over Israel Radio. Another long-time student of hers recalled that on February 1, 1948, the night that the *Palestine Post* was bombed, she was scheduled to teach from the Book of Jeremiah. With the bombing fresh in her mind, she slipped into her broadcast the comment that the king had tried to destroy Jeremiah's prophesies by burning his scrolls. She also noted that the prophet had made sure to dictate his prophesies to a scribe to ensure their preservation. Then, under the watchful eye and ear of the British mandatory censor, she added: "Neither fire nor explosives can succeed in suppressing the truth." A second later, her broadcast was abruptly cut off. The next morning, people on the street greeted her enthusiastically, shouting, "They [the British] can't succeed."

In 1951 Leibowitz began distributing mimeographed self-instruction study guides on a weekly basis. They were designed to inform the study of the weekly Bible portion. Those who received the sheets, whether kibbutzniks, teachers, soldiers, factory workers, or students abroad, answered questions about the Torah portion that Leibowitz featured, then received her corrections—in red ink.

In 1957, Nehama Leibowitz was awarded the Israel Prize, the nation's highest honor, for education. Beginning that year, she taught Bible at Tel Aviv University. In 1968 she became a professor there. Students who have studied with her said she often appeared in their dreams.

"To have studied with Nehama," wrote Vanessa L. Ochs in *Words on Fire* (New York, 1990), "is to have been in analysis with Freud, to have been educated in nursery school by Maria Montessori, to have been inoculated against polio by Dr. Salk."

Nehama Leibowitz has put her studies of the Bible and classical and modern commentators in a series of pamphlets and books that cover the entire Torah. They have been translated into English, French, Spanish and Dutch.

Rabbi Pinchas Peli, the late professor of Jewish thought and literature at Ben-Gurion University of the Negev, once described Nehama as Israel's most outstanding living rabbi.

In 1982, Leibowitz received the Bialik Prize in Literature and Jewish Studies.

When Nehama Leibowitz received an honorary doctorate from Bar-Ilan University in 1983, she refused to wear a cap and gown. She wore her usual outfit, including the famous brown suit and beret. In her remarks, demonstrating her customary firmness, she said that she was pleased that a simple teacher—a "Melamed," in her words—was being so honored.

As a female Biblical scholar, Leibowitz has at times fought uphill battles. In May 1987, Rabbi Shlomo Riskin asked her to teach Bible at a rabbinical seminary. Riskin was immediately condemned by ultra-Orthodox Jewish leaders for asking a woman to teach Bible. Ovadia Yosef, the former Sephardi Chief Rabbi of Israel, proposed a compromise: Leibowitz could lecture, but from behind a screen. Rejecting this arrangement, Leibowitz still taught at the seminary as asked—without the barrier!

During the 1980s, Leibowitz was invited to teach Torah at a yeshiva in Gush Etzion on the West Bank. This was a rarity since women had been permitted until then only to teach secular subjects at yeshivas. She continued to break new ground.

Leibowitz is as renowned for her teaching skills as for her Biblical commentary. Part of her teaching style is to make sure that each student attains maximum involvement in the lesson. Though she used one technique rarely, one English-language professor, entering her course in 1970, learned the hard way how to succeed in Leibowitz's class. The professor had had difficulty pronouncing the words of the Torah correctly. When her turn came to read aloud, Nehama Leibowitz asked her to leave the room. Soon, a second person joined her. Finally Leibowitz stepped outside the class and made it clear that the two could only rejoin her class after reading the entire Torah aloud to one another!

Another Leibowitz teaching technique was to ask a question, then require every student in class to write the answer in his or her notebook. She then went around and checked the replies.

Nehama Leibowitz's older brother Yeshayahu, an Israeli scientist, philosopher and political liberal, has been a controversial figure for years. She, however, has succeeded in staying out of the political limelight, continuing to share her knowledge and understanding of the Bible with so many people.

Nehama Leibowitz continues teaching university classes and seminars in her home. The walls are lined with thirty years of her weekly study sheets, which continue to make their way to all parts of Israel and the world. Her disciples of all ages gather in her home and include many teachers and rabbis who are themselves passing on Leibowitz's methods and insights to others throughout the Jewish world.

ANNIE LEIBOVITZ
Photographer of Celebrities

Born October 2, 1949 in Westbury, Connecticut. American photographer. In taking unusually powerful photo portraits of celebrities, Annie Leibovitz herself became a celebrity. Only twenty-three years old when she became chief photographer for *Rolling Stone* magazine, she acquired a reputation for catching the famous in uncommon, unexpected poses.

Anna-Lou Leibovitz was born on October 2, 1949 in Westbury, Connecticut. Her father Sam Leibovitz, is an Air Force lieutenant colonel and her mother Marilyn Leibovitz, a modern-dance instructor who has performed with Martha Graham's dance company.

As a child, Annie moved often, from one military base to another. She has five brothers and sisters. "We protected ourselves against the world," she remembered. While a student at Northwood High School in Silver Spring, Maryland, Annie painted, played the guitar, wrote music, and was in charge of a folk-singing group.

In 1967, Annie enrolled at the San Francisco Art Institute in California with the hope of eventually teaching painting. One night course in photography, however, caused her to change her plans. She bought her first camera in 1968 while in Japan en route to visiting her father in the Philippines.

Annie spent five months during her junior year living at Kibbutz Amir in northern Israel. While there she photographed her experiences, including an archeological dig.

In 1970, she showed the editors of *Rolling Stone* magazine her photographs of Israel plus her photograph of the poet Allen Ginsberg smoking a marijuana cigarette at a San Francisco peace march. The magazine purchased the Ginsberg photograph for $25. Leibovitz was immediately assigned to shoot photos of Grace Slick, a member of the music group Jefferson Airplane. She was also given a forty-seven-dollar-a week retainer. She had not yet graduated from college.

Leibovitz asked *Rolling Stone*'s editor to send her to New York City to photograph John Lennon. Her photograph of Lennon made the magazine's cover, one of many such Leibovitz photos of Lennon taken during the next thirteen years. Her last photo of him was taken on December 8, 1980, two hours before he was murdered. The photograph remains one of Leibovitz's best-known shots: It depicts a naked John Lennon curled in the fetal position around a fully clothed Yoko Ono, who seems distant from him.

Annie Leibovitz was *Rolling Stone*'s chief photographer from 1973 to 1983. Traveling all over the world, she shot dozens of covers for the magazine. Before photographing a subject, often a two-day project at the person's home, she carefully researched their books, movies or performances. Once inside her subject's home, she observed each detail of the person's daily life. She acknowledges that she spends a great deal of time with her photographic subjects because she didn't have much of a home life herself.

Robert Mapplethorpe

Not being awe struck by celebrities may explain why Leibovitz has been able to put her subjects at ease. Once relaxed and comfortable with her, Leibovitz's subjects let their hair down. Annie Leibovitz herself is shy and awkward, qualities that may have helped her win over some of her photographic subjects.

In 1975, at the height of their popularity, the Rolling Stones rock group went on a six-month concert tour. They hired Annie Leibovitz to document the tour. The project brought her much attention and made her better-known as a professional.

Among the celebrities Leibovitz shot for *Rolling Stone* (and sometimes for other publications, including *Time, Newsweek,* and *Vogue*) during the 1970s and early 1980s were Bob Dylan, Stevie Wonder, John Belushi, Bruce Springsteen, Woody Allen, Dolly Parton, and Arnold Schwarzenegger.

Until she photographed Linda Ronstadt in red lingerie, Leibovitz had been more comfortable photographing men. "That was an important picture for me because it was a start of being able to enjoy looking at women. It's weird now. I can look at women and really appreciate them. [And] I can look at men and really appreciate them."

Annie Leibovitz was more than a mere celebrity photographer. She did unusual shoots with her famous subjects. She photographed the Blues Brothers painted blue. She covered Bette Midler in roses. She wrapped the artist Christo in his own traditional wrapping cloth. "If the 1970s were about New Celebrity," Peter Wilkinson wrote in *New York Woman* in September 1988, "and a lot of very conscientious but aimless thrashing about in the dark, Annie was the decade's most perceptive voyeur, skipping across the country, setting up her lights in that gloom, and freezing the action."

In 1983, Leibovitz decided that she had nearly burned herself out. She took time off, then moved from *Rolling Stone* to *Vanity Fair.* And, she also had her first major exhibit. The sixty-print show, which opened that fall at the Sidney Janis Gallery in New York, also toured the United States and Europe through 1985.

A book called *Annie Leibovitz: Photographs* accompanied the exhibit and sold very well. The exhibit and book included some of her most striking portraits, including those of Robert Redford, John Lennon, Norman Mailer, and Meryl Streep in white face, Woody Allen in a pink-tiled bathroom, and Debra Winger posing topless with a dog.

Reviewing the book for *The New York Times,* Andy Grundberg noted: "Miss Leibovitz's flash reinforces the message of decay and diminution, turning skin into a shiny plastic version of itself and giving the environment around her subjects a twilight-of-the gods pallor....What we get, if we look closely, is a portrait of the 1960s generation gone to seed."

At *Vanity Fair,* Leibovitz turned her lens away from the world of rock to other arenas ranging from Hollywood to high society. Her shooting style, however, did not change. She took portraits of novelist and poet Robert Penn Warren bare-chested. She caught Roseanne Arnold mud-wrestling with her husband; photographed actress Whoopi Goldberg with her arms, legs and face protruding from a tub of warm milk; and caught actor John Cleese hanging upside down from a tree.

In her words, Leibovitz felt "underutilized" although she did a series of posters for the 1986 World Cup Games in Mexico expanding her subject matter into the sports world. She then moved into advertising, taking assignments for American Express, *U.S. News & World Report,* Rose's Lime Juice (one photograph showed the writer Tama Janowitz crouching on historian Arthur Schlesinger, Jr.'s desk), Honda, the Beef Industry Council, and the Gap.

Annie Leibovitz continued to do her own unique up-close portraits of the famous. However, this time they were for American Express ads. She shot the former House Speaker (Thomas P. "Tip") O'Neill in a beach chair with his cigar snuffed out in the sand; music producer Quincy Jones in sweatshirt and shorts; crime writer Elmore Leonard on a beach at sunset, with his manual typewriter in hand; and jazz singer Ella Fitzgerald in a red suit in front of her 1959 Mercedes. The American Express series of print ads won her the prestigious Clio Award, the "Oscar" of the advertising business.

In the spring of 1991, Annie Leibovitz's first museum exhibit opened at the National Portrait Gallery in Washington, D.C.

Annie Leibovitz is five feet, eleven inches tall, has long chestnut brown hair, and wears large-frame glasses. She lives in an apartment on upper Fifth Avenue overlooking Central Park in New York City.

She enjoys shooting her photographs to music. When she started to set up in the Oval Office for a *Vanity Fair* portrait of President Bill Clinton just after his swearing-in on January 20, 1993, she set up her radio and plugged it in near the portrait of George Washington. A displeased White House official informed her, "We've never had music in the Oval Office."

The new President, however, overruled his colleague, making one of his first decisions as chief executive:

"Sure," said Bill, when Leibovitz asked if it was all right. Songs from Eric Clapton's album *Unplugged* wafted through the White House. "I told you we were gonna miss the other guy," a Secret Service agent whispered to a fellow agent.

RITA LEVI-MONTALCINI

Nobel Prize Winner in Medicine

Born April 22, 1909 in Turin, Italy. Italian research scientist and neurobiologist. In October 1986, Rita Levi-Montalcini became the fourth woman to be awarded the Nobel prize for physiology or medicine. She won it in the early 1950s for her groundbreaking discovery of the Nerve Growth Factor, a protein which is instrumental in the growth and differentiation of cells in the nervous system. The discovery has had implications for research into cures for diseases such as Parkinson's and Alzheimer's, which attack the nervous system, and for research into the relationship between nerve cells and the immunological defence system.

Rita Levi-Montalcini was born in Turin, Italy on April 22, 1909 with a fraternal twin sister, Paola. Her father, Adamo Levi, was an engineer and factory manager. The twins had a brother, Gino, seven years older, and a sister, Anna, five years older.

Rita described her father as a dynamic, hot-tempered man, the undisputed master of the household. Her mother, Adele Montalcini, on the other hand, was serene and sweet.

Rita was serious and hardworking in school yet she received only a limited secular education and no Jewish education. Her family were not observant Jews. She was determined to make something of herself, convinced that she was not cut out to be a wife.

At age twenty, a turning point occurred when her former governess Giovanna was diagnosed as having cancer. The news shocked Rita and she resolved to resume her studies. She hoped to become a doctor. When her governess died, she brought up her plans to her father who grudgingly gave his consent.

With her cousin Eugenia helping her, Rita started a program of remedial studies. She was accepted at the Turin School of Medicine in the fall of 1930. One of her second-year teachers was a widely renowned professor of human anatomy and histology named Dr. Giuseppe Levi who later became her mentor.

Studying under Dr. Levi, Levi-Montalcini did her initial work on nervous-system cells, which became her lifelong area of expertise. She graduated from medical school in the summer of 1936 and decided to specialize in neurology, working as Dr. Levi's assistant.

Fascist government decrees in 1938

Courtesy of Rita Levi-Montalcini

King Gustav of Sweden presenting Levi-Montalicini (left) the Nobel prize in 1986.

barred Jews from all university posts and forbade them to practice medicine. Levi-Montalcini was therefore dismissed from her academic post at the Institute of Anatomy as well as from the Neurology Clinic.

In March 1939, Levi-Montalcini left Italy for Belgium, as Dr. Levi had already done. There, she began doing neurological research at the Neurologie Institute of Brussels. Upon the Nazis' invasion of Belgium, she and Dr. Levi moved to Turin, Italy, where they worked together, beginning in the winter of 1940, in her laboratory.

Under a microscope, she operated on chicken embryos, obtained from ordinary eggs. She analyzed the way in which the removal of peripheral limb tissues still lacking nerves affected the differentiation and development of motor cells in the spinal cord and sensory cells in the ganglia at the rear of the spinal cord.

Levi-Montalcini and her family moved to a farmhouse outside Turin in the fall of 1942 in order to escape the Allied bombardment of the city. Her research studies continued and she discovered that nervous-system cells in the first stages of differentiation move "toward distant locations along rigidly programmed routes."

Levi-Montalcini wrote: "Now the nervous system appeared to me in a different light from its description in textbooks of neuroanatomy, where its structure is described as rigid and unchangeable."

Levi-Montalcini's essay on the results of her experiments on chicken embryos was rejected for publication in Fascist Italy because she "belonged to the Jewish race." But it was published in Belgium and, as a result, her fame spread.

After German troops began to occupy Turin in July 1943, Levi-Montalcini and her family escaped to Florence, even though it was in German hands, remaining there until September 1944. After the war Levi-Montalcini continued her biology research. Levi-Montalcini's work had been aided by the research of Dr. Victor Hamberger, chairman of the Zoology Department at Washington University in St. Louis, where she arrived in September 1946 for a semester of study. Doubting the value of her research at first, she achieved a breakthrough late in 1947 that changed her mind.

One day, sitting before her microscope, looking at silver-salt-impregnated chicken-embryo sections, Levi-Montalcini watched the cells as they seemed to behave in ways that she had not noticed before. She compared what she saw to what takes place on a battlefield; it seemed to her that groups of cells were advancing, retreating, being killed, and then cleared away. "It struck me that the discovery of great migratory and degenerative processes affecting nerve cell populations at the early stages of their development might offer a tenuous yet valid path to follow into the fascinating and uncharted labyrinth of the nervous system."

In January 1950, Elmer Bueker, a former student of Dr. Hamburger's, wrote to him, outlining experiments in which mouse tumors had been grafted onto chicken embryos. Bueker had discovered that nerve fibers had infiltrated the tumor cellular mass after being incubated for eight days. He concluded that the tumor provided more favorable conditions for the fiber growth.

Dr. Levi and Rita Levi-Montalcini decided to repeat Bueker's experiments. They grafted cancer tumors taken from mice onto chicken embryos. On June 15, 1951, they watched as bundles of nerve fibers started to grow. This was in apparent response to the tumors' release of a chemical they called the Nerve Growth Factor (NGF). More experiments followed, confirming Levi-Montalcini's hypothesis.

The discovery "offered scientific proof" said Levi-Montalcini "for the intuition first expressed in a Latin proverb: that there is a physical connection between a sound mind and a sound body, namely the NGF protein. Soon NGF will be produced synthetically."

Rita Levi-Montalcini presented these findings to the New York Academy of Sciences. This was only the beginning, however. Her research efforts continued full-speed ahead. Convinced that tumors transplanted into embryos would stimulate fiber growth, she examined cultures showing halo-shaped outgrowths of fibers around sensory and sympathetic ganglia grown near the transplanted tumors. In later experiments, Levi-Montalcini also noticed that the fibers were oriented toward the neoplastic tissue, which she saw as evidence of a neurotropic—or directional—effect.

Working with biochemist Stanley Cohen, Levi-Montalcini and he were able to extract NGF in larger quantities from snake venom and mouse salivary glands, identifying the factor as a protein molecule. Those NGF experiments were conducted between 1953 and 1959.

Levi-Montalcini remained in St. Louis for thirty years. From 1947 to 1951, she worked as a research associate; from 1951 to 1958, as an associate professor of zoology; and from 1958 to 1977, as a full professor. She became an American citizen in 1956, retaining her Italian citizenship.

In the spring of 1961, Levi-Montalcini returned to Rome to establish a research laboratory.

She and Stanley Cohen were named winners of the Albert Lasker Medical Research Award in 1986. Seven weeks later, on October 13, 1986, Levi-Montalcini and Cohen were the joint recipients of the 1986 Nobel prize in physiology or medicine for discovering NGF which, in the words of the Nobel prize committee, "...held out the prospect of shedding light on many disorders, such as cancers, the delayed healing of wounds, and senile dementia, including Alzheimer's disease."

Levi-Montalcini, who has never married, is a short, slender woman with gray-green eyes and silver-gray hair.

In June 1987, she received the National Medal of Science, the highest American scientific award. She was the first woman member of the Pontifical Academy of Sciences in Rome.

Rosa Luxemburg

Famous European Revolutionary

Born in 1871 in Zamost, Russian Poland; died in 1919. German economist and revolutionary. Even as a student, Rosa Luxemburg was attracted to the revolutionary movement in Poland. Smuggled into Switzerland, she earned her doctorate, and then helped to found the Social Democratic Party of Poland, Lithuania, and Germany. She was well-known for her theory of imperialism, which described how capitalism would eventually disappear. She helped found the Spartacists in 1916 to help further her revolutionary aims, then led an unsuccessful revolt in Germany after the war during which she was killed.

Rosa descended from rabbis going back to the twelfth century. She came from a family of wealthy timber merchants. Her mother, who was the daughter and sister of rabbis, quoted from the Bible frequently. Rosa, however, never showed any interest in Judaism or in Yiddish culture.

She grew up in Warsaw and was sent to an exclusive school attended mainly by the children of Russian officials. Rosa was barely five feet tall, but she was nevertheless a bundle of energy with an aggressive streak.

Her familial history of generations of rabbinical scholarship fostered in Rosa a great concern for social justice as well as a fascination with dialectic argument. Impassioned, argumentative, she also had the enormous physical energy to take on causes and debates. As a student, she joined the Polish revolutionary movement.

Upon graduating from high school at the age of fifteen, Rosa worked in the illegal Polish party called "The Proletariat." A year later, the government suppressed the party, and Luxemburg was smuggled across the Polish frontier to escape from being detained.

Just sixteen, she traveled to Zurich where she completed her education, studying political economy and history at the University of Zurich. She also worked in the underground socialist movement of Polish emigres in Switzerland. That movement cooperated for a while with the Marxist Russian Social Democratic movement. In the early 1890s Rosa Luxemburg helped to found the Social Democratic Party of Poland and Lithuania.

By the close of the decade, in 1898, she had earned her doctorate degree from the University of Zurich, writing her dissertation on "The Industrial Development of Poland." Polish Communists cited this document as a treatise about Poland's future. They observed that, according to Luxemburg, because an independent Poland was not feasible, Polish nationalism was a futile goal.

That same year, Rosa Luxemburg moved to Germany and obtained German citizenship by entering into a formal marriage with a German printer Georg Lubecki. The marriage was immediately dissolved and, from that point on, she devoted her life to revolutionary politics.

162

Luxemburg was an acquaintance of Lenin, the Soviet leader, although sometimes they had major ideological scrabbles. For example, they disagreed about the place of nationalism in the Communist revolution. To Lenin, nationalism was viable, an emotional reality, a potential force for revolution. Rosa Luxemburg begged to differ, as she made clear in a 1916 pamphlet, "The Crisis in Socialist Democracy."

Still, Luxemburg admired Lenin. "Have a good look at that man," she once told a friend. "That's Lenin. Observe his obstinate, self-willed skull."

Luxemburg became a major critic of the Bolshevik reign of terror in the Soviet Union. She became active among Polish workers and joined the editorial staff of the *Saxony Arbiter-Zeitung*. Later, she worked for the *Leipziger Volkszeitung*. She was also a frequent contributor to the *Neu Zeit*.

Diaspora Museum

Rosa Luxemburg became a leading figure in the revolutionary left wing of the German Socialist movement. She was jailed in 1900, and again in 1904 for delivering anti-war messages.

Luxemburg took part in the revolution of 1905-1906 in Warsaw. She was sent to jail again for one year. After three months she escaped and resumed her political activities in Germany. Active in both the Polish and the German Labor movements, she became a prominent figure in the Socialist International.

Rosa Luxemburg was well-known for her theory of imperialism. She was convinced that in a pure capitalist society, the inadequacy of the local market would lead to a search for markets in countries with more primitive methods of production. A struggle for these foreign markets would then ensue; imperialism would become the guiding principle of foreign policy. Capitalism would automatically disappear with the exhaustion of external non-capitalist markets. Indeed, it would disappear even before this limit had been reached because expanding capitalism would produce deep social conflicts leading to a triumphant proletarian revolution.

Luxemburg's greatest intellectual contribution to the theory of class struggle was her thesis that when international imperialism struggles with international socialism, nationalism disappears as an important concept. However, she believed, in a strong democratic system. In 1918, she wrote, in a comment on the Bolshevik revolution: "With the repression of political life in the land as a whole, life in the Soviets must also become more and more crippled. Without general elections, without unrestricted freedom of the press and assembly, without a free struggle of opinion, life dies out in every public institution, becomes a mere semblance of life in which only the bureaucracy remains as the active element."

Rosa Luxemburg was indifferent to the frequent anti-Semitic attacks on her despite appalling caricatures of her that appeared in the German press. She believed that the "Jewish problem" did not exist at all. She thought anti-Semitism was a function of capitalism. She never referred to her Jewish ancestry. She had no interest in a specifically Jewish labor movement. She believed only in the international working class; her aim was to bring about the Socialist revolution.

Yet, while she rejected Jewish nationalism and favored universal internationalism, she spoke Yiddish and refused to deny that she was Jewish. She was not alone among Russian women in playing a role that led to the overthrow of the Russian Czar.

Viewing World War I as nothing more than an imperialist enterprise, Rosa Luxemburg founded the *Spartakusbund* ("Spartacus League") in 1916, along with Karl Liebknecht and Franz Mehring.

This was a revolutionary organization that was meant one day to spearhead an overhaul of German society. These Spartacists, supporters of Karl Marx and Friedrich Engels, believed that the only good that might come from the war would be the furthering of their own revolutionary aims. Luxemburg and her colleagues sought to build, in her words, "a great, united German republic" that would come under the control of the proletarian masses.

Rosa Luxemburg's reward, however, was to spend most of the war in prison. Only with the advent of revolution in Germany in 1918 was Rosa Luxemburg released. Toward the end of that year, she and Karl Liebknecht transformed the Spartacus League into the German Communist party. Liebknecht began planning a Spartacist *putsch* in Berlin. Luxemburg felt negative toward such a step.

World War I ended on November 11, 1918. An atmosphere of anarchy and revolution pervaded Germany. Liebknecht sought to declare a German Soviet Republic. Friedrich Ebert, the last chancellor of the German empire, wanted to quash the anarchic spirit and so he aimed his fire at the Spartacists.

The revolt was put down on January 16, 1919. The day before, Rosa Luxemburg had been arrested along with Liebknecht in Berlin. She was questioned at the Hotel Eden, then dragged from there, and beaten unconscious. She was shot in the head and her body thrown into a canal. It was later recovered. Liebknecht was driven away by car and on the way to the Moabit Prison, his captor shot him too.

GOLDA MEIR

World's Most Famous Grandmother

Born May 3, 1898 in Kiev, the Ukraine; died December 12, 1978.
Israeli political leader. Golda Meir served as the first Israeli ambassador to the Soviet Union in the late 1940s, then as foreign minister during the late 1950s and early 1960s, finally as prime minister of Israel from 1969 to 1974. She was a heroine to world Jewry, the symbol of the Jewish people's quest for survival, and the most prominent woman politician of her era. To millions of Jews she was Golda, and to Israelis, *Golda Shelanu*—Hebrew for "Our Golda."

A heroine to world Jewry, a woman whose worldwide popularity exceeded that of royalty and first ladies, Golda Meir proved the most remarkable woman of the modern era. Her secret was that she possessed a rare mixture of sincerity and courage. In the modern age of television, when political leaders package themselves for vast audiences, Golda achieved international fame through the simplicity and candor of her words.

Though politics had been a male domain in the state of Israel, Meir led her country in times of peace as well as war. Her world was filled with drama and violence, yet she retained the image of a warm, loving grandmother. Whether she was meeting secretly with Jordan's King Abdullah to avoid war once the state of Israel was established, or presiding over the Jewish state during the 1973 Yom Kippur War, Golda Meir displayed great political adroitness and nerves of steel.

Although Meir became a role model for the modern feminist movement, she was uncomfortable with the designation. Her trademarks were her prominent nose, and simple black or gray dress. She carried only a plain handbag.

Golda Meir chain-smoked, gazed at her audiences with laser-beam eyes, spoke simply but passionately. She had the ability to win an audience over, whether through logic or emotion. Perhaps her most famous utterance came after the Yom Kippur War: "When peace comes, we will perhaps in time be able to forgive the Arabs for killing our sons. But it will be harder for us to forgive them for having forced us to kill their sons."

To her, protecting the Jewish people and the state of Israel was paramount. "If we have to have a choice between being dead, and pitied, and being alive with a bad image," she once said, "we'd rather be alive and have the bad image."

Born Goldie Mabovitz in Kiev, the Ukraine, on May 3, 1898, she was one of eight children of Moshe and Bluma Mabovitz. Five brothers died in childhood. She was haunted during childhood by the fear of cossacks and peasant mobs bent on pogroms. "If there is any logical explanation...for the direction which my life has taken," she noted, "it is the desire and determination to save Jewish children...from a similar experience."

When Golda was five, her father, a cabinetmaker and skilled carpenter, left Kiev to seek his fortune in the United States. In 1906, the family was reunited in Milwaukee.

Politics appealed to Golda even at the age of twelve when she organized a fundraising event to aid needy students.

In 1917, at the age of nineteen, Golda married a sign painter named Morris Myerson. Convinced that her future lay in the Jewish homeland, Golda Myerson persuaded her reluctant husband to sail to Palestine in 1921. They joined Kibbutz Merhavia, set in a marshy malaria-ridden region south of Nazareth. The future Israeli Prime Minister picked almonds and raised chickens. After Morris failed to adjust to kibbutz life, the Myersons moved to Tel Aviv. Golda and Morris separated in 1945. They had two children, Menachem, a cellist, and Sarah, a kibbutznik.

Meir held various posts with the burgeoning labor movement of the Yishuv (Jewish community) during the 1920s and 1930s. By 1940 she had become head of the Political Department of the Histadrut, the major Jewish labor federation. When, in June 1946, the British arrested most of the Yishuv's political leadership, Meir became acting head of the Jewish Agency's Political Department, in effect, "acting Prime Minister" of the Yishuv. Just prior to Israel's statehood, Golda Meir traveled to the United States and collected from American Jews the huge sum of fifty million dollars for the new state's coffers. She told one audience in the U.S., "You cannot decide whether we should fight or not. We will.... You can only decide one thing: whether we shall be victorious in this fight..." A signer of the Proclamation of Independence on May 14, 1948, Golda Meir was the only woman member of the Provisional Council of State, the Jewish state's first legislature.

Soon after Golda Meir reached the Soviet Union in September 1948, there as her country's ambassador to Russia, her presence at Rosh Hashanah services in Moscow's only synagogue ignited a spontaneous pro-Israeli demonstration of 40,000 Russian Jews. Elected to the first Knesset in January 1949, as a member of David Ben-Gurion's Mapai party, she returned to Israel. In April of that year she became Minister of Labor in Ben-Gurion's government and remained in that post until 1956.

Golda, who in that year adopted the Hebraicized version of Myerson, Meir, as her surname, was appointed Foreign Minister in June 1956. So unwavering was Meir's support of Ben-Gurion's policy of swift retaliation against Arab attacks that the Prime Minister called her, much to Meir's displeasure, "the only man in my Cabinet."

One of Golda Meir's saddest tasks as Foreign Minister was to stand before the United Nations in 1957 and announce that Israel would comply with the demand to withdraw its troops from the Sinai Peninsula after the Jewish state's triumphant Sinai Campaign.

Golda Meir became ill with cancer in the 1960s but she kept it a secret until her dying day, fearing that its revelation would lead others to judge her unfit for office. Tired, and ready for retirement, Meir resigned her Cabinet post in early 1966 and took on the less challenging assignment of Secretary General of the Mapai party. Two years later she resigned from that post as well due to failing health and advancing age. Her retirement was interrupted when Prime Minister Levi Eshkol died suddenly in February 1969, and the party chose Golda Meir to replace him.

National elections were held on October 28, 1969, and this time Golda Meir won election as Prime Minister in her own right. Four years later, when Egyptian and Syrian armies surprised Israel by launching the Yom Kippur War, many of her countrymen held Prime Minister Meir responsible for her country's lack of preparedness. Though she successfully led her country in counter attacking, nothing could erase the fact that 2,552 Israeli soldiers died and another 3,000 were wounded. Blamed by the country for the army's failure to be prepared for the war, she was forced to step down as prime minister in April 1974 under mounting public pressure. Though tainted by the surprise attack of the Yom Kippur War, Golda Meir remained a powerful symbol of the Jewish people. She died four years later at age 80 in December 1978.

Upon her death in 1978, Walter Cronkite of CBS Television told the American nation that "she lived a life under pressure that we, in this country, would find impossible to understand. She is the strongest woman to head a government in our time and for a very long time past."

LISE MEITNER

Setting the Stage for the Nuclear Era

Born November 7, 1878 in Vienna; died October 27, 1968. Austrian nuclear physicist. Lise Meitner is credited with laying the theoretical groundwork for the atomic bomb, although she did not participate directly in its production. For thirty years, she was the partner of Dr. Otto Hahn, a German chemist who discovered nuclear fission. In 1938, Meitner fled from Austria to escape Nazi persecution, which forced her to leave Hahn's laboratory when it was on the verge of one of the most momentous events of the twentieth century—the discovery that uranium atoms could be split. Though her work had been crucial in unraveling the secrets of nuclear fission, Meitner's partner Otto Hahn was the one who won the Nobel prize for the effort.

One of seven children, Lise was encouraged by her father, a highly-respected attorney, to study, especially the sciences. He laid down a tough rule to follow: "A Meitner must have at least one doctor's degree." Lise managed to follow the rule.

Reading newspaper accounts of the Curies' discovery of radium, Lise grew excited about studying atomic physics. Although women, as a rule, did not study physics at that time, Lise was not deterred.

In 1906, Lise Meitner became one of the first women to earn a doctorate from the University of Vienna. That year she moved to Berlin to study under Nobel physicist Max Planck, the originator of quantum theory and a Nobel prize winner. Her long association with Otto Hahn, a Nobel prize-winning German nuclear physicist, began in 1908. He has been credited with discovering nuclear fission.

Meitner and Dr. Hahn were great friends. She often called him her "cockerel," a play on the name Hahn, which means "rooster" in German.

As a woman, Meitner, who never married, suffered discrimination. Max Planck, taken back when she declared that she wanted to engage in scientific research, once said to her: "You have a doctor's degree? What more do you want?" Recognizing her talents, however, Planck hired her as an assistant lecturer at his Institute of Theoretical Physics in Berlin.

To perform radiation experiments in Berlin from 1907 to 1909, Meitner had to work in the basement laboratory in the chemistry institute because no females were allowed upstairs with the male scientists.

Meitner served as an X-ray nurse for the Austrian army during World War I, continuing her research during furloughs.

In 1918, Lise Meitner and Otto Hahn discovered protactinium, which is the chemical element ninety-one and appears between thorium and uranium on the periodic table.

Returning to Germany after the war, Lise Meitner worked at the Kaiser Wilhelm Institute in Berlin along with Hahn. She and Hahn came close to discovering that the

uranium atom could be split, but she was forced to flee to Sweden in 1938 due to mounting Nazi persecution.

Meitner took a train to the Netherlands on the pretext of needing a week's vacation. Although she had a close call with a Nazi guard, she managed to slip across the Dutch border, continuing to Denmark, then Sweden, which became her home for the next twenty years. Had she remained behind, some have speculated, the Germans might have been the first to get the atomic bomb.

After becoming a Swedish citizen, Lise Meitner worked at the Nobel Institute and the Atomic Energy Laboratory.

Nine months after Lise Meitner left Austria, Hahn announced his discovery that uranium could be split. Fearing that he had made a mistake, he sent the details of his labors to her in a letter dated December 1939, in which he also asked her for comments and analysis.

Meitner read the letter over and over. Its implications were startling. She wanted to make sure that Hahn had gotten his science right so she showed the letter to her nephew Otto Frisch, a physicist, who at first was skeptical.

Meitner calculated and calculated. Finally she realized that Hahn had indeed discovered atomic fission. Most importantly, she determined that the energy released by bombarding one uranium nucleus with a neutron was 200 million electron volts, or twenty times the explosive energy of an equivalent amount of TNT. Thus, Lise Meitner was the first scientist to calculate the enormous energy released by splitting the uranium atom, leading others to credit Meitner with providing the theoretical basis for the atom bomb.

No one had used the phrase "atomic fission" before. Physicists of the day thought atomic fission was impossible to achieve. Lise Meitner now knew differently. She had no idea that, when she had concluded that Hahn's work was credible, she had essentially paved the way for nuclear weapons.

Meitner's findings appeared in the January 1939 British journal *Nature* along with this historic passage: "It seems therefore possible that the uranium nucleus has only small stability of form and may, after neutron capture, divide itself into two nuclei of roughly equal size. These two nuclei will repel each other (because they both carry large positive charges) and should gain a total of kinetic energy of about 200 million electron volts." In effect, this sentence was the start of the nuclear age.

By explaining that the nucleus of an atom could be split and release enormous amounts of energy, Lise Meitner has been credited with deciphering the experiment of the century. Yet, for the fission experiment that she began and explained, Hahn was the scientist to receive the Nobel prize for the discovery.

Meitner informed the Danish physicist Niels Bohr of her discovery, who in turn told

American scientists. In August 1945, six and a half years later, the United States dropped an atomic bomb on Hiroshima.

Meitner was taken by surprise when the atom bomb was created. "I must stress," she said in an interview after World War II, "that I, myself, have not in any way worked on the smashing of the atom with the idea of producing death-dealing weapons. You must not blame us scientists for the use to which war technicians have put our discoveries."

After the war, Meitner said: "I do not see why everybody is making such a fuss over me. "I have not designed any atomic bomb. I don't even know what one looks like nor how it works technically." Meitner refused to discuss her role in the development of the bomb, insisting, "I am a theoretical physicist. I know nothing about technical matters."

After the war, Meitner continued to work in Stockholm at the Nobel Institute and at the Atomic Energy Laboratory, retiring in 1958 and moving to Cambridge, England to be with her nephews and nieces. In 1946 she came to the United States (she spoke English well, but with a heavy accent) where she became a visiting professor for a year at Catholic University in Washington.

The widow of one of Meitner's brothers, Mrs. Clarisse Meitner-Priszner, wrote in the *Christian Science Monitor* in April 1959, during the time her sister-in-law was lecturing in the United States: "Extremely orderly and self-disciplined in her speech, Lise always concentrated instantly on the task before her—whether it was darning a pair of stockings or an important laboratory experiment....Though slightly built, she always had an inner strength and determination which has kept her young in body and spirit."

In 1966, Meitner was a co-recipient of the American Atomic Energy Commission's prestigious Enrico Fermi award in recognition of her contribution to science.

Lise Meitner died on October 27, 1968, just days short of her ninetieth birthday.

ADAH ISAACS MENKEN

First American Actress to Wear Flesh-Colored Tights

> **Born June 15, 1835 in Milneburg, Louisiana; died August 10, 1868.** Nineteenth-century American actress. Adah Isaacs Menken wrote poetry on Jewish themes, but was best known for her splashy acting on the stage. When she performed in *Mazeppa* in 1861, she was the first American actress to wear flesh-colored tights on the stage, bringing her fame and the interest of countless fans.

Born Adah Bertha Theodore, she was called Adah McCord, Adelaide McCord, and Dolores Adios Fuertes at various times. Most accounts agree that, upon her father's death, the family moved to New Orleans and her mother gave birth to Adah in the living quarters of her family's general store in Milneburg, a suburb of New Orleans, in 1835. As a child, Adah helped to support her sickly mother.

Adah's actual origins, if different from these accounts, have been hard to uncover because she recounted so many different versions of her early days. Once, she claimed to have been the daughter of a New Orleans merchant. On various occasions, however, she insisted that her mother had either been an Irish woman, a French settler of Louisiana, or a Portuguese rabbinical scholar.

Historians have had an equally hard time pinning down whether she was born Jewish, yet there is no disagreement that, as an adult, she was an incontrovertibly enthusiastic Jewess.

As a teen-ager, Adah received an excellent education, demonstrating a love of poetry and a marvelous grasp of the Bible, literature, and language, including Hebrew and Latin. She was small, but amply proportioned, with dark hair. A strikingly beautiful woman, she had numerous male admirers. At one point, Adah traveled to Havana, hoping that others would believe she had gone there to act and dance, although she had no formal training in either profession. In fact, she was in Havana as the mistress of an Austrian nobleman. Later, she was rumored to be the mistress of kings and princes.

Returning to America in 1855, Adah searched for work as an actress. A year later she was traveling in Texas when her stagecoach broke down. As a result of this event she met Alexander Isaac Menken, who became the first of her four husbands. He was the son of wealthy Cincinnati Jews. Adopting his surname, she later changed Isaac to Isaacs, apparently for euphonic reasons, and kept that name even after their divorce.

Adah Menken and her new husband settled in Cincinnati where she studied Judaism and Hebrew, and wrote poetry, some of which utilized Judaism as a theme. She also published essays in the *Israelite*.

Adah Menken exhibited a militant pride in being Jewish. When, in 1857, Lionel Rothschild was refused a seat in the British House of Commons, after refusing to swear the Christian oath required for admission to the House, she protested by writing an essay about the controversy.

Adah Menken kept a Hebrew Bible under her pillow. Her two books of poems, *Memoirs* (1856) and *Infelicia* (1868), were filled with biblical allusions. Later, as an actress, she refused to perform on Yom Kippur.

In 1858, Menken finally landed an acting role, debuting in Shrevesport, Louisiana, as Pauline in *The Lady of Lyons*. She had an eye-catching stage personality that made her a sensation on stage. Though clearly lacking any acting talent, Menken hoped that her sex appeal and flamboyant personality would suffice on the stage. It did. She loved to flaunt convention. She smoked in public and loved to gamble, both acts considered off limits for nice women of that day. Nor did she adhere to what was fashionable in dress. Actresses did not wear skirts above the ankles nor did they wear flashy wardrobes. Menken did.

American Jewish Archives, Cincinnati Campus, Hebrew Union College, Jewish Institute of Religion

Considered an intellect, Menken attracted such literary greats as Walt Whitman, Algernon Charles Swinburne, Charles Dickens, George Sand, Alèxandre Dumas Sr., and Charles Reade.

If her stage audiences could not get enough of Adah Menken's showy acting, her husband had had quite enough. Disgruntled about her "independent behavior" (as he called it), Alexander demanded that she return to Cincinnati. She complied and he greeted her with word that he was serving her with a rabbinical divorce.

In 1859, the same year in which she made her theatrical debut in New York, considering herself legally divorced, she married the boxer John C. Heenan.

However, a scandal ensued when newspaper articles contended that she had never legally divorced her first husband. Adding to her troubles, Heenan denied being her husband. Her chances of finding work became slim. Pregnant and poor by that time, Menken sought succor from loyal relatives. A miscarriage followed. In December 1860, sitting in her home in Jersey City, New Jersey, she penned a suicide note.

Adah Menken's luck improved soon after this episode of desperation. A theater director, who had attended Menken's performance in a vaudeville act, asked her to star in a performance of *Mazeppa,* a dramatization of a Byron poem, in Albany, New York. She opened in June 1861. Audiences flocked to the show, not merely because they were theater-lovers. Word had spread that Menken appeared nude in the play!

In the past, actors playing Menken's part had stepped aside so that a dummy could be used as the hero goes on a wild ride on a horse into the hills. Not Adah Menken. She chose to do the riding herself. Dressed in flesh-colored tights that gave the illusion of nudity, she ascended a steep ramp strapped to a fiery horse. She became the first American actress to wear flesh-colored tights on the stage, an act that won her international notoriety.

Controversy followed Menken wherever she went. "There were wild, unfounded rumors that Adah was a *femme fatale,* a vampire bent on the destruction of as many men as she could attract," wrote Allen Lesser, in *Enchanting Rebel,* published in 1947. "Her name became the butt of many a lewd remark, and among themselves, women gossiped about her in hushed whispers."

Adah Menken toured American cities from coast to coast in *Mazeppa* for the next four years. One theater critic observed that "Miss Menken places the male in her audience at a disadvantage. She is so lovely that she numbs the mind, and the senses reel." Menken married for a third time, this time to the journalist Robert Henry Newell who wrote that his wife was "a symbol of Desire Awakened to every man who set eyes on her. All who saw her wanted her, immediately." She soon discarded Newell.

Touring London in 1864, Adah Menken angered the British press with her seemingly too explicit performance in *Mazeppa.* This, after all, was Victorian England.

After returning to the United States in 1865, she met "Captain" James Barkely, who became her fourth husband. Their marriage lasted only twenty-four hours after Menken realized that the "Captain" was simply a fortune hunter, and not a military man at all. Learning that Adah Menken's small fortune was considerably smaller than he had imagined, he at once grew distant and the marriage failed.

In 1866, traveling to Paris to perform there, though pregnant and by whom not clear, she had a triumphant visit. She gave birth to a son. The boy's godmother was George Sand (pseodonym of Amandine Aurore Lucie Dupin). Right after the delivery, Menken starred in another successful run of *Mazeppa.* Another stage triumph followed in 1867 when she performed in *Les Pirates de la Savane.* An adventure story, the play allowed Adah Menken once again to appear in meager costumes, pleasing her fans.

Rehearsing in July 1868, while at the height of her popularity, she collapsed, dying a month later at the age of thirty-three.

BETTE MIDLER

"The Divine Miss M"

Born December 1, 1945, in Honolulu, Hawaii. American comedienne. She began her career as a singer and comedienne in New York City. In the early 1970s she became a regular on the Johnny Carson *Tonight Show*, did cross-country concert tours, and released numerous record albums. There followed an incredibly successful film career in the 1980s and 1990s. Midler received an Academy Award nomination for best actress for her performance in *The Rose* (1979). Among her best-known movies are the 1986 films *Down and Out in Beverly Hills* and *Ruthless People*; *Outrageous Fortune* (1987); *Beaches* and *Big Business* (1988); *Scenes from a Mall* (1990); and *For the Boys* (1991).

Bette Midler's father, a house painter, and her mother migrated to Honolulu, Hawaii, from Paterson, New Jersey, in 1940. Five years later they had a child whom they named after actress Bette Davis. The child's first name was pronounced "Bet" because Midler's mother, a movie fanatic, mistakenly believed that was how Bette Davis pronounced her name.

Bette grew up near Pearl Harbor as a member of the only Jewish and only white family in an all Samoan neighborhood. The young Bette was a lonely child, overweight and plain looking. "That's why I went so far to make people laugh—to find some comfort, to be part of the group, and to be accepted," she said. And that's why, at age twelve, she thought of becoming an actress.

One of Bette Midler's important early onstage experiences came in first grade, when she won a prize for singing the Christmas carol "Silent Night." Later, and throughout her youth, she sang at local shows and parties.

Bette attended the University of Hawaii, hoping to study drama, but she dropped out after a year and took odd jobs—one of which included a stint as a secretary at a radio station and another separating pineapple slices in a canning factory.

In 1965, she landed a bit role in a film called *Hawaii*. She was on the screen for only seven seconds, though she was paid $300 a week and $70 a day in expense money. Immediately thereafter, she left Hawaii to live in New York, where she studied acting at the Berghof Studio. To help sustain herself, she once again worked at odd jobs, which included being a hatcheck girl, a typist at Columbia University, and a salesgirl for Stern's Department Store (selling gloves). She also

United Artists Corporation

Bette Midler in a scene from Jinxed *(1982).*

worked briefly as a go-go dancer at a bar in Union City, New Jersey.

In 1966, Bette won a place in the chorus for the Broadway production of *Fiddler on the Roof.* When the actress playing the eldest of Tevye's daughters, Tzeitel, left the show, Bette assumed the role and played it for the next three years. In 1969, leaving *Fiddler* and believing her career to be on the skids, she spent a year in psychoanalysis. She worked on her singing, however, and continued her acting lessons. In 1970 she took a job as a weekend singer for $50 a night at the newly refurbished Continental Baths, a gay Turkish bathhouse in the basement of the Ansonia Hotel on Broadway in New York City. She played to audiences of towel-clad male homosexuals.

Before her appearances at the Baths, Bette's singing style had been straight, dramatic, serious. But then she adopted a new style, becoming "The Divine Miss M," a gaudy and vulgar parody of a drag queen. Bette explained later that "she's an exaggeration of all the things I never thought I wanted to be. Though I tell you, since I've started doing her I've become much more like her than I ever thought was possible."

Bette's conservative father was disturbed by his daughter's show business career. He refused to watch her perform, but Bette was not terribly disappointed. She knew that her father would never approve of her brassy, raunchy style of entertaining, nor would he have enjoyed catching one of her performances at the Baths.

The customers at the Baths encouraged Bette's outrageousness: "They gave me the confidence to be tacky, cheesy, to take risks.... They encouraged my spur-of-the-moment improvisations." Bette admitted that she had to work hard to keep the audience's attention. "If I'd keep my distance," she said, "they'd have lost interest because there were too many other things going on in the building that were more fun." She always showed great affection for the baths: "Those tubs [as she called the Baths] became the showplace of the nation. I made 'em respectable."

Bette Midler's growing reputation won her a guest spot on the Johnny Carson *Tonight Show;* she appeared frequently as a guest on that program. In 1971, she did concerts and nightclubs around the country, often to sell-out audiences. Her onstage outfits were bizarre: satin and sequined gowns from eras gone by, a black lace corset, toreador pants, and scarlet platform shoes. She sang sixties music at a noise level that she described as "about that of World War II." That same year she appeared in the rock opera *Tommy* with the Seattle Opera Company.

In 1972, Midler released her first record album, *The Divine Miss M,* which quickly went gold. The next year she did a concert tour of thirty-two cities. With so much attention focused on her unusual personality, entertainment style, and comedy routines, it was only natural that Hollywood would beckon.

Bette Midler's first starring movie role was in *The Rose* (1979), in which she plays a self-destructive rock singer hooked on alcohol and drugs; the story parallels the life of the late Janis Joplin. For that performance Midler received an Academy Award nomination for best actress.

In 1979 and 1982 Bette did concert tours, the 1982 tour grossing $8 million. Her image remained outlandish, vulgar, dressing in mermaid tails and parrot hats. In 1985, however, she signed to do three films for Disney's Touchstone Pictures, and by 1986 she was the top female box office attraction. On the screen, she has been compared to Mae

Bette Midler is The Divine Miss M.

West, Sophie Tucker, and Rosalind Russell—"larger-than-life, brassy, cynical, aggressive, humorous, and bawdy" wrote one critic.

Although Midler's film characters may start out that way, once the actress develops relationships with other characters, she usually winds up genteel, cooperative, even ingratiating. That is how her portrayal of a crass, nouveau riche struggling with sexual frigidity in the 1986 film *Down and Out in Beverly Hills* has been described. After being "cured" by a homeless man, she starts to contribute to the fight against social injustice.

In the 1986 move *Outrageous Fortune,* she plays a woman who becomes involved in adventures with an upper-class actress. She has also had starring roles in the films *Beaches* and *Big Business* (1988), *Scenes from a Mall* (1990) and *For the Boys* (1991).

In December 1984, Bette interupted her very busy show business career to marry Martin von Haselberg (alias Harry Kipper), a performing artist and commodities trader. Since the birth of her daughter, Sophie, in November 1986, Midler has shifted the center of her life to her child. The belated mom sings and performs hula dances for the little one. "When I'm not working, I'm a real haus frau," she declares.

In 1993 Bette Midler went on a highly successful concert tour, her first in ten years. Richard Corliss, writing in *Time* magazine, said, "It may be mild hyperbole to call Midler the greatest entertainer in the universe—there are, after all, other galaxies yet to be explored, but who can doubt she's the hardest-working woman in show biz?"

LILIAN MONTAGU

First Jewish Woman Lay Minister

Born in 1874 in London, England; died in 1963. English social worker and religious leader. Lilian Montagu was regarded as the dominant spiritual figure in social work in England, more particularly in Jewish social work. She was the first Jewish female lay minister. Lilian Montagu helped found the Liberal Jewish Movement, which was part of the Reform Movement in England. A member of the English banking family of Montagu, who were prominent in politics and public life, Lilian Montagu was born to wealth and a high social position. She worked as a social worker and was also a magistrate.

Lilian, known as Lily to many in her life, was born in London, England, in 1874. She was the daughter of the Orthodox Jewish banker Samuel Montagu, the first Lord Swaythling, and a leading member of the English banking family of Montagu, who were prominent in politics and public life. After completing her education in exclusive private schools, Lilian entered the field of social work. She devoted her life to working for the poor children and young girls of London.

Sensing that the children of the Russian immigrants who had reached England had become apathetic to religion, Montagu was convinced that it was essential to revitalize Judaism in order to make it more of a living faith.

At age seventeen, Lilian held Sabbath services in English for children. She also started evening classes for working girls; two years later those classes became the Western Central Jewish Club for girls. At the club, girls found friendship, they were given advice and care, and they were able to make something of themselves rather than being destined for jails or asylums. It developed into the West Central Jewish Day Settlement, which was founded in 1893. Montagu led this institution for the rest of her life. Even German bombs, which destroyed its premises during World War II, did not interrupt her efforts.

In 1900, Lilian Montagu became affiliated with the National Council of Women in Britain and in 1908, with the Women's Industrial Council. She was also chairman of the West Central Jewish Club.

Influenced by the writings of Claude Montefiore, she took up the cause of Liberal Judaism. One of its first proponents, she helped to secure a place for it in England.

Montagu had seen the value of Jewish piety in her own home and that led her to become concerned with the difficulties of adapting the ritual of Jewish tradition to modern life. In July 1899, she wrote an article for the *Jewish Quarterly Review*, on "The Spiritual Possibilities of Judaism Today," suggesting that the tenets of Judaism could be practiced in a way that would make them suited to the demands of that day.

So sincere and kind was she in helping young delinquents after she became a magistrate that they were motivated to reform themselves in order to win her approval. They wrote her "fan letters" even though she was sometimes the judge who sent them to jail.

In her replies, Montagu encouraged them and was heartened at their rehabilitation.

In 1902, Lilian Montagu, along with Claude Goldsmid Montefiore, founded the Jewish Religious Union. That in turn led to the establishment of a separate religious movement, which was represented by the Liberal Jewish Synagogue. Then, in 1926, Montagu established the World Union for Progressive Judaism. She conducted Liberal Jewish services, wrote on religious subjects, and also published a biography of her father.

In 1926, Lilian Montagu set up headquarters for the World Union at her home, and its office remained there until 1959. She became the honorary secretary and served in that role until her death. Through her, the World Union was especially helpful to Liberal rabbis who had been displaced due to Nazi persecution in Europe.

Montagu's published writings included novels, stories, prayers, and religious pamphlets. *The Faith of a Jewish Woman* and *My Club and I* contained autobiographical material. Among her books were *Naomi's Exodus, Broken Stalks, What Can a Mother Do?* and *Thoughts on Judaism*. Despite her many published works, she did not think of herself as a professional writer.

Deeply religious, Montagu was one of the first women to preach in the synagogue. A regular preacher at services of the Liberal synagogue, Lilian Montagu ministered to the affiliated synagogues that she promoted. She preached for the first time at the Liberal Jewish Synagogue on June 15, 1918 on "Kinship with God." That event was history-making. She became the first Jewish woman to be formally recognized as a "lay minister."

In "The Expression of My Personal Faith," a part of her book, *The Faith of a Jewish Woman,* she noted: "I believe in God as the God of truth.... It matters infinitely what we think and believe, for thought and belief do affect conduct. We know that some of the best Jews the world has produced have been unlearned and that learning and the love of truth are not necessarily the same thing."

In 1926, she was made a lay minister of the West Central Congregation. She was the first woman to perform this function. She spoke, not only as a preacher, but as an advocate of Liberal Judaism, throughout the United Kingdom, the United States, and other countries. That same year she called the first international conference of Liberal Judaism.

Montagu scored another first in 1928 when she spoke at the Reform Synagogue in Berlin; she became the first woman to preach from a rabbinic pulpit in Germany.

In 1929, Montagu was awarded an honorary Doctor of Hebrew Law degree by the Hebrew Union College in Cincinnati, Ohio.

In 1937, she received the Order of the British Empire for her club work. She was one of the first women in England to be a justice of the peace. In 1942, she became president of the Jewish Religious Union of England.

Lilian Montagu was regarded as the dominant spiritual figure in social work in England, more particularly in the realm of Jewish social work.

Rabbi Leo Baeck said of her: "She holds a singular place which she has made her own through great perseverance and devotion, as well as through the revolution which allowed women to identify themselves in new ways."

Montagu's biographer Eric Conrad noted in his 1953 book, *Lily H. Montagu, Prophet of a Living Judaism,* that "By teaching others, she taught herself. By praying with others, she was helped to formulate her own thoughts and to put into words the yearning for the Indefinable that was smoldering within her."

Among the quotes attributed to Montagu is: "Kinship with God is derived from the actual experience of prayer and from the effort after righteousness." And: "We have no power to explain God. If we could, we should be God ourselves."

One of the prayers which she composed seemed to reflect her philosophy very well:

"O God, be thou praised. All around us are revelations of Thy loving kindness ...We fix our minds on the day when Thou wilt make Thyself known to all nations of the world, and all men will seek together to do Thy service."

Lilian Montagu preaching in 1928.

Schwadron Collection, Hebrew University, Jerusalem

There is an intriguing footnote to her life. Ellen Umansky, a professor of religion and modern Jewish thought, and one of Montagu's biographers, was looking through a promotion piece that announced a forthcoming multi-volume *Encyclopedia of Religion*. Searching for references to Judaism, she found that one hundred Jewish personalities had been chosen as subjects for profiles, but none were women. She contacted the publisher, Macmillan Publishing Company, and won their agreement to include Henrietta Szold, Sarah Schenirer, and Lilian Montagu!

BELLE MOSKOWITZ

"What Do You Think, Mrs. M.?"

Born in 1877 in New York, New York; died in 1933. Social service executive and civic worker. An almost legendary figure in politics, Belle Moskowitz possessed greater power and influence than any woman in the United States at the height of her career in the 1920s. She was among the first American Jewish women to play such an important role in politics. She was New York Governor Alfred E. Smith's most important adviser, working for him from 1918 until 1928.

Born Belle Lindner, she was the daughter of a poor Jewish watchmaker from Eastern Europe. Slender, dark-eyed, beautiful, zealously idealistic, she was intensely interested in social work and pursued her education at Columbia University's Teachers College. She took every course imaginable that she thought might help her understand and aid the underprivileged. She wrote, produced and directed plays for New York City's Education Alliance, a downtown settlement house.

In 1900, Belle began her career in community work as the $500-a-year director for amusements and exhibitions at the Educational Alliance. She held that post for three years.

In 1903, Belle married one of the young men with whom she had worked at the Alliance. He was an artist and architect named Charles H. Israels. The rearing of her three children kept Belle Moskowitz from professional work for five years. In 1908, she began a two-year stint on the staff of *The Survey,* a publication of the Russell Sage Foundation.

A committed social reformer, Moskowitz selected certain causes and fought for them with all her strength. In 1909 she undertook a probe of the city's so-called "dancing academies." Poor girls from the Lower East Side who worked in garment-center sweatshops gravitated to these places of recreation even though the academies were likely to bring about what the reformers called "the downfall of young women." Liquor was sold on their premises; rooms were available for rent. Past efforts to clean up the academies had failed. Reformers had tried to deal with the academies for years, but despite the investigations and the newspaper articles, nothing had happened.

Moskowitz had an ace up her sleeve. She, too, could have chosen the path of running to the newspapers, loudly denouncing what was going on at the academies. But she thought that avenue was a waste of time. She decided that she needed to find some pressure points she could exert on the politicians. Discovering that Tammany Hall and community leaders were among the academies' owners, she informed them that she would avoid running to the newspapers with the story of their role in the academies if they made sure that regulatory legislation was adopted and enforced.

The ploy worked and the legislation was passed and implemented. "These laws," wrote *The New York Times,* "did more to improve the moral surroundings of young girls" than any other single social reform of the era. She also fought for workmen's compensation, decent housing for young women, and pure milk for babies.

In 1911, Belle Moskowitz's husband died. After his death, she became field secretary of the Playground and Recreation Association of America.

In 1913, the garment workers' union forced dress manufacturers to accept the appointment of an impartial arbitrator to listen to workers' grievances. The union leaders sensed that appointing a routine reformer would only alienate the employers. So they suggested Belle Moskowitz. "No one could fool her," grudgingly acknowledged the employers' association attorney.

The employers agreed, and they were pleased to find that Moskowitz decided each case on its own merits. "She understood the union leaders perfectly," the attorney for the employers' association conceded.

American Jewish Archives, Cincinnati Campus, Hebrew Union College, Jewish Institute of Religion

She married Henry Moskowitz, a social worker and community leader. With him, she helped arbitrate strikes in the garment industry. Closely associated with New York Governor Alfred E. Smith, Henry Moskowitz, together with Norman Hapgood, wrote Smith's biography, *Up From City Streets*, which was published in 1927.

By now everyone who counted in New York knew Belle Moskowitz. She was, some said, already a legendary figure. With her new-found connections, Belle Moskowitz was counted among the inner circle of reform leaders, many of whom attended her wedding.

Her political activities grew. In 1917, she became a public relations counselor. From 1919 to 1921 Moskowitz was secretary of the New York State Reconstruction Committee; in 1920 and 1921, secretary of the Governor's Labor Board; and from 1921 until her death in 1933, secretary of the Educational Council of the Port of New York Authority.

Belle Moskowitz's most important role was as confidante and adviser to New York's Governor Alfred Smith. So great was her influence that she only had to suggest someone she thought qualified and the person could wind up in the New York Assembly, State Senate, or selected for a senior state-agency post. She helped Smith implement his social welfare programs by giving him a social vision.

The governor called her "Mrs. M.," as did the social workers and reformers she recruited to work for the governor. She would sit inconspicuously in a corner of the governor's office, knitting. When Smith needed advice on important decisions, he turned to her and asked: "What do you think, Mrs. M.?"

The Irish leaders of Tammany Hall, who sneeringly called her "Moxie," resented Belle Moskowitz's influence over the Governor. They would have loved to prove that she was performing a sexual service for him, but could not. Her Jewishness, and that of other Smith associates such as Joseph Proskauer, bothered them. Out of her hearing, they sang an anti-Semitic tune: "Moskie and Proskie/Are the brains of Tammany Hall."

Moskowitz was called "Lady Belle" by the young social workers, a nickname they gave her after she refused to recruit them into good political jobs. They resented it when she sat against the wall at settlement-house receptions on the Lower East Side, and signaling to someone, asking if that person would be interested in a certain political post. Belle Moskowitz had that kind of power.

During the 1928 presidential campaign, when Smith was the Democratic nominee, Belle Moskowitz was the publicity chairman of the party.

She also served as director of both the National Council of Jewish Women and the Women's City Club, as well as secretary to the Mayor's Commission of Women on National Defense. She decided to leave politics after Smith lost the presidential campaign in 1928.

Moskowitz became the president of Publicity Associates, where she worked until her death in 1933.

When Smith learned of Belle Moskowitz's death from a heart attack, he rushed from Albany, where he was about to attend the inauguration of Governor Herbert Lehman, to New York City.

Alfred Smith, writing in the *Universal Jewish Encyclopedia,* noted that Belle Moskowitz "combined to a rare degree the qualities of statesmanship, executive ability and clear social thinking which made her an extremely valuable adviser and friend through many of my years of public life, particularly during the time in which I served as governor of New York."

BESS MYERSON

Miss America and Consumer Advocate

Born July 16, 1924 in New York, New York. Former Miss America, consumer advocate, and television personality. Bess Myerson rose from a lower middle-class background to become the first Jewish woman to be crowned Miss America, capturing the title in 1945. Subsequently, she became a much-admired consumer activist, although in later years an aura of scandal hung over her personal life.

Bess was born in 1924, one of three daughters, to Russian immigrant parents in New York City. Her father Louis was a struggling house painter who believed that to become successful, one needed some musical skills. Therefore, he provided musical training for his daughters. Bess studied the flute, then the piano.

Bess grew up in the Sholem Aleichem housing project in the Bronx. She attended the High School of Music and Art where she studied piano. She earned extra money as a babysitter and camp counselor, and graduated from Hunter College in 1945.

She was five feet, ten inches tall, brunette, and beautiful. After college, Bess entered the Miss America contest to capture the $5,000 scholarship that would allow her to purchase a new piano so that she could continue her musical education.

While competing in beauty contests, she was the object of a string of anti-Semitic acts that rendered the experience "painful." On the afternoon of the finals for the Miss New York City beauty pageant just prior to the Miss America contest, officials urged her

to change her name to Beth Meredith. "I couldn't imagine why," she said. Her instincts, however, led her to say no. Later, she called her refusal "the most important decision I have ever made."

In September 1945, Bess Myerson became the first—and to this date only—Jewish woman to be crowned Miss America. Her triumph, which gave America Jews great pride, launched her on a career that included television and public service.

On a tour promoting World War II bonds in Wilmington, Delaware, her non-Jewish hostess complained in Bess Myerson's hearing: "We cannot have Miss Myerson at the country club reception in her honor...We never had a Jew in the country club." Packing her bags quickly, the new Miss America left the house immediately.

Plans for her to visit veterans' hospitals had to be cancelled because, as Myerson recalled, "some

Courtesy of Bess Myerson

of the parents didn't want me—[even though] their sons had lost arms and legs fighting a war to save the Jews."

She found the experience shocking. "I had never been deprived of anything because of my last name, and I didn't want to be out there, being insulted. I couldn't handle it." So, when officers of the Anti-Defamation League proposed that, rather than ride at the head of a certain parade, she speak out against bigotry and prejudice, she accepted. For two weeks out of every month during her year as Miss America, Myerson made speeches for the ADL.

Myerson completed her musical studies and, in 1946, made her concert debut at Carnegie Recital Hall. Critics were not enthusiastic. In time, she abandoned her original plans to become a concert pianist.

Unlike most Miss Americas, Bess Myerson did not fade from the public scene. In 1947, hired by WOR-TV, a New York City station, she began a long career as a television announcer and commentator. From 1951 to 1957, she was emcee for CBS-TV's *The Big Payoff*. During the 1954-55 season, she was the hostess on NBC's *Philco Playhouse*.

Bess Myerson married Allen Wayne in 1947, but divorced him in 1958. They had a daughter named Barra. In 1962, she married Arnold Grant, a well-connected tax attorney, but they divorced in 1967.

From 1960 to 1968, Myerson served as commentator for the Tournament of Roses annual parade on New Year's Day. She was also a commentator for the Miss America Pageant from 1964 to 1968. Her best-known television appearances were as a regular panelist on CBS-TV's long-running program *I've Got a Secret*, beginning in 1958.

In 1969, Bess Myerson became New York City's Commissioner of Consumer Affairs, turning what was formerly a low-profile position into an effective, aggressive crusading force on behalf of the "little person." She continually exposed dishonest business practices. For example, she clamped down on restaurants that falsely claimed to serve one hundred percent beef hamburgers. Because of her efforts, New York City adopted some of the toughest consumer protection laws in the country.

Next to Mayor John Lindsay, she was New York City's most visible public figure. Leaving office in 1973, Myerson considered running for office, but instead wrote consumer columns for the New York *Daily News,* and taught political science courses at Hunter College. She developed ovarian cancer and underwent eighteen months of chemotherapy treatment. Concerned about how others would react ("in those days, people thought cancer was catching"), she kept the cancer a secret.

In 1977, when Edward Koch, then running for mayor of New York, was accused of being a homosexual, Bess Myerson proposed to him that she accompany him to rallies, arm-in-arm. "Within a week, the press will write that we're going to be married," she told him. Koch agreed and so she campaigned intensively for him, staying by his side to help squelch rumors and lend him her support. Many credited her with helping Koch obtain victory.

Myerson made her first bid for public office in 1980, running in the Democratic primary contest for U.S. Senator from New York. Among her rivals were her former boss, John Lindsay. She lost the primary to U.S. Representative Elizabeth Holtzman who then went on to lose the November election.

Myerson enjoyed politics and her associations with the high-placed. Introduced once to Golda Meir, Israel's Prime Minister from 1969 to 1974, Bess Myerson embraced the Israeli leader. At one time, both women had the same last name (Golda's original surname from her first marriage had been Myerson). This led Golda to quip: "So you're the famous Myerson girl I've been hearing so much about!"

Always involved in a number of projects at once, Myerson published the *I Love NY Diet Book*, written with Bill Adler, in 1982.

In 1983, after being turned down by Jacqueline Onassis and Beverly Sills, Mayor Koch named Myerson commissioner of the city's Department of Cultural Affairs. "Community leaders and shopkeepers will come out to see Bess Myerson," she said the day she was appointed, adding with a laugh, "if only to see what I look like now. They'll never say, 'Bess Who?'"

On January 13, 1987 Bess Myerson announced that she would take a ninety-day unpaid leave after becoming the subject of a special city probe. She had invoked her Fifth Amendment rights before a grand jury that was looking into the business practices of her regular companion, Carl A. Capasso, a contractor. She eventually resigned. The tabloids, describing her as an aging beauty queen, called the tale "the Bess Mess" and two books were written about Myerson's court case.

"For a long time Bess Myerson was a woman who could do no wrong and who sort of symbolized New York City success," wrote City Councilwoman Ruth Messinger in October 1988. "In an era when there was a great deal of question about how high Jews could rise, there was Bess Myerson as proof you could get to the top. She achieved a kind of permanent fame. She became a quasi-mythic character. Then it begins to crumble...That stirs the juices of people who said, 'I always knew she couldn't be that perfect.'" Myerson's trial got under way on October 4, 1988. She was charged with fixing her lover's divorce case by giving a city job to the emotionally disturbed daughter of the presiding judge. If she had been found guilty, she could have faced a thirty-seven-year jail sentence.

Myerson and Capasso were acquitted of charges of conspiracy, mail fraud and bribery. Eager to put the experience behind her, especially the unpleasant memories of being hounded by the media, Myerson asked writers to omit that part of her life in profiles of her. "It was an enlightening experience," she told the authors of this book. "It fed my courage and my survival instinct."

As of the summer of 1993, Bess Myerson was working as a phobia treatment specialist, helping people to get over their obsessive fears. In the fall of that year, she began visits to the Sloan-Kettering Institute where she works with cancer patients.

"I always wanted to be a doctor. My mother used to say I'd marry one."

Doña Gracia Nasi

Sixteenth-century Marrano Activist

Born in 1510 in Lisbon, Portugal; died in 1569. Sixteenth-century Marrano champion of Jewish rights. Doña Gracia Nasi was the most remarkable Jewish woman of her time. She took over a large, complex business empire in Europe, ran it well, and retained her fortune despite efforts by kings and others to wrest it from her. She saved hundreds of Marranos from death and persecution. Her efforts to wield Jewish economic and political power foundered, however, she was simply ahead of her time. Nasi sought in vain to punish anti-Semitism by imposing an economic boycott on the Italian town of Ancona. She sought unsuccessfully to build a Jewish homeland in Palestine, using Tiberias as her base.

Doña Gracia Nasi was the daughter of wealthy, aristocratic Marrano parents whose last name was de Luna. As a Marrano, Beatrice (that was her Christian name) was forced to behave as a devout Christian. She shared in the double life of Marrano families who were forced to behave as devout Christians yet held on to their Jewish faith.

Beatrice later changed her name to Gracia. She was born in 1510 in Lisbon, Portugal. Her family carried the prestigious Jewish name Nasi.

Beatrice's goal was to practice her Judaism openly. Her early life is largely a mystery although it is known that she was conscious of her Jewish origins and kept in touch with other Marrano families in Lisbon. When her brother Samuel Nasi died in 1525, she took over responsibility for raising his two sons.

At age eighteen, Gracia Nasi married a Spanish descendant, a man several years older, Francisco Mendes. Two years later, they had a child named Reyna. Establishing themselves in the highly-profitable spice trade, the Mendes family built a commercial empire that reached into England and Western Europe. Their extensive financial network also served the secret purpose of providing escape routes for Marranos threatened by the Spanish Inquisition, as well as allowing them to transfer their funds elsewhere.

In 1536, Francisco Mendes became ill and died, leaving Gracia Nasi-Mendes, now just twenty-six, in a most precarious situation. She was forced to give her husband a Christian burial. Departing Lisbon, she, along with her six year-old daughter Reyna, her sister Reyna, and her two nephews, Joseph and Samuel, sought refuge in England, sailing there on a trading vessel with her entire fortune stowed among

Doña Gracia Nasi and Joseph Nasi.

From Arthur Szyk's illustrations in *The Last Days of Shylock* by Ludwig Lewisohn

Top: Doña Gracia Nasi as she appears on Israeli postage stamps. Center: Israeli postage stamp. Bottom: The earliest Jewish medal with Hebrew inscription depicts Doña Gracia Nasi.

the cargo. The House of Mendes had a solid reputation in London as the dominant trading establishment.

After a few months, Gracia, and her daughter, fled England and reached Antwerp, Belgium, safely where she joined her brother-in-law, Diego, the top commercial figure in that city, and became a full partner in his enterprises.

Over the next six years Gracia mixed with rich bankers and aristocrats, writers, artists and scholars, many of them Spanish or Portuguese emigrés. She and her brother-in-law sought to persuade the Pope to stop the Inquisition in Portugal. Their efforts were partly successful. Gracia wanted to discard her pretense of being a Christian and practice Judaism freely.

Nasi urged Diego to move his business elsewhere. Failing that, she wanted him to give her the property that was due her so that she could move to a place where she could live freely as a Jewess. Diego died in 1542 before it was possible to do either. Diego left his entire estate and the assets of the Mendes banking house in Gracia's possession, effectively making her head of the Mendes family.

Meanwhile, charges that had been brought by jealous business rivals against Diego lingered even after his death. Gracia felt compelled to defend her dead brother-in-law against those charges in order to make sure that the authorities would not confiscate her property. She managed to have the charges dropped.

In 1547, Gracia reached Venice with most of her fortune intact. Her sister Reyna gave her trouble, demanding her own and her daughter's share of the estate. Gracia refused. In revenge, the younger sister disclosed to the Venetian government that Doña Gracia was about to emigrate to Turkey, taking all of her wealth with her, and that she planned to practice Judaism openly there. To prevent her supposed flight, the authorities arrested Gracia. Fortunately for Gracia, the Turkish Sultan Suleiman intervened on her behalf. He managed to secure her release so that she could depart for Turkey. Negotiations over the release of her property, however, dragged on for several years.

Reaching Ferrara, Italy, Gracia openly espoused Judaism for the first time in her life. She assumed her Jewish name of Gracia (Hannah) Nasi. There she organized the flight of hundreds of fugitive Marranos; she operated an underground railroad from Portugal. In appreciation of her work, the famous Ferrara Bible, published in 1533 by two Marranos, was dedicated to her. During the sixteenth and seventeenth centuries, that Bible sustained hope for many Marranos who hoped to return to their faith, but only understood the

Spanish of that Bible translation.

Gracia reconciled with her sister and arranged the marriage of her sister's daughter to Gracia's nephew Samuel. She also provided generously for the young couple.

In 1553, Gracia settled in Constantinople along with her daughter Reyna. She expanded her efforts on behalf of fellow Jews, helping the poor and financing the building of schools. Reyna married her cousin Joao Miquez, who openly avowed Judaism and assumed his Jewish name of Joseph Nasi. He became associated with Doña Gracia in all of her political and commercial activities, including shipping, banking, and trading, among which was the crucial wine monopoly.

In 1556, Doña Gracia confronted Pope Paul IV, considered one of the most anti-Semitic Popes in history. The Pope had imprisoned the Marranos of the papal port of Ancona and burned twenty-six of them at the stake. To punish the Pope, Gracia organized a boycott of Ancona. Controlling a large portion of world trade, the Jewish merchants of Turkey used Ancona as the main port of entry for shipping wares from Turkey to Europe. The Pope threatened the Jews of Italy with expulsion if they complied with Doña Gracia. When only a part of the Jewish community supported the boycott, the plan fell apart.

Doña Gracia believed that Palestine was the best sanctuary for persecuted Jewry. She decided to set up a settlement in Tiberias on the Sea of Galilee as the start of a Jewish homeland.

About 1558, the Sultan, Suleiman, leased the city of Tiberias and some seven nearby villages to Doña Gracia for 1,000 ducats a year. A wall was built, completed in the winter of 1564-65, to protect residents from roving bands of thieves. Doña Gracia built a mansion for her private use outside the city walls. She planned to settle there in 1566. It is not clear whether she actually did settle in Tiberias. But she was absent from Constantinople from 1566 until 1569, the year of her death, suggesting that she may well have settled in Tiberias.

With her death, Gracia's settlement plan fell apart. Faced with a possible outbreak of violence, wealthy Jews left the city. It was not until 1740 that Jews rebuilt the city and made Tiberias a permanent settlement.

In December 1990 a commemorative gathering of one thousand people was held in Tiberias in honor of Doña Gracia.

$\mathscr{L}$OUISE $\mathscr{N}$EVELSON

Outstanding American Sculptor

Born September 23, 1899 in Kiev, Ukraine; died April 17, 1988.
American sculptor. Louise Nevelson was one of America's best sculptors and the most important American woman sculptor, although recognition eluded her until late in her career. She is considered the chief originator and exponent of environmental sculpture. Many of her large abstract sculptures adorn plazas in New York City and museums around the world. Her main contribution has been to blur the boundaries between sculpture and painting.

$\mathscr{L}$ouise Berliawsky was born in Kiev, Russia, the second of four children. Her father Isaac journeyed to the United States in 1902 and went into the lumber business in Rockland, Maine, a small town with only twenty Jewish families. The business prospered and he sent for his wife, Minna, and children two years later.

Louise's father often brought home pieces of wood from his lumberyard which Louise played with and carved. Shy at first, Louise showed artistic ability early when, in second grade, the children were asked to draw a sunflower and hers was considered the most original. She exhibited little interest in most academic subjects, but became a good athlete and excellent dancer. She wanted, however, to become a sculptor.

The combination of being Jewish and an aspiring artist in Rockland gave Louise a double stigma; she always felt as if she were an outsider.

Louise graduated from high school in 1918, and that year met a New Yorker named Charles Nevelson who had been visiting Maine. Two years later they were married. Settling in New York City with her husband, Louise studied drawing, painting, drama and dance. In 1922, the birth of the couple's son Myron led to a domestic crisis. Charles insisted that his wife stay home with the baby. She resented being tied to both baby and husband. When Myron was school age between 1928 and 1930, Louise Nevelson studied at the Art Students League. Charles grew resentful of her remaining at the League late at night, not returning for supper. In 1931 they were divorced.

Nevelson then left her son with her parents in Maine and traveled to Munich where she studied for one year with the

Louise Nevelson among some of her work.

Painted wood sculpture "Homage to the Six Million."

painter Hans Hofmann. When the Nazis closed his school, she moved to Vienna, and then to Paris. During her stay there, she visited the *Musée d l'Homme*. She was deeply impressed with the African sculptures she saw there.

Returning to New York, Nevelson and another artist, Ben Shahn, became assistants to the Mexican muralist Diego Rivera on his Rockefeller Center social protest murals. Nevelson hated reproducing the small sketches as murals and hated even more the incredible amount of research required for creating these paintings.

Louise Nevelson's first exhibition of her own sculpture opened in 1933. She was influenced by the cubism of Picasso, the forms of pre-Columbian Central American and African design, which was reflected in her sculptures. Two years later some of her work was featured at the Brooklyn Museum.

On September 12, 1936, a *New York Times* critic wrote that "She uses color as it has never been used before…applies it abstractly so to speak, even as though she was working on canvas instead of in the round." That critique bolstered Nevelson's self-confidence as an artist.

In 1937, Nevelson taught sculpture at the Educational Alliance Art School on the Lower East Side as part of a Works Project Administration-funded program. She literally found her unique medium when she happened across discarded wooden cases inside of which were rolls of carpeting that had been packed. She used these odds and ends of wood and began constructing rhythmic, collage-influenced works in three dimensions.

Nevelson survived by selling her work to artist-friends and by accepting family aid. Most of her work was in clay or plaster models which she never cast into the permanent medium of bronze for lack of funds.

Louise Nevelson's first one-person show was in September 1941 in New York. She received mostly favorable reviews; few, however, bought her art. Nevelson spent the next fifteen years developing her skills, destroying many of her works, saving only those she treasured.

Home to Nevelson was the SoHo section in New York City. There, she painted one wall gold and began collecting and assembling gold works. She had one studio for black work, one studio for white.

During one thirteen-year span, she worked on a series of black-painted wood pieces and called this "Mrs. N's Palace." It was supposed to be a permanent environment in which the pieces are attached to a black mirror-glass base.

She thought of her sculptures as "environments" and tried to merge the sculpture with the environment in such a way that the two had one identity. As she put it, she searched for a "reality that was factual, in an area where there was an unlimited source, to reach what for me would be reality."

Louise Nevelson worked in many mediums including wood, plaster, terra cotta, stone, aluminum, and bronze. She became especially associated with wooden sculpture. It was after a visit to Mexico that Nevelson's works focused on the sculptural landscapes of painted wood.

During the mid-1950s, the Whitney Museum began buying Nevelson's sculpture. Her works grew larger; her reputation blossomed. Some were freestanding sculptures. But her trademark sculptures were monochromatic (often all-black or all-white) "sculptured murals"—large relief works that are meant to hang on a wall.

In 1957, observing the lines of a wooden case of liquor, Nevelson decided to put together a number of wooden boxes, one on top of another—and then examine the effect. This was her first "wall." Often her "walls" are monochromatic, either white, black or gold; they consist of square boxes mounted in rows and stacks that resemble a large modular bookcase. Abstract carvings of wood are mounted inside each of these squares. Nevelson's two major works from the late 1950s are "Moon Garden Plus One" and "Sky Cathedrals," two landscape arrangements of abstract wooden pieces.

In 1963, Nevelson became the first woman and first American sculptor to work under contract to Sidney Janis, who represented the noted artists Jackson Pollock, Robert Motherwell, and Willem de Kooning. Nevelson had assembled three "environments," but later, when she had an argument with Janis, he claimed that she owed him $20,000. He claimed he would only turn over her works when he was paid. She paid off the debt, but became so severely depressed that she considered suicide. She eventually recovered.

Nevelson became increasingly aware of her Jewish background. Her first work upon returning to New York in 1964 was "Homage, 6,000,000," a large wall that demonstrated an aggressive use of space. It served as a memorial piece to the Holocaust and was purchased by the Israel Museum.

In January 1977, the French government released Palestinian terrorist Abu Daoud, who had planned the massacre of the Israeli athletes at the 1972 Munich Olympics. That prompted Louise Nevelson to withdraw her promised work, "Homage to the Baroque," worth $125,000, which she had planned to donate to the new French art facility, *Le Centre National d'Art et Culture George Pompidou*. She urged other artists to boycott this new museum as well.

Nevelson was awarded the National Medal of Arts in recognition of her outstanding contribution to American art.

Louise Nevelson was considered somewhat eccentric. She rarely entertained, always dressed in outlandish clothes and wore dark glasses in order not to be recognized. She died in 1988 at the age of eighty-nine.

IDA NUDEL

The Guardian Angel

> **Born April 27, 1931, in Novorosis in the Crimea, former Soviet Union.** Russian Jewish activist. Known as the "Guardian Angel" for her efforts on behalf of Soviet Jewish prisoners of conscience, Ida Nudel was arrested in 1978. Suffering through prison and exile, she was released in 1987 and immediately flew to Israel.

Ida Nudel lives in Carmei Yosef, a quiet suburb of Rehovot, Israel. Her graying hair is still tied back in her trademark ponytail. Her loud, infectious laugh and piercingly high voice fill the room. This is the woman the KGB could not tame or break, one of the great symbols of the struggle of Soviet Jews for their right to emigrate to Israel.

Throughout her captivity in Russia from 1978 to 1987, she had feared for her life, but never despaired. "Kafka, Kafka, where are you?" she asked in a tape-recorded message that had been smuggled to Israel in 1979. "Even your imagination could not create a situation like this."

In the midst of her meeting with the authors of this book in April 1993, the phone rang. Someone had found Ida Nudel's Israeli credit card after she had misplaced it. She was pleased that it had turned up, but disturbed with herself for losing it. "It's the first time in my life that I've done that. I'm usually so disciplined." Indeed, she had been that.

Nudel had first sought an exit visa to leave the former Soviet Union in 1970, telling friends that she could not stand the discrimination against Jews in the USSR. The authorities said she could not leave because she possessed state secrets, having learned them at the Moscow Institute of Planning and Production, where she worked checking hygiene at food stores.

Her sister Elana, her only living relative, won permission to leave Russia with her husband and son in 1972.

Soon after that, Ida Nudel's "punishment" began. She lost her job, and in June 1978 she was sentenced to five years of internal exile on charges of "malicious hooliganism." She had placed a banner in her Moscow apartment window demanding that she be permitted to go to Israel.

Her actual "crime" was her one-woman campaign to keep contact with, and look after, "Prisoners of Zion," many of whom she had never met. Those "Prisoners of Zion" affectionately called her "ma-

Ida Nudel (left) with Israeli actress Aviva Marks.

192

State of Israel Government Press Office

Ida Nudel being greeted upon arrival in Israel. Pictured: Shimon Peres (left), Natan Sharansky (behind her), and Yitzhak Shamir (second from right).

ma" or "the angel of mercy." In prison, she was the only female among sixty male criminals.

Following an international outcry, she was permitted to move to a one-room hut in the summer of 1979.

Nudel was released from exile on March 20, 1982, but was warned not to socialize with "refuseniks" or foreigners. She was granted a permit that forced her to live for five years in the remote town of Bendary in Moldavia. Her only explanation of how she endured her hardships: "Motivation."

Jane Fonda, the actress, visited her for the first time in April 1984, and the two began a close friendship; Fonda campaigned aggressively for Ida Nudel's release. In July of that year, Nudel's Moscow residence permit was permanently revoked. By February 1985, she was barred from entering Moscow.

"I cannot wait any more. Take me out," she told the *Jerusalem Post's* Louis Rapoport in June 1986. "I want Israel now." Rapoport, meeting her in her exile state in Bendary, described her: "At fifty-five, her bespectacled face is a map of where she has been and what she has gone through: cracked country lips, a furrowed intelligent brow, black hair streaked with gray, penetrating Gloria Swanson eyes, and an aura that alternates between massive strength and obvious vulnerability. She is warm, inspiring, and indomitable, yet the wear and tear of Soviet persecution is evident."

Ida Nudel had no desire to be heroic during her imprisonment. She told the authors of this book:" I didn't want to stay. But I don't regret it. They were the best years of my life. There's no free lunch." She was at various times surrounded by rats, poisoned, and made to live with male ex-convicts. She put a knife under her pillow to take her own life, if necessary.

In the spring of 1993, Ida Nudel sounded proud of what her plight had meant for others. "I knew what I was doing, I represented the essence of the struggle."

Nudel's struggle ended on October 15, 1987 when she reached Israel. The first person she saw was her sister, Elana Friedman, two years her junior. "It is the moment of my life," Ida rejoiced breezily. "I am home at the soul of my Jewish people. I am a free person among my own people." Ida Nudel was in tears. Greeting her at the airport were Prime Minister Yitzhak Shamir and Jane Fonda.

Jane Fonda summed her up on that day: "She was most hated by the KGB. She was a woman fighting not just for herself but for all Jews in the Soviet Union who want to leave. She would not stop despite ill health and terrible difficulties. Ida is little, but she is beautiful."

Nudel spent her first three years in Israel writing her autobiography, *A Hand in the Darkness,* and giving speeches on the needs of new immigrants.

Ida Nudel's struggle makes her seem older than her years. Yet she is "just" sixty-one [1993], born in the Crimea in 1931. "I was a strange bird," she explained. "My teachers thought I would be an actress because I recited poems about the suffering people of World War II very emotionally. When I read poems loudly, everyone cried."

Her parents were "idealistic Communists," in Ida Nudel's words, and although her mother came from a religious family, neither parent was observant. "I'm second-generation non-religious," Nudel quipped lightly. When she was ten months old, her parents turned her over to her mother's parents in the first Jewish *kolkhoz* (a Russian collective farm) called Jankhio. "My parents had no place for me. They were building a new world." Nudel reached Moscow when she was three years old, going to live with her parents again. She spoke Yiddish fluently, thanks to her grandparents. Her father, a colonel in the Russian army during World War II, was killed at the battle for Leningrad in August 1942.

From her mother, who died in 1963, Nudel learned that being Jewish could be problematic in Russia. "She used to say, `Remember, you're Jewish. If you have nothing to do, take a book. Never get into a conflict.'" Nudel followed that rule throughout her youth. "My first conflict was with the KGB," she says now.

After she completed high school in Moscow, she went to a university there for five years and studied economics. She worked for three years in the Ural Mountains region. She returned to Moscow to work in an office where she dealt with finances connected with the building industry.

Ida Nudel insists that she is unmarried, but there is a twinkle in her eye that may indicate that there is a part of her past she apparently wishes not to divulge.

Now, after being released from her Russian exile, Ida Nudel lives on an Israeli pension and on "back-pay" for her days in prison. She is helping single Russian mothers to cope through education and moral support, and is busy trying to push the Israeli government to do more for Russian immigrants. She is concerned that unless more is done to help them integrate, Israel will lose the chance to take in the two-million Russian Jews who still want to emigrate.

State of Israel Government Press Office

Ida Nudel greeting her sister upon Ida's arrival in Israel.

CHANA ORLOFF

Outstanding Twentieth-Century Sculptor

Born in 1888 in Tsare, Ukraine; died December 18, 1968. French/Israeli sculptor. Chana Orloff has been called one of the greatest women artists of all time and one of the great sculptors of her day. Her massive figures are found in museums from New York to Oslo to Tel Aviv. Her style was unique, distinguished by its simplicity of form, which she adapted to Cubism. She did portraits of numerous, leading Parisians and well-known figures in the art world, including Pablo Picasso and Henry Matisse. Her favorite medium was wood, but she also worked with stone, marble, bronze, and cement. Her "Fèmmà La Guitare" is her most admired piece.

Born in the Ukraine, Chana Orloff moved with her family to the settlement of Petah Tikva in Palestine when she was sixteen. She lived there for the next six years; while her father worked in the fields, she was employed as a seamstress.

"I am a Jewess born in Russia and rooted in Israel," she used to say. Though she spent much of her time in Paris, she considered herself an Israeli.

At the age of twenty-two, Orloff moved to Paris to study dressmaking. She had many friends among the avant-garde artists of the day. While there, her talent for design was observed, then encouraged. She studied sculpture at the *Ecole des Arts Decoratifs,* making her home in France.

While a student, in 1912, she modelled for Amedeo Modigliani who sketched her and inscribed the drawing in Hebrew, "Chana, daughter of Raphael."

In 1913, two of Chana Orloff's wooden sculptures were accepted by the *Salon D'Automne.* She was only twenty-five years old. During the next twelve years, her work received considerable recognition. Exhibitions of her sculptures appeared from time to time in, among other places, New York and Boston.

In 1916, Orloff married the poet Ary Justman. He died two years later in an influenza epidemic, leaving her with a one-year-old son.

One of her better-known efforts is her 1924 sculpture, "Man with the Pipe," which was purchased by the French Government. *The Jerusalem Post* noted of the sculpture: "There is that strong feeling for plastic, three-dimensional form, a unity of mood that is carried through the entire work from feet to head, and at the same time a keen insight into character that makes us feel that we know this man as he sits so solidly smoking his pipe. In other words, she has been able to make a complete and convincing statement."

Chana Orloff as drawn by Amedeo Modigliani.

In 1925, when she was only thirty-seven years old, Orloff was made a chevalier of the French Legion of Honor. The next year she became a naturalized French citizen. Her work was exhibited at the School of the Museum of Fine Arts in Boston and at the Marie Sterner Gallery in New York City and on both occasions American critics offered admiring comments.

Orloff's first commission for a monument came in 1931. In the following years she was commissioned to do portraits of numerous, important Parisians and well-known figures in the art world, including Pablo Picasso and Henri Matisse.

Even during the Nazi occupation of France Chana Orloff kept working on what she called her "pocket sculptures." In December 1942, Orloff was warned that her arrest was imminent. She fled with her son to Switzerland. Her Paris studio was vandalized and a good deal of her work was either stolen or destroyed. Orloff returned to Paris when the war was over.

Orloff's art departed from all formal French tradition. Her sculpture, whether it was bronze, marble, iron or wood, was highly individualistic.

George S. Hellman, writing in the *Universal Jewish Encyclopedia,* said that her work, "has force, robustness, humor; it has freshness, subtlety and at times mystery. In her portraits of men and women she seeks and achieves not the obvious likeness, but the truth of character, which is most revelatory. She exaggerates and simplifies, but her portraits are not caricatures that lessen or deride her subjects; they magnify the essential."

Orloff sculptured hundreds of figures, including Israel's first prime minister, David Ben-Gurion, and the Yiddish dramatist and novelist, Sholem Asch. She also sculpted pregnant women, women with children, ordinary men and women, and birds. Her favorite medium was wood because its smooth rounded surfaces glided into one another. She found it "warm and friendly."

Orloff also worked with stone, marble, bronze, and cement. Her work was described as realistic and influenced by Cubism. For her, she once said, the important thing was "to create a living work of art."

Karl Schwartz, in the book *Jewish Arts,* wrote: "One sometimes finds something cruelly ironic and glaringly frank in her busts. In her portrayals of women, she knows how to unfold a tender lyricism and in her child studies, the naivete of the child-world. Her statues of animals are masterpieces of plastic forms. Never verging on the sentimental, dramatic, or pathetic, Chana Orloff displays a sense of humor, and is, at the same time, original, real-

"The Pipesmoker", 1924.

istic and always expressive."

Orloff's series of drawings and sculptures called *Retour* depicted the sufferings of a deportee.

Art critic Meir Ronnen, writing in *The Jerusalem Post* in April 1961, reviewed an Orloff exhibit in Israel covering fifty years of her work, among which were seventy-eight pieces of sculpture. "Orloff's work," he wrote rhapsodically, "is characterized by a voluptuousness of form and a sense of construction, without which, of course, a sculptor can accomplish little. She has also remained remarkably true to her own personality. But it is not unnatural that the work of the Cubists, Gaudier and Brancusi, should not have passed unnoticed by her."

In Orloff's later years, numerous major exhibitions of her art work were mounted. These included a retrospective in the Tel

The Diaspora Museum

"The Horsewoman."

Aviv Museum in 1969. She visited Israel often and created a number of public monuments there, the best-known of which is the roaring lion statue in memory of Dov Gruner, which is placed in a busy thoroughfare in Ramat Gan. Other monuments by Orloff are in such kibbutzim as Revivim, Ein Gev, and Beit Oren.

Orloff maintained a home in Tel Aviv, and once, later in life, declared that she wanted to die in Israel. She could not have known that she was about to get her wish.

Chana Orloff arrived in Israel in December 1968 to plan an exhibition. Meant to celebrate her 80th birthday, it was the largest and most comprehensive of her independent exhibitions.

She was physically well. "I hope not to be late for the opening," she remarked. "But woe to who will cry if I am not there."

While in Israel, she said she had had a bad dream and wrote to her son and daughter-in-law to come immediately. By the time they arrived, however, she had already had a stroke and was hospitalized. When she regained consciousness, shortly before her death, she asked to see Eli, her son. She died on December 18, before the exhibition opened.

In all, Orloff created nearly 400 sculptures. Her last work has been placed at the entrance to the exhibition hall at the Tel Aviv Museum. It is a bust of the late Israeli Prime Minister Levi Eshkol.

BERTHA PAPPENHEIM

Sigmund Freud's Famous "Anna O"

> **Born in 1859 in Vienna; died in 1936.** Feminist leader and German Jewish community activist. Bertha Pappenheim founded the Jewish feminist movement in Germany and led it from 1904 to 1924. Educating an entire generation of German-Jewish women in radical ideas, she encouraged those women to seek political, economic, and social rights. She pioneered in organizing a nation wide network of Jewish social workers to protect and free women. She was the first to raise publicly the problems of unwed mothers, illegitimate children and prostitutes in the German Jewish community.

Bertha was the third daughter born to a wealthy Orthodox family in Vienna. Her mother came from Frankfurt, Germany. Unable to continue her education beyond high school, Bertha was forced to spend most of her time embroidering and daydreaming despite her great energy and intelligence.

At age twenty-one, Bertha suffered serious psychological problems and was referred to the well-known physician Josef Breuer who informed his colleague, Sigmund Freud, of his treatment of her.

Pappenheim became the famous "Anna O"—the person whom Freud most discussed, though he never treated her. Hers was the most prominent illustration of major hysteria. Most of what is known of Bertha Pappenheim's early years has come from Breuer's famous essays in *Studie in Hysteria* (1908), which was compiled with Sigmund Freud. Breuer considered her case a major breakthrough in psychoanalysis. In one essay, Pappenheim is described as a young woman who suffers from psychosomatic paralysis brought on by the stress of nursing her father during a fatal illness.

Breuer was unable to solve Pappenheim's problems. Her mental health was restored only when she put aside the role of being the dutiful daughter who was searching for a husband and became a feminist and social worker.

Following her recovery, Pappenheim and her mother moved to Frankfurt. There her female relatives encouraged her to become involved with charity work. It took little coaxing for Pappenheim had a strong social consciousness and a great sensitivity to injustice. She was strongly influenced by a popular feminist periodical called *The Woman*.

Bertha Pappenheim sought equal justice for Jewish women. She herself resented being denied higher education because of the Jewish prejudice that expected girls to marry and boys to achieve scholarly success.

In the early 1890s Pappenheim started to work in Jewish charities, beginning by dishing out soup to poor immigrants from Eastern Europe. In 1895, she became housemother in an orphanage for Jewish girls, retaining that post for twelve years.

Pappenheim began writing in the 1890s. Her first book was called *In the Secondhand Shop*. It was a collection of short stories, reflecting her concern for the poor and her love of children. In 1899, by now a clearly identified feminist, she wrote a play called *Women's Rights,* which focused on the political, economic, and sexual exploitation of women.

The role of Jewish women was a constant theme in Pappenheim's stories. One of her heroines said sadly: "I would have...enjoyed learning about art and politics, if I had been educated to understand them."

In 1900, she wrote a pamphlet, "The Jewish Problem in Galicia," arguing that the lack of education for Jewish women led to poverty and vice. Four years later, while a member of the welfare board of the city, she organized a social-work branch to aid Jewish women.

Pappenheim felt that women needed to form their own national organization, that such an instrument could become a focus for feminism, and that feminism could reinvigorate Judaism in Germany.

As part of the International Women's Congress in Berlin in 1904, Bertha Pappenheim founded the national *Judischer Frauenbund,* a social service agency of German Jewish women that aided women in the early part of the twentieth century. *The Frauenbund* grew to a membership of 50,000 women by 1929. Pappenheim served not only as its president, but also as its main personality and driving force for the next twenty years.

Pappenheim believed that girls should learn home economics—that housekeeping was a legitimate career. Thus the *Frauenbund* provided courses in this area. She also believed, however, that many injustices inflicted on Jewish girls could be corrected if Jewish women played a larger role in their community. Because of this idea, she sought political equality for these Jewish women. By reeducating and rehabilitating the poor, the *Frauenbund* would, Bertha Pappenheim hoped, prevent Judaism's demise in Germany.

Pappenheim, who never married, also founded a home for delinquent and disturbed girls, and for unwed mothers in 1907. She admitted that much of her efforts had their basis in her wish to achieve surrogate motherhood.

The white slave trade became yet a new passion for Pappenheim. Many Jews from Eastern Europe had been moving westward at the turn of the century, and among them were girls who had been turned into "white slaves." Pappenheim's best-known publication was *Sisyphus Work,* a study of Jewish prostitution and white slavery in Eastern Europe and the Middle East.

Through the book, she hoped to end the sexual abuse of women, likening women's struggle in this issue to that of Sisyphus. He was the ancient king of Corinth who had been condemned to roll a huge stone up a hill in Hades, only to find the stone rolling down all the time.

In 1902, Bertha Pappenheim attended a conference on white slavery and recalled to the group horrible tales of the traffic in women: "I remember the time when—despite the fact that I had been involved in social work for several years—the words 'white slavery' rang in my ears.... I did not know what they meant, could not grasp that there were people who bought and sold... "girls and children."

Bertha Pappenheim cited women's inferior legal status in Judaism as one cause of white slavery. Pappenheim begged the rabbinic and lay Jewish leaders in Germany and Eastern Europe to raise their voices against the practice. Her plea fell on deaf ears because the leaders feared that their criticism would unleash a new wave of anti-Semitism. She also petitioned rabbis to modernize marriage, divorce and inheritance laws. Her pleas went unanswered.

Pappenheim was a descendant of Glueckel of Hameln. In 1910, Bertha Pappenheim translated Glueckel's memoirs from Yiddish to German. Pappenheim admired her ancestor's piety and her strength. Glueckel was not only a wife and mother (of thirteen children!), but an equal partner in her marriage. That impressed Pappenheim.

Bertha Pappenheim tried to teach women about their cultural and religious heritage by translating the *Tzenah Ureenah,* a sixteenth-century women's Bible, and the *Mayse Bukh,* a collection of medieval folk tales.

Although she became ill as she grew older, Glueckel continued to travel and to remain involved in her social activities. During this time, she met Lillian D. Wald and visited the settlement house Wald had founded. In a conversation with Henrietta Szold, Pappenheim tried to persuade her that Zionism and Youth Aliyah would lead to the dissolution of families.

When Hitler came to power, his cohorts used reprints of Bertha Pappenheim's early expositions of Jewish connections to the white slave trade to encourage anti-Semitism.

Pappenheim wrote her own obituary: "In 1904 she founded the J.F. B. *(the Judischer Frauenbund)*—its importance is not yet fully understood. The Jews of the entire world—men and women—owe her [their] thanks for this social achievement. But they withhold it. What a pity!"

MOLLIE PARNIS

Fashion Designer for First Ladies

Born March 18, circa 1905 in New York, New York; died July 18, 1992. American dress designer. Even as a teen-ager, dress designing seemed to be in Mollie Parnis's blood. As an adult, U.S. First Ladies like Mamie Eisenhower, Betty Ford, and Lady Bird Johnson wore her dresses, and Parnis built a multimillion-dollar business. Through the contacts she made by visiting the White House and elsewhere, Parnis also became one of America's great hostesses. Her Park Avenue apartment was one of the country's most famous salons.

Born on the Lower East Side of New York City, Mollie Parnis had no difficulty revealing the day of her birth (March 18), but found it impossible to divulge the exact year. The best guess: 1905. "Close, but not precise," was all Mollie would say.

Mollie was the eldest of Abraham and Sara Parnis' five children. Her parents had emigrated from Austria sometime before 1900. Mollie began working at odd jobs at eight years old. One was tutoring foreigners in English at twenty-five cents an hour.

While in high school, Mollie decided that she wanted to work in women's fashion. When a young man named Leonard Livingston invited her to a football game, she insisted that her mother buy her a new outfit. Sara Parnis took Mollie to Division Street and bought a navy-blue dress for her.

The football game over, the young man offered to take Mollie dancing. Rather brazenly, he suggested she go home and change into a different dress. He did not realize that she was wearing the only dress she owned.

Taking a pair of scissors in hand, Parnis cut the neckline, borrowing a lace collar from her mother's blouse and adding an artificial flower. It was Mollie Parnis's first design.

Livingston's nerve had no adverse effect on Mollie. The couple was married in 1930.

As an eighteen year-old, Parnis had become an assistant saleswoman in the showroom of a blouse manufacturer. At times, she made suggestions to the designers—change a neckline, a jabot, a frill, a sleeve. Once, due to her growing expertise in the business, she rang up a $20,000 sale to one customer. When she sought a raise, her boss responded instead by putting her name in the lobby directory.

"You don't know what that did for me," Mollie said many years later. "I got so excited

over it, I had all my friends come over to Seventh Avenue to look at 'Mollie Parnis, fourth floor.' It was like an actress having her name up in lights the first time."

In 1933, she and her husband became business partners as well—he handling the finances, Mollie Parnis dealing with clothing design, even though she could not sketch, cut, or drape. From the beginning, the company, called Parnis-Livingston, prospered. Volume for the first year was, in Parnis' words, "near a million."

Mollie Parnis hired other designers as the business grew. She remained the fashion director, designing versatile, comfortable dresses in good fabrics—fashionable, but not trendy. She urged women to avoid fads. "I've always had a theory," she once said, "that good designing doesn't mean dresses you have to throw away every year. Things shouldn't go out of date overnight."

Parnis had no desire to start trends in fashion design. "I don't try to design like St. Laurent," she said in 1977. "I tell everyone at work, we are trying to dress only ten percent of the women in America with a certain taste level. I am not the most trendy designer, but I am never far behind."

In 1941, she and her husband moved the company into a loft at 530 Seventh Avenue near 39th Street, located in the fashion district of New York City.

Leonard Livingston died in 1962, and Parnis went out of business—but just for three months. She went to dinner one night with a man who asked when she was going to open her showroom again.

"Maybe never," she said.

"Oh, my God," he replied. "The only thing that made you a little different was that you worked. Don't you know that widows in this town with a little money are a dime a dozen?"

The remark had an immediate effect on Parnis. She returned to business at once.

When Parnis reopened the business, it was renamed Mollie Parnis, Inc. She began to design dresses for a number of U.S. First Ladies, including Mamie Eisenhower, Lady Bird Johnson, and Betty Ford. Parnis kept photographs of First Ladies wearing her designs in her office. She once designed a shirt for Lyndon B. Johnson.

A green-and-blue silk taffeta Parnis dress, which Mamie Eisenhower wore at a reception in 1955, made headlines when a guest appeared wearing the same dress. Undisturbed, Parnis noted, "I do not sell directly to any wearer. Nor do I usually make one of a kind; that's what makes this country a great democracy."

In 1976, the business's volume was nine-million dollars. Parnis's dresses in her better ready-to-wear line averaged $395.00 retail. Her boutique clothes cost an average of $250.00 retail.

Apart from fashion designing, Mollie Parnis built a life for herself as a New York hostess, running one of the country's better-known salons. "The last thing I want to talk about is what people are wearing," she once told an interviewer. She cultivated important people and invited them to her Park Avenue duplex.

Among those she befriended were Hollywood stars, including Kirk Douglas and his wife Anne, as well as media stars like Barbara Walters and Mike Wallace. She tended to socialize mostly with Democrats, but she made an exception in befriending Republican presidential advisor Henry Kissinger and his wife Nancy.

Hanging around such bright individuals, Parnis felt sorely her own lack of education. "I admire people who are able to express themselves well and who grasp facts fast. I read very slowly and have no background in literature or history or anything. When I'm reading, I often stop to look up a word that should be part of my vocabulary," she once lamented.

Parnis gave her formal dinners about twice a month; informal dinners more often. For years, her election-night parties drew celebrities and political figures from New York, California, and Washington. She gave up hostessing the parties when her son Robert Livingston, a theatrical producer, died in 1979.

Though she had made it in the fashion world, as well as in high society, Mollie Parnis had one enduring frustration: never having been a journalist. She was enamored of them and of their world. "If I had a choice of being president of the United States or Kay Graham [publisher of *The Washington Post*] I'd rather be Graham," she said.

In the early 1980s, Parnis dresses were selling for from $300.00 to several thousand dollars. Mollie Parnis closed down the business in 1984, partly because she was in her seventies and also because she found the business had changed, and not to her liking. "I don't like talking to a computer," she explained. "The fashion element has gone out of the business. It's so impersonal. I remember a time when, if I had a problem, I'd just call up Adam Gimbel, or Andrew Goodman, and we'd talk it over."

Mollie Parnis became a great collector of art during her lifetime and she was also interested in projects that would help both New York City and Jerusalem. She contributed part of her fortune to beautifying those two cities. She gave away at least $1.5 million through the Mollie Parnis Livingston Foundation of New York. One of her early projects was giving "Dress Up Your Neighborhood" prizes to help create vest-pocket parks and green areas in decaying New York neighborhoods.

Molly Parnis died on July 18, 1992.

$\mathcal{A}$NA $\mathcal{P}$AUKER

Romanian Communist Leader

Born in 1890 in Bucharest, Romania; died in June 1960. Romanian political leader. When Ana Pauker was appointed foreign minister of Romania in 1947, she was the first woman in modern history to achieve that position. As the intellectual leader of the Romanian Communist Party, she was the main strategist of Romanian Communism. She spent her final years under house arrest and died in obscurity.

She was born Hannah Rabinsohn. Her father, who was a rabbi, was an Orthodox kosher butcher in Bucharest, Romania. Ana, as she was known, was an excellent student. She received a traditional Jewish education, and hoped to become a physician. After a brief time in medical school she developed an interest in socialism. She taught Hebrew at a Jewish Primary School in Bucharest, but was fired for teaching more socialism than Judaism.

"She was full of spirit and utterly devoted to her ideals," according to someone who knew her then. "She was not sentimental. She never wept."

In 1918, at the age of twenty-eight, Ana was arrested for aiding the publication of secret manifestos. She spent the next two years in and out of prison, organizing Communist units and labor unions when she was free. Meanwhile, she read vociferously about Communist ideology. Her political activities led to her expulsion from Romania in 1920.

Pauker found refuge in Switzerland where she met and married Marcel Pauker, a Romanian student at the Zurich Institute of Technology. A fellow Communist, who was also Jewish, he became a journalist after completing his engineering studies.

In 1921, Pauker formally joined the Communist Party. A year later, returning to Romania, she became a member of the party's Central Committee.

The Communist Party was banned in Romania in 1924. Again, Pauker was arrested and imprisoned. Upon her release, she joined her husband in the United States where he worked with Amtorg, the Soviet trading agency. During the late 1920s, the Paukers returned to Romania. Pauker organized anti-fascist and anti-monarchist groups. She played a major role in the Grivitsa railway shop strike. Sentenced to jail once again, she escaped.

By the early 1930s, the Paukers had three children, a son and two daughters. One of the daughters died in infancy. Pauker saw very little of her children, preferring to devote herself to party affairs.

In 1935, a policeman shot her in the leg during the general anti-Communist purge. The bullet was never removed. She was charged with treason, and with leading Communist activity in Romania. Though wounded, Ana Pauker conducted her own defense. Her gallantry won her international attention. She was sentenced to ten years of hard labor.

When the Soviets occupied Bessarabia in 1940, they arranged an exchange with the

Germans, trading two Romanian members of Parliament for Ana Pauker, then the most prominent Romanian Communist being held by Germany. Soviet leader Joseph Stalin welcomed her to Moscow in 1942.

Ana and Marcel were divorced about this time. Her husband was the victim of Stalin's purge of veteran Bolsheviks. He was denounced and sent into exile as a political deviationist. Some say he was denounced with Ana Pauker's consent, perhaps even at her instigation. He was executed, accused of being a Western spy. Ana Pauker's reputation for adhering to the Party's dictates without mercy began with this incident.

Pauker remained in the Soviet Union until 1944 when Romania was invaded by the Soviets. She returned to her homeland that year during the Soviet occupation. Ana Pauker was one of the leaders of the Roman-

Courtesy of *The Jewish Chronicle*

ian Communist division of the Red Army. She wore the uniform of a major but was in fact a political commissar.

Ana Pauker attracted the attention of Europe's leading Communists, among them Russia's Stalin and Andre Vishinsky. They installed her as their watchdog in the new Eastern European satellite. She personally instigated purges.

Rising swiftly to leadership in the Romanian Communist Party after the war, Ana Pauker was a formidable speaker. She had a strong, passionate voice. She was well-versed in Socialist and Communist political theory and she was also fluent in French.

Ana Pauker was one of the most important and effective Communist leaders in postwar Romania. She organized a coalition government, the Democratic Front, under Petre Groza, which existed from 1944 to 1947. She became the secretary of the Communist party's Central Committee.

Pauker spearheaded the Communist takeover of Romania in 1946. She organized a national congress of anti-fascist women, speculating that, since women had only recently received the right to vote, they would prove an important force at the balloting box. She was right. The Communists won.

By the end of 1947, Ana Pauker was the most powerful Communist leader in Romania, the only one with direct access to Stalin. Politically, she ranked as high as Marshal Tito of Yugoslavia and Premier Georgi Dimitroff of Bulgaria.

On November 7, 1947, Pauker was appointed foreign minister. She quickly dismissed the old guard and brought Communists into key spots. She was also first deputy prime minister in the cabinet of Petre Groza.

Victorious in her political aspirations, Ana Pauker moved into a fashionable district of Bucharest, and bought a lakeside villa at Snagov. She traveled in a chauffeur-driven, bullet proof limousine. She wore expensive clothes, but no jewelry.

As Foreign Minister, Ana Pauker signed a treaty of mutual assistance with Hungary in January 1948 and with Czechoslovakia in July 1948. But she never became prime minister because her party colleagues apparently feared an anti-Semitic backlash.

Throughout 1948 and the early part of 1949, some five thousand Romanian Jews, including some members of Ana Pauker's family, were permitted to leave Romania each month for Israel.

Pauker's precise role in fostering Jewish emigration from Romania to Israel is murky. Word spread that she was unsympathetic to Zionism because she was an avowed atheist and seemingly had no strong ties to the Jewish community. In January 1950, Israeli Prime Minister David Ben-Gurion denounced her by saying, "Ana Pauker, the daughter of a rabbi, is preventing her own brethren from returning to the Promised Land." Some have said that Ben-Gurion's comment might have actually been made on Pauker's behalf to strengthen her credibility with the Romanian authorities.

However, emigration to Israel was eventually halted.

Ironically, because of this earlier period of mass emigration, Ana Pauker was expelled from the Communist Party in 1952, deprived of all her posts, and arrested. Among the charges against her was one that she favored mass emigration to Israel between 1948 and 1951. Indeed, evidence exists that suggests that she did favor emigration and had worked quietly on behalf of the Romanian Jewish Communists. One former Romanian minister noted that Pauker justified the Jewish exit by saying that she believed that aiding the Israeli struggle against British imperialism was a righteous cause, which, when implemented, applied Stalin's principle of national self-determination.

Not much is known of Pauker's life after her fall from power. She spent two years in various prisons, suffered a nervous breakdown, and was taken to a Russian sanatorium for treatment.

After Pauker was returned to Bucharest, she was placed under house arrest. It was rumored that she would have to stand trial, but in December 1954, clearly no longer a threat to the Romanian government, she was given a minor post in the Foreign Ministry. In 1959, she was listed as an employee of the Bucharest Public Library.

She lived long enough to see her former proteges in the Foreign Office come to power in Romania after Stalin's death. Ana Pauker died in June 1960.

ROBERTA PETERS

Opera Singer Who Sells Coffee

Born May 4, 1930 in New York, New York. American opera singer. Roberta Peters is one of the great coloraturas of the twentieth century. She became one of the most popular concert artists of the day and as the Metropolitan Opera's prima donna held the record for appearances by a singer on television's *The Ed Sullivan Show*, performing on his weekly show sixty-five times. Ironically, once she began making television commercials, she became better known for that than for singing opera.

The daughter of a shoe salesman, Solomon Peterman, and a milliner, Ruth (Hirsch) Peterman, Roberta was born in 1930 in New York. Her parents took notice of the child's singing abilities, but nothing came of it until she was "discovered" at the age of thirteen by the famous tenor Jan Peerce, a family friend. He advised her not to become a child prodigy, not to sing in public until she was truly ready. Upon hearing that, her parents took her to the studio of a renowned voice teacher, William Hermann.

Peters credited Hermann with helping her learn tricks that kept her voice strong for years. She noted that "He gave me the technique and taught me the ability to maintain and hold on to it. One of the things he had me sing was the Klose clarinet studies which require a sense of movement and agility." (She was still doing those exercises in the 1980s.)

Under Hermann's tutelage, Roberta devoted herself nearly full-time to developing her skills in singing, as well as taking classes in ballet, drama, and foreign languages. After she graduated from junior high school, she was given private tutoring. She does not have a high school diploma.

After six years of intensive study, the famous impresario Sol Hurok visited Hermann's studio, heard Peters sing, and promptly signed her to a contract, although she had not yet made a professional appearance. In 1950, he arranged for her to audition for Metropolitan Opera boss Rudolf Bing. Peters was only nineteen years old.

The audition was traumatic and exhausting for Peters. She recalled that "Mr. Bing made me sing 'The Queen of the Night' four times that day. He asked me if I had maybe one more high F and would I mind doing it again. I found out afterward that he had brought in a different conductor for each time around."

Bing hired her, but Peters was not scheduled to debut until the following January, 1952, in the difficult role of the Queen of the Night in Mozart's *The Magic Flute*.

But then on November 17, 1950 the phone rang in the Bronx apartment of twenty year-old Roberta Peters. On the line was Rudolf Bing. That morning, Roberta and her mother had made plans to attend a performance at the Met as standees, since they were unable to afford the price of regular tickets.

"Get into a cab immediately and come down to see me," ordered Bing. "It's important," he added mysteriously.

What could he possibly want? .

An hour later, Peters reached Broadway and 39th Street, rushed into Bing's office at the Met and, to her shock, heard him announce that prima donna Nadine Connor had taken ill suddenly. He asked her to replace Connor, playing Zerline in Mozart's *Don Giovanni.*

Peters' face turned white. Searching for breath, her heart began to race. Never before had she faced an opera audience, nor had she sung with a company of other singers, never had she sung with an orchestra.

No matter.

"Yes," she whispered to Bing, she would take the prima donna's place.

Consulting with the renowned conductor Fritz Reiner, Bing made preparations for Peters' debut. Costumes had to be altered or improvised. Peters would have to wear Connor's shoes. "We're going to the opera tonight," Peters informed her mother. "But not as standees. I'll be on the stage and you'll have a seat in the front."

Roberta Peters' performance created a sensation. The audience stood and cheered; the critics loved her. Peters' career was launched. With her even, warm tone, and her ability to sing the most difficult roles, Peters took on important coloratura parts, winning praise whenever she sang. She has been hailed as well for her memorable performances in Puccini's *La Boheme* and Verdi's *La Traviata.*

Leading composers, such as Roy Harris and Aram Khachaturian, have dedicated works to Peters. She has also appeared in lighter fare: operettas on tour and summer theater including productions of *The King and I* and *The Merry Widow.*

In April 1955 she married Bertram Fields, a hotel executive. They have two sons, Paul Adam, born in April 1957 and Bruce Eric, born in December 1959. Neither son went into opera as a profession, but they frequently went to hear their mother sing.

When Peters became pregnant the first time, Sol Hurok threw a fit. "He turned green, blue and purple," Peters remembered. "He was terribly upset—he said I'd lose my voice." She did not lose her voice, but she did drop out of the Met for that season.

In 1960, Peters appeared on stage in Russia during the American U-2 spy plane crisis, when an American espionage plane was caught spying over Russian territory. "Despite the bitter propaganda drive against the United States, the Russian audiences were among the friendliest and warmest I've ever encountered," she recalled.

Showing up in Israel at the time of the 1967 Six-Day War, Peters was deeply impressed: "Its people—soldiers, civilians, men and women—were magnificent—all ready to fight and die for their country. I'm filled with admiration for them."

Broadening her public appeal across the U.S. were her many appearances on *The Ed Sullivan Show,* the Sunday night television variety program, on which Peters performed sixty-five times. She also appeared twenty-five times on the *Voice of Firestone,* another popular television show of the 1950s.

Among contemporary sopranos, few could equal Roberta Peters' record for endurance: In 1980, when she was fifty years old, she celebrated her thirtieth year with the Metropolitan Opera, the longest career of any coloratura in the Met's history.

By the 1980s, recitals and concerts occupied much of Peters' time, as she was eager to demonstrate that she was more than just an opera singer. She averaged forty recitals and concerts a season.

Feeling vocally "stretched" in 1981, Peters began to sense a tightness in her sound when she performed. She returned to study with her old accompanist George Trovillo, who had retired to San Diego. Why did she need a trainer so late in the game? "I need someone with ears just for me, someone to go over things—refresh and refine." After a few sessions, Peters declared: "Now I feel wonderful and am singing as well as I want to."

In 1985, Peters no longer sang "The Queen of the Night" arias—they were restricted to the practice room. But she still performs the role of Lucia in *Lucia di Lammermoor* and did Gilda in Verdi's *Rigoletto* at the Met.

Courtesy of ICM Artists, New York

Peters is best known to many Americans who do not go to the Metropolitan Opera, but who do watch television, for a series of television commercials she did for a type of credit card and a coffee manufacturer. To many viewers, she was "the coffee lady."

Peters believes that young singers do not give themselves sufficient time before starting a career, but she acknowledges that she herself appeared in public when "barely out of puberty. It's a tribute to my teachers. You have to have the voice to begin with—that is perhaps inborn. But you also have to have the intelligence to understand what is being taught."

MOLLY PICON

First Lady of the Yiddish Theater

> **Born June 1, 1898 in New York, New York; died April 5, 1992.**
> American actress. Molly Picon was the darling of the Yiddish musical
> stage when it flourished in America between the 1920s and 1950s,
> performing mostly at the Second Avenue Theatre in Manhattan. She
> has been called the "First Lady of the Yiddish Theater." Small, slight,
> with an impish face, she starred in the Broadway musical *Milk and
> Honey* in 1961.

Molly Picon was born in New York City in 1898. Her father Lewis, who had been a rabbinical student in his native Warsaw, worked in the garment industry after immigrating to the United States. Molly's mother Clara (Ostrow) Picon was a seamstress from Kiev who sewed costumes for actresses performing in Yiddish theater productions in Philadelphia, where the family had settled. Because of her mother's connection to the theater, Molly began acting on stage as a child.

At the age of five, Molly performed in a children's amateur night at the local Bijou Theater, which was usually a burlesque house. "I always had a bit of ham in me, God forgive me," she said in 1980, "and I'd sing and dance and do somersaults in front of them when they came for fittings." An actress had suggested that Molly's mother take the five-year-old to the burlesque theater where they had amateur nights for children. A five-dollar gold piece was first prize. Molly's mother dressed her in a fancy dress and they set out.

"Why is the child all dressed up?" an inebriated man asked Molly's mother as they made their way to the theater on the trolley. "So she can sing and dance and win five dollars," Molly's mother replied. The man was skeptical, so Molly's mother urged the child to perform right then and there.

Impressed, the man passed a hat and collected money. "That was my first paid professional performance," Molly Picon recalled. Later that evening she won the gold piece, taking home a grand total of ten dollars counting the coins the audience threw on stage after her performance.

For the next three years, Molly appeared in Yiddish versions of *Uncle Tom's Cabin*, *Shulamite Gabriel*, *Sappho*, and other productions.

By the age of seventeen, Molly had finished three years at William Penn High School in Philadelphia, but had quit to join an English-language stock company in Philadelphia. She appeared in a Boston vaudeville act during the 1918-1919 season, but an outbreak of influenza forced the Boston theaters to close. Picon suddenly found herself unemployed and broke. She sought aid through the local Yiddish troupe, which was still performing. And so she returned to the Yiddish theater where she then spent most of her early career, becoming a major comic star. She wrote or contributed to creating some of her own songs and character sketches.

Molly Picon rose to prominence under the management of her husband Jacob

Kalich, whom she married in 1919 at the age of twenty-one. She became the star of the Yiddish musical stage, which performed on lower Second Avenue in Manhattan from the 1920s to the 1950s. During those years twelve downtown Yiddish theaters produced many plays.

From 1921 to 1923, Kalich arranged for Picon to tour throughout Europe. Returning to New York afterward, she

Molly Picon appearing in the 1923 movie East and West.

starred on Second Avenue for eight more years, in *Zipke* in 1924; *Mamele* in 1925; *Molly Dolly* in 1926, and other well-received plays.

Kalich wrote or adapted more than forty of Picon's starring vehicles, starting with the operetta *Yankele,* which was a smash hit when it opened at the Second Avenue Theater in 1923.

In the early years of the Yiddish theater the first act of many plays took place in Europe, the second in America, essentially focusing on the theme of immigration, which included acknowledging the longing that families had for what had been left behind. However, "After the Holocaust," said Molly Picon, "there wasn't anything that anyone looked for any more, so the themes became more American."

In 1949, Molly Picon retired, for the first but not the only time, as she would "return" countless more times later. "We decided we had enough for what we want, so we bought a beautiful house in New York state with a swimming pool and a Turkish bath. I love gardening and I raised some beautiful tomatoes. One day a few weeks after we retired, I brought one into the house. I was so proud of growing it myself. And Yankele (her husband) said, 'It's beautiful, Molly, but there's only one trouble with it. Tomatoes don't applaud.'"

Molly Picon boasted that she had the only Yiddish swimming pool in the world. At three feet the poolside sign said: A *mechaye;* at five, *Oi vei* and at ten feet, *Gevalt.*

Picon also performed "uptown" on stages in Manhattan's theater district in vaudeville, and on singing tours. She became a radio personality and was featured on *Maxwell Hour Coffee Time,* which aired on WEVD from 1932 to 1951. Picon's first starring role on Broadway came in *Morning Star* in 1940. She played the role of a Jewish immigrant mother. Although the play received only fair reviews, Picon's performance was praised.

211

Molly Picon in the movie Come Blow Your Horn.

In the 1930s Picon toured abroad again—to Europe, Palestine, South Africa, and Latin America. In 1936, in Warsaw, she acted in a film called *Yiddle with His Fiddle* for a Polish-Yiddish film company.

After World War II, Picon, with her husband, again traveled throughout Europe, this time to perform for Jews who had survived the Holocaust. With them, Molly Picon and her husband brought several hundred packages of cosmetics, jewelry, and candy to give the people they met in displaced-persons camps, hospitals, and orphanages. To Picon, those were her greatest days. "We met people who hadn't laughed in seven years and who laughed for the first time. It gave them a sense of normalcy again, to come together and see who was still alive. That was six months of great nights."

Back in the United States, she appeared on Broadway in the comedy *For Heaven's Sake, Mother* in 1948. In 1949 she returned to Second Avenue to star in *Abi Gezunt,* her first Yiddish play in many years. During the early 1950s she toured Israel, performing Yiddish shows. In the late 1950s she was featured in such plays as *Farblonjet Honeymoon* and *The Kosher Woman.*

Picon bemoaned the waning of the Yiddish theater in the early 1960s: "Yiddish is more than a language. It means warmth, family feeling, togetherness, the custom of charity. We were raised from childhood to take care of our own, to spend Friday nights with grandma and participate in the services. We were not very religious, but we were very Yiddish-minded, and it kept us together." As the Yiddish theater declined, Picon turned to ethnic Jewish roles offered her on Broadway and in films.

Picon's most successful role was as the American widow Clara Weiss searching for a husband in Israel in the 1961 hit Broadway musical *Milk and Honey.* It ran for two seasons.

In 1967, she appeared in an off-off-Broadway review entitled *How to Be a Jewish Mother.* Four years later, she appeared as Dolly Gallagher Levi in *Hello, Dolly!* in a touring company of the popular musical.

Picon's autobiography, *So Laugh a Little* appeared in 1962. It detailed the first sixty-four years of her acting life. But there was still more to come.

Picon's film roles in the 1960s and 1970s included parts in *Come Blow Your Horn* in 1963; *Fiddler on the Roof,* playing the colorful character role of Yente, *The Matchmaker* in 1970; and *For Pete's Sake* in 1974.

Molly Picon died in April 1992 at the age of ninety-four.

SYLVIA PORTER

America's Most Famous Economic Reporter

Born June 18, 1913 in Patchogue, New York; died June 5, 1991. American journalist, financial expert and consumers' advocate. Sylvia Porter was America's most widely read economic reporter for four decades. Her personal-finance column was syndicated by the *Los Angeles Times* in over four-hundred newspapers and had an estimated readership of forty million people. Porter began writing her daily column of financial information and advice in 1936 while she was financial editor of the *New York Post*. She wrote over twenty books, including *Sylvia Porter's Money Book*. In 1979, for the third straight year, she was named by the *World Almanac* as one of America's twenty-five most influential women. She was chosen by the *Ladies' Home Journal* as one of the eleven most important women of the 1970s.

Born in Patchogue on Long Island, New York in 1913, Sylvia was the only daughter of Russian-Jewish immigrants, Louis Feldman, a physician, and Rose (Maisel) Feldman.

According to Porter, she and her brother had a secure, middle-class childhood within a family that "didn't think it was unfeminine for a girl to think. If anything we rather thought that intelligence added to womanliness." Her mother encouraged Sylvia to take up a career. At age six, Sylvia wrote a piece of fiction called *My Public,* an early indication that she might want to become a writer.

While Sylvia was still a child, her father moved the family to Brooklyn. He practiced medicine there until he died of a heart attack in 1925. Sylvia attended Public School 99, skipping the sixth grade. She went to James Madison High School in Brooklyn, graduating in 1929. Though only sixteen, she enrolled at the all-female Hunter College where she planned to major in English literature and history as preparation for becoming a writer.

In the fall of 1929, while Porter was a college freshman, the stock market crashed. Her mother lost $30,000 in the crash, after which Porter decided to study the American financial system in order to find out how people had managed to lose so much money. She immediately switched her major to economics.

Porter won every cash prize given to economics students. In her junior year she was named a Phi Beta Kappa. In 1931, she married Reed R. Porter, a bank employee. The next year, she graduated from Hunter

magna cum laude with a bachelor of arts degree.

Porter became an assistant to Arthur William Glass of the just-opened investment counseling firm Glass & Krey on Wall Street. Working there, and later for other firms, she acquired her knowledge of the bond markets, business cycles, and currency fluctuations. She also took graduate courses at New York University's School of Business Administration.

Porter wrote for some financial journals under the byline S.F. Porter, concealing the fact that she was a woman, trying to penetrate the mostly-male domain of economics. Early in 1934, Porter began a weekly column on the American government securities market that was published in *American Banker* magazine. That year and the next, she operated her own advisory service on United States government bonds.

In 1935, *The New York Post* hired Porter to write an occasional column of financial news. She was soon given the regular Wall Street beat. In 1938 she became financial editor, the same year she began writing a daily column called "Financial Post Marks". It was soon changed to "S. F. Porter Says."

In her columns, Porter tried to educate her readers about the stock market during a period when that institution had suffered a loss of self-confidence. She pointed to economic injustices, which was easy, she said later, "because there were so many of them."

One of her most famous assaults was unleashed against the U.S. Secretary of the Treasury, Henry Morgenthau, Jr. in an article in *American Banker*. She took him to task for his handling of the new government bonds market and asked if his annual "lapses into disharmony" were due to his "obstinacy, stupidity, or sheer ill advice."

Morgenthau, upon discovering that Sylvia Porter was a woman, sent her roses. Senator Edwin Johnson sent no roses after she attacked his silver policy. He called her "the biggest liar in the United States."

In 1936, she exposed a bond market racket, succeeding in getting the U.S. Treasury Department to intervene.

Porter's first book, *How to Make Money in Government Bonds,* published in 1939, offered advice on investing to both average citizens and investment counselors.

In her second book, written in 1941 and called *If War Comes to the American Home,* she advised readers how to adjust their finances to a war economy. "Facts, figures, broad word pictures and succinct arguments are all presented with conversational ease," wrote a reviewer for *The New York Times* on May 2, 1941.

In 1942, Porter's editor at *The New York Post* decided that her gender was an asset, so that it was acceptable to change her byline to Sylvia F. Porter. With the change of byline, Porter became even more prominent. In 1947, her newspaper column became nationally syndicated.

Porter's column was titled simply "Sylvia Porter" and attracted some forty million readers. Economists, business people, and politicians had great respect for her. One of her syndicated columns once received 150,000 letters.

In 1944, Porter founded a weekly newsletter for the banking and securities community, and called it "Report on Governments." She became a consumer advocate long before others used the term. She tried to clarify financial matters for the average person and to cut through what she termed "bafflegab"—the obscure terminology of finance and government. She refused to call herself a true economist, but tried to speak to consumers directly. "They should all be able to understand what I write," she told *The New York Daily News* on July 24, 1979. "I'm insulted when somebody doesn't."

In her column, Porter gave advice on such topics as to how and when to take vacations for less money; how to finance higher-quality medical care without getting into financial trouble; how to structure a budget for a family that was growing; how to decorate a home or an apartment. Beginning in 1960, Porter published an annual tax guide. In 1962, President John F. Kennedy named her to his newly created Consumer Advisory Council. During the Johnson Administration, the President often invited her to dinner at the White House until she grew to dislike the Vietnam War, of which Lyndon B. Johnson had been the chief architect. Vowing from that point on to remain aloof from politics, in 1974 she broke her promise to herself and agreed to participate in President Gerald R. Ford's economic summit.

Porter spent five years preparing a 1,105-page book called *Sylvia Porter's Money Book: How to Earn It, Spend It, Invest It, Borrow It, and Use It to Better Your Life*. Published in 1975, it was a bestseller.

Porter was named a contributing editor to the *Ladies Home Journal* magazine in 1965. From 1961 to 1979 she served on the board of editors of *The World Encyclopedia Yearbook*.

In 1978, after more than thirty years with *The New York Post*, Sylvia Porter moved to *The New York Daily News* where she continued to write her column five times a week.

The next year, Porter was named Woman of the Year in Finance by the first annual Women in Finance Conference. For the third straight year, in 1979 she was named by the *World Almanac* as one of America's twenty-five most influential women.

Porter was married three times. She had a daughter and a stepson. Porter died in 1991 at the age of seventy-eight.

SALLY PRIESAND

First Female Rabbi in the United States

Born June 27, 1946 in Cleveland, Ohio. American Reform rabbi. In 1972, Sally Priesand became the first female rabbi in the United States and the first woman to be ordained by a theological seminary. She encountered resistance to the idea of her holding a pulpit initially, but eventually she was accepted, paving the way for other women to serve in the rabbinate. In 1979, Priesand became the rabbi at Congregation Beth El in Elizabeth, New Jersey. Rabbi Priesand's ordination revolutionized Judaism and helped the Conservative movement to decide to ordain women as rabbis in 1981.

Sally Priesand was born in Cleveland, Ohio, the daughter of Irving Welch, a construction engineer, and his wife Rosetta. She attended a Conservative synagogue, experiencing the traditional attitude that a woman's place was in the home, raising children.

As a child Sally wanted to become a teacher. By the age of sixteen, she had decided that it was Judaism she that wanted to teach. Priesand received a B.A. degree in English from the University of Cincinnati in 1968 and a Bachelor of Hebrew Letters in 1971 from the Hebrew Union College-Jewish Institute of Religion (HUC-JIR) in Cincinnati. She received a Master of Arts in Hebrew Letters in 1972, also from HUC-JIR.

When Priesand entered HUC-JIR, she thought little of her role as a pioneer, only that she wanted to become a rabbi. "I didn't do this to champion women's rights," Priesand said. "My feminism came a little bit later. I think it was there, but when you're trying to accomplish a goal, you have to focus in on what you're doing."

Sally's parents supported her goals enthusiastically. "My decision was an affirmation of my belief in God, in the worth of each individual, and in Judaism as a way of life," Sally Priesand commented. "It was a tangible action declaring my commitment to the preservation and renewal of our tradition."

How did she find the determination and courage to be the only woman student at HUC-JIR? She displayed the answer, four words engraved on a letter opener someone gave her as a gift: "Say little, do much."

Since HUC-JIR had no housing for women, Priesand lived off-campus. Her male colleagues taped lectures she missed when making speeches as the first woman rabbinical student. Of her ambitions, she wrote: "Undoubtedly, many believed that I was studying at HUC-JIR to become a *rebbezin* (the wife of a rabbi) rather than a rabbi. Four years passed before people began to realize that I was serious about entering the rabbinate." Priesand felt that she had to outshine her classmates so that no one would question her academic ability. "I was always conscious of being the best," she told the authors of this book. "I had very high standards. I felt if they were going to get rid of me, it wouldn't be because of my grades." Priesand judged her professors to be fair, but on occasion she sensed that some "would not be overly upset" if she had failed.

Priesand served as a visiting student rabbi—a requirement of rabbinical students at HUC-JIR—at synagogues in Hattiesburg, Mississippi and Jackson, Michigan.

When she was ordained on June 3, 1972, Sally Priesand became the first female rabbi in the United States. She was also the first woman to be ordained by a theological seminary. Other women have served as rabbis, ordained by rabbis in private, but none had been ordained in public at a theological seminary. Classmates gave her a standing ovation at the ordination ceremony.

As Priesand sat in the historic Plum Street Temple, waiting to accept *s'micha* (ordination), she reflected on the implications of this act. "For thousands of years women in Judaism had been second-class citizens," she wrote later. "They were not

Rabbi Priesand greets Passover in 1973.

permitted to own property. They could not serve as witnesses. They did not have the right to initiate divorce proceedings. They were not counted in the *minyan*. Even in Reform Judaism, they were not permitted to participate fully in the life of the synagogue. With my ordination all that was going to change; one more barrier was about to be broken."

Playing down her personal ambitions, Priesand insisted that "I didn't decide to do this so that I would be the first woman rabbi or to carry a torch for the feminist movement. I had always wanted to teach, and simply realized that what I wanted to teach was Judaism."

In her first pulpit Priesand served as assistant rabbi at the Stephen Wise Free Synagogue in New York City; later she became an associate rabbi there. During her seven years at Stephen Wise, she conducted services, giving a sermon on each Sabbath, and taught in the adult institute, supervised the youth program, and attended all committee meetings.

Seeking her own pulpit was not easy for Priesand. Of the twelve synagogues to which she applied, nine rejected her without an interview. That led her to write that "We tread on dangerous ground when we separate the contributions that women can make from those that men can make....When congregations hire women rabbis, they ought to be asking 'What does she as an individual have to offer?'" rather than, "What does she as a woman have to offer?"

In August 1979, Priesand was offered and took the pulpit of Congregation Beth El in Elizabeth, New Jersey, serving there for four years. She also served as chaplain at Manhattan's Lenox Hill Hospital.

Despite her own achievement, Priesand knew that much more needed to be done to give women equal status with men within Judaism. "Words must be supplemented by deeds," she argued. "If the Reform Jewish community is unable to install women in roles of leadership, as examples to others, then what we're doing is giving a double message to our congregations...disproportionately few women are represented in the upper echelons of the Reform Movement."

She added: "Men and women must learn to overcome their own psychological and emotional objections and regard every human being as a real person with talents and skills and with the option of fulfilling his or her creative potential in any way he or she finds meaningful. Women can aid this process—not by arguing but by doing and becoming, for accomplishments bring respect and respect leads to acceptance. Women must now take the initiative. They should seek and willingly accept new positions of authority in synagogue life."

Since 1981, Priesand has served as the full-time rabbi of the Monmouth, New Jersey, Reform Temple. She is single and lives in Eatontown, New Jersey.

Being the "first" woman rabbi in America, Sally Priesand was expected to have an expert opinion on a wide range of issues. "Surprisingly enough, though I have always considered myself an introvert, I somehow managed to cope with these new pressures," she said. An avid supporter of the Equal Rights Amendment, Priesand has been politically active on a number of fronts. For instance, she opposes the spread of nuclear power plants.

She has written numerous articles and in 1975, authored a book called *Judaism and the New Woman.*

Since 1972, the Hebrew Union College-Jewish Institute of Religion has ordained 771 rabbis, 185 of them women, a figure Rabbi Priesand describes as "good." The entering classes at HUC-JIR in the early 1990s were fifty percent female.

In 1978, Priesand was named as one of the Extraordinary Women of Achievement by the National Conference of Christians and Jews.

HANNAH RACHEL

The Maid of Ludomir

Born in 1815 in Ludomir, Poland; died in 1892. Hasidic rebbe. The most famous of the Hasidic women rebbes, "The Maid of Ludomir," as Hannah Rachel came to be called, became legendary. Thousands of men and women made pilgrimages to her *bet ha-midrash*, among them learned men, rabbis and other *tsaddikim* (righteous ones). Eventually, a special group of Hasidim formed a group calling itself "Hasidim of The Maid of Ludomir." The first Hasidic leader to settle in the Holy Land, Hannah dreamt of hastening the arrival of the Messiah and sought to accomplish it in her time. Known as a miracle worker, she had curative powers.

Hasidism was founded in the early eighteenth century in the Ukraine by a man named Israel Baal Shem Tov (or, in abbreviated form, the Besht). He taught that all Jews were valued equally before God, scholars as well as the uneducated. He also taught that prayers and humility were as important and perhaps more important to God than intellectual achievements. The true way to serve God, he taught, was through happiness and joyous song.

After the death of the Besht, his disciples, known as rebbes or tsaddikim, continued the movement. The most important of all the Hasidic women rebbes was Hannah Rachel. She was born in Ludomir, Poland, in 1815 and was described in Hasidic legends as "The Maid of Ludomir."

Hannah was an only child. Her father Monesh Webemacher was prosperous and educated. The parental attention usually given to an eldest son was focused on her. Accordingly, she received far more education than the other young girls who were her contemporaries. She excelled in all her Jewish studies, including Midrash (the ethical and devotional explanation of biblical texts). She also studied Aggadah and Musar. She prayed with ecstatic emotion, which was seen as an early sign of her mystical powers.

Numerous matchmakers, knowing of her father's wealth and position, approached him to secure Hannah's hand in marriage.

Hannah, however, fell in love with someone. She wanted to be with him alone, to tell him of her feelings for him, but couples could not meet privately before marriage. She urged her father to let her marry her hearts' choice. Moved by her pleas, he agreed to let Hannah marry her young man from Ludomir.

When Hannah Rachel's mother died, Hannah Rachel was morose, remaining in her room throughout each day, leaving only to visit the grave of her mother. At the gravesite, Hannah wept uncontrollably.

Legend tells that at one especially emotional visit to her mother's grave, she fell asleep, then awoke amidst darkness and the eerie shapes and shadows of the graveyard. Running home, she stumbled over a headstone and fell into a partially dug grave, a frightening experience. She began screaming, then fainted. An old sexton heard her and carried her back home where she went into shock, and hovered near death for a long time. She did not speak for days. The doctors lost all hope for her survival. One day she asked for her father, and told him that she had just returned from Heaven, where she had sat before the highest court and received a fresh, exalted soul. A few days later, she totally recovered.

Although only men wore fringes and prayer shawls, Hannah, too, donned these garments and put on *tefillin*, the small leather boxes which contain parchment on which biblical selections are inscribed. She passed the entire day studying the Torah and praying. Despite Hannah's love for her betrothed, the marriage was called off. She began to observe the religious duties of Jewish males.

Soon thereafter, her father died. Hannah Rachel recited the traditional mourner's prayer, the *Kaddish*, for him, again taking on the role reserved by Jewish law for male mourners. With her father's fortune, Hannah built a new *bet ha-midrash* (prayer and study house) and adjoining living quarters for herself.

Hannah spent all week praying and studying the Torah in her quarters. Each Sabbath, at the *Se'udah Shelishit* (third meal of the Sabbath), she opened the door to her apartment and gave scholarly discourses to the Hasidim who had gathered there to listen.

The Maid of Ludomir, as she was now called, became renowned. Men and women by the thousands made pilgrimages to her *bet ha-midrash*, among them learned men, rabbis and other *tsaddikim*. In time, a Hasidic group called "Hasidim of The Maid of Ludomir" was formed.

Hannah Rachel acquired the reputation of being a miracle worker who could cure the sick. To those ill people who visited her, she gave curative herbs. Praying in her bet *ha-midrash*, her followers treated her as a *tsaddik* (righteous one).

Some *tsaddikim* were discomfited by The Maid of Ludomir, convinced an evil spirit lurked inside her. Some may have simply been jealous or fearful that other Jewish women would imitate her, especially by not marrying, thus threatening Jewish survival. Hence, The Maid of Ludomir was encouraged to marry but she spurned all offers.

At the age of forty, Hannah finally gave in to the pressure of a celebrated *tsaddik*, Rabbi Mordechai of Czernobiel, and agreed to marry his choice for a husband—a Talmudic scholar. It is not clear why she succumbed to pressure at this time, at an advanced age for women of her time. Some speculated that she may have wanted to give birth to a "savior of Israel."

After her marriage, Hannah's influence declined. The marriage soon ended in divorce. She then emigrated to Palestine. Once in the Holy Land, she met a well-known Kabbalist. They resolved to end the Jewish exile and hasten the coming of the Messiah. Both prepared painstakingly for that day.

The time was set. The Maid of Ludomir arrived on time at a cave outside Jerusalem that was to serve as the appointed place for the arrival of the Messiah. A third man arrived as well; Jewish law required him to be present since a man and woman could not be alone in a secluded place.

But, the story goes, the Kabbalist, who was elderly, did not reach the cave although he had left in time for the rendezvous. Near his home he met an elderly Jew with a flowing, white beard who asked the Kabbalist for some food. The Kabbalist invited the stranger into his home, eager to be hospitable. Once the two men started to talk, the Kabbalist totally forgot his appointment with the Maid of Ludomir. The old man, who sabotaged the meeting with Hannah was Elijah, the prophet, in disguise. And thus the Maid of Ludomir's plan to hasten the Messianic era failed.

The Maid of Ludomir fit into the tradition of mysticism, which was the foundation of Hasidism. She was scholarly and she possessed incredible charisma. Most importantly, she was able to overcome the limitations imposed on Jewish women of the time. Some contend that had she remained married, she might have become one of the greatest of the rebbes. Nonetheless, she was a remarkable Hasidic leader and the first to settle in the Holy Land.

JUDITH RESNICK

"Being an Astronaut was Her Religion"

Born April 5, 1949 in Cleveland, Ohio; died January 29, 1986.
American astronaut. One of three mission specialists, Judith Resnick was on the ill-fated American space shuttle Challenger, which exploded in space on January 29, 1986. The seven astronauts aboard all died. While she was the first Jewish astronaut, Judith Resnick disliked being labeled as such. She was neither the first woman in space, nor the first American woman, but she was unquestionably the first Jewish astronaut.

Judith Resnick was the granddaughter of Jacob Resnick of Kiev who, with his wife, fled Ukraine in 1924 and emigrated to Palestine. Their son, Judith's father Marvin, grew up in an Orthodox Jewish environment and studied in a yeshiva in Hebron in Palestine as a child. He survived the Arab attack against the Hebron Jewish community in 1929. That same year, Judith's grandparents moved to Cleveland where Jacob became a *shochet* (or ritual slaughterer).

Though born in Cleveland, Judith grew up in Akron, Ohio. Her parents made sure that she received a Jewish education. She had a bat mitzvah and attended Sunday and Hebrew school classes until her high school graduation. Resnick's parents were divorced when she was seventeen.

Judith practiced the piano for an hour each day, although sometimes she hated it. In time, however, she became proficient in playing classical music.

At Akron's Firestone High School, Judith was a member of the school's honor society, the French club, the chemistry club and the math club (the only girl among fifteen boys). Known for her incredible math ability, Judith had perfect scores of 800 on both her verbal and math Scholastic Aptitude Tests. "I can still see this little, short brunette in bobby socks and saddle shoes, quiet as a mouse," her math teacher Donald Nutter said in 1986. "If you had a question no one else could answer, you could call on her."

Courtesy of NASA

Because of her math and science skills, many colleges wanted Judith. She chose Carnegie-Mellon University in Pittsburgh where she received her degree in electrical engineering in 1970. Resnick's personal goals were, as she said: "To learn a lot about quite a number of different technologies, to be able to use them somehow, to do something that required a concerted team effort and, finally, a great individual effort."

She got her wish in March 1978. While working for Xerox, Judith Resnick was chosen as one of six women in a group of thirty-five space-shuttle astronaut candidates. More than 8,000 people applied for the program. Judith Resnick noted that "This is the first semester since I was four that I haven't been in school." That same year, she married a fellow engineering student, Michael Radak, but they separated five years later.

Resnick obtained work as a design engineer with the RCA Corporation in Moorestown, New Jersey. She also worked as a biomedical engineer at the National Institutes of Health in Bethesda, Maryland. In 1977, Judith received her doctorate from the University of Maryland. She then went to work for the Xerox Corporation as a senior systems engineer in El Segunda, California.

According to one of Judith's professors in graduate school, she was consistently the first to begin work in the morning, and always the most industrious. She was very knowledgeable about computers at a time when few others were.

Though not a practicing Jew, Judith said in an interview that her Jewish roots were strong. As an adult, she no longer attended synagogue. She had never visited Israel, but she retained a rudimentary knowledge of Hebrew later in life. When it became clear that Judith was to become an astronaut, Jewish scholars thought it prudent to decide on what kind of Jew she should be in space. According to former Chief Rabbi Shlomo Goren, it would not be necessary for Judith to light Sabbath candles while there. Goren explained that, since time is calculated on earth according to the sun and moon, it cannot have an effect on persons traveling in space. Hence, a Jew cannot celebrate the Sabbath and holidays in space.

"Astronauts," Judith Resnick once said, "don't have to be either very feminine or very masculine women, or very superhuman males, or any color or anything. It's about people in space." Dr. Marvin Resnick, Judith's father, said soon after her death in early 1986 that "while religion played no part in Judy's life and she resented being referred to as 'the Jewish astronaut,' there is no question that she felt Jewish and knew she was Jewish, but she didn't want to...participate in the amenities of Jewish life. Judy was totally dedicated to her life as an astronaut. That was her whole religion. Her life was dedicated to the exploration of space. She was doing the thing she loved."

In 1984, Judith Resnick went into space for the first time. Aboard her first shuttle flight, on the Discovery, she served as a mission specialist, operating the spacecraft's remote-control arm and performing solar-power experiments with a 102-foot-high solar sail. One of the tasks was to point a camera on the orbiting craft's long robotic arm to inspect initial efforts to shake a chunk of ice off the side of the shuttle.

"The earth looks great," she commented over the radio after going into orbit.

Television cameras aboard Discovery caught her — in polo shirt and shorts — focusing on her tasks, with her long, curly, dark brown hair wafting above her head at zero gravity. That image proved one of the best-known in space program history. On the ill-

Courtesy of NASA

Judith Resnick in a T-38 aircraft at the Ellington Air Force base in 1978.

fated American space shuttle Challenger, Resnick was one of three mission specialists. Her assignment was to help take photographs of Halley's Comet, among other tasks. She was also carrying a signet ring for a nephew and a heart-shaped locket for a niece. "I think something is only dangerous if you are not prepared for it," she said of space travel, "or if you don't have control over it or if you can't think through how to get yourself out of a problem."

Until then, Resnick had spent 144 hours and 57 minutes in space.

The Challenger exploded into a huge fireball moments after it lifted off at Cape Canaveral, Florida, the worst disaster in the American space program's history.

Among the mourners was Ohio Governor Richard Celeste who spoke at Temple Israel in Akron, telling Resnick's parents and friends: "She knew she would be at home in space. And she was. And she is."

Resnick's father noted in an interview then that "Despite what happened yesterday, I felt that the space program definitely should continue, and I know Judy would feel the same way. One little mistake or whatever it was that caused [the explosion] should not interfere with a program that has produced such fantastic results in the sciences."

Not the first woman in space (that was the Soviet Union's Valentina Tereshkova in 1963). And not the first American woman in space (that was Sally Ride in 1983). Resnick, however, was perhaps the most determined. "I want to do everything there is to be done."

ERNESTINE ROSE

Queen of the Platform

Born January 13, 1810 in Pyeterkow, Poland; died August 4, 1892. Nineteenth-century suffragette. A headstrong rebel from childhood, Ernestine Rose petitioned a Polish court successfully to have her inheritance reinstated after her father forfeited it when she refused to marry the man of his choice. She also circulated the first petition for the property rights of women. In 1837 she appeared before the New York State Legislature, championing the passage of this statute, a fight she pursued for nine years. She was called radical for espousing such unpopular causes as women's rights, the abolition of slavery, and free public education.

Ernestine Rose was born in 1810 in the Jewish ghetto in Pyeterkow, Poland and named Sismondi Potowski. She was the daughter of a rabbi. She preferred reading and studying to sewing and cooking and begged her father to give her an education.

Going against the traditional role of women, Ernestine spent long hours studying the Scriptures. At the age of fourteen, she shocked her Orthodox Jewish community by revealing many doubts about her religion. She questioned the purpose of self-denial as an act that gave pleasure to God. She began to advocate equal rights for women in all phases of communal life.

At the age of sixteen, Ernestine won her father's consent to study on her own. He engaged a private tutor for her.

Her mother died that same year. Ernestine inherited a large dowry. Her father wanted her to marry someone much older than she, but she pleaded with the prospective groom not to marry her. Ernestine's father told her that if she refused to marry the man, her dowry would automatically be forfeited to the suitor. She brought suit before the Polish High Tribunal at Kalish, making history by pleading her own case. The court accepted her arguments; she received her mother's inheritance.

Ernestine's father decided to marry a woman about Ernestine's age. With her own money, Ernestine was able to buy her way out of Pyeterkow, Poland, never to return. Thus, at the age of seventeen, she left home, hoping to become a supporter of humanitarian causes. Ernestine traveled throughout Western Europe at her own expense, speaking out about a wide variety of reforms she supported. She visited Poland, Russia, Germany, Holland, Belgium, France, and England.

Ernestine Rose was shocked to find that Polish Jews could not reside in Germany. While traveling through Europe, Rose sought an audience with the Prussian monarch Frederick III to complain about his harsh treatment of Jews. When the king agreed to see her, she told him that his treatment of the Jews was both inhumane and unjust. Impressed, the king permitted her to remain in Germany for as long as she wished. She invented an air freshener and lived on the profits from the sales.

In June 1829, Rose left Germany, at age nineteen, and traveled on to Holland, Belgium, and France. In Paris, she witnessed the 1830 Revolution. Three years later, she traveled to London, living there and studying English as well as teaching Hebrew and German.

In 1832, Rose came under the influence of the renowned social reformer Robert Owen, the founder of Utopian Socialism, who was sixty years old at the time. Owen believed that man was the product of his environment. Surround him with poor conditions, and he will turn to evil; surround him with good, and he will be good. He set up communes—a good environment that would encourage people to be good — to prove his point. Following Owen's doctrine, Ernestine established the Association of All Classes of All Nations, a pioneer group that championed human rights for all. The group rejected formal religion; by adopting this radical creed, Rose broke with her own religion though she always considered herself part of the Jewish people. Ernestine met William H. Rose, a jeweler and silversmith who was a fervent disciple of Owen. They married and left England for the United States in 1836.

In America, Ernestine Rose focused her efforts on promoting racial and sexual equality. She was disappointed to find that American women were not much better off then their European counterparts. She became an abolitionist and spoke out against slavery despite the dangers involved in lecturing on the subject, particularly in the South.

She campaigned for property rights for women, women's suffrage, and more liberal divorce laws. The press and clergy were anti-feminist at the time. Women's rights were conveniently equated with the advocating of "free love." Clergymen would appear at rallies and use biblical quotes to "prove" that women were inferior to men.

In 1850, Rose was elected a delegate to the first National Women's Rights Convention in Worcester, Massachusetts. There she met such liberal leaders as William Lloyd Garrison, Julia Ward Howe and Wendell Phillips. Rose was a delegate to all the Women's Rights conventions for the next thirty years.

Ernestine Rose was often in the center of controversy. For example, in Bangor, Maine, a heated fight broke out between two clergymen, one who did not want Ernestine Rose to speak in the town, the other who did. Rose's critic accused her of being both an atheist and a Jewess. He called her lower than a prostitute. But once Rose was given an opportunity to speak, she won over the audience.

In 1856, a bill was introduced in the New York State Legislature to protect the rights and property of married women. Rose tried to get enough signatures for a petition endorsing the bill so that it would be passed by the State Legislature. She was able to obtain only five signatures in five months. For the next four years she worked getting signatures on the petition. In 1868, the bill finally became law.

Rose became a public spokeswoman for the abolitionist movement. People flocked to her lectures, which for many was a relatively new experience: hearing a woman express opinions in public. Rose was dubbed "Queen of the Platform."

Rose supplemented the family income by selling perfumes. By 1860, women had achieved some rights, but the right to vote remained elusive. Ernestine Rose told other women: "Freedom, my friends, does not come from the clouds, like a meteor; it does not bloom in one night; it does not come without great efforts and great sacrifices; all who love liberty have to labor for it."

Rose was one of the first women to fight for suffrage in the western states. She was largely responsible for the adoption of women's suffrage by the state of Wyoming in 1869. Sadly, she died before the Nineteenth Amendment, which gave nationwide suffrage to women, was passed in 1920.

Ernestine Rose had no contact with Jews. But she did rise to their defense when her friend Horace Seaver, a radical and editor of *The Boston Investigator,* editorialized that Jews "were about the worst people of whom we have any account." Her reply was published in two installments, which were followed by anti-Semitic rebuttals. Only after this episode did Ernestine Rose's Jewish background become widely known.

In 1882 William Rose died and was buried in England. Ernestine Rose died ten years later at the age of eighty-two in Brighton, England where she was spending the summer.

MIRIAM ROTHSCHILD

Lady of the Fleas

Born August 5, 1908 in Peterborough, England. British naturalist and writer. Largely self-taught, possessing no university degree, Miriam Rothschild has become the world's leading authority on fleas. She is best-known for her studies on the plant-derived defense poisons of insects. In 1985, she became a Fellow of the Royal Society, one of the highest honors a British scientist can attain. She has published more than three hundred scientific papers.

*M*iriam Rothschild is the first child of Nathaniel Charles Rothschild, who was senior partner in the London-based merchant banking firm of N.M. Rothschild & Sons. Her mother was the former Rozsika von Wertheimstein.

Miriam was born on August 5, 1908 at Ashton Wold, her parents' huge estate near Peterborough, England. During the next five years, three more children were born: two girls and a boy. "I owe everything to my parents," she recalled. "My father was a great man. His idealism was what I followed. My mother was a brilliant person."

Until 1935, Miriam spent six months of every year at Tring Park, an estate thirty miles northwest of London, with her grandfather Nathan Mayer (Natty) Rothschild—the first Lord Rothschild and the first Jewish peer in England.

Miriam's parents were, in her words, "broad-minded" about their Jewishness. "My father really believed that assimilation was a better solution," she said. She had, however, always been conscious of her Jewishness. "I was terribly conscious of anti-Semitism," she commented. "I lost my husband's whole family and my mother's whole family in the Holocaust.... Some people find it difficult to be Jewish. I was one of the lucky people. I was always glad to be Jewish. I always liked being Jewish. I was proud to be Jewish." From childhood, Miriam went to synagogue on Yom Kippur (though her parents did not).

Many of the members of her family with whom she spent much time had a strong interest in animals. Miriam's uncle, Walter, became the second Lord Rothschild. He had amassed one of the greatest collections of animals, ranging from starfish to gorillas and he housed the collection in a museum at Tring Park. Miriam grew up in close proximity to 2.25 million butterflies, 300,000 bird skins, 144 giant tortoises, 200,000 birds' eggs, and many other preserved beasts.

At four years old, Miriam began breeding ladybugs and caterpillars. She took a tame quail to bed with her. "I just always loved animals and I was passionately fond of flowers," she wrote in 1990.

When Miriam was fifteen, her father died. His death was so great a shock to Miriam that it curbed her enthusiasm for natural history for a time. Two years later, her interest in nature was rekindled when she assisted her brother in dissecting a frog. "I had never before seen fresh, internal organs, blood vessels, and nerves," she wrote in 1990. "Their extreme beauty was a revelation. That experience...was my road to Damascus."

Miriam Rothschild had no formal education until she was seventeen. Her father had disliked schools. "I was educated up to age fifteen by talking to my father. After he died, I was educated from books. At her own insistence, Miriam briefly attended a few classes in biology and literature. Hanging around the Tring Museum, and soaking up the rich scientific lore contained there, proved invaluable to her. Because of her background, Miriam Rothschild prefers referring to herself as a naturalist rather than a scientist. "My scientific investigations were not based on science, but on natural history, learning about the animals in the fields and being passionately fond of them," she explained.

Courtesy of *The Jewish Chronicle*

In the late 1920s, a naturalist at the British Natural History Museum recommended her for the University of London's research table at the Biological Station in Naples, Italy. There she became acquainted for the first time with what she described as "some of the most beautiful marine animals in existence."

In 1932, Rothschild became a student researcher at the Marine Biological Station in Plymouth, England. She uncovered a previously undescribed specimen infested with larval trematodes (parasitic flatworms). "My fate was sealed," she claimed. "I was completely hooked." For the next seven years Rothschild studied the life cycle of trematodes. In November 1939, a German bomb dropped on England at the start of World War II destroyed all her equipment.

Miriam Rothschild returned to Ashton Wold, and, inspired by the safety belts American aviators who were taking off at a nearby airfield were using, installed seat belts in a motorcar. Her effort to patent the idea failed.

During these war years, Rothschild also worked at Bletchley on the top-secret Enigma project, which was aimed at cracking the German war code.

Her first love was her naturalist work. Each evening she reached for her microscope and worked at her specimens for five hours. Miriam Rothschild became a specialist in fleas—of which some 1,500 specimens are known. With her mother's encouragement, she completed her father's project of cataloguing 30,000 fleas. She labeled 6,000 drawings. "It was a very sound piece of work, which is going to endure," she said proudly.

Miriam Rothschild became fascinated by fleas. "If you were a flea," she said in 1985, "you could jump to the height of Rockefeller Center and you could do that about thirty thousand times without stopping." She spent two years trying to figure out how fleas jump. She solved the problem while on a flight to Israel. Thinking about all her research, she determined that they crouch and contract their bodies and draw upon the energy yielded by resilin, an extremely efficient and elastic protein.

In "Fleas," a December 1965 *Scientific American* article, Rothschild described how fleas, which subsist entirely on blood, have adapted to their furred and feathered hosts. Her widely acclaimed research revealed that female rabbit fleas cannot breed unless they are attached to the flesh of a pregnant rabbit.

Rothschild has also researched the relationship between insects and plants, especially the ways in which insects use plant-derived poisons to ward off predatory birds. She discovered that when a white butterfly lays its eggs, it exudes a chemical over the eggs to prevent other butterflies from laying their eggs on the same plant, thus protecting its offspring. That chemical has been named Miriamide in her honor. She hopes that this chemical might prove beneficial in shielding certain plants, such as cabbages from butterflies, and thus prove a good, natural alternative to dangerous insecticides.

In 1983, her book *The Butterfly Gardener,* written with Clive Farrell, was published. It offered practical advice on how to create gardens designed to attract butterflies. "You can really abandon any romantic idea of creating a home for these angelic creatures," she advised her readers. "The best you can do is to provide them with a good pub. And like all popular wayside inns, it must have a plentiful supply of standard drinks always on tap."

In 1992, the Royal Horticultural Society presented her with the Victorian Medal of Honor; her grandfather, the first Lord Rothschild (Nathan Mayer), was an early recipient. Miriam Rothschild was elected president of the Royal Entomological Society that same year. Her late father, Nathaniel Charles Rothschild, had been a past president.

Gratified at all she has accomplished, Miriam Rothschild still had hoped for an even greater achievement in her lifetime. "I've always wished I could discover some general principle in science" she explained.

At the age of eighty-five [1993], she still puts in a full day's work, caring for her animals and continuing her research. She has been researching a chemical substance she discovered in insects which she believes must stimulate the recall system of predators. "It helps you remember things that have happened in the past," she said, noting that it was too early to tell if this had applications for human beings.

ANGELICA ROZEANU

World's Greatest Woman Table Tennis Player

Born October 15, 1921, in Bucharest, Romania. Romanian table tennis player. Angelica Rozeanu is regarded as the world's greatest woman table-tennis player in history. She won seventeen world titles in table tennis, including six straight singles titles, from 1950 to 1956. She was the first Romanian woman to win a world title in any sport. She led Romania to five Corbillon Cup victories. She also won the women's doubles crown twice and the mixed doubles crown three times.

Angelica Adelstein was born into a wealthy home in Bucharest, the capital of Romania, in October 1921. At the age of nine, Angelica's sixteen year-old brother Gaston taught her how to play table tennis at home on her dining room table. She loved the game and two years later could beat most of the neighborhood boys and girls.

At age twelve, Angelica entered the Romanian Cup competition, and to everyone's surprise, including hers, she won. A few months later, she reached the finals of the Romanian national championship, although she lost in the final games. "This was a lesson to me," she said later. "I realized that if one wanted to be a champion in sport, one had to work much harder...which I did."

Two years later, a YMCA club opened near her house, and there she started to play table tennis with strong male players. At fifteen, Angelica was good enough to win her first important event, the Romanian National Women's championship in Chernovitz, Romania. She captured that title every year thereafter until 1957 (except during the war years 1940 to 1945).

In 1936, she appeared in the world championships, in Prague, for the first time. She won her first two rounds, then lost in the third. She was fifteen years old but looked ten, and since children were not admitted to the table-tennis halls in the evening, she had to explain that she was a competitor.

The year she won her first title, Angelica met the great Hungarian table-tennis star Victor Barna. She decided to copy his backhand drive. Young Angelica was an eager devotee of all sports, including tennis, cycling, and swimming. She came to regard table tennis as her favorite, perhaps because she excelled at it.

In 1938, Angelica captured her first major international victory, the Hungarian Open in Czegled, Hungary. The Romanian government, apparently with anti-Semitic motives, barred her from participating in the world championships in London that year. In March, Rozeanu traveled to the world championships in Cairo. There, she reached the quarterfinals where she lost to the current world champion. By the time Angelica Rozeanu had returned to Romania, the Nazis had taken control of the country and one of their new anti-Jewish measures was to ban Jews from entering sports centers, effectively preventing Rozeanu from playing table tennis. She was unable to play throughout the

Zvi Nishri, Physical Education and Sport Archives of the Wingate Institute of Physical Education and Sport, Netanya, Israel

Angelica Rozeanu (right) during a practice session.

war. She did not hold a table-tennis racquet for five years.

Angelica renewed her training after the war and played with male players to strengthen herself. In 1944, she married fellow Romanian Lou Rozeanu.

In 1948, Rozeanu played a grueling match at the World Championships in Wembley, London against Giselle Farkas. Rozeanu used a defensive strategy and lost by a narrow margin. Thereafter, she decided to change her tactics from defensive to offensive play and began to practice a surprise attack from both sides. Her strong forehand drive was now complemented by an excellent backhand.

Angelica Rozeanu reached her peak comparatively late. In 1950, in Budapest, Hungary, when she captured the first of her six consecutive world singles titles, she was twenty-nine years old. She also aided the Romanian team's victory in the Corbillon Cup, which was given to the world's best women's table tennis team.

In 1951, in Vienna, Rozeanu played even better, repeating her singles performance and adding the mixed doubles title. In 1952, she took the world singles title in Bombay, India. That year she became Romania's national table-tennis coach, holding the post until 1958.

In 1953, in Bucharest, she captured the women's world singles title and helped Romania win another Corbillon Cup.

Between 1948 and 1950, Rozeanu was a sports reporter at the Romanian newspaper *Romania Libera.* She was also president of the Romanian Table Tennis Commission from 1950 to 1960. She was given the highest sports distinction in Romania—the coveted title of "Merited Master of Sport"—in 1954. In addition, she has received four "Order of Work" honors from the government. In 1955, she was appointed a deputy of the Bucharest Municipality. In 1956, Rozeanu played in the women's World Championships in Tokyo, where she was hoping to win an unprecedented seventh straight world title. In a tense, close match, which some have called the best in the history of table tennis, she lost to an unknown Japanese player, Kiyoko Tasaka. The score was 21-19, 22-20, and 32-30. Calling the defeat the worst of her career, Rozeanu still impressed the Japanese with her performance.

In 1958, the post of chairman of the National Table Tennis Federation in Romania was held by a Nazi-oriented Communist. A purge of Jewish table-tennis players started. Rozeanu was forbidden to play in international matches. She was accused of engaging in the "cult of personality." When the chairman himself was purged, Rozeanu returned to favor.

In March 1960, Rozeanu traveled to Russia and won three titles there, in singles, doubles, and mixed doubles.

Rozeanu divorced her husband in 1959. In February 1960, he immigrated to Israel, hoping that Angelica and their daughter Michaela, then fourteen, would follow. In August of 1960, Angelica and Michaela went to Vienna as tourists, then on to Israel. The Romanian government promptly withdrew all the honors bestowed on her.

Upon arriving in Israel, Angelica Rozeanu moved in with her former husband, who is now a professor of thermodynamics at the Technion in Haifa. They lived together until they separated permanently in 1969.

In 1961, Rozeanu won the Maccabiah Games table tennis championship. She continued to win singles and doubles titles in matches played in Europe.

Even at the "advanced age" of forty (for table-tennis players), no one could beat Rozeanu on her South African tour. However, in 1962, Israel could no longer afford to send her abroad to play in tournaments. Angry and disappointed, Rozeanu decided to give up the game. She had won approximately one hundred international titles by that time.

Rozeanu became a coach for a Tel Aviv sports club, Mercaz Hapoel. She became disillusioned when, rather than being asked to serve in the top echelons of table tennis leadership as she had in Romania (she had been a national coach in the 1950s), she was asked to give exhibitions with youngsters in different parts of the country.

In February 1969, Rozeanu married Dr. Eliezer Lopacki, a Polish-born psychiatrist who came to Israel in 1950. He died in June 1979.

Rozeanu's daughter Michaela became an engineer at Elbit Computers in Haifa, and Angelica Rozeanu started working there in 1969. In 1980, she was chosen as one of the firm's "outstanding workers." In April 1983, Angelica retired from the computer company.

Rozeanu is a member of the Jewish Sports Hall of Fame.

HELENA RUBINSTEIN

America's Most Incredible Jewish Businesswoman

> **Born December 25, 1872 in Cracow, Poland; died April 1, 1965.**
> American businesswoman. Helena Rubinstein was one of the wealthiest self-made women in history. Singlehandedly, she established a new business—cosmetics—which became one of America's ten most important industries. With little knowledge of English, chemistry, or business, she transformed her beauty creams into a 500-item business with over $100 million in sales.

Born to a poor family in Cracow, Poland, Helena was the eldest of eight daughters. After studying at the University of Cracow, she went to a medical school briefly in Zurich. There she met a fellow medical student whom she wanted to marry but her father refused to give his permission.

Distressed, Helena dropped out of school, and in 1902 she departed for her uncle's ranch in Australia. She took with her twelve jars of beauty cream she had acquired from a friend of her mother's, a Hungarian physician. That cream became the basis of her cosmetics empire. She moved in with her oculist uncle Louis Silberfeld who lived in Coleraine, a small town with a population of only 2,000, eighty miles from Melbourne.

Helena quickly realized that the harsh, hot climate caused dry, flaky skin among Australian women and that her beauty cream would help them. Admiring Helena's skin, Australians flocked to her for her special cream. To keep Helena in supplies, her mother sent her a dozen jars of her homemade cold cream each month from Poland.

Helped by a small loan from a fellow passenger on the boat to Australia, Rubinstein eventually opened a beauty salon in Melbourne and began selling her special cold cream.

Within three years, Helena Rubinstein had amassed $100,000. The secret of her success was the realization that dry and oily skins required different products; she was a trend-setter in offering clients a personal skin analysis with each jar of cream. Whenever she was asked how she made "creme valaz," the cream she sold in Australia, she offered only vague responses. She kept her recipes a secret.

In 1908, Helena left Australia for London and there she opened the first modern beauty salon in Western Europe. It was located in the city's Mayfair section. Until then, women had made their own beauty aids. Some people were skeptical that she would succeed. Before she left Australia, one Englishman had told her: "My little girl, you don't know how conservative London is. You'll lose all your money." It turned out quite the opposite. Queen Alexandra was among her clients. From the start, Rubinstein employed her relatives in the major positions in her business. In London, two of her sisters became the shop's managers as the business grew larger and Rubinstein opened more shops.

In 1912, Helena Rubinstein opened a salon in Paris. There her customers included the novelist Colette and the actress Sarah Bernhardt. She established branches in other European cities, and became one of the continent's most important entrepreneurs in the beauty business. The artist Pablo Picasso once said of Helena Rubinstein: "She is as much a genius as I."

Two years later, in 1914, Helena moved to the United States, where her business ventures made her even wealthier. By this time she was married to the American journalist Edward Titus. Noting that American women had purplish noses, grayish lips and chalk-white faces from "terrible powder," she realized that she had much work to do.

Rubinstein opened a salon at 15 East 49th Street in New York City and soon had salons all over the United States. She made all her products personally. She sent saleswomen on the road and urged them to insist that the make-up they were selling would "transform" the ordinary woman. Among the beauty items they sold were waterproof mascara and medicated face creams.

An early portrait of Helena Rubinstein.

American Jewish Archives, Cincinnati Campus, Hebrew Union College, Jewish Institute of Religion

Cosmetics maker Elizabeth Arden became Rubinstein's chief and much-publicized rival as both their businesses grew quickly and successfully.

Helena Rubinstein was tiny—four feet, ten inches tall. She wore her dark hair pulled back in a chignon. Rubinstein had two sons, Roy, born in 1909, and Horace, born three years later. In 1916, she separated from her husband. She finally divorced Titus in 1938.

Following World War I, Rubinstein was back in Paris, recognized by now as Europe's leading cosmetician. Rubinstein spent most of her time in her laboratories working on her products. Over a thousand different cosmetics eventually bore her name.

Just before the stock market crashed in 1929, Helena Rubinstein sold two-thirds of her business to Lehman Brothers for $7.33 million. With the crash, the Rubinstein stock fell. She wrote letters to women stockholders, noting that men, especially bankers, could not appreciate the beauty needs of American women, and that these men were ruining her business.

Lehman was forced to sell the business back to her at the low price of $1.5 million. When asked how she had made $6 million so simply, she replied, "All it took was a little *chutzpa*." In 1938, Helena married a Russian prince from Georgia, Artchill Gourielli-Tchkonia, who was twenty years her junior, and of questionable credentials.

In 1941, having returned to America, she discovered a thirty-room triplex on Park Avenue that she liked (normally she lived only in apartments on the top floor). Helena phoned the agent only to be informed that the building was "restricted." Jews could not live there. In response, she bought the entire building.

After World War II, Helena Rubinstein started branches of her businesses and opened manufacturing facilities around the world. Due in part to her efforts, the beauty industry

Helena Rubinstein arriving at the opening of the art gallery in her name at the Tel Aviv Museum on January 22, 1958.

had reached out to the middle class. Because of her burgeoning business and marketing genius, her personal fortune had become immense. She had homes in America and France and amassed impressive collections of jewelry and art. She had over one-million-dollar's worth of jewelry and an art collection that sold for four-million dollars after her death.

In 1951, Rubinstein decided to offer products for men. She opened one of the first men's boutiques in New York. It was twenty years before its time; it closed one year later.

She was called glamorous and tempestuous. She traveled in international society and was a patron of the arts. She founded the Helena Rubinstein Foundation which provided grants to museums, colleges, artists, and institutions for the needy. In 1958, she arrived in Israel as part of a world tour. She had little feeling for her Jewish background, but she did want to build a cosmetics factory there. The government insisted that she either build or donate a museum as part of the deal. Grudgingly, she donated $500,000 and the Helena Rubinstein Pavilion was built in Tel Aviv. She gave it only two pictures from her huge collection.

When she died in 1965, she failed to leave the rest of her art collection to the museum.

Just before her death at the age of 92, three gunmen invaded her 26-room Park Avenue apartment, bound and gagged her butler, maid and secretary, and demanded that she open the safe which contained her jewels. She snapped back: "I'm an old woman. You can kill me. I'm not going to let you rob me. Now get out." They did—empty-handed.

At the time of her death in 1965, her estate was valued at $100 million and the company's annual sales exceeded $60 million. Her son, Roy Titus, succeeded her as head of the Rubinstein empire. Her autobiography, *My Life for Beauty*, appeared in 1966.

NELLY SACHS

First Jewish Woman to Win a Nobel Prize

Born December 10, 1891 in Berlin, Germany; died May 12, 1970.
German poet. Nelly Sachs shared the Nobel prize for literature with
S. Y. Agnon in 1966. One of the major Jewish poets and a refugee
who fled from Nazi Germany to Sweden in 1940, she was the first
Jewish woman to win a Nobel prize. Her best-known poetry deals
with the Holocaust.

Nelly (she was called Leone at birth) Sachs was the only child of a wealthy Berlin
industrialist. The family lived in the Tiergartenviertel, one of Berlin's better neighbor-
hoods. Because of her family's wealth, Nelly was educated by private tutors. She studied
music and dancing. Her early love of literature came from home.

By the age of seventeen, Nelly began writing poems in traditional, rhymed forms.
She also wrote plays for puppets that had a fairy-tale flavor. Although some of her early
work appeared in newspapers. She wrote mainly for her own enjoyment.

In 1921, Nelly Sachs published her first full-length work, a volume entitled *Legenden
und Erzaehlungen* (*Legends and Stories*). The stories in the book reflected the influence of
Christian mysticism in both the world of German Romanticism and the Catholic Middle
Ages.

In the decade before Hitler came to power, Sachs had been renowned in Germany for
her expressionist lyrics. With Hitler's rise, she rediscovered her Jewish heritage and began
searching for mystical ideas in the *Zohar* (a mystical interpretation of the Torah written in
Aramaic which she utilized in her poetry).

Every member of her family, with the exception of her elderly mother, was killed in
the concentration camps of the Holocaust. She, too, might have met such a fate and indeed, in 1940 Nelly Sachs herself was ordered to report to a "work camp."

Fortunately, a German friend of Sachs's, at great risk to herself, journeyed to Sweden
and met with the great Swedish poet and 1909 Nobel prize-winner, Selma Lagerlöf, then
on her deathbed. Sachs and Lagerlöf had corresponded with each other for many years. In
one of Lagerlöf's final acts, she made a special appeal on Sachs's behalf to Prince Eugene
of the Swedish Royal House. Though virtually no Jews were permitted to leave Germany,
Prince Eugene arranged a visa for Nelly Sachs and her mother so that they could travel to
Sweden. Sadly, Selma Lagerlöf died before Nelly's arrival in Stockholm.

Many of Nelly Sachs's works, among them the writings for the puppet theater, were
lost after her flight to Sweden. Her early work is therefore largely unknown. Her reputation has been based on her creative output since the start of World War II. During the
war years, Nelly Sachs wrote some of her most impressive poetry. At the center of her
poetry is the motif of flight and pursuit, the symbol of the hunter and his quarry. Her
poetry has been described as ecstatic, mystical, and visionary.

She wrote her best-known play, *Eli, A Mystery of the Sorrows of Israel,* in 1943. It was published eight years later. The play is made up of seventeen loosely connected scenes, which tell the tragic story of an eight-year-old Polish shepherd boy. The boy poignantly raises his flute heavenward in anguish when his parents are taken away and then murdered by a German soldier. A cobbler named Michael traces the culprit to the next village. Filled with remorse, the soldier collapses at Michael's feet. The play is interwoven with the themes from the Jewish legend of the *Lamed Vav Zaddikim* ("The 36 Hidden Saints").

Nelly Sachs said she wrote *Eli*, later presented as a radio play and an opera, "under the impression of the dreadful experience of the Hitler period while smoke was still commingled with fire."

Concentrating on the Holocaust, Nelly Sachs combined elements of Jewish mysticism with traditions of German Romanticism. She tried to convey the incomprehensible horror of the Holocaust, making constant use of two words: *tod* and *nacht*, German for death and night, respectively.

American Jewish Archives, Cincinnati Campus, Hebrew Union College, Jewish Institute of Religion

Although her adult poems were largely composed in free verse, Nelly Sachs wrote with careful craftsmanship and utilized a German that was influenced by the language of the Psalms and was full of mystical imagery of Hasidic origin. "If I could not have written, I could not have survived," she wrote. "Death was my teacher...my metaphors are my sounds."

Nelly Sachs was almost fifty years old when she reached Sweden. She shared a two-bedroom apartment on the third floor of a building with her mother.

At the outset, living in exile in Sweden, Nelly Sachs made a modest living by translating Swedish poetry into German. She eventually published several successful volumes of her translations.

Of her own poems, her best-known one was *O die Schornsteine* ("O the Chimneys") with its poignant lines:

> O the chimneys, On the cleverly devised abodes of death, As Israel's
> body drew, dissolved in smoke, Through the air, As a chimney-sweep a
> star received it, Turning black, Or was it a sunbeam?

In that poem, the body of Israel is in the smoke emitted by the chimneys of the Nazi concentration camps.

In her book *In den Wohnungen des Todes* (*In the Habitations of Death*), dedicated "to my dead brothers and sisters," Nelly Sachs included cycles entitled "Prayers for the Dead

Fiance," "Epitaphs Written On Air," and "Choruses After Midnight."

Sternverdunkelung (1949) contains poetry that expressed an unyielding faith in the survivability of the people of Israel and the importance of its mission.

Sachs recognized the existence of evil and accepted the tragedy that flows from that evil. But she did not believe in being vindictive or plotting retaliation against evildoers. When Sachs was awarded the peace prize from the German Book Publishers Association in October 1965, she said, "In spite of all the horrors of the past, I believe in you.... Let us remember the victims and then let us walk together into the future to seek again a new beginning."

Her *Spaete Gedichte* (*Late Poems*) (1965) contained the extended poetic sequence *Gluehende Raestsel* (*Glowing Riddles*) (1964).

Sharing the 1966 Nobel prize for literature with the Israeli novelist and short-story writer S.Y. Agnon, Nelly Sachs noted, "Agnon represents the state of Israel. I represent the tragedy of the Jewish people."

The Nobel prize citation declared: "With moving intensity of feeling she has given voice to the worldwide tragedy of the Jewish people, which she has expressed in lyrical laments of painful beauty and in dramatic legends. Her symbolic language body combines an inspired modern idiom with echoes of ancient biblical poetry. Identifying herself totally with the faith and ritual mysticism of her people, Miss Sachs has created a world of imagery, which does not shun the terrible truths of the extermination camps and corpse factories, but which at the same time rises above all hatred of the persecutors, merely revealing a genuine sorrow at man's debasement."

Explaining her writing, Nelly Sachs said: "I have constantly striven to raise the unutterable to a transcendental level, in order to make it tolerable, and in this night of nights, to give some idea of the holy darkness in which the quiver and the arrow are hidden."

Nelly Sachs's later work examined the relationship of the dead and the living, the fate of innocence, and the state of suffering.

She died in 1970 at the age of seventy-eight.

$\mathcal{S}$ARAH

Mother of the Jewish People

Born and died around the nineteenth century B.C.E. Biblical figure. Sarah is considered the ancestral mother of the Jewish people. Because of her central role in Judaism—she is the first of the four matriarchs—Jewish women are referred to as "daughters of Sarah." Sarah's name is mentioned in the parental blessing of girls on Sabbaths and holidays. The story of her life is related in the Bible in Genesis 11 to 23. At first, she was named Sarai, but her name was changed to Sarah when Abraham accepted circumcision. Marked by both her beauty and barrenness, she was Abraham's niece as well as his wife.

$\mathcal{T}$he biblical story of Sarah revolves around a woman who acts, makes decisions, and has feelings. She is not merely an uninteresting or undelineated appendage of her husband. She is the earliest example we have of such a woman.

She was the first of the four matriarchs of the Jewish people, wife of Abraham, who is regarded as the Father of the Jewish People.

When the Bible discusses the patriarchs and their wives, there is, scholars have noted, a certain disparity between the men and the women. The men lord it over most of the women, even the great women of the Bible. Not Sarah, however.

She enjoyed a special position, which arose perhaps from her strong, independent personality. Her relationship with her husband is an equal one, not one of a wife who is subservient to her husband. Some attributed this to the fact that Sarah and Abraham were not only husband and wife, but close relatives. (Sarah was the daughter of Haran, Abraham's elder brother, making Sarah not only Abraham's wife but his niece as well.)

Interestingly, Abraham refers to Sarah as his sister, not his niece, but he may have simply been trying to describe how close the two were. It was not uncommon during biblical times for a man to call his wife "my sister."

There is one other version, as described in Genesis 20:12, which cites Sarah as Abraham's half-sister, the daughter of his father, but not of his mother.

The matriarchs may have had greater prophetic powers than the patriarchs. This might account for the patriarchs appearing to be dependent upon their wives for making the crucial decisions affecting family life, children, and family succession.

So dominant and independent was Sarah that she, like other male figures in the Bible, was granted the privilege of changing her name—from Sarai ("my princess," as in Abraham's) to Sarah ("princess," as in for the entire race). Here, too, the Bible reinforces the notion that Sarah is Abraham's partner in far more than name by referring to "Abraham and Sarah," not to one or the other separately as it does with the other patriarchs and their spouses.

Sarah lived around the nineteenth century B.C.E. She grew up north of Canaan (the area which became Israel), a land that was controlled by the Hurrians. She moved south with Abraham, and their household.

Sarah first appears prominently in the Bible when she made a journey to Egypt with Abraham during a famine in Canaan. Just prior to entering Egypt, Abraham worried that Sarah's uncommon beauty, astonishing considering that she was sixty-five years old at the time, might encourage the Egyptians to kill him in order to acquire her. Abraham told Sarah to claim that she was his sister. Sarah obeyed.

Nonetheless, when courtiers reported Sarah's beauty to the Pharaoh, she was taken to the royal palace. Abraham was apparently generously rewarded for his "sister's" hand. However, the Pharaoh realized that Sarah was indeed Abraham's wife. He returned her to her husband, ordering both Sarah and Abraham to leave Egypt.

A later text, known as the Genesis Apocryphon, and discovered among the Dead Sea Scrolls, gave a detailed description of Sarah's legendary beauty.

"How splendid and beautiful the form of her face, and how soft the hair of her head; how lovely are her eyes and how pleasant is her nose and all the radiance of her face; how lovely is her breast and how beautiful is all her whiteness! Her arms, how beautiful! And her hands, how perfect! And how attractive all the appearance of her hands. How lovely are her palms, and how long and dainty all the fingers of her hands. Her feet, how beautiful! How perfect are her legs! There are no virgins or brides who enter a bridal chamber more beautiful than she."

Sarah's relationship to Abraham—that of an equivalent partner—appears to belong to a later age.

No greater example exists of Sarah's remarkable relationship to Abraham than the fact that, being barren, she was prepared to let Abraham father children with another woman, children whom Sarah would then adopt. Biblical scholars note that, owing to Sarah's larger mission, the forging of a nation, she was ready to make this rather unusual sacrifice.

She suggested that Abraham procreate a child by her Egyptian handmaid, Hagar, a child who would become his heir. So strong was her relationship with Abraham that she knew that such an offering would not affect their ties. Sarah seemed able to cope with the reality of not being able to bear children.

Hagar bore Abraham a son, Ishmael. Once Hagar had conceived, however, she became contemptuous of Sarah. In return, Sarah treated her handmaiden harshly. Perhaps Sarah felt that Hagar had replaced her in Abraham's affections. While still pregnant, Hagar fled, returning only due to a divine order, comforted by being told that she would bear a son who would eventually found a great nation.

When Sarah was ninety years old, and Abraham ninety-nine, she and Abraham were informed by divine messengers that they would have a child. Sarah's response to being told she would give birth was disbelief and so she "laughed within herself, saying, 'After I have grown old, and my husband is old, shall I have pleasure?'" (Genesis 18:12) It is, however, not at all clear whether Sarah was laughing out of joy, or fear that others would mock her for giving birth at such an advanced age.

When her son was born, he was called Isaac from the Hebrew root that means "laugh."

Ultimately, after Sarah had given birth to Isaac, not wishing Ishmael to share Isaac's inheritance, Sarah saw to it that Hagar and her son were permanently expelled from Abraham's household. Biblical scholars suggest that Sarah's behavior here shows that, unlike other females in the Bible, she was not a passive woman. When circumstances required, she acted.

Abraham was reluctant to banish Hagar and Ishmael. God told him, however, "Whatever Sarah says to you, do as she tells you, for through Isaac shall your descendants be named." After this divine messenger, Abraham sent Hagar away.

Sarah died in Kiryat Arba (now Hebron) at the age of 127, twenty-eight years before her husband's death. For her burial plot, Abraham purchased the cave of Machpelah. Abraham and the other patriarchs and some of their wives were also buried there.

SARAH SCHENIRER

Founder of the Beth Jacob Schools

Born in 1883 in Cracow, Poland; died in 1935. Pioneer in religious education for Orthodox Jewish girls, Sarah Schenirer was the first person to believe in combining general and religious education for Jewish girls. She founded the Bet Jacob (House of Jacob) school network for young religious women, first in Poland, then throughout all of Europe.

Born in Cracow, Poland, Sarah came from a chassidic family. Her father, a merchant, was a follower of the Rabbi of Belz. Sarah's only religious instruction came from a rabbi who visited her school once or twice a week. He also handed out some popular moralist works in Judeo-German, written for women.

The lack of education for Orthodox women like herself bothered Sarah. Having no formal education, and without an intellectual focus, she was convinced that these women would eventually adopt non-Orthodox ways. It seemed absurd to Sarah that while Jewish boys were given a thorough Jewish education, young women were barred from obtaining such religious knowledge, and were even sent to Christian Polish schools.

Sarah was considered pious as a child. A seamstress by day, during her teens, she studied the Bible and Rabbinic texts by night, unusual even for religious girls at the time. She developed quite a clientele in her small but flourishing dressmaking business.

Schenirer realized that, when it came to picking out a dress, her customers knew precisely what they wanted; but they had no idea how to meet their spiritual needs. She thought it imperative to find a way of helping them.

"I felt," she said later, "I must help them to see that they were ready to give up, not a shell, but the very substance without which they and their dear ones would perish. But I was without education. I lacked the gift of speech to convey my convictions."

She knew what these young women faced. She had seen them often at synagogue. "When the father comes home from the Rebbe," she wrote, "he is too dazzled to see what will come out one day into the glaring light, revealing a breach that has gone beyond repair. While the men bend and sway in the rhythm that tradition has created, and their heads are held aloft into almost visionary heights, the girls go dancing, skipping, dreaming on in their own way, along the path of a world which is wide open, unfenced, and pitiless. Their paths and the parents' paths may never meet." Schenirer was troubled by her sense that Jewish fathers and daughters lived in different worlds. She believed that education would keep these girls within the religious fold.

With the start of World War I, Sarah and her family fled to Vienna. Schenirer attended the religious services and lectures of Rabbi Dr. Flesch, an advocate of modern, progressive Judaism. In 1917, she returned to Cracow with vague plans for the religious education of women.

She sought the approval of the Rebbe of Belz. Sarah Schenirer and her brother sent a note to him, when he was at Marienbad, asking whether she might educate Jewish women in the Torah. "May the Lord bless your work with success," was the answer.

Sarah received similar encouragement later from the Rebbe of Ger and the Hafetz Hayyim, a noted Rabbinic scholar.

How did these learned men circumvent the Shulhan Arukh's ban on women learning the Torah? They did so by arguing that it was only fair to teach their Jewish daughters what non-Jewish girls who wanted to convert had to be taught (laws, rituals, and other essential ingredients of Judaism).

Sarah Schenirer abandoned her dressmaking business to teach full-time. She brought a blackboard and some benches into the small room at home that she had used as a dressmaker. At first, young women refused to attend. Schenirer decided to concentrate her efforts on young children.

In 1918, Schenirer opened a school for young girls whose education had been ignored. The school had twenty-five students, all under seventeen years of age. The school was called Beth Jacob (the House of Jacob). By the end of the year, the school had grown to eighty students. She moved it into a three-room flat. Yiddish was the language of instruction.

Sarah Schenirer sent two of her assistants to open schools in other places. Agudat Israel of Cracow, the ultra-Orthodox movement, adopted her program of schools for girls. This was the start of the network of Beth Jacob schools in Poland.

In 1923, at her own initiative and from her own small funds, Schenirer began to train teachers for these schools. By 1925, twenty schools were functioning, some at a high school level. She occasionally journeyed to other towns where she spoke to large groups of women, hoping to encourage them to found Beth Jacob schools for their daughters.

During the summers, Schenirer organized courses outside of the cities for girls to train as teachers; there they could escape from the blistering hot ghetto of Cracow.

By 1937, in Poland alone, 248 Beth Jacob institutions had 35,000 girls enrolled. Two years later, hundreds more of these schools had been set up in Poland.

Sarah Schenirer's educational movement grew in part because of the perceived need for such institutions. But it also grew because of Schenirer's personality. Her pupils were moved by her piety, sincerity and integrity.

Schenirer also began the Bnos ("Daughters") Youth Organization for religious girls, allowing girls to enter environments that had once been solely male precincts.

Not much is known about Sarah Schenirer's personal life. She married and eventually divorced a man who was less observant than she. Cheerful, charismatic, possessing a sense of humor, Schenirer was quite popular with her students.

Beth Jacob schools were opened in other countries, including Palestine; there, teachers' training colleges were established in Tel Aviv and Jerusalem.

As a result of World War II, and the Nazis' destruction of so many Jewish communities, Sarah Schenirer's efforts were nearly wiped out. Following the war, the network was resurrected, particularly in the United States.

The stress shifted, from adapting Jewish tradition to modern circumstances to an emphasis on preserving Jewish tradition. One criticism of Schenirer's schools had to do with the fact that the education level was inferior to boys' schools. Sarah Schenirer's collected writings, translated into Hebrew from the original Yiddish, were published in Tel Aviv in the late 1950s. Schenirer's last testament read in part: "My dear girls, you are going out into the great world. Your task is to plant the holy seed in the souls of pure children. In a sense, the destiny of Israel of old is in your hands.

"Be strong and of good courage. Don't tire. Don't slacken your efforts. You have heard of the Hasid who came to his rabbi and said joyfully, 'Rabbi, I have finished the whole Talmud.' 'What has the Talmud taught you?' asked the rabbi. 'Your learning is fine but your practical task is the main thing.'"

Sarah Schenirer died in 1935 after a brief illness in a Vienna Hospital. She was fifty-two years old.

ROSE SCHNEIDERMAN

Bombshell of a Speaker

> **Born April 6, 1884 in Saven, Russian-ruled Poland; died August 11, 1972.** American labor organizer. A diminutive, (four feet, six inches) red-haired firebrand, Rose Schneiderman pioneered the task of emancipating women at the beginning of the twentieth century; her efforts reached their height in the campaign for women's suffrage and the current feminist movement. She helped to organize the National Women's Trade Union League and was its first president in 1928. She was the secretary of the New York State Labor Department from 1937 to 1944. Schneiderman was described as a "bombshell of a speaker."

Rose Schneiderman was born in the small village of Saven, in Russian-ruled Poland, in 1884. She moved with her family, to the Lower East Side of New York six years later. Soon after the move, her father died. Rose and her two brothers were temporarily placed in orphanages because her pregnant mother could not provide for her children.

When she was thirteen, Rose returned home to live with her mother. She stopped going to school and began working, becoming the family's main breadwinner. She earned $2.16 a week working a sixty-four-hour week as a cashier in a downtown department store in New York City.

A few years later, she took a job as a machine operator in a factory that manufactured caps. The work was less genteel than her previous job, but the wages were higher. In this job, Rose encountered the all-male world of unions. "After I had been working as a cap-maker for three years," she said later, "it began to dawn on me that we girls needed an organization."

From the moment, in 1903, that she organized Local 23 of the United Cloth, Hat, Cap and Millinery Workers Union, and became its secretary, Rose Schneiderman was totally preoccupied with union organizing.

"It was such an exciting time," she wrote in her 1967 memoirs, *All For One*. "A new life opened up for me. All of a sudden I was not lonely anymore. I had shop and executive board meetings to attend as well as the meetings of our unit." Schneiderman and a fellow worker recruited a sufficient number of women to create their own chapter. Eager to attain social justice, she felt that labor unions provided an opportunity for her to advance, and for other working women to advance with her. She championed the fight for minimum wages, maximum working hours and legislation that would prevent child labor. One sign of her success was the appearance of well-to-do women joining picket lines at her side.

In 1904, Schneiderman was chosen secretary of the union's national executive board. She also helped organize the White Goods Workers Union. She was put in charge of the union's general strike in 1913.

She found organizing labor unions difficult—and frustrating. "You work and work and work and seem to be getting nowhere," she wrote in her memoirs. "Just when you feel that it is no use going on, something happens. There is a reduction in pay or a faithful worker is discharged. Then the workers remember that there is help waiting for them. But there are always setbacks ahead. You organize a group and set up a local. Then you have to nurse the members along so they won't get discouraged and quit before the union is strong enough to make demands on the employers. All this could be terribly discouraging if you didn't have faith in trade unionism and didn't believe with every cell in your body that what you were doing in urging them to organize was absolutely right for them."

Schneiderman noted that "the only cloud in the picture was Mother's attitude toward my becoming a trade unionist. She kept saying I'd never get married because I was so busy—a prophesy which came true."

After the tragic Triangle Shirtwaist fire of March 1911, in which 147 women perished, Schneiderman was at a meeting when someone cautioned the large audience against feeling bitter and urging peace and harmony. Rose Schneiderman was incensed. She lectured the crowd in response, using words that have been long remembered: "To speak of peace and harmony now would be treason to the dead!"

In 1906, Schneiderman helped found the National Women's Trade Union League (WTUL) and from 1914 to 1917, she was a general organizer of the International Ladies Garment Workers Union.

From 1918 to 1926, Rose Schneiderman served as vice-president of the national WTUL; she remained president of the New York branch of the WTUL until she retired in 1949.

In 1919, she was a delegate to the First National Working Women's Congress in Washington, D.C., and one of two delegates sent by the Women's Trade Union League to the Paris Peace Conference. There she presented a list of labor standards affecting the working women of America.

Another strong interest of Schneiderman's was the Women's Suffrage Association. To her, votes for women meant more than political equality with men—the vote was a weapon that could be used to benefit wage-earning women.

After women gained the vote in 1920, the Women's Party's worked for an equal rights amendment. A problem arose: Achieving equal rights with men would have required the abrogation of all the protective legislation for women that Rose Schneiderman had fought for and had obtained, since these new laws did not apply to men. Among the laws in question were ones guaranteeing women minimum wages, maximum hours, and compensation for pregnancy.

Though she was at odds with her old friends with whom she had struggled in the pre-suffrage period, Rose Schneiderman defended protective legislation.

After World War I, Rose Schneiderman's career took a decidedly political turn. In 1920, she was an unsuccessful candidate for the Senate seat from New York on the Farm Labor party ticket. In 1937, Governor Herbert Lehman appointed her secretary of the New York State Department of Labor. She worked there until 1943 and served as labor adviser to several national labor and other government agencies.

From 1933 to 1945, Schneiderman was the only female member of the Labor Advisory Board to the National Recovery Administration under President Franklin Roosevelt.

Her friendship with Franklin D. and Eleanor Roosevelt lasted until their deaths. The two Roosevelts learned a good deal about unions from Rose Schneiderman, lessons that influenced such New Deal legislation as the Wagner Act and the National Industry Recovery Act.

Rose Schneiderman died in New York City in 1972. The obituary in *The New York Times* on August 14, 1972, read in part: "A tiny, red-haired bundle of social dynamite, Rose Schneiderman did more to upgrade the dignity and living standards of working women than any other American."

The obituary commented on the irony that many of the pioneering laws she helped legislate became the targets a half-century later of pro-ERA (Equal Rights Amendment) women. "There was less paradox in that shift than appeared, however," the obituary noted. "The upward march that Rose Schneiderman did so much to start had now progressed to a point where women felt able to stand on their own feet, with walls of special protection as unwelcome as walls of prejudice. That progress is her monument."

NAOMI SHEMER

Israel's Irving Berlin

Born July 13, 1930 at Kibbutz Kinneret. Israeli songwriter. Israel's most famous songwriter, Naomi Shemer has written nearly 400 songs. She won international recognition when her song "Jerusalem of Gold" became something of a national anthem after Jerusalem was united during Israel's spectacular 1967 Six-Day War triumph. In 1983, she won the Israel Prize, the country's most prestigious honor. Shemer has written some of Israel's best-known songs, including *Machar* ("Tomorrow"), *Al Ha'dvash ve Al Ha'Oketz* ("The Honey and the Sting"), and *Lu Yehi*. ("Let It Be").

Naomi's parents, Meir and Rivka Sapir, came from Vilna, Lithuania (then Poland), her father arriving in Palestine in 1920, her mother five years later. Her parents met at Kibbutz Kinneret on Lake Kinneret (the Sea of Galilee). Her parents were Zionists and Socialists, ideologically opposed to traditional Jewish observances. But they had a rich Jewish education and deep sensitivity to Jewish history and customs.

Naomi was born at Kibbutz Kinneret on July 13, 1930. She has one brother and one sister. Her father was the commander of the *Briha,* the illegal organization that smuggled Jewish survivors out of Europe to Palestine after World War II.

Both of Naomi's parents loved music. Her mother played the flute and harmonica and her father loved to sing. Eager to encourage her daughter to develop her musical talents, Naomi's mother arranged for a piano to be donated to the kibbutz by her American friends for Naomi to play. The child was only six years old.

Despite her young age, Naomi's task was to conduct the "sing-along" at the kibbutz on Friday evenings and on Jewish holidays. "No one taught me how to do that," she recalled. "This was my real university." Her great talent was an ability to improvise.

At the age of fourteen, she traveled once every two weeks to Haifa where she studied with pianist Hans Neumann. She then studied music at Jerusalem's Music (now Rubin) Academy. Eventually she returned to the kibbutz to teach music and began composing children's songs based on kibbutz life.

In 1956, she left the kibbutz and moved to Tel Aviv with her first husband, Gideon Shemer, an actor and director. Her songwriting skills were in great demand. As she notes, "This is the only country in the world in which the singers run after the composers."

Naomi divorced Shemer in 1967 and married a writer and attorney, Mordechai Horowitz, two years later. She has a daughter Leli from her first marriage; a son Ariel from the second. Singing together was always an important part of Israel's cultural life. Shemer remembered: "There was a mish-mash, songs from Germany, Russia, Bedouin songs, songs in Yiddish. Everything was turned into Hebrew and it became ours. We would sing endlessly." Shemer began translating songs, mostly from French. "Two things influenced me," she said. "One was this cocktail (the variety of songs that she and her friends sang) and the idea that anything was possible. I don't feel I have to worry about a style, or where a song comes from. This is my credo, the feeling that you can make every song Jewish by putting it into Hebrew. Then it becomes ours."

Her most famous song is *Yerushalayim Shel Zahav* ("Jerusalem of Gold"). In the winter before the 1967 war, Israel Radio commissioned Shemer to write a song that would be performed, though not be part of, the annual Independence Day song contest. It had to be about Jerusalem. Working at the song for months, she recalled that "I worked desperately hard on this because I was scared. It was too great a responsibility because so many beautiful things had already been written about Jerusalem. I thought about it, I searched my soul."

Then around Purim, feeling forlorn about the task she'd been given, she called the radio managers to ask to be

Courtesy of Naomi Shemer/Yael Rosen-Horen

released from writing a song about Jerusalem. The festival director Gil Aldena told her: "All right, don't write about Jerusalem. But please don't leave this festival without a song of yours. Write whatever you want." She agreed. The director put the phone down and told his colleague: "Now, she's going to write about Jerusalem."

He was right. What inspired—and saved—her was her recollection from her school days of a Talmudic story in which Rabbi Akiva promises his wife that they will emerge from their poverty and he will buy her "Jerusalem of Gold," a jewel in the shape of Jerusalem made out of gold. That very night she wrote the song.

Naomi Shemer's song, when sung at the festival, immediately touched the audience. It was about the longing for Jerusalem's Old City and the Western Wall. And when the Israeli army conquered the Holy City only three weeks later, the song seemed prophetic. In the national euphoria over the military victory, the composition, which was recorded by a twenty-year-old soldier named Shuli Natan, became the most popular expression of the nation's felings.

Naomi Shemer's haunting song, *Lu Yehi* has come to be identified with the 1973 Yom Kippur War. Several months before that war, Shemer wanted to do a Hebrew version of the famous Beatles' song, "Let It Be," and she wanted to translate the title as *Lu Yehi*. On the third day of the war, she wrote the song.

"I put on paper all the anxiety that we felt during those first three days of the war," she observed, recalling the heavy losses Israel suffered when Egyptian and Syrian forces caught the Israeli army off-guard. "I sat at the piano and I sang the painful lines, still with the original tune of 'Let It Be.' My husband returned from the war and told me: 'I won't let you use a foreign melody. It's a Jewish war and you'll compose a Jewish tune for it.'"

Naomi Shemer accepted that "request." The next night she sang the song for the first time on Israel television. One Naomi Shemer song has become identified with a painful moment in Israel's history. As part of the 1979 Peace Treaty signed with Egypt, Israel had to evacuate the settlement of Yamit on the Sinai coast. Shemer's song, *Al Ha'd-vash ve Al Ha'Oketz* ("The Honey and the Sting"), became the theme song of the Israeli resistance movement to that evacuation. Shemer had written the song eighteen months before the evacuation to convey her feelings for her sister Ruth, who had lost her husband Avraham Nussbaum a few months earlier. One line went, "Don't uproot anything which has been planted," and when the Yamit activists heard the song, they phoned her to say, "This is our song."

Is there a Naomi Shemer style of songwriting? Answering this question herself, Shemer grows emotional. "I dislike even the search for style in my work. It disturbs my work. You have to be free and open to do all that you want to do. I don't want to write into a mold, to get to be stylish. I hate it. I try for each song to come from a different corner, a different color, from different cloth. It's not my business to worry about style, it's not my duty."

Her favorite Naomi Shemer song? "The most recent one," she replies easily. Shemer had been traveling to Lake Kinneret. "There is one place near the Poriyya Hospital where the Kinneret is never the same color. The lake was purple and turquoise. That gave me the germ for a new song."

For Naomi Shemer, being Jewish and Israeli are inseparable. Throughout her career, she has written the songs that capture and reflect Israel's national moods, from the euphoria of the Six-Day War (*Yerushalayim Shel Zahav*) to the longing for peace (*Lu Yehi*) during the Yom Kippur War.

BEVERLY SILLS

More Important to See than the Statue of Liberty

Born May 25, 1929 in Brooklyn, New York. American opera singer. One of the great success stories of America opera, Beverly Sills rose in stature as an opera singer from being a dependable performer with the New York City Opera to becoming a top-ranked coloratura soprano which won her international recognition. When she was fifty years old and at the height of her profession, she retired. In July 1979 she was named director of the New York City Opera, a position she held for ten years. The *Ladies' Home Journal* chose her as one of the eleven most important women of the 1970s. In January 1994 Sills was named chairwoman of New York City's Lincoln Center.

Beverly Sills was born Belle Miriam Silverman on May 25, 1929 in Brooklyn, New York. Her father Morris Silverman, was an immigrant from Romania. He was a broker for the Metropolitan Life Insurance Company. Her mother, Shirley (Bahn) Silverman, emigrated to the United States from the Ukraine.

In her autobiography, *Bubbles: A Self-Portrait,* published in 1977, Sills described a childhood incident when her father objected to her musical aspirations.

"No, Morris," replied Mom. "The two boys (Beverly's older brothers) will go to college and be smart. This one will be an opera singer."

Mom, it turned out, was prescient.

"Beverly was born with a bubble in her mouth," her mother said in 1979. "That has something to do with God. The doctor punctured it and he called her `Bubbly.' She's been 'bubbly' all her life—as eager, as willing, as loving now as ever." Hence Sills's nickname, Bubbles.

A child star, Beverly performed on radio and television programs for the first time when she was three years old. She had golden curls like Shirley Temple and was a precocious stage talent. Beverly won first prize in the "Miss Beautiful Baby of 1932" contest at Brooklyn's Tompkins Park by singing the catchy tune, "The Wedding of Jack and Jill."

Certain that her daughter had musical talent, Shirley Silverman saw to it that Beverly had dance, voice, and elocution lessons and that she attended numerous concerts. At a Lily Pons concert, Beverly, still a preschooler, declared: "I want to sit up very close. I want to see what she does with her mouth. Momma, someday I want to sing like Lily Pons."

In the early 1930s, Beverly, calling herself Bubbles Silverman, performed professionally. Singing and tap dancing, she appeared on radio station WOR's *Uncle Bob's Rainbow House.* Before she was seven years old, she had memorized twenty-two arias, which she sang in Italian, from her mother's record collection.

In 1936, Beverly auditioned before voice coach Estelle Liebling. After singing for Liebling, Beverly burst into tears, thinking she had been awful. Liebling, however, said:

"You're the first seven-year-old I ever heard with a trill."

Liebling agreed to give the child a weekly fifteen-minute vocal lesson, beginning a long relationship between voice coach and pupil.

Liebling encouraged Beverly to audition for CBS-radio's *Major Bowes Amateur Hour*. Sills sang "Caro Nome" from Verdi's *Rigoletto*. From that day on, Sills was a regular member of the *Major Bowes Capitol Family Hour*, which was broadcast nationally each Sunday from New York City.

"Retiring" at age twelve, Beverly resumed a normal childhood. In 1942, she graduated from Public School 91 in Brooklyn and was selected by classmates as the "Prettiest," the "Most Likely to Succeed," and the "One with the Most Personality." She studied at

Brooklyn's Erasmus Hall High School, then at Manhattan's Professional Children's School.

Sills's full-time career began in the fall of 1945 when Broadway producer J.J. Shubert tried to turn Beverly into a musical theater star. She became a member of the Gilbert and Sullivan national touring company, playing a variety of leading roles in one-night stands at theaters throughout the U.S.

The next year, while a member of the same company, Beverly Sills had leads in the operettas *Rosemarie, Countess Martiz,* and *The Merry Widow.* Her father, however, expressed great disappointment in her performances. "That wasn't singing to his mind," Sills recalled, "it was putting on false eyelashes."

After Sills's father died in 1949, she experienced a new emptiness in her life. Beverly and her mother lived a "lonely, close existence" in a one-bedroom apartment in New York. Sills sang in a private club to help make ends meet.

In 1951 and 1952, however, her career revived and she toured coast-to-coast, doing one-night stands again, this time with the Charles L. Wagner Opera Company.

Sills auditioned repeatedly for the New York City Opera, and finally joined the company in 1955. She made a successful debut on October 29 of that year as Rosalinde in Johann Strauss's *Die Fledermaus.* What fully established her as a promising young soprano was her performance as Baby on April 3, 1958 in the New York premiere of Douglas Moore's modern opera, *The Ballad of Baby Doe.*

On November 17, 1956 Sills married Peter Greenough, the associate editor of *The Cleveland Plain Dealer.* She commuted routinely to New York City—first from Cleveland, then from Boston, where the family moved in 1959. The couple's first child, a daughter named Meredith, born in 1959, was born almost entirely deaf; a son, Peter Jr., arrived in 1961. He was born deaf, mentally retarded and epileptic. Sills virtually retired from her career at that point. She decided to devote herself to helping afflicted children. "I can't sing anymore," she said in 1961. "I have too many other things on my mind."

Sills had to overcome bitterness and self-pity before she could resume her career. "I felt if I could survive my grief," she said later, "I could survive anything."

When she did return to the stage almost ten years later, she became a superstar with her performance as Cleopatra in Handel's *Julius Caesar.* According to Sills: "*Julius Caesar* was the turning point of my career. It was—and I don't mean to be immodest, but after all these years I am a pretty good judge of performances—one of the great performances of all time in the opera house."

Sills received superlatives for her singing. Winthrop Sergeant wrote in *The New Yorker* (March 1, 1969): "If I were recommending the wonders of New York to a tourist, I would place Beverly Sills at the top of the list—way ahead of such things as the Statue of Liberty and the Empire State Building."

Beverly Sills won her first real foreign recognition as Pamira in Rossini's *The Siege of Corinth* at Milan's La Scala Opera House on April 11, 1969. The Milanese termed her *La Fenomena* (the phenomenon) and *Il Mostro* (a progidy of nature). *La Stampa's* headlines stated that *bel canto* (literally, "fine singing" in Italian) had finally returned to La Scala.

Eventually, Sills also debuted the role of Pamira at the Metropolitan Opera on April 8, 1975 appearing in *The Siege of Corinth,* there winning an eighteen-minute ovation.

"Miss Sills looked beautiful," wrote *The New Yorker* magazine critic. "She bore herself with dignity and pathos, and rippled through her roulades with a facility that set the audience cheering." For the next ten years Sills sang on stage both at home in the U.S. and overseas. She was credited with incredible interpretive skills and wonderful musicianship, exemplified by her mastering the lighter bel canto roles of Bellini and Donizetti.

Beverly Sills retired from professional singing on January 9, 1978. She became co-director of the New York City Opera, sharing the position with Julius Rudel, starting in the fall of 1980. Sills said she wanted to "put [my voice] to bed, so it would go quietly, with pride."

Sills assumed sole directorship of the New York City Opera on July 1, 1979 after Rudel resigned suddenly. She held that post until 1989.

In 1980, Beverly Sills received the Presidential Medal of Freedom. Five years later, she won a Kennedy Center Honor.

In January 1994 Sills was named chairwoman of New York City's Lincoln Center, one of America's greatest showcases for opera, classical music and ballet. Sills is the first woman elected to that unsalaried post.

HANNAH G. SOLOMON

Founder of the National Council of Jewish Women

Born in 1858 in Chicago, Illinois; died December 7, 1942. Communal worker. Hannah Solomon, almost singlehandedly, founded the National Council of Jewish Women, the first national Jewish women's organization in America and the world. It was the forerunner of all national Jewish women's organizations. Elected president in 1893, Hannah Solomon held the post for twelve years.

Hannah's father Michael Greenebaum came to the U.S. from a small town in Germany in July 1845. He had been trained as a tinsmith, but unable to find work in his homestead, he emigrated to the United States, planning to stay no more than four or five years. Reaching Chicago two years after he arrived in America, he was among the first Jews to settle in that city. He became a hardware store salesman, and faring well, persuaded his family to join him. In time he became a wealthy hardware merchant.

Michael and his wife Sarah had ten children; Hannah was the fourth child. A fervent believer in Reform Judaism, Michael initiated the idea of Sunday worship so that men who worked Saturdays would not miss the rabbi's sermon.

Rather than attend the public schools, Hannah went to the Zion Temple, a Reform synagogue school where she studied German and Hebrew. Gifted in music and an excellent pianist, she was given private piano lessons, studying with Carl Wolfsohn. She became an accomplished musician very quickly.

Being a member of the Chicago Greenbaum clan, a family of means and influence, Hannah naturally drifted into the cultural and musical circles of the larger Chicago community. In 1877, just eighteen years old, Hannah became the first Jewish woman invited to join the Chicago Women's Club. While it was not clear what brought about the invitation, it was the start of Hannah's career in public activities. She and her sister were the first two Jewish members of the prestigious club.

On May 14, 1879, at the age of twenty-one, she married Henry Solomon, a businessman in the clothing industry. She had three children, two sons, one of whom died in 1899 at age nineteen, and a daughter. While she raised her children, Hannah Solomon refrained from work outside the home. She read widely, kept a diary, and retained her musical interests.

By the age of thirty-two, Hannah Solomon, a dynamo of activity at just under five feet tall, was ready to take part in public life. She was one of a growing number of Jewish women who, feeling unwelcome among non-Jews, wanted to improve their status as women, and thought the way to do it was by forming their own organizations.

In the early 1890s, American Jewish women were eager to improve their status. They were unsure about how they wanted to proceed, or for that matter, what precisely they wanted. They knew that they had to organize and assert themselves in order to make their collective voice heard. Excluded from non-Jewish women's clubs, these women wanted their own organizations, their own clubs, a place to go where they would be accepted for themselves and what they were.

In 1890, Hannah Solomon had been appointed a member of the Parliament of Religions, which was to be held as part of the 1893 Chicago Exposition. Authorized to represent American Jewish women, along with sixteen other American women, for a year, Hannah Solomon worked on forming a Jewish Women's Religious Congress for the Parliament. This would be the first national assembly of American Jewish women.

A Jewish women's board was formed in 1891 and Solomon was chosen as its chairwoman. To reach the outstanding Jewish women of America, she obtained a list of the leading rabbis and wrote to them asking them to name women in their congregations who would have the most to offer the Parliament of Religions pavilion.

Solomon received ninety-three names, representing twenty-three cities, and the Congress she had envisioned became a reality. Solomon asked for two places for Jewish women on the general Parliament program. The Jewish women's board had selected as speakers Henrietta Szold, then secretary of the Jewish Publication Society, and writer Josephine Lazarus, sister of the poet Emma Lazarus.

The Jewish men of Chicago invited Solomon to merge the Jewish women's group with theirs. She agreed to this with the provision that the men permit the women's group to have active participation in the program. When the men refused, Hannah Solomon withdrew her group from the plan.

Solomon became concerned with what would happen next. She wanted to get Jewish women out of the kitchen. Sensing that middle-class, culturally-minded American Jewish women would not be permitted inside the "better" (read, "non-Jewish") civil and sociocultural clubs, Solomon thought of building an organization where Jewish women would feel free to express themselves honestly and openly. "In a flash, my thoughts crystallized to a decision," she said. "We will have a congress out of which must grow a permanent organization!"

On September 7, 1893 the congress turned itself into the National Council of Jewish Women. Hannah Solomon traveled around the country to set it up. Elected the group's president, Hannah Solomon held the post for twelve years. At the next convention in New York, there were 3,000 members.

The council was the first national Jewish women's organization in the United States. It sought to encourage women to work in religion, philanthropy, and education. The Jewish Council remained neutral politically. Its members did not advocate the right of women to vote apparently because their husbands did not believe in that right for women.

At first, the founding mothers of the organization pleaded for social welfare changes that were broad and nonparochial. But Hannah Solomon wanted to move faster than her followers. It took until after she retired for the council to begin their work toward such specific gains as slum clearance, low-cost housing, better public schools, and safer child-labor laws.

Solomon had support from other women, including Sadie American. Sadie, a crucial figure in the social-welfare world of Chicago and New York, did most of the organizing work for the National Council of Jewish Women.

Visiting England, Hannah Solomon aided an English Jewish women's group that developed into the Union of Jewish Women of England. In 1904, she was chosen as a delegate of the National Council of Women to attend a meeting of the International Council of Women in Berlin. Her fluency in the three official languages—English, German, and French—won her fame.

After resigning in 1905 as president of the Council, Solomon continued her public activities. She was also among the leaders of the Bureau of the Associated Charities of Chicago (later, the Bureau of Personal Services) and president of the Illinois Industrial School for Girls.

While serving on one of these local civic committees, Hannah Solomon inspected a garbage dump while dressed in a gown of white cotton lace and held a matching parasol in her white-gloved hand. Even if her attire was a bit strange, she carried out her task with her usual professional flair.

Solomon visited Palestine in 1923, although she did not believe in Zionism or in the formation of a Zionist state. Even so, she had nothing but praise for the labors of the local Jewish community there.

As for her own brand of Judaism, Solomon was once criticized by a member of the National Council of Women for failing to observe the Jewish Sabbath in the traditional way. "I consecrate every day," was Solomon's tart, concise answer.

Hannah Solomon died on December 7, 1942 at the age of eighty-four.

SUSAN SONTAG

Leading American Intellectual

Born January 16, 1933 in New York City. American writer. Considered one of America's leading intellectuals, Susan Sontag became widely-known in the 1960s for writing controversial essays about the war in Vietnam, photography, pornography, and the meaning of art. By late in the decade she ranked as the major spokesperson of the American avant-garde. She has written five novels, the latest of which, *The Volcano Lover,* was published in 1992.

Susan Sontag was born in 1933 in New York City. She and her younger sister lived with their grandmother from an early age. Their parents, who were fur traders, had gone to China where, in 1938, their father died. A year later, their mother returned to New York to take care of her children. Severely asthmatic, Susan traveled to the healthier climate of Tucson, Arizona, with her mother and sister. Their mother remarried and the family moved to Canoga Park, a Los Angeles suburb.

At an early age, Susan displayed signs of a budding intellect. In high school she bought *Partisan Review* at a newsstand at Hollywood and Vine and read Lionel Trilling, Harold Rosenberg and Hannah Arendt.

Susan felt different as a child, not because she was Jewish, but rather because she was solitary and bookish. She had no Jewish content in her family life as a child. In fact, her family always displayed a Christmas tree.

Although Sontag was raised at least nominally as a Jew, she said: "I identify as a Jew but I'm not religious at all. I come from an assimilated family that's been here [in the United States] for several generations. My identification is within the concept of secular America."

Graduating from North Hollywood High School at age fifteen in 1948, Susan entered the University of California at Berkeley. A year later she transferred to the University of Chicago. There she met Philip Rieff, who was an important social psychologist and cultural historian. They were married in 1950, and were divorced in 1959.

It took Sontag only two years to obtain her B.A. degree in philosophy from Chicago. In 1951, she and Rieff moved to Cambridge, Massachusetts, where she became a teaching fellow at Harvard University. She earned two Master's degrees, first in English in 1954, then in philosophy in 1955, both from Harvard. From 1955 to 1957 Sontag was a doctoral candidate at Harvard but did not complete her Ph.D. degree.

After studying at St. Anne's College at Oxford University in London and the University of Paris in 1959, Sontag then returned to New York where she took a job on the editorial staff of *Commentary,* the neoconservative-opinion journal. She also taught philosophy and religion at City College, Sarah Lawrence College, the University of Connecticut, and Columbia University over the next few years.

Sontag's first novel, *The Benefactor,* was published in 1963 and was well-received. It

Russell Court, Coram 51

is the story of a rootless man in his mid-60s who cannot distinguish his dreams from his waking life. Her second novel, *Death Kit*, was published in 1967. Its main character, Diddy, takes a train trip and thinks he has seen a murder; he may even have committed it.

It was Sontag's essays, not her novels, that turned her into a major literary figure in the 1960s. Her early essays were discussions of the works of artists and filmmakers. Literary fame came to her in 1964 when an article she wrote, "Notes on Camp," was published in *The Partisan Review*. She argued that "a good taste of bad taste" exists—and that, by implication, an "awful" work of art can and should be appreciated because of its intrinsic outrageousness, frivolity, and meaninglessness rather than in spite of those things. "Notes on Camp" prefigured the intellectual stance called "post-modernism."

In 1966, "Notes on Camp," along with many other early Sontag essays, were republished in *Against Interpretation and Other Essays*. Rejecting traditional notions regarding artistic criticism, she came up with her own "aesthetic sensibility," which stressed the "form" or "style" in which a certain work was rendered, no matter what its content. In the book's title essay, she urged the viewer of a work of art to try to "experience" its "sensory" qualities and not be overly concerned about its "meaning."

Sontag's second collection of criticism, *Styles of Radical Will*, appeared in 1969. In "The Pornographic Imagination," she argued that pornography was a valid literary genre.

Another essay, "Trip to Hanoi," was her first overtly political essay. One of the earliest opponents of the American war in Vietnam, Sontag traveled to North Vietnam in 1968 and, in this essay about her experiences she assailed the United States for its military involvement in Southeast Asia. She called North Vietnam an "ethical society," and termed America a "passionately racist country."

Sontag had become so preoccupied with Vietnam that by 1969 she developed difficulty in writing. She began to make films, writing and directing *Duet for Cannibals*, a Swedish film screened at the New York Film Festival in 1969. That was followed by *Brother Karl*, which was released in 1971.

By 1973, Sontag tried to focus once again on her writing. She wrote short stories for *The New Yorker, The Atlantic* and *The American Review*. Reviewers thought she had finally found her true literary genre.

In 1975, Susan Sontag was hospitalized and diagnosed with breast cancer. Her doctors told her she had two years to live. She searched for the right treatment, which she finally obtained from a doctor in France.

Two years later, Sontag's essays on the art of photography were republished in a book called *On Photography*. She examined the role of the photographic image in modern society, especially the curiously entrancing power it has over subject and object. *On Photography* won a National Book Critics Circle Award.

Illness as Metaphor was published in 1978 and is considered one of Sontag's most important books. In it she explored the kinds of language used to describe certain diseases, explaining that the metaphorical descriptions of cancer usually blamed the victims for being "repressed" or emotionally unbalanced, making those suffering from diseases feel responsible for their illnesses. This book also won a National Book Critics Circle Award.

Another collection of Sontag essays called *Under the Sign of Saturn* was published in

1980. In her essay, "Fascinating Fascism," she rejected her earlier view that advocated style over content, suggesting now that ideas could sometimes be poisonous no matter how remarkable or appealing the style in which they were presented.

In February 1982, Sontag set off a bitter controversy among left-wing intellectuals when she spoke at a Town Hall rally in New York City held in support of the Solidarity labor movement in Poland. Stating that "Communism is fascism—successful fascism, if you will," she was attacked by other Western intellectuals who found the notion that Communist regimes were inherently totalitarian a disagreeable idea. She was denounced as an ideological turncoat by some American progressives.

In 1988, Sontag published *AIDS and Its Metaphors,* a sort of sequel to *Illness as Metaphor.* She railed against the way society had turned AIDS into the "dregs" disease which, so the perception went, largely afflicted the lower classes. She attacked the notion that AIDS was a judgment on the guilty.

In 1990, Sontag received a five-year fellowship from the MacArthur Foundation. Two years later, in 1992, her fifth novel, *The Volcano Lover,* was published. The subject is the scandalous late eighteenth-century romance between Lord Nelson, Britain's greatest naval hero, and Lady Emma Hamilton.

During the summer of 1993, Sontag directed a production of Samuel Beckett's *Waiting for Godot* in the ruined city of Sarajevo. She believed that the play, concerning two homeless and hungry outcasts waiting for aid that never comes, was a fitting metaphor for the plight of the citizens of the Bosnian capital. "I didn't want to be a tourist here," she said of her visit there. "I want to give something, to contribute."

Sontag lives in a duplex town house in lower Manhattan in New York City, not far from the offices of Farrar, Straus & Giroux, her publisher for nearly thirty years. Her son David Rieff is his mother's editor at her longtime publishing house.

GERTRUDE STEIN

Presiding over the Lost Generation

Born February 13, 1874 in Allegheny, Pennsylvania; died July 27, 1946. American writer. One of the most famous writers and important personalities of the twentieth century, Gertrude Stein won acclaim not only for her forty books, but also for being a shrewd, discerning critic and a patron of the arts. What truly established her place in art and literature was her friendship with the great literary and artistic figures whom she called, in a phrase that became famous, the "Lost Generation."

Gertrude Stein was the youngest of five children. She was the daughter of Daniel and Amelia Keyser Stein, middle-class German Jewish immigrants. Born on February 13, 1874 in Allegheny, Pennsylvania, Gertrude grew up in Vienna, Paris, and then in East Oakland, California, where her father was vice president of a street car concern. Gertrude was an omnivorous reader, frequently taking books out of the public library.

Few Jewish families lived in East Oakland. Stein's father sometimes attended synagogue services. Gertrude went to Sunday school for awhile, her sole contact with Judaism. She did read the Old Testament.

Both her parents died while she was an adolescent. Michael, her brother who was nine years older, took charge of the family. His careful management of the Stein estate, plus his quick climb up the ladder of the street railway business, assured Gertrude a decent income for the rest of her life.

Gertrude's brother Leo, an exceptional but erratic student of the arts, was her main companion well into her thirties. The two often discussed philosophy, ideas, and literature. Gertrude was also extremely fond of her brother Michael. He frequently took Gertrude and Leo to plays and operas.

Stein was educated at Radcliffe College from 1893 to 1897. One acquaintance described her as heavyset, ungainly and mannish, with short hair. Stein always dressed in black. Her large figure was never corseted. She frequented museums plays and as always, she read, especially the French psychologists.

Stein studied psychology under the famous philosopher and psychologist William James. Although James rarely admitted undergraduates to his graduate seminar, he made an exception in Stein's case. Along with another student, Leon Solomons, Gertrude Stein published several papers in psychology.

From 1897 to 1902, Stein studied neurology at the Johns Hopkins Medical School, but became increasingly undisciplined in her work. She contended that she had no interest in getting degrees and that exams bored her.

In 1903, in her fourth year, after failing her exams, Stein was offered the opportunity to make up the work during summer sessions. During the past few summers, she had been spending time with Leo, who had moved to Europe and worked as a painter and art critic,

and a number of his fascinating friends. The choice between make-up work in medical school and another summer of fun with Leo and his friends was an easy one for Stein. She went off to Europe and dropped out of medical school.

Stein took her secretary and lifelong companion Alice B. Toklas with her. After the summer in Paris, Stein spent a year in London studying Elizabethan prose.

From then on, Stein lived for the most part with Leo in Paris at 27, *Rue de Fleurus,* which became the site of her legendary salon. Under Leo's guidance, Stein and Leo purchased modern paintings from such then obscure artists as Pablo Picasso, Georges Braque and Henri Matisse. Stein's Paris home turned into a center of artistic life in the 1920s, drawing to it such aspiring American writers as Ernest Hemingway and F. Scott Fitzgerald.

It was Gertrude Stein who coined the phrase the "lost generation" to describe the plight of these seemingly aimless expatriates.

Stein's Paris apartment was a place that became a forum for the exchange of gossip, ideas, and news. Stein sat in her chair by the stove, talking, listening, and above all, serving as hostess to everyone who visited, most of whom were notable in the arts. Among those who visited were Matisse, Picasso, Bertrand Russell, Edith Sitwell, Sherwood Anderson, Hemingway, Fitzgerald, Virgil Thomson, Thornton Wilder, and Alfred North Whitehead.

Stein's relationship with Alice B. Toklas evolved into a romantic one, beginning in 1907. Two years later, Toklas moved to the apartment on *Rue de Fleurus.* In 1913, Leo moved out of the apartment, while Alice stayed on. Other than one visit to the United States in 1934-35, Stein spent the rest of her life in Europe.

Stein's first full-length work, written in 1903, and published posthumously in 1950, discussed a lesbian love triangle. It was called *Q.E.D.* Stein believed that character determined events, which differed from the view of contemporary naturalistic and realistic writers who were concerned with the effects of deterministic forces beyond the control of the individual.

Stein's first book, *Three Lives,* published in 1909, was a collection of three stories of lower-class women. The most famous sketch was called "Melanctha," and was the study of a black woman's unhappy love affair. Stein's sympathetic portrayal of black characters was considered remarkable for the time.

Following the publication of *Three Lives,* critics called her writing increasingly incoherent. One even compared her style to Chinese torture: "It never stops and it is always the same." Someone else wrote that, much of the time, Stein's concrete meaning was "inaccessible to the reader." Her publisher once said he had no idea what her books were about.

Stein's style of writing was called associative. It was considered illogical and repetitive. "Steinese" is the phrase that has been coined to suggest her strange literary idiom. Often parodied and derided, Stein's writing has been termed a precursor of modern American literature's stream of consciousness style. Her best-known line is: "Rose is a rose is a rose is a rose."

Stein's second book, containing a set of profiles, published in 1914, was titled *Tender Buttons.* She wrote a number of memoirs, the most famous of which appeared in 1933 and was called *The Autobiography of Alice B. Toklas.* Stein pretended that Toklas had written it; Toklas's actual contribution remains unclear.

In 1934, Stein's operatic libretto, *Four Saints in Three Acts,* was set to music by Virgil Thompson. It contained one of her most famous lines, "Pigeons on the grass alas."

Stein also wrote works of criticism that included sweeping generalizations about countries. Her book *The Geographical History of America: The Relation of Human Nature to the Human Mind* was published in 1936.

"In the United States," she wrote, "there is more space where nobody is than where anybody is. That is what makes America what it is."

Stein also wrote *Everybody's Autobiography,* published in 1937.

Stein lived in Paris until World War II. During the war she lived with Toklas in the French countryside where French villagers shielded them from the Nazi occupiers. Once Paris was liberated, Stein and Toklas returned there.

Two of Stein's books, *Wars I have Seen* (1945) and *Brewside and Wilie,* published a week before her death in 1946, described her wartime experiences.

Stein discussed her literary theories in many lectures and books. "A sentence is not emotional, a paragraph is," she wrote in *How to Write,* which was published in 1931. "A sentence has not really any beginning or middle or ending because each part is its part as its part," she wrote in *Narration* (1935). Stein avoided using punctuation. It interfered, she said, with what was "going on."

On her deathbed in the American hospital in Paris, she asked Toklas, "What is the answer?" Toklas said nothing. Stein's last words were, "In that case, what is the question?"

$\mathcal{L}$INA $\mathcal{S}$TERN

The Woman Who Revived the Dead

Born in 1878 in Irany, Lithuania, Russia; died March 8, 1968. Russian physiologist and biologist. In 1939, Lina Stern became the first woman to be admitted to the Soviet Academy of Sciences. The author of over four hundred works on physiology and other medical subjects, she was awarded the coveted Stalin Prize in 1943. A pioneer in the study of chemical foundations of physiological processes in humans, especially of the central nervous system, Lina Stern discovered the "hematoencephalic barrier," a filtering membrane that protects the nerves and spinal fluid from harmful substances. During World War II, after giving brain injections to shock victims given up for dead, 301 of the first 383 "hopeless" patients recovered. Her lifesaving treatment became standard in many Soviet hospitals.

$\mathcal{L}$ittle is known about the role of Soviet Jewish women in the arts and sciences, their achievements obscured and minimized by a Communist regime that made it all but impossible to gain an insight into what these women were doing. One Soviet Jewish scientist has become known to the West, though even her story is in some parts sketchy.

Her name was Lina Stern. Born in Irany, Lithuania, in Russia in 1878, Lina was educated in Riga, then taken to Switzerland as a child. She graduated from the University of Geneva Medical Faculty in 1903.

From 1917 to 1925, Stern worked in Geneva as an assistant in biochemistry. Fellow scientists recalled her as a plump, dark-eyed colleague who loved to putter in her lab by day, and dance all night. Considered a brilliant scientist, she became the friend of many academicians who passed through the Swiss city.

In 1925, Lina Stern made a fateful decision choosing to return to her homeland. Already a renowned figure in the West, she must have surprised most of her colleagues when she broke the news to them. Why abandon the West where the atmosphere was so much better for scientists, they asked her? Her answer was simple: In Moscow, she was confident that she could take up science in "a society built on scientific principles." She became a Soviet citizen at once.

That same year she was appointed professor of physiology at the Second Medical Institute of Moscow University. In 1929, Stern was appointed director and chief professor at the Physiological Scientific Research Institute in Moscow and the director of the Department of General Physiology at the All-Union Institute of Experimental Medicine.

In 1932, Lina Stern was elected a member of the German Academy of Natural Sciences. Seven years later, she became the first woman to be admitted to the Soviet Academy of Sciences. In 1943, she was the recipient of the Stalin Prize and several Orders of Merit.

Stern specialized in the physiology of the brain and central nervous system. For a long time she was concerned with the fundamental medical problem of why it was that certain medicines and serums injected into the bloodstream did not get through to the brain nerve centers. For example, intravenous injections of anti-tetanus serums failed to stop tetanus from occurring once the poison got into the central nervous system. Stern concluded that there had to be a barrier (in fact, a filtering membrane) that had developed in order to protect the nerves and spinal fluid from dangerous substances and most germs. She called this block the "hematoencephalic barrier."

In her effort to determine how to get around this barrier, Stern asked herself: Why not inject medicines directly into the nerve centers in the brain? This was a dangerous experiment so she tried it first on dogs. She got amazing results. Calcium solutions, injected into the bloodstream in large doses, acted as stimulants. When Lina Stern injected a few drops of a calcium salt solution into a dog's brain, the effect was precisely opposite from the one that would have been expected: rather than being stimulated, the dog tottered, collapsed, and after a few minutes fell sound asleep. When Stern injected potassium phosphate, the dog had a case of frenzied jitters for thirty minutes.

Even though she had experimented thus far only on animals, what she had learned through her experiments gave her hope that perhaps there might be relevance in her research to treating human beings. Would a brain injection of this solution revive a dying patient with low blood pressure, weak pulse, and feeble breathing? she asked herself. During World War II, she got the chance to test her theory out on people. She gave brain injections to shock victims who had been given up for dead. The treatment worked incredibly well: Of the first 383 "hopeless" cases, 301 recovered.

By the end of the war, Dr. Stern's treatment was standard in many Soviet hospitals. She began to try brain injections (of vitamins, sedatives, medicines, etc.) for numerous other illnesses and achieved excellent results against tetanus, ulcers, skin diseases, inflammation of the brain, and mental disorders.

Perhaps, Stern theorized, her discoveries might explain the physiology of anger. An angry man, she noted, sometimes calmed down all of a sudden. Why was that? When the anger-stimulating adrenaline, a natural chemical in the blood, passed a certain concentration, she argued, it broke through the hematoencephalic barrier into the brain, reversing its effect. The barrier thus served as a kind of safety valve. "It keeps the man from—what do you say?—from blowing his top," Lina Stern explained.

Between 1910 and 1947, Stern wrote over four hundred scientific papers on biology and physiology in Russian and German. Among her papers were *Die Katalase* (with F. Battelli, 1910); and *Ueber den Mechanismus der Oxydationsvorgaenge in Tierorganismus* (1944).

Time magazine wrote on March 3, 1947 that "U.S. doctors who have studied her solid, imaginative work agree that her discoveries may well be a milestone in the treatment of shock, tetanus, high blood pressure and many other disorders involving the central nervous system."

After World War II, matters grew bad for Stern personally. Though she had won several important Soviet scientific awards for her studies of the physiology of the brain and central nervous system, she fell victim to the notorious Jewish doctors' plot, which the Soviet regime had dreamt up in order to suppress its Jewish population. In 1948, Lina Stern was accused of "rootless cosmopolitanism" (that was the phrase used by the Soviets to accuse Jews of committing the "crime" of being Jewish).

Removed from all her positions during the purges that followed, and stripped of all her honors, Stern had to await the death of Joseph Stalin for an improvement in her personal status. With Stalin's death in 1953, she was reinstated professionally; all her honors were restored.

Lina Stern made significant contributions to the study of the physiology of the central nervous system, the problems of sleep, the endocrine system, catalase, oxidation ferments, oxidizing processes in animals, neurohormone regulation, the blood-brain barrier, cerebrospinal fluid, and defense mechanism and blood plexuses in the brain.

Stern was described as a "lover of science and art, a tireless research worker, a highly gifted and cultivated woman of letters, a brilliant investigator, and a vivid lecturer."

Lina Stern died in 1968, a Jewish personality of little fame in the West, but of great significance in the field of medicine.

BARBRA STREISAND

Greatest Entertainer of Her Generation

Born April 24, 1942 in the Williamsburg section of Brooklyn, New York. American singer, actress, and director. Barbra Streisand is the most famous Jewish entertainer of the 1970s, 1980s and 1990s, and among the most powerful women in Hollywood. She is the top-selling female recording artist in the world having sold sixty-million albums. Known primarily as a remarkable singer in her early days, Streisand became a fine actress and director as well.

The youngest of two children, Barbra was born Barbara Joan Streisand on April 24, 1942 in the largely-Jewish Williamsburg section of Brooklyn. Her father Emanuel was a high school English teacher. When Barbra was fifteen months old, her father died. Her mother, Diana Rosen Streisand, worked as a secretary, but had trouble making ends meet. "We never had a living room, never had a couch," Streisand said in 1991.

Six years later, Streisand's mother married a used-car salesman. Barbra attended a Jewish religious school in Brooklyn and grew up in a kosher home.

From the time she was a child, Barbra wanted an entertainment career, perhaps as an actress or professional singer. Her mother wanted her to take secretarial courses in case acting did not work out. Diane Streisand thought her daughter was not beautiful and that that would hinder her.

Barbra Streisand was determined to prove her mother wrong. She developed great will power. Her grandmother called her *farbrent* (Yiddish for "on fire.") "I just couldn't accept *no* for an answer," Streisand said in 1991.

After her 1959 graduation at age seventeen as an honors student at Erasmus Hall High School, she moved to Manhattan. She went to New York City's Forty-second Street library and read the work of the major French dramatists. "That was the most exciting time of my life," Streisand recalled.

She tried to make it as a singer in Greenwich Village coffeehouses. Her style has been described as spontaneous, earthy, sexy-yet-little-girlish, romantic. Barbra dropped the second "a" in her first name when she became a professional singer.

Streisand made her New York stage debut on October 21, 1961 in the Off-Broadway revue *Another Evening with Harry Stoones*. It opened and closed the same night. While trying to make it as an entertainer, she worked as a switchboard operator and theater usherette.

Barbra's real break came that same year when David Merrick saw her perform at the Blue Angel nightclub in Greenwich Village. He signed her at once for the role of Miss Mermelstein, the lovelorn secretary Barbra Streisand never became in real life, in the Broadway musical *I Can Get It for You Wholesale*. The show opened on March 22, 1962 when Barbra was not yet twenty years old. It ran for nine months largely due to Barbra's singing and comedic talents. She won the New York Critics Award for her performance.

In 1963, she married her *Wholesale* co-star Elliott Gould; they were divorced six years later.

Streisand was above all, a first-class singer with a voice that has been described as throbbing, and with great range. Almost all her albums, including *People* (1965), *My Name is Barbra* (1965), *Color Me Barbra* (1966), *Stoney End* (1971), *The Way We Were* (1974), *A Star is Born* (1976) and *Superman* (1977) have become platinum record albums (one million or more in sales).

In 1964, Streisand received an Emmy Award for outstanding individual achievement in entertainment, for her CBS television special *My Name is Barbra*. That same year, she earned her first two Grammy awards, for best album and best female solo vocal, both for *The Barbra Streisand Album*. She collected the best female solo vocal award again in 1965 (for *People*) and in 1966 (for *My Name is Barbra*).

Barbra Streisand appearing in the movie Nuts.

Israel Film Archive, Jerusalem/Warner Brothers

On Broadway, in 1964, she rose to even greater fame with her first dramatic leading role as Fanny Brice in *Funny Girl,* one of Broadway's most successful musicals. Two songs from the show, "People" and "Don't Rain On My Parade" became her signature numbers. In 1964, CBS signed Streisand to a multi-year, multi-million-dollar contract.

For the 1968 movie, *Funny Girl,* Streisand won an Oscar for best actress. In 1970, she was given a special Broadway Tony Award as "Actress of the Decade." In Hollywood, she starred in the films *Hello Dolly* (1969); *The Owl and the Pussycat* (1970); *The Way We Were* (1973), one of her most successful films; *Yentl* (1983), the first movie she directed; and *Nuts* (1987), one of her most critically-acclaimed movies. She established some records with *Yentl*. She was the first woman to produce, direct, write and star in a film.

Her film, *The Prince of Tides* (1991), which she directed and starred in, earned seven Oscar nominations, including best picture of the year. It did not win any of the awards, but it did gross over $100 million. As of 1992, Barbra has starred in fifteen films.

One key to Barbra Streisand's success has been her unwillingness to compromise. She refused to change her last name or fix her nose or teeth for the sake of appearances.

She won an Oscar for best song in 1977 for composing the music for the song "Evergreen" for the film *A Star is Born*. She received a Grammy for best female vocalist and

State of Israel Government Press Office

Meeting with then Prime Minister Yitzhak Shamir, April 1984.

songwriter in 1978, again for "Evergreen."

In 1981, Streisand won a Grammy in the best vocal duo or group category for "Guilty," in which she collaborated with Barry Gibb, and in 1987 *The Broadway Album* brought her the Grammy for best female pop vocalist.

Streisand is aggressive about her Judaism. She resisted advice to downplay the Jewish themes in the movie *Yentl*. She even went to Hebrew classes with her son, Jason, in preparation for his bar mitzvah.

Barbra Streisand is an equally assertive feminist. When she met Queen Elizabeth in March 1975 in London at the preview of her film, *Funny Lady* she asked the monarch: "Why do the women have to wear gloves to meet you and the men don't?"

A flustered queen replied, "Well, I don't really know. It's just tradition, I suppose."

Streisand told the press that the regulation was most anti-feminist. "It's the men's sweaty hands that ought to be covered, not ours."

Fearful of singing in public, she has rarely done so since her early appearances. On New Year's Eve, 1993 she performed at her first paid public concerts in twenty-seven years in two shows in Las Vegas.

She made one live appearance between 1967 and 1993—when she sang for 500 guests at her Malibu, California, home in a special fund-raising performance. But generally she avoided singing in front of large audiences. Later, she revealed that her fear stemmed from a death threat she had received just prior to the 1967 concert. "It did scare me," she said in 1993. "I forgot my words, in front of 135,000 people. I went blank."

When Colorado approved Amendment Two, banning laws protecting the rights of homosexuals in November 1992, Streisand called for what many interpreted as a boycott of the state. Her initiative on supporting a boycott put Hollywood figures, some of whom enjoy skiing there, on the spot. Her stand got a mixed reaction. John Denver, a longtime Aspenite, said: "I resent Barbra Streisand, who only comes to Colorado at Christmastime, telling us how to do things." When she learned of Hollywood's cool response, she said she had not actually called for a boycott, but would agree to one if asked.

In late December 1992, Streisand signed a long-term film and recording contract with Sony Corporation, estimated to be worth sixty-million

Appearing in the movie Yentl.

Israel Fil Archives/Jerusalem Cinematheque.

dollars—two-million dollars a year for ten years to develop film projects, three-million dollars for each film Streisand directs herself, and five-million dollars for each of six musical albums.

A *People* magazine cover story published on May 31, 1993 noted that Streisand's personal fortune had reached more than $100 million, and that she was "possibly the most powerful woman in Hollywood."

Her fiftieth album, *Back to Broadway* was released in 1993. She has been hard at work directing a film version of Larry Kramer's play about AIDS called *The Normal Heart*.

In June 1993 Streisand and fellow actor Robert De Niro announced they would star together in the life story of abstract painter Jackson Pollock.

HELEN SUZMAN

Best-known White Critic of Apartheid in South Africa

Born November 7, 1917 in Germiston, Transvaal, South Africa.
South African politician. Helen Suzman is considered South Africa's
most distinguished parliamentarian. She was the longest serving
member of the South African parliament, and the best-known white
critic of her country. Considered a first-rate debater, she has fought
discrimination based on race or color and been a champion of the
rights of the African people. She helped the Liberal wing break away
in 1959 to form the Progressive Federal Party (PFP) and served as its
lone legislator for thirteen years, from 1961 to 1974, before the
PFP's ranks slowly grew to twenty-seven of the 165 seats. She retired
from politics in 1989.

Helen Suzman was born Helen Gavronsky on November 7, 1917 outside Johannesburg, South Africa. After attending the Park Town convent near Johannesburg, she obtained a Bachelor of Commerce degree from the University of Witwatersrand.

Helen was not interested in politics until she was an adult and World War II erupted. "...As a Jew, I was particularly worried about what was going to happen if Hitler were to win the war." Her husband Mosie, a physician, was in the army. They had two daughters, both born during the war.

With the government of Jan Smuts in power, Suzman hoped that after the war there would be "liberating ideas in South Africa so far as color was concerned. All the indications were there." Just prior to the end of the war, she began lecturing at Witwatersrand, focusing on the economic history of South Africa. Suzman was asked to prepare evidence for a government commission appointed by Smuts to investigate the laws applying to urban Africans. After six months of intensive research, she stated: "I was so appalled by what I had learned—the handicaps on mobility, the restrictions on the right to live with one's family, all the aspects that affected the right of Africans to enter the modern industrial economy and I thought to myself that I must get into politics and do something about this."

Helen Suzman could not turn her eye from the injustices in the political and social system. "Let me assure you that I have no sentimentality about Blacks," she said in 1977. "I'm not a bleeding heart Liberal who goes around moaning about the noble savage and all that rubbish....But the injustices are so patently obvious to anybody who has the eyes to see, and it has always worried me."

Suzman joined a branch of the United Party, attending party congresses and initiating resolutions. The party soon lost power, leaving Helen Suzman no longer able to influence from within. In 1952, by now well-known within the party, Helen Suzman was asked to run for election.

"At first I refused because I had a job that I enjoyed at the University and I had a husband and two children (then 13 and 19)," she said. Her home was in Johannesburg but Parliament was in Capetown, which meant spending five or six months a thousand miles away from home. Her husband insisted she run for office anyway and so she did. Although she ran against an incumbent of fourteen years, she won. She was now in the official opposition camp.

As a new "backbencher," Suzman had little chance to speak, and her style, when she did, was too reminiscent of a lecturer. A minister even complained that she had read too many books! Suzman worked on improving her technique as a debater. It took her three years before she felt comfortable speaking in Parliament. "Work [in parliament] is certainly much harder than I had realized," she wrote. "There is also a tendency which I am determined to guard against of becoming cloistered in the atmosphere of the House—of forgetting the outside world."

In 1959 she was re-elected. That year, along with twelve other members, she broke away from the United Party over differences on race policies and, as she explained, "because we wanted a party that would be unequivocally opposed to race discrimination of any kind on the statue books."

Forming themselves into the Progressive Party, they remained part of the opposition in Parliament. In 1961, Suzman was re-elected as a candidate of the Progressives. All twelve of her colleagues who had left the United Party to form the Progressives were defeated; only she was returned to Parliament.

Her opponents were bewildered by her. One said, "You simply want to hand over [the country to the blacks]. I forgive you, you are very naive; you are a woman." A well-known rightwing member of Parliament said that he "did not wish to attack Mrs. Suzman—she is much too enchanting to attack hard."

Suzman's continuing credo was this: "If we are serious about wanting to restore our position as a respected member of the Western community of nations, we have simply got to

Courtesy of Helen Suzman

realize that our old prejudices and practice of discrimination must go. We have got to give individual equality of opportunity....It is our basic belief as Progressives that merit, not color, should be the measure of a man's ability to exercise responsibility."

Suzman served as the Progressive's lone legislator in Parliament from 1961 to 1974. During that time, she asked thousands of questions, made hundreds of speeches, and single-handedly did the work of the political opposition. She championed abortion reform, the ending of detention without trial, and improvement of prison conditions.

She won elections in 1966, 1974, and 1977. By 1977, she was joined by another fifteen members (out of the 165-member Parliament) in the official opposition.

Suzman's autobiography, *Time Remembered,* was published in 1968.

In her introduction to *Value Alive, a Tribute to Helen Suzman,* Suzman's colleague and close friend Irene Menell wrote: "She has been far more than an exemplary public representative; far more than a witty and incisive debater; far more than a clear-sighted analyst of our social, political and economic ills. She has maintained an unwavering commitment to Liberalism at its best, and done so in a way that has always been singularly un-selfconscious."

The South African leader P. W. Botha once told Helen Suzman that she was "a busybody creating trouble throughout the country," while another of her country's leaders, F.W. de Klerk, called her "a saboteur of the police."

In 1989, Suzman retired from politics, having suffered many frustrations, yet still remaining optimistic. She had served thirty-six years in Parliament and was seventy-one years old. Helen Suzman had fostered a belief in liberal values at a crucial stage in South Africa's political history. She demonstrated the value of the parliamentary system of government; and she set a standard of excellence in opposition. Colin Edglin, a South African parliamentarian, said of her: "Throughout the darkest of days Helen succeeded in keeping alive in South Africa a belief in the fundamental liberal values of human dignity, individual freedom, and the rule of law."

Suzman fought the racial pass laws and job reservation as well as the Group Areas Act, forced removals, unequal education, and a thousand other kinds of race discrimination. A great moment for her came on June 19, 1986 when the House of Assembly voted 126-16 to scrap the pass laws. Her colleagues in the PFP clustered around her and even government MPs crossed the floor to congratulate her on her fight against these laws.

Suzman's showed respect for both sides, but she had a subtle degree of irreverence. She was never overawed by those who held high office. Helen Suzman lived to see apartheid cast aside when free democractic elections were held in South Africa in the spring of 1994.

HANNAH SZENES

A Lesson in Courage

Born July 17, 1921 in Budapest, Hungary; died November 7, 1944. Poet and heroine of World War II. During the war, Hannah Szenes served as a paratrooper in the British army. Parachuting behind Nazi lines into the former Yugoslavia, she volunteered to cross the border into Hungary to warn Jews of the Nazis. She was captured, and after terrible torture, executed. She was only twenty-three years old. Her wartime heroics turned her into an enduring symbol of courage for the state of Israel and the Jewish people.

Hannah Szenes was born in 1921 in Budapest where her father, Bela Szenes, was a well-known journalist and playwright. Assimilated, middle-class Jews, Hannah's parents were not observant. Hannah, therefore, learned little of Judaism during her childhood. Her father died when she was six years old. She continued to live with her mother and brother.

Hannah was an excellent student at the local public school, excelling especially in composition and poetry. It was there that she gained some appreciation of Judaism and learned of the existence of anti-Semitism.

When she was ten years old, she entered a private Protestant girls' high school. The school had recently begun to admit Catholics and Jews. Catholic youngsters paid double the normal tuition; Jews, triple. Nonetheless, Hannah's mother never considered sending her daughter to the Jewish high school.

Her first year, Hannah received excellent grades. But, her mother complained to the principal about the discrimination practiced against Hannah despite her academic success. The principal showed some flexibility; he lowered Hannah's tuition so that it equaled that paid by the Catholics. One instructor at the school was the chief rabbi of Budapest, Imre Benoschofsky, who was a great scholar and a zealous Zionist. He had a good deal of influence on Hannah's burgeoning interest in Judaism and Zionism. At the age of thirteen, Hannah began a diary.

Official anti-Semitism grew in Hungary. Anti-Jewish legislation was passed. Elected president of the high school's literary society, Hannah, now seventeen, was informed that she could not take office. She was told that a Jew could not hold the presidency. What should she do, fight or hold her peace?

"You have to be someone exceptional to fight anti-Semitism...," she confided to her diary. "Only now am I beginning to see what it really means to be a Jew in a Christian society. But I don't mind at all. It is because we have to struggle, because it is more difficult for us to reach our goal, that we develop outstanding qualities. Had I been born a Christian, every profession would be open to me."

Hannah thought about converting to Christianity in order to be able to take office. Rather than convert, however, she decided to sever her connection with the literary society. As a young woman, Hannah was tall, blue-eyed, with brown, curly hair flowing about her elongated face. She was a determined person who stuck to her beliefs.

Hannah joined Maccabea, the most established Zionist student organization in Hungary. Toward the end of October 1938, she wrote in her diary: "I've become a Zionist. This word stands for a tremendous number of things. To me it means, in short, that I now consciously and strongly feel I am a Jew, and am proud of it. My primary aim is to go to Palestine, to work for it." Hannah's teachers tried to dissuade her from leaving for Palestine. Graduating at the top of her class in March 1939, she could easily have entered the university. Instead, she applied for a place at the Girls' Agricultural School at Nahalal in Palestine.

Hannah reached Nahalal that September. In her first letter to her mother, she wrote: "I am home....This is where my life's ambition—I might even say my vocation—binds me, because I would like to feel that by being here I am fulfilling a mission, not just vegetating. Here almost every life is the fulfillment of a mission."

In 1941, Szenes joined both Kibbutz Sedot Yam and the Haganah (the Jewish underground). By 1942, she was eager to enlist in the Palmach, the commando wing of the Haganah. She also thought of returning to Hungary to help organize youth emigration and to rescue her mother.

She enlisted in the British army in 1943.

In January 1944, Hannah Szenes began training in Egypt as a paratrooper who would operate behind enemy lines. She was the first woman volunteer in the parachutist group. To her comrades she asserted: "We are the only ones who can possibly help, we don't have the right to think of our own safety; we don't have the right to hesitate....It's better to die and free our conscience than to return with the knowledge that we didn't even try."

In June of that year Hannah Szenes was parachuted into the former Yugoslavia, where she crossed the Hungarian border with the aid of a partisan group. The Germans

Central Zionist Archives, Jerusalem

captured her at once and sent her to Budapest. While in prison there, she found an ingenious way of communicating with prisoners whose cell windows faced hers: she cut out large letters and placed them, one after the other, in her window to form words.

A comrade wrote about her: "Her behavior before members of the Gestapo and SS was quite remarkable. She always stood up to them, warning them plainly of the bitter fate they would suffer after their defeat. Curiously, these wild animals, in whom every spark of humanity had been extinguished, felt awed in the presence of this refined, fearless young girl."

This observation notwithstanding, both the Gestapo and Hungarian counter-espionage officers brutally tortured Szenes. They demanded her radio code; she refused. They threatened to torture her mother in front of her eyes, then kill her. She still would not buckle. Her mother, whom they had also imprisoned, was, in the end, released rather than tortured.

A "trial" was held on October 28, and Hannah Szenes was executed by a firing squad ten days later. Eyewitnesses from among her prison mates testified to her bravery. Her final words to her comrades were: "Continue on the way, don't be deterred. Continue the struggle til the end, until the day of liberty comes, the day of victory for our people."

Her remains, along with those of six other fellow paratroopers who also died, were brought to Israel in 1950. They are buried together in the military cemetery on Mount Herzl, Jerusalem.

Hannah Szenes's diary and poems were published in Hebrew in 1945. They have been translated and published in other languages including Hungarian. The last poem she wrote in prison in Budapest was:

> One—two—three… eight feet long,
> Two strides across, the rest is dark…
> Life hangs over me like a question mark.
> One—two—three… maybe another week,
> Or next month may still find me here,
> But death, I feel, is very near.
> I could have been twenty-three next July;
> I gambled on what mattered most, The dice were cast. I lost.

Nearly every Israeli can recite from memory Szenes's poem "Blessed is the Match," part of which goes:

> Blessed is the match consumed in kindling flame.
> Blessed is the flame that burns in the secret fastness of the heart.

Another of her poems has become a popular prayer among Jews:

> *Eli, Eli, shelo y'gamer l'olam*
> *Hachol v'hayam,*
> *Rish-rush shel hamayim,*
> *B'rak hashamyaim,*
> *Tefillat haadam*

Lord, my God, I pray that these things never end:

The sand and the sea,
The rush of the waters,
The crash of the heavens,
The human prayer.

In a fitting footnote, on November 5, 1993 Hannah Szenes's family in Israel received a copy of a Hungarian military court's verdict exonerating Szenes of the treason charges for which she was executed. Israel's Prime Minister Yitzhak Rabin, attending the Tel Aviv ceremony where the document was turned over to the family, noted that for Hannah Szenes, "there is little use for the new verdict. Nor does it offer much comfort to her family. But historic justice is also a value and the new verdict…represents a measure of reason triumphing over evil."

HENRIETTA SZOLD

Founder of Hadassah

Born December 21, 1860 in Baltimore, Maryland; died February 13, 1945. Teacher and social worker. One of the greatest Jewesses of her generation, Henrietta Szold was one of the pioneer builders of Jewish culture in America. Her greatest accomplishment was the founding of Hadassah, the Women's Zionist Organization of America, with 400,000 members, one of the pillars of American Jewry. She also set up Youth Aliyah (Youth Immigration to Palestine).

Henrietta Szold was born shortly after her family arrived in the United States from Hungary. She was the oldest of the eight daughters of Rabbi Benjamin Szold, a prominent leader of the Baltimore Jewish community.

Although few girls went beyond a nominal Jewish education, Henrietta's father taught her Hebrew, the Bible, Talmud, and Jewish history. She attended the Jewish school in Baltimore where the language of study was German.

The Russian pogroms of the early 1880s proved to have had crucial influence on Henrietta. When Russian immigrants began streaming into Baltimore, Henrietta decided to help them. She worried that being a girl would handicap her in her efforts to aid the immigrants. In a letter she expressed concern for "my Russians": "I have gone back to my early girlish longing to be a man. I am sure that if I were one I could mature plans of great benefit to [the immigrants]."

She was also a correspondent for the New York *Jewish Messenger,* signing her articles "Sulamith."

Carrying on with her regular teaching by day, Szold conceived the idea of a night school where immigrant adults could study English and the basics of American life. In 1898, renting a room above a store in the cheaper section of town, she began classes with thirty pupils. Eventually the public school system incorporated the program she developed.

In 1893, Henrietta Szold became secretary to the editorial board of the Jewish Publication Society (JPS). Her main task was editing the earliest annual editions of the *American Jewish Year Book.* In time she became JPS's dominant figure, functioning unofficially as the society's editor until 1916.

Szold had an incredible intellect, a nearly

Central Zionist Archives, Jerusalem

Henrietta Szold (center) with Hadassah personnel in Jerusalem, 1922.

perfect memory, wide-ranging Jewish as well as basic knowledge, fluency in Hebrew, German, French, and a working knowledge of Yiddish. Remarkably industrious, she was modest and without great ambition so that much of her editing went unnoticed.

Forty years old and unmarried, Henrietta Szold began helping scholar Louis Ginsburg with his major literary effort, *The Legends of the Jews*. Her affection for him grew and when he returned from a vacation in Germany with a much younger wife, she felt betrayed. Over the next few months Szold had a severe physical breakdown.

Szold's father died in 1902. She wanted to gather, edit, and publish his scholarly writing. Sensing that she needed an appropriate education for such a task, she applied to the Jewish Theological Seminary in New York. At age forty-three, she was the first female student to study there, permitted to attend only on the condition that she not seek accreditation for her studies. She and her mother made their first visit to Palestine on July 30, 1909 where Henrietta Szold wrestled with the question of whether to stay or leave. "If I were ten years younger," she wrote, "I would feel that my field is here. I think Zionism a more difficult aim to realize than I ever did before...[but] if not Zionism, then nothing...then extinction for the Jews."

Szold returned home early in 1910 and resumed work at the JPS.

Gnawing at her was the sight of Jews suffering from malaria and trachoma, and the absence of basic hygienic standards in Palestine. Back in the United States, Henrietta Szold wanted to do something about all the negative things she had seen in Palestine. She began by addressing forty women in a Jewish study circle meeting in the vestry rooms of the old Temple Emanu-El in New York. It was Purim—February 24, 1912—the Jewish festival that celebrates Queen Esther's victory over Haman:

"If we are Zionists, as we say we are," Szold said, "what is the good of meeting and talking and drinking tea? Let us do something real and practical—let us organize the Jewish women of America and send nurses and doctors to Palestine."

The organization that Henrietta Szold founded was given the name Hadassah, the Hebrew name for Queen Esther. Szold became Hadassah's first president and remained in that post until 1926. Hadassah became the largest of all Zionist groups in the United States and the largest Jewish woman's organization in the world. In 1916, Federal Judge Julian Mack became a key benefactor to Szold. In order to permit her to devote all of her time to Jewish philanthropy, Mack and other friends assured her of an income for life.

Szold resigned as secretary of the publications committee of the JPS, then began to proofread its English translation of the Bible. She put in sixteen-hour days, but complained that part of her life was empty. "I have always held that I should have had children, many children." Henrietta Szold never married.

In 1920, she returned to Palestine to begin two years of supervising the Zionist Medical Unit sent there by Hadassah. Although she had originally planned to return to America, she spent the rest of her life in Palestine.

Hadassah began with a nursing service in 1913; by 1918, it sent a medical unit to Palestine. At that juncture, four out of ten babies did not survive their first year.

Szold encountered difficulties with the medical unit. Forty-five doctors resigned and seventeen student nurses went on strike during Szold's first week in Palestine. She was able to achieve calm quickly, and soon a well-run network of welfare stations, dispensaries, and laboratories was operating efficiently throughout the Yishuv. It was supported by Hadassah and the Jerusalem Nurses' Training School—the entire effort operating under Henrietta Szold's direction.

This network provided health services both to Arabs and Jews and taught them preventative medicine in homes and schools. In 1934, Szold spoke at the cornerstone laying of the Hadassah Hospital on Mount Scopus in Jerusalem.

Szold was appointed one of the three leaders of the nation in embryo in 1927. Placed on the Zionist Executive, the Jewish self-governing body responsible for the Yishuv's internal affairs under the British Mandate, she was given the portfolios of health and education. Sometimes, for months at a time, she was left in Jerusalem as the committee's sole representative.

As she turned seventy years old, Szold began to organize a Central Bureau for the social work that was being done in all of Palestine. She concentrated on the youth, particularly juvenile offenders. Hitler was gaining power in Germany during this time. Szold went to the London Conference on the German Jewish situation in October 1933 and began to organize the settling of German youngsters among the kibbutzim in Palestine. She returned to Palestine and held two important posts: She organized social services and she supervised the immigration of German-Jewish children from Germany to Palestine.

Szold was a founder of Youth Aliyah, which from 1933 to 1945 located 30,000 orphans and unaccompanied children, who might have been killed in concentration camps, and took them to Palestine. The program succeeded, largely because of Henrietta Szold's talents as a manager. She remained vigorous to the end, sitting on hot buses for hours in order to greet each new arrival personally and escort him or her to their new homes.

During the Arab riots of the late 1930s, Szold took responsibility for accommodating over 5,000 refugees from Jaffa and Hebron. On the Arab-Israeli conflict, she wrote: "I believe there is a solution; and if we cannot find it, then I consider that Zionism has failed utterly."

BARBARA TUCHMAN

One of America's Greatest Historians

Born January 30, 1912 in New York, New York; died February 6, 1989. American biographer and historian. One of America's most outstanding historians of the twentieth century. Barbara Tuchman made scholarly history readable to the general public. In 1962, she won the Pulitzer prize for *The Guns of August,* a diplomatic and military history of the outbreak of World War I; and for *Stillwell and the American Experience in China,* 1911-1945, a 1971 biography of General Joseph W. Stillwell set in the context of modern China.

Born in New York City, Barbara Tuchman was the daughter of Maurice and Alma (Morgenthau) Wertheim. Barbara came from a distinguished family. Her father was a banker, publisher, and philanthropist who was president of the American Jewish Committee from 1941 to 1943. Her maternal grandfather was Henry Morgenthau Sr., who served as American ambassador to Turkey. Her uncle was Henry Morgenthau Jr., Secretary of the Treasury during Franklin Roosevelt's presidency.

Barbara experienced her initial encounter with World War I in early August 1914 although she was too young to really remember it. Accompanying her parents on a visit to her grandfather, then the American ambassador to Turkey, she was on board an Italian ship in the Mediterranean, heading for Constantinople. During the journey, there was an exchange of shots between the *Gloucester,* a British warship, and two German naval vessels, the *Breslau* and the *Goeben.* Years later Barbara Tuchman devoted an entire chapter in *The Guns of August* to this historic event, the first naval engagement of the war.

By the age of six, Barbara had already developed an interest in history. A major influence in her interest in history was the *Twins* series of children's books by Lucy Fitch Perkins. Barbara was also influenced by the historical novels of Alexander Dumas.

Barbara graduated from the Walden School in New York in 1929 and enrolled at Radcliffe, where she was uncertain what she wanted to study. She chose to major in history and literature. "I experienced at college no moment of revelation that determined me to write historical narrative," she wrote in her book *Practicing History.* "When that precise moment occurred I cannot say; it just developed...."

In 1933, Barbara received a B.A. degree from Radcliffe College. She had written her honors thesis on "The Moral Justification for the British Empire." She never continued her education to receive a doctorate.

Determined to see the world, Barbara Tuchman joined her grandfather at the World Economic Conference in London in 1933. She started her first job the next year as a research assistant with the Institute of Pacific Relations. In 1935, she was sent to the Institute's Tokyo office to help produce an economic handbook of the Pacific area.

Later that year she began working for *The Nation,* a magazine owned by her father. At first, she clipped newspaper articles; later she moved on to writing and editing. In

1937 she reported on the Spanish Civil War for the magazine. Max Lerner, a *Nation* editor then, recalled her as a "petite, dark, intense girl."

At the age of twenty-three, Barbara Tuchman wrote an essay on the Japanese character that was published in the prestigious journal, *Foreign Affairs*. In 1938, when she was just twenty-six, her first book, *The Lost British Policy: Britain and Spain Since 1700,* was published in England. She returned home to America in September of that year. In 1939, now back in the United States, she became the American correspondent for two British magazines, the *New Statesman* and *Nation*.

In June, 1940, Barbara married a physician, Lester R. Tuchman. They had three children.

From 1943 to 1945, Barbara Tuchman worked on the Far Eastern desk of the Office of War Information.

Bert Verhoeff

Tuchman's second book, *Bible and Sword,* was published in 1956 by New York University Press. It discussed relations between Britain and Zionism and was sympathetic to the Zionist cause. "With all its problems," she wrote after visiting the Jewish state in 1967, "Israel has one commanding advantage—a sense of purpose: to survive."

In a comment about Judaism, she also wrote that "the fossilized rules of Orthodoxy hamper progress and conveniences in the nation out of proportion to the number who take them seriously.... Orthodoxy strikes the visitor as the most stultifying of Israel's self-made problems."

In 1958, Viking Press published Tuchman's book, *The Zimmerman Telegram*. It dealt with the repercussions of a message that had been intercepted and publicized by the British. The message had been sent from Germany to a German diplomat in Mexico. It proposed that Mexico reconquer certain territories in the southwestern part of the United States.

Tuchman called herself a "late developer," chiefly because her first renowned work, the best-selling *The Guns of August,* was published in January 1962 when she was fifty years old. It dealt with the diplomatic prelude to World War I and the military history of the war's first thirty days, from the invasion of Belgium on August 4 to the eve of the Battle of the Marne on September 4, 1914. To do the research, Tuchman drove around battlefields in a rented Renault sedan and took notes on index cards which she kept in her purse.

In the book, Tuchman stressed the human factor, the weaknesses of national leaders in a time of crisis. "One of the finest books in years," William L. Shirer stated. John F. Kennedy gave the book to Harold Macmillan as a sobering account of the ease with which nations drift into war.

Tuchman's 1966 book, *The Proud Tower*, was a study of the years 1890-1914, which included a chapter on the Dreyfus Affair. *Stillwell and the American Experience in China, 1911-1945* was published in 1971.

Two other Tuchman books—*A Distant Mirror: The Calamitous 14th Century* (1975) and *The First Salute* (published in 1988)—were best sellers. *The First Salute* dealt with the European roots of the American revolution.

The March of Folly, published in 1984, dealt with a number of historical crises from the fall of Troy to Vietnam.

Tuchman preferred writing history to fiction, believing that it offered a greater challenge and responsibility to the writer. She felt that historians should seek to write history as it actually happened, however unattainable such a goal might be. Tuchman once explained what kind of historian she was: "I belong to the 'How' school rather than the 'Why.' I am a seeker of the small facts, not the big explanations; a narrator, not a philosopher." She said that she tried to have action in every paragraph. She found great happiness, she said, when she sat working at the National Archives and the manuscript division of the Library of Congress. However, she had other interests, too. Tuchman's hobbies were skiing, playing poker, and gardening at her home in Cos Cob, Connecticut.

Some have accused her of omissions, misinterpretations, and oversimplifications. Critics, however, praised her for her intelligence, clarity and great narrative skill.

"...It is this quality of being in love with your subject that is indispensable for writing good history—or good anything for that matter," she once said.

In 1979, Tuchman became the first woman president of The American Academy and Institute of Arts and Letters.

Tuchman was once asked what history had taught her: "The most dispiriting thing is that we, I mean, man, society, don't seem to have learned anything from the past. Oh, we learn to manage better in a certain set of circumstances. The management of World War II was better handled than that of the First World War. But the fundamental drives within society haven't changed much."

$\mathcal{S}$OPHIE $\mathcal{T}$UCKER

Last of the Red Hot Mamas

Born in 1884 in Russian Poland; died February 9, 1966. American entertainer. Sophie Tucker was affectionately known as "the last of the red-hot mamas." Performing in burlesque, vaudeville, and night clubs, she appeared in the United States and Europe during a sixty-two-year career. She was especially loved in England. Among the songs she made famous were: *My Yiddishe Mama,* and her theme song, *Some of These Days.* One writer described her as "blonde, blue-eyed and built like a battleship."

$\mathcal{S}$ophie Tucker was born Sophie Abuza somewhere in Russian Poland in a peasant home. Her mother, traveling with her two year-old son and heading for the United States ,where she planned to join her husband, gave birth to Sophie during the journey.

Until she was eight years old, Sophie lived in Boston. She was raised in a religiously observant and Yiddish-speaking home. Two more children were born to the family. The family then moved to Hartford, Connecticut, where Sophie's parents opened a restaurant and a rooming house. Kosher meals were served for up to fifty cents. Awakening before dawn, young Sophie prepared lunches for workers.

The show people who frequented her parents' restaurant had a positive impact on Sophie. She loved what they did and possessed some of the same talent that they had. She had a strong voice and a good ear.

Often she was asked to lead the singing in school. At thirteen, she appeared at outdoor concerts in the local Riverside Park. She was a big person even as a teenager, weighing 145 pounds. Sophie had great confidence in her singing, and she garnered prizes for her vocal talent. Schoolmasters also called her "the girl with personality."

While Sophie was singing for customers' tips at the restaurant, her father was gambling in the back room. Her mother dutifully cooked the food even as her husband drained the family's hard-earned resources.

After graduating from high school, Sophie, though only sixteen years old, married Louis Tuck. Soon the Tucks had a baby boy. Sophie's husband, however, seemed satisfied to live off her family's income. History was repeating itself. Sophie Tucker was perplexed.

Though Orthodox Jews had little taste for divorces, she believed firmly that she had to separate from her husband. And, that she had to leave Hartford if she was going to make something of herself. She had no desire to be like her mother. She left her son with her parents and headed for New York City. Vowing to return, she promised herself that she would one day improve the quality of her parents' lives.

With only $100 in her pocket, Tucker found simple, cheap lodgings. Searching in vain for singing jobs in Tin Pan Alley, she grew desperate. Finally, she got a break. The Cafe Monopol hired her. She changed her last name to Tucker, and appeared before audiences decked out in jewelry, belting out song after song in a huge, brassy voice. She sang

fifty to one hundred songs a night, often taking customers' requests for tunes to sing.

Considered too rotund and unattractive to make it as a white singer, Sophie donned blackface, the popular style of the day for entertainers. She was billed as "Sophie Tucker, Manipulator of Coon Melodies." She hated her new persona, and hated the four years she was billed as America's most prominent coon singer. (Others were Eddie Cantor, Al Jolson, and Fannie Brice.) Audiences, however, loved her and were shocked when she removed her gloves to show white wrists. Her black dialect had convinced them she was black.

Sophie Tucker's first engagement in *The Ziegfeld Follies of 1909* led to her being fired on the spot. Hired as a fill-in, she was let go because her booming voice drowned out the show's star! She went on to achieve great popularity and to earn a large income through appearances in vaudeville and night clubs.

Among the songs she made famous was *My Yiddishe Mama*. Sophie Tucker developed the persona of the aggressive woman, the woman who initiates sexual encounters with men and never loses. She sang her signature tune, *Some of These Days,* for the first time in 1911. Three years later, she was a sensation at the Palace Theater in New York.

Tucker never forget her poverty-stricken past. "The happiest thing of all is that in becoming a success I hurt nobody. Some people get ruthless. Some hurt others, but I did it the hardest way, and the longest way, too."

Tucker was married and divorced three times. Her only child was the son from her first marriage who was raised by her parents.

Instrumental in introducing jazz to England, Sophie Tucker was often invited to perform before appreciative British audiences. She counted members of the British royal family and English nobility among her close friends.

One highlight of her career was her royal command performance at the London Palladium to aid the King George V Memorial Fund. The event coincided with the announcement of Edward VIII's abdication in 1934. At one point, she cocked her head towards the Royal Box, waved and shouted: "Hi yah, King."

From 1919 to 1941, Tucker appeared in half a dozen Broadway musicals including, *Leave It To Me* (1938), Cole Porter's long-running musical. That year, she served as president of the American Federation of Actors. Her Hollywood movie credits included *Broadway Melody* and *Follow the Boys.*

Sophie Tucker was occasionally heard on the radio. She did not like the medium: "You can't do this, you can't do that," she told one interviewer. "I couldn't even say 'hell', or 'damn', and nothing, honey, is more expressive than the way I say 'hell or damn.'"

Vaudeville historians Charles and Louise Samuels wrote that Tucker "had the biggest, brassiest voice of all. The beat in her voice made your heart pound with it, and in syncopated time. With the same gusto, she sang everything from the sentimental ballad *Mammy's Little Coal Black Rose* to her cathouse special, *There's Company in the Parlor, Girls, Come on Down.*

In 1945, the same year in which her autobiography *Some of These Days,* appeared, Sophie established the Sophie Tucker Foundation, which distributed millions of dollars to various charities. Always proud of her Jewish background, Tucker returned home whenever possible to celebrate the Jewish holidays. She visited Israel three times. She once declared that Zionism was her only activity other than singing. While in Israel she set up two youth centers bearing her name, one in Beit Shemesh, the other in Kibbutz Be'eri in the Negev. An Israeli reporter asked her, during a 1962 visit to Israel, whether she had ever considered living in Israel. "No," she replied. "I'm too busy raising money in New York—for Israel. How could I do that here?"

In 1963, *Sophie,* a musical based on her life, opened on Broadway. It had run into trouble in its tryouts in Philadelphia. Sophie put money into it, saying: "I could not let them kill me while I am so much alive."

Even late in life Tucker held her audiences. In the 1950s she appealed to the new generation with her self-effacing humor: "I'm the 3-D Mama with the Big Wide Screen." In 1962 she gave another command performance in London. And in late 1965, at nearly eighty-two years of age, she made a successful appearance in the Latin Quarter of New York City. Tucker died a few months later in the same city on February 9, 1966.

SIMONE VEIL

France's Most Important Jewish Politician

> **Born July 13, 1927 in Nice, France.** French politician. Simone Veil
> is the most prominent Jewish political figure in France. At the end of
> her five year term as Minister of Health in France in 1979, she was
> described as the most popular politician in France and touted as a
> possible prime minister. She was the first female French cabinet
> member in twenty-eight years. Veil (pronounced Vay) was president
> of the European Parliament from 1979 to 1982.

Born Simone Annie Jacob on July 13, 1927, Veil was the youngest of the four children of André Jacob, an architect, and Yvonne (Steinmetz) Jacob.

In March 1944, the day after Simone graduated from the Lycée de Nice, roughly equivalent to an American high school, Simone, her sister and her mother were sent to the concentration camp at Auschwitz, Poland where Simone's mother died of typhus.

The following winter, with Russian troops advancing on Auschwitz, Simone, her sister and other survivors were crowded into cold cattle cars and shipped to the Bergen-Belsen concentration camp in Germany.

In May 1945, Simone and her sister were liberated from the death camp by British soldiers. Her thirteen-month ordeal (including a bout with typhus) made her look forty years old, though she was only seventeen. Simone and her sister tried in vain to locate their father and brother, who had been deported elsewhere.

Simone has been reluctant to talk about her experiences during the Holocaust. To cover the identification number (78651), tattooed on her left arm at Auschwitz, she often wears long-sleeved clothing.

Seeking to resume a normal life in 1945, Simone studied law and political science at the Institute for Political Studies in Paris. There she met Antoine Veil, whose sister had been a fellow inmate of Simone's at Auschwitz.

Antoine Veil and Simone were married on October 26, 1946. Simone Veil became the mother of three sons and a homemaker, delaying her formal education for a few years, while her husband moved up in the ranks of the French civil service. In 1956, ten years after her marriage, Simone Veil received her law degree. She hoped to become a trial lawyer.

That year, Simone Veil qualified as a magistrate. The following year (1957) she became an attaché with the Ministry of Justice where she worked for the next seventeen years. She helped to draft reform legislation dealing with prison administration and prisoners' rights as well as social measures affecting mental patients, and adopted illegitimate children.

In 1969, Veil served as technical adviser to Minister of Justice Rene Plevan in his work as the Keeper of the Seals. From 1970 to 1974, she was secretary-general of the High Council of the Magistrature. During this time, she also served as a member of the

administrative council of the Office of French Radio and Television.

Although Veil was little known outside legal circles, the newly elected President of France, Valéry Giscard d'Estaing, appointed Simone Veil the Minister of Health. She thus became the only woman in France to hold full Cabinet rank since 1948. "I don't at all reject being a woman," she insisted in 1976. "On the contrary, I profit from it. I exploit it even!"

Veil's first major task was to defend the Giscard government's bill to legalize birth-control devices. After that measure passed the National Assembly in November 1974, she tackled an even more controversial bill—permitting abortions during the first ten weeks of pregnancy. During a nationally televised debate in the Assembly, she lost her composure only once. An angry legislator shouted at her, "Madame Minister, do you want to send children to the ovens?"

Veil's head slumped forward. Tears came to her eyes. "You have no right to say that, to me, of all people," she replied angrily. The deputy who had accused her seemed unaware that Veil and her family had suffered in the Holocaust; the television audience and the other lawmakers knew. "Do you wish a recess?" the President of the Assembly asked her. Calming down, Veil said it was not necessary.

The bill was adopted on December 20, 1974, leading President Giscard to say proudly, "She passed the unpassable." France became the first Catholic country with legalized abortion.

To help dramatize the need for new anti-smoking legislation, Health Minister Veil cut her own consumption of cigarettes from two packs to one pack a day. She also stopped smoking in public. In addition, she promoted the distribution of contraceptive devices, and improved maternity services for the poor. To meet the cost of France's health insurance program, she championed a sharp increase in social security taxes. No one seemed to hold it against her.

Despite Veil's sometimes unpopular stances on controversial issues, she was France's most popular political figure. Enhancing her credibility was the fact that she did not belong to any one political party.

In the spring of 1979 Veil led Giscard's party slate in the election of the French delegation to the European Parliament. The Parliament has a role in deciding the budget of the European Community and supervises the commission of the intergovernmental organizations.

During the campaign, Veil advocated integrating Europe even more, by greater

French participation in the Common Market, and a larger effort in dealing with such common European problems as the environment, employment, and women's rights.

Veil was elected to the European Parliament on June 10, 1979 and she resigned as French Minister of Health.

"Madame Simone Veil has symbolized the rise of women to the highest positions of responsibility in French society," declared President Giscard d'Estaing. "By her simplicity, her dignity, her competence, she has illustrated the indispensable contribution of women in the public life."

The European Parliament's first task was to elect a President. Simone Veil won on the second ballot. In this capacity, she had become the so-called "President of Europe."

In her inaugural address on July 18, 1979 Veil emphasized the need for the parliament to be a leader in European affairs. "The European public will not forgive us if we don't assume this responsibility," she warned. Veil was president of the Parliament from 1979 to 1982.

Media analysts noted the irony of a Holocaust survivor presiding over the European Parliament. In October 1979, Veil told the Associated Press, "As a Jew, as a concentration camp survivor, as a woman, you feel very much that you belong to a minority that has been bullied for a long time. As for the deportation, what remains with you most is the memory of humiliation, and that's a feeling many women have, too, of trampled dignity....If this parliament has a Jew, a woman, for its president, it means everyone has the same rights."

In 1983, Simone Veil took an unorthodox approach to the question of tracking down former Nazis. "Eichmann was a case apart—he had become a symbol," she said. "I also think that if Mengele were found, that would justify some special measures. As for the rest, I have had enough of these trials."

She has never been affiliated with the women's liberation movement in France. "Sexual liberation doesn't help a woman," she said in 1978, "if she hasn't got economic liberation...[and] psychological liberation...."

Judaism, however, did not appear to loom large in her later life. In a January 1993 letter, Veil wrote: "I have not received any Jewish education and have not frequented any established religion. My parents were totally ignorant of religious traditions. I add that for my part I have not given any religious education to my children."

However, in March 1993, she canceled a planned visit to Jordan after she learned that her invitation to a human rights conference there carried the stricture that no one could attend whose passport had been stamped in Israel.

LINDA WACHNER

America's Most Successful Businesswoman

> **Born February 3, 1946 in New York, New York.** American businesswoman. Linda Wachner is the only female CEO of a *Fortune 500* industrial company. She is also the only woman to head a public company in America that she neither inherited nor founded. In fact, she won the company, Warnaco, in a bitter takeover battle in the 1980s. She is one of the few CEOs to take her company private, then public again. Warnaco, once an unexciting apparel maker, had sales of $625 million in 1992 and profits of $89.8 million.

Linda Wachner is in the forefront of a new generation of women who have reached the upper echelons of American management. From age eleven, Linda Wachner knew that she wanted to be in charge of something. That year, lying flat on her back at home in Forest Hills, New York, encased in a plaster cast from head to knees, she had just undergone a surgical procedure to correct a serious case of scoliosis. She could barely move, and she faced the grim prospect that she might never walk again.

The experience made her determined that, no matter what she did with her life, *she* would call the shots—not her parents, not her doctors, not her physical therapist. "The focus I have today comes from when I was sick," she said in later life. "When you want to walk again, you learn how to focus on that with all your might, and you don't stop until you do it."

Her resolve helped her succeed. In 1966, when she was twenty, she graduated from the University of Buffalo with a bachelor's degree in business administration. She was hired at ninety-dollars-a-week by the Associated Merchandising Corporation, the New York City buying arm of Federated and other department stores.

Robert Nesbit, a divisional merchandise manager at the time, recalled: "Linda used to come flying through my door every morning hitting me with ideas on how we could run the business better. She wanted to tell our manufacturers how they could do more business with the stores. It was the right move, but she was pissing people off because she was going about it so forcefully. I thought, 'Either they are going to run this girl right out of here or else she's going to be running the place.'"

Linda Wachner become an assistant buyer at Foley's department store in Houston; she moved later into the position of bra and girdle buyer at Macy's in New York City. She then married Seymour Appelbaum, who was thirty-one years her elder. Appelbaum had a serious heart condition, which made the marriage difficult. Wachner remembered: "I felt like we were fighting for his life the whole time." He died in 1983 at the age of seventy-one.

By 1974, Wachner had taken a job in marketing at Warnaco. When she was promoted to vice president a year later, Philip Lamoureux, her boss, told her that it had taken one hundred years for a woman to rise that high in the company. The comment embittered

Wachner: "He knew how aggressive I was, and I think he was telling me I had better not expect too much more."

David Mahoney, the CEO of Norton Simon, recruited her in 1978 to run the American division of his cosmetic company, Max Factor. The business was losing money and she dissected it, figuring out where costs could be cut, and listening attentively to the buyers in the stores. By her second year, she had achieved a five-million-dollar operating profit. Mahoney called Linda Wachner "a problem-solver. If she gave you numbers for the business, you could go to bed at night and be able to sleep because you knew she'd make them."

Wachner spent five years as president and CEO of Max Factor. Managing was interesting, but not sufficient for her. She wanted to own her own company. She got off to a shaky start, however. With Beatrice taking over Max Factor, Linda Wachner spotted a chance to take charge. Raising $280 million, she sought to persuade Beatrice's management to sell the company to her. But Beatrice did not want to part with Max Factor and within a month Wachner was forced out.

Wachner would not be counted out, however. A California investor named Andrew G. Galef made a hostile bid for Warnaco Inc. Wachner had read that Robert Matura, the CEO of Warnaco, planned to take Warnaco private. She wanted to weigh in with a competing bid. Galef does not remember who called whom, "but I do recall Linda being very excited and asking me, 'Where else are you going to find that many great brands under one roof?'"

On March 17, 1986 Wachner and Galef offered thirty-six dollars a share for the company, and a bidding war erupted between them and Matura. By the end of April, Wachner and Galef won with an offer of $46.50 a share. The total price was $550 million, of which $500 million was borrowed with the aid of investment banking firm Drexel Burnham Lambert. When Wachner was asked whether she planned to keep the former management on board, she replied, "They put those golden parachutes in themselves." With those few words, she had pulled their rip cords.

In those early days at Warnaco, Wachner was a whirlwind— meeting employees and visiting plants. She pared down the portfolio of businesses from about fifteen weaklings to two main cash generators: intimate apparel, as lingerie is known in the rag trade, and menswear. Out went the $25 million-a-year women's apparel business, consisting mainly of White Stag and Geoffrey Beene sportswear and Pringle of Scotland sweaters.

Under Linda Wachner, Warnaco's sales have grown from $427 million in 1987 to $625 million in 1991. The business has 12,500 employees. Warnaco owns the licenses for products that range from Valentino-designed nighties to Fruit of the Loom cotton underwear. Warnaco also has thirty percent of the brassiere market, with leading brands such as Warner's.

Linda Wachner says: "I want to make Warner's the Coca-Cola of the bra business."

Wachner is not the typical CEO. She answers her own phone. She keeps a small greenhouse stocked with orchids in her office.

Fortune magazine called her "part mogul and part Jewish mother," adding that she "has injected a once sleepy apparel maker with energy, focus, financial discipline, and fashion flair."

Her guiding business principles are: stay close to the customer, keep on top of the business, and watch the till. She owns ten percent of the company.

Linda Wachner has acquired a reputation as a tough boss, one who does not brook dissent. She was asked if a sexual double standard existed, if she would not have acquired such a tough image if she had been a man. Her response: "Do I think there are jealousies out there in the world and people who aren't satisfied? Sure, but it's not against women. If I thought that way, it would slow me down."

Aware that others are infuriated at her toughness, Linda Wachner offers no apologies. "Have I yelled at meetings? No question. Do I think I've ever hurt anybody? I hope not. Look, I just want people to be good...."

In 1991, Linda Wachner earned three million dollars, which made her one of the highest paid women executives in the United States.

As of October 1993, she had increased the value of Warnaco for the stockholder by $140 million. Her own Warnaco holdings, according to *Fortune* magazine, were worth $72 million.

LILLIAN D. WALD

Angel of Henry Street

Born March 10, 1867 in Cincinnati, Ohio; died September 1, 1940. American social worker. A pioneer in public health nursing, Lillian chose as her main vocation helping Eastern European immigrants who had crowded into New York's Lower East Side. She established the Henry Street Settlement House in New York City and was known as "the Angel of Henry Street." Considered one of the most outstanding social workers of the twentieth century, she was American Jewry's best-known social worker and a prototype for all who followed in her footsteps.

Lillian's parents, Max D. Wald and Minni Schwartz Wald, emigrated from Germany after the 1848 uprisings. Well-off and assimilated, they lived in Cincinnati at first, then Rochester, New York. Max Wald traveled widely, dealing in optical goods. The Walds had four children, including Lillian. The death of Lillian's older brother Alfred, to whom she was very close, left her in shock.

She did not have to work, but she refused to be idle. For a brief time, Lillian worked obtaining credit ratings of firms in the Rochester area for Dun & Bradstreet. The work did not appeal to her.

Lillian sought a different direction for her life. One summer, while visiting her sister Julia, Julia became ill. The doctor recommended that a trained nurse look after her. Lillian was sent to bring such a nurse to the house. Lillian and the registered nurse became close friends and Lillian grew fascinated with the profession.

Although nursing was not a popular career for young women from her social background, Lillian decided to apply for a nurse's training course at the Bellevue School of Nursing in New York City. She won the backing of her family. To gain entry into the course, which admitted women over 25 years of age, Lillian lied on the application form, stating that she was twenty-five, not her real age of twenty-two.

After Wald graduated the nursing school in 1891, she worked for a year at the New York Juvenile Asylum. Sensing that she could accomplish little there as a nurse, Wald applied to medical school. She also began teaching a class on nursing, hoping to encourage young immigrant girls to become nurses.

One day, in March 1893, a small child came to the class and asked for help for her sick mother. Wald volunteered to see what she could do. The child led her through tenements where for the first time Lillian saw the filthy, unsanitary conditions in which immigrants lived. Nursing the child's mother back to health, Lillian Wald saw how sickness frightened these new immigrants to America and made them feel helpless. She was shocked by the lack of nursing services and the lack of hygiene. She vowed to improve the situation.

Lillian Wald approached Mrs. Solomon Loeb, wife of the wealthy German-Jewish financier, and asked her to sponsor two nurses to live and work on the Lower East Side. Mrs. Loeb and her son-in-law Jacob Schiff, the financier and philanthropist, agreed in 1893, to support two nurses for the task.

Lillian Wald worked with a friend, another nurse named Mary Brewster. To find those who needed nursing care, they moved into the tenements. People began knocking on their door at all hours of the day asking for help. Wald and Brewster founded a nurses' service, which offered the first visiting nurses in the world (growing to more than 20,000 visiting nurses a half-century later.)

To maintain the immigrant patient's self-respect, a fee of ten cents per visit was charged. The new service was of special value in preventative care for

Courtesy of The Library of Congress

children. This was a time when there were no school doctors. Wald grabbed a boy suffering from scarlet fever out of a school room and brought him to the director of the city health department who promptly ordered that 150 school doctors begin working in New York City schools.

Meanwhile, more space was needed for Wald's social-service work. In 1893, she turned to Jacob Schiff, who then purchased a house at 265 Henry Street for Wald and her nurses. It became a settlement house as well as the headquarters of the Visiting Nurse Service. The backyard became the first playground in the area and served as a model for city playgrounds established all over the country. "The House on Henry Street," as it was soon called, was not restricted to Jews or to whites.

Lillian Wald did not think of herself as Jewish per se. When she was approached by an editor for an autobiographical statement, she said: "All my work has been non-sectarian and my interests are entirely non-sectarian." She thought Jewish identity unimportant for the new immigrants to America and might even be a threat to their becoming Americanized. She persuaded many Orthodox Jewish women to discard their wigs.

Wald kept a daily record of her work. Here is an extract from one July day in 1893:

> "Visit and care of typhoid patient, 182 Ludlow Street. Visit to 7 Hester Street where in rooms of Nathan S. found two children with measles. After much argument succeeded in bathing these two patients and the sick baby, the first time in their experience.... Brought clean dresses to the older children."

The Henry Street settlement became one of New York's best-known landmarks. It acquired an international reputation as a center for social work. Among its prominent visitors were Franklin and Eleanor Roosevelt, Al Smith, and the Gershwins.

In 1898, Wald helped form the Outdoor Recreation League, which built and supervised public parks and playgrounds. She also established the first convalescent home for women, children, and workers; and the first special education classes.

In 1902 Wald organized the first city school for nursing in the world and, as a result, the United States became the first nation to begin regular medical care for schoolchildren. That same year, Wald founded the first "bedside school" for handicapped children, a model for many such schools later established in the country.

President Theodore Roosevelt asked Wald to arrange a conference on the care of dependent children in 1909. Because of her experience and the needs she saw, Wald urged authorities to organize a Federal Children's Bureau, which was set up by Congress in 1912.

Lillian Wald was a pacifist when America entered World War I and she was listed by American military intelligence as one of sixty-two Americans "active in movements which did not help the United States when the country was fighting."

In April 1917, with the nation at war, Wald was serving as president of the American Union against Militarism. She found that funding for her settlement house and her Visiting Nurse Service began to dry up. Despite her political feelings, however, she decided to allow her settlement house—by now expanded to three buildings—to be used in the war effort. At her suggestion, one of her nurses was made director of the U.S. Army School for Nursing.

Wald's mother died in 1923. A few months later she lost her biggest supporter, Jacob Schiff. She herself then suffered a heart attack and was plagued by poor health until her death. Lillian Wald wrote *The House on Henry Street* (1915), and *Windows on Henry Street* (1934).

During the Depression, in the early 1930s, the Henry Street Settlement House issued thousands of food tickets and provided other forms of relief.

Lillian Wald retired in 1933 and died at her home in Westport, Connecticut on September 1, 1940. She was seventy-three years old.

BARBARA WALTERS

First Woman Anchor in Television News

Born September 25, 1931 in Boston, Massachusetts. American television broadcaster. Barbara Walters was the first female anchor on a network newscast and the highest-paid news performer in TV, achieving both in 1976 when ABC wooed her away from NBC with a five-year contract that guaranteed her one million dollars a year. She has turned the television interview into a unique art form. Her *20/20* program remains a hit, and in 1993, she was paid three-million dollars a year to do the weekly show plus two *Barbara Walters Specials*. *The Ladies' Home Journal* chose her as one of the eleven most important women of the 1970s. In 1992, *TV Guide* named her Newsperson of the Decade for the 1980s.

She was born Barbara Jill Walters in Boston, Massachusetts, on September 25, 1931. Barbara is the daughter of Lou and Dena (Selett) Walters. Barbara's father owned the Latin Quarter and other night clubs. A sister, Jacqueline, who was three years older than Barbara, was mentally retarded.

Barbara attended Miami Beach High School and two private schools in New York City—the Fieldston School and Birch Wathen School.

Neither of Barbara's parents was especially Jewish-minded. Candles were lit at home for the Sabbath, although the family did not belong to a synagogue. "The only way Judaism was important," Walters said, "was socially. Our friends were Jewish."

Through her father and his work as a well-known impresario, from an early age Barbara became acquainted with many celebrities. They never intimidated her and meeting so many kinds of people had an impact on her. "I grew up very unprejudiced," she said. Attending Sarah Lawrence College in Bronxville, New York, she received a Bachelor of Arts degree in English in 1954.

The "dominant force" (her words) in her life was the fact that her sister was retarded. "I always knew," she recalled, "that I had to take care of her financially. I had tremendous guilt and sadness about her. [Her retardation] made our lives different. Maybe that's what interested me so much about people. My heroes are those who work with the handicapped."

Barbara's goal was to become an actress. But being more realistic, she decided on teaching and, after moving to New York City, began a master's degree program in education. She worked as a secretary in an advertising agency, which influenced her to eventually set her sights on a television career.

Barbara Walters started her career at WNBC-TV, the local New York City affiliate of the NBC television network. She was assistant to the publicity director. Selected to participate in the station's training program for television producers, she moved on to become a producer and writer at WRCA-TV. She then moved to WPIX-TV as the women's-program producer.

During the 1950s, few opportunities existed for women in the broadcasting profession. Walters helped change that. CBS-TV hired her as a news and public affairs producer and writer. Assigned to the network's morning show, she wrote material for Dick Van Dyke, Will Rogers Jr., Jack Parr, and Anita Colby. Disappointed with the size of her job responsibility, she took a job with a theatrical public relations firm.

Walters's first big television break came in 1961. Dave Garroway, the first host of NBC's long-running *Today* show, invited her to join the staff as a writer. Her news sense was quickly recognized, and she was given on-air assignments. In 1962, she covered First Lady Jacqueline Kennedy's trip to India. The idea that women should do hard news was still in the distant future. The show spotlighted the "*Today* girl," using recognized names, among whom were Lee Ann Meriwether, Maureen O'Sullivan, Florence Henderson, and Betsy Palmer. Smiling, engaging in small talk, the "girls" were not newswomen. Walters, however, considered herself one.

One day, veteran actress Maureen O'Sullivan, *Today's* latest "girl," was abruptly dismissed. Host Hugh Downs and producer Al Morgan gave Barbara a trial run as a newscaster: They did not call her the *Today* "girl." They worried, however, that an educated female on the show might backfire.

Walters was a success. Her interviewing skills were excellent, and by 1963 her interviews became a featured part of the program. Her reputation grew; she became known for luring big names to the show.

Able to get access to interview presidents, when other reporters could not, Walters was as much at ease with movie stars as with politicians. She was the first to get TV interviews with Truman Capote, the notoriously shy Fred Astaire, and the painter Andrew Wyeth.

Barbara Walters's forte was getting her subjects to speak candidly. "I have developed a particular type of interview," she said. "I'm good at drawing people out—there's a thin line between asking critical questions well and making someone mad."

According to Walters, part of the secret of her interviewing technique, is this: "You have to do your homework. I don't like to wing it. And, you have to listen and be ready to ask a follow-up question. It's good to start by asking people about their childhood. It relaxes them."

On December 8, 1963, Walters married Lee Guber, a theatrical producer and owner of theaters-in-the-round. Their daughter, Jacqueline, was born in 1968. Guber died in 1989.

With the death of Aline Saarinen in 1971, Barbara Walters took over as daily host of the syndicated program *For Women Only,* changing the name to *Not For Women Only.* She also covered such major news events as President Richard Nixon's first visit to the People's Republic of China in 1972.

Her career got a boost in April 1974 when she was elevated to the position of co-host of the *Today* show with Jim Hartz, becoming the first female co-host of any of the morning programs. Despite a speech fault that turned her "r"s into "w"s, Barbara Walters became a star. *Ladies' Home Journal* chose her "Woman of the Year" in Communications in 1974.

Courtesy of *The Jewish Week*

In the spring of 1976, when ABC offered her one-million dollars a year, Walters was front-page news around the country. NBC would not make her an anchor of its evening news; ABC offered her the chance to co-anchor the evening newscast with Harry Reasoner. She went with ABC, becoming the first woman news anchor. Walters' ABC contract also called for a number of prime-time interview specials. On her first one, she interviewed then President and Mrs. Carter and Barbra Streisand.

As a result of Reasoner resenting her "intrusion," Walters' experience as co-anchor ended after a year. She began doing special interviews.

Most likely because she is Jewish, and thus feels closer to the state of Israel than to other countries, the news coverage of which Barbara Walters is most proud is her work during the Middle East peace process in the 1970s. "The most memorable person I ever interviewed was (the late Egyptian President) Anwar Sadat," she said. Her close contacts with Israelis helped her coverage enormously.

Barbara Walters's greatest coup came in November 1977 when she set up a joint interview with Egyptian President Anwar Sadat and Israeli Prime Minister Menachem Begin after their historic meeting. Traveling on the memorable plane ride that took Sadat from Cairo to Tel Aviv that November 19, Walters passed a note to Sadat, asking "Will you do an interview with me?" She provided space for four possible answers: yes, no, alone, with Begin. Sadat handed the paper to her at the end of the journey, having marked "Yes" and "alone" as his answers.

Later, Begin said to Sadat, "For the sake of our friendship with Barbara, will you do a joint interview with me?" and Sadat said, yes. The interview, the only joint one the two men would give, was held in the Knesset (Parliament) building in Jerusalem right after Sadat delivered his address there.

In subsequent years, Walters interviewed both men separately many times. Once, ending a Sadat interview, Walters, as was her custom, thanked him.

"Thank you, Barbara," came the president's reply. "And how do you like a one-million-dollar job? Do you know that the salary for my job is only twelve-thousand dollars a year? And I work day and night."

In 1986, Walters married Merv Adelson, the onetime chairman of Lorimar Telepictures. They were divorced six years later. As of early 1993, Walters was receiving three-million dollars a year for co-anchoring *20/20* and at least two *Barbara Walters Specials*. Both *20/20* and her interview specials continue to receive strong ratings.

WENDY WASSERSTEIN

Chronicling the Age of Feminism

Born October 18, 1950 in Brooklyn, New York. American playwright. In the late 1980s, Wendy Wasserstein was called the most important theatrical chronicler of the impact of feminism on the younger generation. Satirical comedies, her plays have serious themes that deal with the ups and downs of the women's movement. In 1989, she enjoyed her greatest success with *The Heidi Chronicles*. It was awarded the Pulitzer Prize and a Tony Award as the best new play of the year. Her latest play *The Sisters Rosensweig* opened in New York in 1992.

Wendy Wasserstein was born on October 18, 1950 in Brooklyn, New York, the youngest of four children. Until the age of eight, she attended a yeshiva in the Flatbush section of Brooklyn.

Wendy's mother, Lola (Schleifer), and father, Morris W. Wasserstein, were Jewish immigrants from Central Europe who arrived in the United States as children in the 1920s. Her father was a well-to-do textile manufacturer; her mother a housewife with a strong interest in dance and theater.

In the early 1960s, Wendy moved with her family from Flatbush to the prosperous Upper East Side of Manhattan.

Wendy's maternal grandfather was an amateur playwright who had acquaintances in the Yiddish Theater. Wendy's mother took her to plays often. Wendy took dancing lessons every Saturday morning from the dancer and choreographer June Taylor. After class, usually she attended a Broadway matinee with her mother. "I was a show biz baby, born in a trunk," she said in 1989. "I always loved the theater." Musicals, especially.

Wendy attended the Calhoun School, an exclusive Manhattan preparatory academy for girls. "We weren't an intellectual family," she recalled. She was editor of the school's newspaper. And she had a sense of humor. "I was always funny," she once said. "I always had friends because I am funny."

By volunteering to write the musical revue for the school's annual mother-daughter luncheon, Wendy was excused from gym classes. She was not an especially good student. "I would show up every day in the same work shirt and the headmistress would call my mother and tell her that I should get dressed up and wear pink," she noted in 1981.

Despite this, Wendy was accepted at Mount Holyoke College in South Hadley, Massachusetts, where she majored in history. She thought about pursuing a law degree. Midway through college, she took a summer playwriting course at nearby Smith College. She spent her junior year at Amherst College where she performed in campus theatrical productions. She continued to take the law boards each year, however.

After graduating from Mount Holyoke College in 1971, Wendy moved back to New York City and studied creative writing at the City College of New York with such writers

Courtesy of Royce Carlton, Inc., New York

as Joseph Heller and Israel Horovitz.

In 1973, her play, *Any Woman Can't,* was produced off-Broadway. It concerned a girl who gets married after failing her audition for tap-dancing class.

Wasserstein received her Master's degree later that same year from City College, and then enrolled at Yale University's School of Drama. She chose it over the Columbia University School of Business, where she had also been admitted.

Wendy claims she was frightened to death during her first few months at Yale. She thrived, in spite of her fears, however. She wrote *Montpelier Pa-zazz,* a collegiate musical, with David Hollister and the musical revue, *When Dinah Shore Ruled the Earth,* a collaboration with fellow student playwright Christopher Durang.

In 1976, Wasserstein graduated from the Yale School of Drama with a Master of Fine Arts degree. For her master's thesis she wrote a one-act version of what became *Uncommon Women and Others.* It opened off-Broadway on November 21, 1977.

Wasserstein's feminism came from her mother. "She never approved of housework though she had a house full of kids," she recalled. "She thought women who stayed at home were wasting their lives." Naturally Wendy's plays touched on feminist themes.

Uncommon Women and Others portrayed five characters at an elite women's college in the early 1970s who come to terms with new choices and fears in the wake of the feminist movement.

The play won a number of awards and was televised by the Public Broadcasting Service.

Wendy Wasserstein was by now the most promising young playwright in the country. In 1980, the Phoenix Theater commissioned her to write a new play. She wrote *Isn't It Romantic,* a near-sequel to *Uncommon Women.* It examined the lives of two longtime friends, former classmates at a women's college, six years after graduating. The play opened to mixed reviews on May 28, 1981. *New York Times* critic Mel Gussow wrote there was no "denying the playwright's comic virtuosity and her ear for contemporary jargon." A reworked version opened off-Broadway on December 15, 1983. It became a box-office hit and ran for 733 performances.

Another Wendy Wasserstein play, *Tender Offer,* was performed in the spring of 1983 to critical praise. It told the story of a disappointed little girl and her father, whose dedication to his job had caused him to miss his daughter's dance recital.

Wasserstein began to write *The Heidi Chronicles* in 1986 in a studio in East Hampton, Long Island. Wasserstein says she works better in small spaces and the closer it seems to a college dorm room, the better.

Heidi, Wasserstein's character, delivers what became one of the most quoted lines about the American female experience. "I feel stranded, and I thought the point was that we wouldn't feel stranded. I thought we were all in this together."

The play traces Heidi's life from adolescence to adulthood. Paralleling this, it tells the history of the women's movement from its early days in the 1960s. "I want to entertain, but I also want to use the theater to shake things up a little bit," Wasserstein said then. "I want to make people think."

The play premiered off-Broadway on December 11, 1988. Three months later it arrived on Broadway. It won the Pulitzer Prize and the Tony Award and earned for Wendy Wasserstein nearly every major New York theater award, including the New York Drama Critics Circle.

Judith Miller, writing in *The New York Times* on October 18, 1992, wrote of Wasserstein: "Slightly disheveled, a little overweight, hair in all directions, she has a smile that is warm, and, above all, vulnerable. She is a New York type—the lovable, witty, anxious, forty-something single Jewish woman."

Wasserstein's latest play, *The Sisters Rosensweig*, opened at Lincoln Center in New York City in October 1992. The play revolves around Sara Rosensweig, a twice-divorced Jewish-American banker who lives in London and is visited on her fifty-fourth birthday by her two sisters. Wendy Wasserstein told the *Times'* Judith Miller that she wrote "*Sisters*" because "it was important to me to write a play about three uncommon women who are not twenty-three...."

Wasserstein is single and believes that part of the reason for that is her career. "All that success intimidates a lot of men," she complained to Judith Miller. "Can't you see the scene in the bar? 'Hi there, I'm Wendy. I won the Pulitzer prize. What do you do?'"

Of her Jewish background, Wasserstein has said: "Jewish writers inspired me, particularly of musical comedy.... Passover is the most meaningful holiday to me, and I spend it with my family.... There is a Jewish tradition of show business which has influenced my career. My Jewishness has made my outlook on life more ironic and earnest."

Sometimes Wasserstein's audiences believe some of her characters (Heidi of *The Heidi Chronicles*, for instance) are Jewish, when they are not. "As far as I could make out, everyone around me was Jewish when I was a child. I didn't know anybody who was Protestant except on television." As for her practicing Judaism today, Wasserstein says, "I'm sort of a High Holy Days Jew."

RUTH WESTHEIMER

First Superstar Sex Therapist

Born June 4, 1928 in Frankfurt-am-Main, Germany. American sex therapist. Ruth Westheimer originally wanted to be a physician, but instead became a kindergarten teacher in Palestine. She took up sex therapy in the 1960s and by the 1980s was giving advice on the subject first over the radio, then on television. America's most popular sex therapist, she is known universally as "Dr. Ruth."

Born Karola Ruth Siegel in Frankfurt, Germany, on June 4, 1928, she was the only child of Orthodox Jewish parents. Her childhood was middle-class; her father, a learned man, was a successful notions wholesaler. "My father," recalled Westheimer, "gave me the attention that other fathers give to a son."

When Ruth was eleven, the Siegels tried to flee Nazi Germany. Ruth was sent to a Swiss school for six months after which she was expected to travel to Palestine. She never saw her family again. She assumed they died at Auschwitz.

The Swiss school turned into an orphanage where Ruth and one hundred other Jewish refugee girls remained until the war was over. The school director thought of Ruth as a welfare case and trained her as a maid. One teacher noted with disapproval, "She is very intelligent, very lively, and doesn't let anybody else talk."

Having learned about sex by sneaking into her father's library where she read his books, Ruth shared her knowledge with the other children. "I taught all the other girls about menstruation," she said in 1983. "And I got into trouble with the directress. She told me to shut up."

Following the war, Westheimer reached Palestine, abandoning her German name Karola and her Orthodox Judaism.

In 1948, when the state of Israel was founded, Ruth joined the Haganah, the Jewish underground movement. Trained as a sniper, she fired a gun only in target practice. She wanted to become a doctor, but lacked the means to further her education. Self-conscious that she was only four feet, seven inches tall, Ruth moaned into her diary, "Nobody is going to want me because I'm short and ugly."

Her Jewish background impelled her to want to help people. "I can't be a physician,"

Gideon Lewin (Courtesy of Ruth Westheimer)

she said to herself, "so I'll be a kindergarten teacher."

In 1950, a young Israeli soldier proposed marriage, and she quickly accepted. They moved to Paris. Her husband studied medicine and Westheimer, though she lacked a high-school diploma, earned a psychology degree from the Sorbonne. Ruth still wanted a career more intellectually stimulating than teaching.

Westheimer's first marriage ended after five years. In 1956, now pregnant, she married the prospective father, a young Frenchman, and moved with him to New York City. They had a daughter Miriam. That marriage failed, too. Westheimer worked as a housemaid while she learned English and attended night classes to get a Master's degree, which she received in 1959 from the New School for Social Research. She then worked as a research assistant at Columbia University's School of Public Health.

In 1961, while skiing in the Catskill Mountains in northern New York, she met her third husband, a telecommunications consultant and German-Jewish refugee, Manfred Westheimer. They had a son Joel in 1964.

In 1967, Westheimer became project director of a Planned Parenthood clinic in Harlem. "I thought these people are crazy. They talk about sex all day long, and then forty-eight hours later, I said, 'That's a very interesting profession.'" Over the next three years, working days at the clinic, she worked evenings at Columbia University toward a doctorate in family counseling. She also took courses in sex counseling. She was awarded her Ph.D. in 1970.

During the early 1970s, Westheimer served as an associate professor for sex counseling at Lehman College in the Bronx. She moved to Brooklyn College in 1977. Dismissed from her job (for reasons she will not reveal), she called it her "big break." She began lecturing to some New York broadcasters on the need for more sex education programming, and was then invited to be a guest on an NBC affiliate's Sunday morning public affairs program.

In late 1980, she was offered twenty-five dollars a week to do *Sexually Speaking,* a fifteen-minute weekly show on Sundays that aired after midnight. The show was a hit. When the station offered listeners a "Sex on Sunday" T-shirt as a promotion, rather than the few hundred requests it expected, 3,500 were received.

In September 1981, the show, now a live phone-in, was expanded to one hour, filling the ten to eleven time slot each Sunday evening. Of the 4,000 phone calls received each night, only thirty were aired. Soon, "Dr. Ruth," as she came to be called, had New York City's top-rated radio show for its time period.

Westheimer's style is infectious. Tom Shales of *The Washington Post* wrote in 1985: "Once you've talked sex with Dr. Ruth, can it ever be as good with anyone else?"

She is nonjudgmental about sex. "Orgasms," she said cheerfully, "are just a reflex, like a sneeze." She condones nearly all nonviolent sex between consenting adults as normal and healthy. "There's nothing wrong with new uses for peanut butter or onion rings as long as you have a relationship," she told one male caller. She won't take phone calls from the under-sixteen age group. (They have to write.)

Eschewing talk about violent sex, she acknowledged, "It's not that I don't know it exists." She's just not interested in it. She has admitted to ambivalence toward homosexuals.

Westheimer attributed her popularity in part to her distinctive accent ("It relieves listeners of any impropriety in talking about sex") and her willingness to describe parts of the anatomy by their correct names; also, in part, to her being an older woman. "I don't sit on television with a short skirt and decolletage. No man feels threatened talking about his erection with me. I don't think I would have been as listened to twenty years ago."

Westheimer has retained a private practice as a psychologist and family counselor.

Dr. Ruth with the authors Elinor and Robert Slater.

In 1984, Westheimer did a forty-minute nationally televised program on the Lifetime cable network called *Good Sex With Dr. Westheimer,* (later renamed *The Dr. Ruth Show*) which aired six nights a week. NBC Radio began syndicating her radio program nationally that year as well. She continued to do television and radio shows into the 1980s. The *Washington Post's* Tom Shales dubbed her "our first true superstar sex therapist."

Westheimer had one literary embarrassment. In her 1985 paperback called *First Love: A Young People's Guide to Sexual Information,* she wrote that "the safe times [for sexual intercourse] are the week before and the week of ovulation." She meant "unsafe times." The typo required a quick recall of 115,000 copies of the book.

On being Jewish, Westheimer has said: "Part of my being able to talk about issues of sexuality has to do with my being so Jewish. Because for us Jews there's never been a question of sex being a sin, but of sex being a *mitzvah* and an obligation."

One of Ruth Westheimer's favorite hobbies is skiing. "I think it's a sexy sport. It moves your body and you have to take a risk."

As of 1993 she was no longer doing radio, but she did a new cable television program called *Dr. Ruth's Never Too Late.* She has also produced documentary films on such subjects as German Jews and Ethiopian Jews.

Ruth Westheimer's most recent book, *The Art of Arousal,* was published in May 1993. It is a look at sensual art through the ages. At a book party at Tavern on the Green in New York, she announced to the crowd: "If any of you take these books [home] and have some good sex tonight, I would like to know all about it."

$\mathscr{S}$HELLEY $\mathscr{W}$INTERS

Two-time Oscar Winner

Born August 18, 1923 in East St. Louis, Illinois. American actress known for her versatility as an actress. Shelley Winters launched her outstanding movie career in 1948 by grabbing an Oscar nomination for *A Double Life*. She subsequently won two Academy Awards in the best supporting actress category for her roles in the 1959 movie *The Diary of Anne Frank* and the 1965 movie, *A Patch of Blue*. Known for her earthy sensuality in her earlier movies, she acquired a reputation for playing Jewish women, sexy matrons, and whores on the screen in later years.

$\mathscr{S}$helley Winters was Shirley Schrift at birth. Her father, Johann Schrift, was a fashion designer; her mother, Rose (Winter) Schrift, sang for the St. Louis Municipal Opera. At the age of two, Winters appeared in an amateur show—and found that she loved the stage.

In 1934, when Shelley was eleven years old, she and her family moved from East St. Louis, Illinois, to Brooklyn, New York where she attended Thomas Jefferson High School and appeared in a production of Gilbert and Sullivan's operetta, *The Mikado*.

In 1939, six months before she was to graduate from high school, Shelley dropped out and took up modeling in New York's garment district in order to finance acting lessons at the New Theater School. She also performed in the chorus line at the La Conga Club. Changing her name to Shelley Winter at that point, she did some summer stock as well. Between 1939 and 1942, Winters continued to act. One key event occurred in 1942 when she played a supporting role in the operetta *Rosalinda*. Because of that performance, she landed a contract with Columbia Pictures at the then handsome salary of $150 a week.

In 1944 and 1945, she played small roles in seven Columbia-produced films, changing her name from Winter to Winters in 1945. Columbia did not renew her contract and so Winters returned to the stage, where she found parts in productions of *The Taming of the Shrew* and *Of Mice and Men*.

Charles Laughton, the renowned actor, gave her acting lessons. More screen tests followed, none successful. Finally, in 1947, Winters won a small role in the film *The Gangster*. That proved important because the director, George Cukor, watched her perform and was impressed enough to cast her for his film, *A Double Life*, starring Ronald Coleman, in 1948. She played a trampy waitress who is strangled by Coleman's character. Enjoying her first film success, Winters also won an Oscar nomination for her role.

Other parts that emphasized her earthy sexuality followed. Later in 1948, she played a mobster's girlfriend in Universal Pictures' *Larceny*. Universal signed her to a contract.

In 1949, Winters was given her first featured role in the musical *South Seas Sinner*. That same year, she played Alice Tripp, a pregnant factory worker drowned by her seducer, in *A Place in the Sun*, a film based on Theodore Dreiser's book, *An American Tragedy*. She

Avco Embassy

Shelley Winters appearing in the movie Diamonds.

received an Oscar nomination for that role, securing her reputation as a great film actress.

One writer described Winters as a method actress "with the uncanny ability to be appealing, obscene, self-centered, domineering, and funny, all at once."

While her film career was skyrocketing, Winters' personal life had its ups and downs. She married Mack Paul Mayer in 1942, and divorced him six years later. Although she was engaged to actor Farley Granger in 1951, they never married. Leaving Granger the next year, she married Italian movie idol Vittorio Gassman. That marriage ended two years later, in 1954. They had a daughter Vittoria (Tory). In 1957, Winters married another actor, Anthony Franciosa, and again the marriage ended in divorce three years later.

Little of note occurred in her career during much of the 1950s. In 1951, she began studying acting, singing and dancing at the Actors Studio under Elia Kazan's direction. With her film career uneventful and seemingly stalled, she returned to Broadway in 1955.

Heavier, more mature, she was back making movies in 1959. In one of her most famous roles, she played the Dutch housewife in *The Diary of Anne Frank*, winning the Oscar for best supporting actress. She donated the statuette to the Anne Frank Museum in Amsterdam.

During the 1960s, Winters portrayed promiscuous matrons, whores, and suffering mothers. In 1965, playing the horrendous Rose-Ann D'Arcy, she won a second Oscar in the best supporting actress category for the movie *A Patch of Blue*. Over the next decade she was frequently chosen to play Jewish women. "I've got the market cornered on Jewish mothers and whores," she told *Newsday*. In *Next Stop, Greenwich Village*, *Minnie's Boys*, and *The Diary of Anne Frank*, she played Jewish mothers. In the 1972 movie, *The Poseidon Adventure*, she played a Jewish grandmother, garnering another Oscar nomination.

Believing her career suffered by playing so many Jewish women, Winters sought to break out of that mold. "Producers feel being a Jewish woman is a *yenta*," she noted. "I have to stop this image." She was very proud to be Jewish.

She made her debut as a playwright with the production *One Night Stands of a Noisy Passenger*, three short semi-autobiographical plays. Critics attacked her play and it closed soon after its debut off Broadway.

Asked about her career in a 1976 interview with the *Jerusalem Post*, Winters observed that "It's the most punishing, wearing, degrading profession I know. Why did I keep at it?

I think sheer pigheadedness on my part and the fact that I always felt I was just as good as the people I saw and only needed the opportunity to prove it."

Any regrets, she was asked in that same interview? "I'm only sorry that I didn't marry a nice Jewish man and have lots of children. I guess when you come down to it, I'm basically a woman looking for a man."

She has devoted much effort to fundraising for the state of Israel. She was once asked why?

Shelley Winters, Wendy Wasserstein, and Marvin Hamlisch.

Helayne Seidman

"Because I'm a Jew, of course, but more than that, because I'm a human being, and I care about what goes on in the world. I think the whole world must be concerned with Israel—this country is the hope of the future. It combines the wisdom of the old and the energy of the young. If Israel goes, the whole free world goes."

Her best-selling memoir, *Also Known as Shirley,* was published in 1980. Winters complained that, because of the book's frankness, members of her family stopped talking to her. To offset the damage, she threw a party for all those she offended in the book and 400 people showed up.

In 1989, she published a second memoir, called *Shelley II,* in which she revealed tidbits from her relationships with famous friends, including James Dean, Marilyn Monroe, and Sean Connery. She has appeared in films and television throughout the 1980s and early 1990s. In 1991, she played the grouchy pianist Mrs. Fraser in the film *Stepping Out.*

ROSALYN S. YALOW

First American Woman to Receive a Nobel Prize in Science

Born July 19, 1921 in New York, New York. American biomedical investigator. Rosalyn Yalow was the first American woman to receive a Nobel prize in science and only the second woman to capture the Nobel prize in medicine, winning in 1977 for her development of radioimmunoassay (RIA) of the peptide hormones. Because of RIA, doctors could for the first time measure the concentration of hundreds of pharmacologic and biologic substances in the blood and other fluids of the human body, as well as in animals and plants. RIA has also allowed doctors to know how patients are responding to treatment. Thanks to RIA, it became possible to produce test-tube babies.

Rosalyn Sussman Yalow was born in the Bronx, New York, on July 19, 1921. She was the younger child of lower-middle-class Jewish parents. Her father, Simon Sussman, who was born on the Lower East Side, ran a small business. He and his wife Clara also had a son, Alexander.

Rosalyn's mother went to work as a cashier in a department store when she was only twelve years old. She told Rosalyn to become a schoolteacher. Even years later, when Rosalyn was an important scientist, her mother would admonish her, "No self-respecting woman goes to work and leaves two small children (a son born in 1952, a daughter in 1954) at home alone with just a maid."

Neither of Rosalyn's parents had much of an education. Her father taught himself bookkeeping; and her mother was an avid reader, a habit Rosalyn adopted even before she entered kindergarten. Rosalyn said her father "taught me I can achieve anything I set out to do."

Yalow attended public elementary schools, then went to Walton High School where a chemistry teacher advised her to study science. She graduated from high school at the age of fifteen. At Hunter College, some professors urged her to pursue a physics career. However, others also cautioned her that she would have to settle for a secretarial job to underwrite her graduate training. She graduated Phi Beta Kappa and magna cum laude from Hunter with a B.A. degree in physics and chemistry and then took shorthand.

However, no steno pad was in store for Rosalyn Yalow. She was accepted as a teaching fellow in physics at the University of Illinois at Urbana, the only woman among 400 men in the faculty of the College of Engineering. In 1945, she became the second woman to receive a Ph.D. degree in physics from the university.

During graduate school, Rosalyn met a fellow physics student, the son of a rabbi from upstate New York, named A. Aaron Yalow. On June 6, 1943 they were married. After completing her Ph.D. degree in January 1945, Yalow worked for a year as an electrical engineer for the Federal Telecommunications Laboratory. She then joined the faculty at Hunter College as a physics lecturer in 1946, holding that post until 1950.

Dr. Yalow was hired in 1947 as a consultant to the Radiotherapy Department in the VA hospital in the Bronx. The department had begun to explore the use of radio isotopes in the diagnosis and treatment of diseases. In 1950, Dr. Solomon A. Berson joined the radioisotope unit and became its chief four years later.

At first Yalow and Berson studied the use of radioactive iodine in the diagnosis and treatment of thyroid disease. Subsequently they measured blood volume by tagging red blood cells or plasma proteins with radioisotopes. They discovered ways in which radioactive iodine could be utilized to tag insulin and other proteins in order to study the body's normal methods of making and destroying such substances.

It was while conducting these studies in 1959 that Dr. Yalow and Dr. Berson came up with their revolutionary method of radioimmunoassay. They invented the RIA

Courtesy of Rosalyn Yalow

technique in order to measure the amount of insulin in the blood of adult diabetics. Subsequently, Yalow and others have utilized RIA to resolve scores of medical problems in thousands of laboratories in the United States and abroad.

When asked when she realized that she had made a major discovery Dr. Yalow responded, "Immediately. We instituted a course in 1961 and for the next four years we trained one hundred and fifty endocrinologists in using the techniques because we knew it would be of major value in determining initially the hormones in the blood."

This ingenious application of nuclear physics to clinical medicine enabled scientists to use radioisotopic tracers to measure the concentration of hundreds of pharmacologic and biologic substances in the blood and other fluids of the human body, as well as in animals and plants. In the past those substances had often been impossible to measure either because they were present in too minute quantities or diluted concentrations, or because their chemical properties were too similar to those of other substances. The discovery of RIA has been called one of the most significant applications of basic research to clinical medicine. Blood collection centers used the RIA to prevent the inclusion of blood contaminated with hepatitis virus.

In 1976, Rosalyn Yalow became the first woman to win the Albert Lasker Prize for Basic Medical Research. She was the first American woman to receive a Nobel prize in science, capturing the coveted prize in 1977 for her development of radioimmunoassay (RIA) of the peptide hormones.

Yalow was presented with an honorary doctor of science degree in 1980 by the University of Hartford in Connecticut. At the university's commencement exercises she

313

Rosalyn Yalow in her laboratory.

noted that "If we are to have faith that mankind will survive and thrive on the face of the earth, we are dependent on continued revolutions brought by science. These revolutions will set us free from hunger and disease and permit us to set our sights on the stars."

Yalow describes herself as a feminist, but does not like "ghetto" jobs or "ghetto" awards, those which single out women. "If we [women] were ever to move upwards we must demonstrate competence, courage, and determination to succeed and must be prepared to challenge and take our place in the Establishment." This book's authors asked Rosalyn Yalow whether there were any special people or institutions that greatly influenced her and that helped her to identify positively as a Jew.

She replied: "In 1943 I married a fellow graduate student in physics at the University of Illinois. He was the son of an Orthodox rabbi and was the source of my Jewish learning. Our house has been strictly Orthodox." Her husband died in August 1992.

The authors also asked Dr. Yalow which Jewish holidays were most meaningful to her and how she observed them. Her answer: "We have had seders in our home since the mid-50s. I.I. Rabi, a noted physicist, was a guest for many years. One year we also had [the well-known novelist] Isaac Bashevis Singer."

Ralph Coslovsky worked in Yalow's lab and reported that Yalow worked day and night, including Sundays. He remarked that she ran her lab "like Napoleon must have run his army. It was small and super-efficient. She streamlined procedures and developed materials that were so effective, we obtained perfect results routinely, which in other labs take longer and numerous trials. She loved to get her hands dirty, labeling the isotopes, caring for the animals—stuff a technician might do....As much as you admire her, she was so overpowering, you felt relief at her absence."

Asked what had pleased her the most about her research, Yalow noted that it had been the fact that "RIA is still used in thousands of labs around the world, including those in developing countries."

Anzia Yezierska

Queen of the Ghetto

Born circa 1880 in Plinsk, Russian Poland; died November 21, 1970. American novelist. Anzia Yezierska was one of the first American Jewish immigrant writers to make an impact on the mass magazines of her day. Drawing upon her experience as an employee in sweatshops and as a waitress, cook, and teacher, she was one of a handful of American Jewish writers who vividly and movingly portrayed the lives of immigrants in the New World.

Anzia, born in Plinsk, Russian Poland, around 1880, was raised in a poor but Orthodox Jewish home. Her parents, Baruch and Pearl Yezierska, took her to New York in the 1890s when she was sixteen years old.

After the family reached the United States, Anzia's father remained a full-time Talmudic scholar. His wife and children were forced to support the family. Rebelling against her family, Anzia ran away from home. She wanted, as she said later, to "make from herself a person."

It is difficult to trace her early days because she has given different accounts of that period. At one stage, she married and had a daughter, but left them so that she could concentrate on her writing.

Eager to learn and be on her own, Anzia was forced to work in sweatshops and a laundry on the Lower East Side in New York. She did gain one advantage from the experience: She acquired a good deal of insight into the life of new immigrants that enriched much of her early writings.

To increase her knowledge, Anzia learned what she could from night-school English classes and from borrowed books. She won a scholarship to a training program for domestic-science teachers. From 1905 to 1913, she taught cooking in an elementary school.

Anzia published her first short story in 1915. During the next ten years her stories appeared in a number of respected magazines. Yezierska was helped and encouraged in her early writing by the author Frank Crane, who was also a Methodist Episcopal clergyman.

Anzia's first piece of writing, a story called "Where Lovers Die," was published in 1918 in the *Metropolitan* magazine.

Critic Edward J. O'Brien praised her short story, "The Fat of the Land," as the best short story of 1919. In it, Yezierska wrote about the children of Jewish immigrants to America, noting how ashamed the children felt over mothers who were uneducated in the ways of their new country.

Anzia Yezierska presented one of the earliest accounts of the tensions that existed between Russian and German-Jewish immigrants during the late nineteenth century in America. She wrote with venom pouring from her pen, and the target of her venom was often the German-Jewish social workers who came from wealthy families and tried to help the less fortunate Jewish families (descendants from Russia and Eastern Europe). Anzia

Yezierska called these social workers bourgeois women, even though they described themselves as "friendly visitors."

Yezierska despised these social workers for belonging to the German-Jewish families who had Americanized themselves decades earlier. She despised them as well for living in comfort in their homes on the Upper West Side, departing once a day to enter the world of the Lower East Side where they provided their "scientific charity" (in Yezierska's words) to the newly-arrived Russian and Eastern European immigrants.

Yezierska took on other groups as well, including older people, sometimes the foreign born and bred, sometimes the religious community. Always she used wit and sarcasm in her writing. She differed from other writers of her time because of her strong bent toward realism. Other writers placed taboos on a variety of subjects, among which were religion, sex, and filth. She did not.

Anzia Yezierska's writing was serious, but tinged with much humor, however bitter. Not counted as an expert in style, or plot development, or characterization, she nonetheless offered readers a good deal of emotion that seemed to make up for other literary defects.

Yezierska's characters came to symbolize the spiritual hunger of America's new immigrants. They also reflected the immigrant's zest for life. She was able to provide an authenticity to her short stories because of her knowledge of conditions on the Lower East Side. This was especially the case with a collection of ten short narratives dealing with East Side life called *Hungry Hearts* (1920); the book established her reputation as a realist writer.

In *Hungry Hearts,* Anzia Yezierska's immigrant characters struggle with an America of poverty and exploitation that disillusions them; they search for the "real" America that will match their ideals. Literary critic Peggy Stinson wrote that "the stories, like all of her fiction, are realistic, passionate, occasionally autobiographical, sometimes formless and overwrought; their effusive language suggests the style and intonation of an immigrant speaker."

Yezierska's main characters are women—women working in sweatshops or at home, women who want to overcome the daily drudgery of their lives and find love, beauty, independence, dignity.

Hollywood bought the film rights to *Hungry Hearts* and hired Yezierska as a salaried writer. The film based on those stories was produced by Samuel Goldwyn in 1922. Yezierska subsequently became a wealthy celebrity. The glamour of Hollywood quickly lost its attraction for Anzia Yezierska. She returned to New York, continuing to write fiction during the 1920s and 1930s.

Her first novel, *Salome of the Tenements* (1922) was about an East Side Russian Jewess, Sonya Vrunsky, who became the wife of an American-born millionaire and philanthropist, John Manning. Unable to share his outlook on life, she leaves him to start a career of her own as a dress designer.

Yezierska's next books, which also dealt with the adjustment of the Jewish immigrant to American life, were *Children of Loneliness* (1923); and *Bread Givers.* (1925) The latter story was an autobiographical novel about her own early years. It was subtitled "A Struggle between a Father of the Old World and a Daughter of the New." She expressed sympathy for the daughter.

In 1927, she wrote *Arrogant Beggar*. Five years later *All I Could Never Be* was published.

Often, Anzia Yezierska relied upon her immigrant background in New York to authenticate her scenes and to give her Yiddishized English dialogue a truthful ring. She was called "Queen of the Ghetto" in appreciation of her successful literary chronicling of the Jewish immigrant's fate.

Hitting a dry spell after those books were published, Yezierska earned little money. It was only when her autobiographical work *Red Ribbon on A White Horse* was published in 1950, as she approached old age, that she had a slight revival of popularity. The title came from one of her father's favorite quotations, "Poverty is an ornament on a Jew like a red ribbon on a white horse."

While her publisher called it an autobiography, Yezierska's daughter, to whom the book was dedicated, called it fiction. The book made no mention of a husband or child. It skipped over that part of Yezierska's life.

Ultimately, Yezierska was unable to win the affection of huge numbers of people. Many readers disliked the intensity of her writing and felt that she harped too much on hunger and loneliness. Yet she achieved a great deal as a new immigrant in a strange land, and her writings have in later years helped many to understand the immigrant's plight.

THUMBNAIL SKETCHES

ALEXANDRA, QUEEN SALOME

BORN 139 B.C.E.; DIED 67 B.C.E.
ANCIENT JEWISH RULER.

Queen Alexandra was the last effective ruler of the independent Hasmonean dynasty in the Land of Israel. Only three women have ruled the Jewish people: Athaliah, during the First Jewish Commonwealth; Golda Meir, Prime Minister of the state of Israel from 1969 to 1974; and Queen Salome Alexandra (known as Shelomzion in Hebrew) during the Second Commonwealth. Alexandra ruled Judea from 76 to 67 B.C.E., succeeding her husband Alexander Yannai. Queen Alexandra reversed his unfriendly policy toward the Pharisees. Alexandra's reign has been called a high point of the Second Commonwealth, her time as queen also important in the history of Jewish internal government. The Sanhedrin, formerly more like today's British House of Lords, was reorganized in accordance with the wishes of the Pharisees, and became a supreme court, administering justice and ruling on religious matters under the Pharisees' guidance. Alexandra acted wisely in foreign affairs by enlarging the size of the army, and making provisions for a variety of fortresses. She virtually eliminated military campaigns. The King of Armenia threatened to fight her kingdom, but she was able to placate him by sending gifts. Yet she made no alliances. Judea remained independent. Upon Alexandra's death, her successors were unable to provide stability and eventually Judea lost its independence to Rome, ending the Hasmonean dynasty. Alexandra has been taken to task by historians for exhibiting a lack of statesmanship because she was more interested in maintaining peace even if it hurt the state in the long run. She was assailed for encouraging conflict among her citizenry rather than uniting the Judean people, and for not trying to settle the disputes between the Sadducees and the Pharisees. Yet, though she ruled only nine years, the queen managed at least to quiet the dissension between the Sadducees and Pharisees.

ARNOLD, ROSEANNE BARR

BORN NOVEMBER 3, 1952 IN SALT LAKE CITY, UTAH.
AMERICAN COMEDIENNE AND ACTRESS.

Roseanne began her career as a stand-up comedienne, which led to her successful television career. Her show *Roseanne,* which debuted in 1988, has become the top comedy show of the late 1980s and early 1990s. "I was just a real weird woman from the day I was born," Roseanne said in 1989. After watching a hobo jump off a train when she was eight, Roseanne fantasized about "goin' on the road." She says she got her love of comedy from her father. While in Colorado, Roseanne met Bill Pentland, a night clerk at a motel. They were married in 1974, and had three children. Roseanne visited a Denver comedy club in August 1981, sat through the routines of several male comedians, then took the stage to deliver a comic rebuttal to the sexist jokes she had just heard. She then played clubs in Kansas, Arizona, Oklahoma, and Texas. After reaching Los Angeles, she was a smash hit when she did her routine in the Comedy Store and two weeks later she was cast in a television special called *Funny.* In 1987, she did her own HBO special called *The Roseanne Barr Show.* It won Ace Awards (cable TV's version of the Emmy) for Best HBO Special and Best Female in a Comedy. Matt Williams, a former writer for *The Cosby Show,* asked her to star in a sitcom with the focus on one working mother. *Roseanne* was born. It debuted in mid-

October of 1988 and since then has continuously been in the Nielson Ratings' top ten. Critics called it "the best thing since Cosby." At the American Comedy Awards ceremony in May 1989, Roseanne was named Best Female Performer in a Leading Role in a Television Series. Her marriage to Pentland ended after fifteen years in July 1989. She married Tom Arnold, a comedian and comedy writer, in 1990. Her autobiography, *Roseanne: My Life as a Woman,* was published in September 1989. In November 1993 Roseanne Arnold won an Emmy for best comedy actress on American television. In early 1994, Roseann published her second autobiography, *My Life.*

ATHALIAH

BORN AND DIED NINTH CENTURY B.C.E.
QUEEN OF JUDAH FROM 842 TO 836 B.C.E.

Athaliah's name in Hebrew means "the Lord is exalted." The daughter of Ahab and Jezebel (or perhaps the daughter of Omir), Athaliah married Jehoram (Joram), the crown prince of Judah, and in so doing, sealed the alliance between Israel and Judah. The marriage also led to the introduction of Baal worship in Jerusalem during the rule of her husband, and her son Ahaziah. Athaliah, the queenmother, grabbed power after Ahaziah was murdered by Jehu during the anti-Omride revolt. She murdered all potential rivals in the royal family (her husband had done the same, perhaps prompted by her). Only the infant son of Ahaziah, Joash, escaped. His aunt Jehosheba, the sister of the dead king and the wife of High Priest Jehoiada, saved Joash. Six years later, Jehoiada conspired to have Joash crowned in the Temple. He became the legitimate king, and Athaliah, who had rushed to the spot yelling "treason," was led to the "horse entrance," also called "The Horse Gate," where she was killed. The Temple of Baal was destroyed. Athaliah's violent end seemed inevitable—the Temple priesthood and others most likely viewed her as a foreign usurper and the murderer of the royal Davidic line. In the *Aggadah,* Athaliah is grouped with Jezebel, Vashti, and Semiramis as one of the four women who gained power in the world. Her violent story was adopted by the French dramatist Jean Racine, whose play *Athalie* (1691) became a classic tragedy. Sarah Bernhardt made the part of the villainous queen one of her great roles.

BLUME, JUDY

BORN FEBRUARY 12, 1938 IN ELIZABETH, NEW JERSEY.
AMERICAN AUTHOR.

One of the most popular and controversial American authors of juvenile fiction, Judy Blume puts her characters, aged nine to twelve, into situations where they are forced to confront such preadolescent traumas as divorce, incipient sexuality, and peer group pressure. Her first fourteen books sold nearly seven million copies. Ten of her best-selling children's books were selected in a kids' poll as among their fifty favorite books, and three of them won first, second and third place. Blume's young readers totalled twenty-seven million by the mid-1980s when she turned to adult fiction. In 1978, Blume wrote her first adult novel, a best seller called *Wifey,* a sexually-frank tale of a suburban housewife who scuttles a stagnant marriage. In 1984 Blume authored another best-selling adult book, *Smart Women.*

Born Judy Sussman, to Orthodox Jewish parents, while a junior at New York University, Judy married attorney John M. Blume. Always a talented storyteller, Blume eased the boredom of doing housework as a suburban housewife in Scotch Plains, New Jersey, by making up rhymed children's stories. She tried her hand at children's novels, but got only rejection slips until 1969 when her picture book, *The One in the Middle is the Green Kangaroo,* was published. It was about a middle child who felt the pressure of being sandwiched between an older brother and a younger sister. *Are You There, God?, It's Me, Margaret* was the first of her first-person novels, written in the voice of a child. The book, published in 1970, was narrated as if experienced by a New Jersey sixth-grader named Margaret. In 1983, Blume was named among America's one hundred "Most Important Women" by the *Ladies' Home Journal* and as one of America's twenty-five "Most Influential Women" by the *World Almanac.*

BUXTON, ANGELA

BORN AUGUST 16, 1934 IN LIVERPOOL, ENGLAND.
BRITISH TENNIS PLAYER.

Angela Buxton

One of the greatest woman tennis players of all time, Angela Buxton remains the only Jewish woman to win a Wimbledon title. She began playing tennis at age eight while attending a convent school in Johannesburg, South Africa. Angela returned to England in 1946, improving her game while living in Los Angeles for six months in the early 1950s. In 1953, she won two gold medals at the Maccabiah Games in Israel. By 1954, Angela was ranked number four in England. Her best season came two years later when she won the English Indoor and Grass championships and the hardcourt doubles title (with Darlene Hard). In addition, Buxton won the doubles (with Althea Gibson) in both the Wimbledon and the French Open. Her greatest accomplishment came when she reached the singles final at Wimbledon that year, only to lose to the American player Shirley Fry. Her tennis career ended in 1956 when she injured her wrist. She then opened the Angela Buxton Center, a tennis school in London's Hampstead section. In recent years, she has been writing and lecturing about the tennis scene.

COPELAND, LILLIAN

BORN NOVEMBER 25, 1904 IN NEW YORK, NEW YORK; DIED FEBRUARY 7, 1964.
AMERICAN TRACK AND FIELD STAR.

Lillian Copeland was an outstanding success in the shot put, discus, and javelin. An all-around athlete at the University of Southern California, she won every woman's track event she entered. Copeland gained the first of her nine national titles in 1925 with a victory in the shot put event. In 1926, Lillian was touted as one of the world's greatest female athletes. She won a silver medal in the discus throw in the 1928 Olympics. She captured a gold medal in the same event in the 1932 Olympics, setting a world record, hurling the discus 133 feet, 1⅝ inches. So eager was she to take part in the 1935 Maccabiah Games in Palestine that she went there to join the competition before receiving an invitation. She paid her own way, and won each of her three specialties. After her retirement from sports competition, Copeland worked with the Los Angeles County Sheriff's Department from August 11, 1936 to January 31, 1960, most of the time as a juvenile officer. She is a member of the Helms Athletic Hall of Fame and of the Jewish Sports Hall of Fame in Israel.

DAWIDOWICZ, LUCY

BORN JUNE 16, 1915 IN NEW YORK, NEW YORK; DIED DECEMBER 4, 1990.
AMERICAN HISTORIAN AND AUTHOR.

Lucy Dawidowicz's towering, award-winning book *The War Against the Jews 1933-1945*, published in 1975, is regarded as the most thorough piece of research into the Holocaust. Born Lucy Schildkret, she received a B.A. in 1936 from Hunter College. Following World War II, she traveled to Europe for the American Jewish Joint Distribution Committee to aid concentration camp survivors. In 1947, she helped writer John Hersey research his 1950 novel, *The Wall*, about the Warsaw Ghetto. Dawidowicz served as research director of the American Jewish Committee until 1969. She then joined the faculty of Yeshiva University as Professor of Holocaust Studies, where she taught there until 1975. In *The War Against the Jews: 1933-1945*, Dawidowicz asserted that Hitler's "final solution" went beyond a vendetta of European bullies and anti-Semites. Rather, it was the result of despotic, authoritarian ideology and was aimed at destroying the alien Jewish outsider. Accordingly, she insisted that the slaughter of the European Jews was inevitable, that resistance was bound to fail. She *forcefully* defended Jewish victims of the Holocaust against accusations that they did not do enough to fight the Nazis. Asked if she thought the Holocaust should be taught to public school students, Dawidowicz replied, "I'd feel a lot safer if they learned the meaning of the Constitution instead." In 1993, Schocken Books published a posthumous collection of her essays called *What Is the Use of Jewish History?*

EPHRON, NORA

BORN MAY 19, 1941 IN NEW YORK, NEW YORK.
AMERICAN WRITER.

In 1963, Nora Ephron began working as a general assignment reporter for *The New York Post*. Eleven years later, Ephron became a senior editor at *Esquire* magazine and wrote a column talking about the media. Three collections of her journalistic essays were published in the 1970s, including one entitled *Scribble, Scribble: Notes on the Media* (1978). In 1967, she married humorist and author Dan Greenburg. "I don't think I'm a great writer," Ephron said in 1983. "I think that I have a voice.... I think I have a way of writing—that, whatever it is, is very clearly me writing it." Her best-selling book *Heartburn* (later a movie with the same name) was a roman à clef based on her second marriage—to Watergate journalist Carl Bernstein. Asked his reaction to *Heartburn*, Bernstein replied, "Obviously, I wish Nora hadn't written it.... The book is like Nora—it's very clever." By the late 1970s Ephron was writing screenplays for the movies, including *Silkwood,* and *When Harry Met Sally.* She also wrote the screenplay and directed the 1993 movie *Sleepless in Seattle.*

EPSTEIN, CHARLOTTE "EPPY"

BORN SEPTEMBER 1884, IN NEW YORK, NEW YORK; DIED AUGUST 27, 1938.
AMERICAN SWIMMING ADMINISTRATOR.

Charlotte Epstein is called the mother of American women's swimming. In 1914, she founded the National Women's Life Saving League, which provided a place for women to meet and swim. Five years later, her league became the New York Women's Swimming Association (WSA). This small group of businesswomen led by Epstein built the WSA into the world's greatest swimming organization. Charlotte established women's swimming as a sport in the United States. She was largely responsible for the inclusion of the first American women's swimming team in the Olympics when a delegation participated in the Antwerp Games in 1920. Among Charlotte's proteges have been Gertrude Ederle, Aileen Riggin, and Eleanor Holme. During her twenty-two years with the Women's Swimming Association, Charlotte's swimmers held fifty-one world records and made up thirty national champion relay teams. Professionally Charlotte Epstein was a court stenographer and legal secretary. She was named a member of the Jewish Sports Hall of Fame in Israel. She never married. Her last assignment was at the Court of Domestic Relations in Brooklyn.

FRANK, RAY

BORN IN 1865 IN CALIFORNIA; DIED IN 1948.
AMERICAN PREACHER.

Ray Frank was an Orthodox Jew whose father was a former Indian agent claiming to be descended from the eighteenth century's most important Talmudic scholar, Elijah of Vilna. A close friend and correspondent of the California journalist and writer Ambrose Bierce, Ray Frank preached frequently and eloquently and taught school in a Nevada village, wrote short stories, lectured and studied to be an elocutionist. In 1892, Rabbi Isaac Mayer Wise used the pages of the *American Israelite* to invite her to become the first female student at Hebrew Union College in Cincinnati, Ohio. She attended classes for one semester at HUC, the Reform movement's rabbinical seminary. After that, she was called the first woman rabbi in the world, which was incorrect. One newspaper referred to her as a female messiah. Frank was never formally employed as a rabbi, but she was often asked to speak from both Jewish and Christian pulpits. She is likely to have been the first American woman to preach from a Jewish pulpit. Based in Oakland, California, Frank traveled throughout the American Northwest, serving as a correspondent for a number of newspapers headquartered in San Francisco and Oakland. Just before Rosh Hashanah in 1890, while stopping off at Spokane Falls, Washington, she was distraught to learn that there were no Jewish religious services planned. In a special edition of the Spokane Falls *Gazette,* she placed an ad to announce that she would preach to Jews at the Opera House that evening, Rosh Hashanah eve. Not only did she preach that evening, but she was there for Yom Kippur services as well. On September 4, 1893, Frank offered the opening prayer at the first Jewish Women's Congress in Chicago, which was held as part of the Parliament of Religions during the World's Fair there. The next morning she gave an address, "Woman in the Synagogue," arguing that because women were spiritually superior to men, they had a responsibility as mothers, wives, sisters or sweethearts to be religious teachers and to lead others to God. Although she thought woman had the right as well as the ability to serve as rabbis or congregational presidents, she adopted the view that a woman's "noblest work will be at home." Because of her activities, the press erroneously called her a "lady rabbi." She was asked by one Reform congregation in Chicago to be its full-time spiritual leader, but she declined, believing that it would mean she would have to give up her independence of thought. In 1901, she married Simon Litman, a professor at the University of Illinois.

FRANKENTHALER, HELEN

BORN DECEMBER 12, 1928 IN NEW YORK, NEW YORK.
AMERICAN PAINTER.

Helen Frankenthaler created a new style in painting, evolving her own form of Abstract Expressionism. Rather than paint on top of an already sealed canvas, Helen poured paint over an unprimed surface, permitting the color to soak into the canvas support. A whole generation of painters, taking their cue from her, began practicing stain, or Color-Field, painting. "She is one of the great artists of the last half of this century," says art critic and friend Eugene Goossen. The youngest daughter of a New York Supreme Court judge, Helen grew up in solid bourgeois comfort in Manhattan. She began painting as a child. She did watercolors and sketches and used Crayolas for drawing. "Like every other kid, I made terrific pictures, but maybe mine had a little more passion," she said. Attending Bennington College in the late 1940s, Frankenthaler studied with artist Paul Feeley, whose seminars brought her in contact with the school of European modernism in art. She became an excellent Cubist painter. She graduated from Bennington in 1949, then studied art history at Columbia University in New York City. She began to paint in a fourteen-dollar-a-month cold water studio located on Twenty-first Street. In the summer of 1950, studying with painter Hans Hofmann at his school in Provincetown, Massachusetts, Frankenthaler began using color in her paintings for the first time. She was particularly impressed with the power of light in painting. She experimented with a new style, inspired by her mentor, Jackson Pollock, who employed the method of directly pouring paint. She used the technique in one of her best-known works, "Mountain and Sea," in 1952. It was a moody, abstract interpretation of the landscape. From 1958 to 1971, Helen was married to the Abstract Expressionist painter Robert Motherwell. In 1978, Frankenthaler's paintings were selling for as much as $30,000 each. In 1985, a retrospective of thirty-five years of her work was shown at the Guggenheim Museum in New York City. It contained seventy-six drawings on paper.

GUGGENHEIM, PEGGY

BORN JANUARY 2, 1900 IN NEW YORK, NEW YORK; DIED DECEMBER 23, 1979.
AMERICAN ART PATRON.

The second daughter of Benjamin Guggenheim (1865-1912), Peggy Guggenheim had a major impact on modern art, both in the United States and in Europe. When her father drowned on the *Titanic* in 1912, Peggy invested her inheritance in what became the largest private collection of modern art. It was housed in Venice's *Palazzo Venier dei Leoni*. Living in Europe during the 1920s and 1930s, Peggy opened the Guggenheim Jeune Gallery in London and exhibited the works of Europe's most important avant-garde artists. With the Nazi invasion of France, she shipped her art collection to New York and later opened the Art of the Century Gallery there. In 1946, Peggy was back in Europe where she opened her art museum in Venice. After her death, the Guggenheim Museum in New York City assumed responsibility for Peggy Guggenheim's Venice art museum. The Italian Government declared the museum a national monument. Peggy wrote two volumes of memoirs, *Out of This Century* and *Confessions of an Art Addict*.

HAUSER, RITA E.

BORN JULY 12, 1934.

AMERICAN LAWYER.

Rita Hauser is an international lawyer who is considered one of the best female attorneys in America. Hauser served as the American representative to the United Nations Commission on Human Rights from 1969 to 1972 and was a member of the U.S. delegation to the U.N. General Assembly in 1969. She has been influential in Republican party circles and in foreign policy groups. Hauser was born Rita Abrams to parents who were Russian immigrants. In 1954, she graduated magna cum laude from Hunter College in New York City with a B.A. degree. A year later she earned a doctorate in political economy at the University of Strasbourg, France, again magna cum laude. In 1959, she began practicing law in New York City, specializing in corporate law for international clients. She has been a partner in the highly respected law firm of Stroock & Stroock & Lavan, which focuses its practice on private and public international law. Fluent in French, Hauser frequently travels to France on business. She played an important behind the scenes role in the election campaigns of presidents Richard Nixon and Ronald Reagan. In 1978, she briefly sought the Republican nomination for attorney general of New York. Reports surfaced at times that she was being considered for the U.S. Supreme Court. In 1988, she was one of five American Jews who met in Stockholm with Yasser Arafat, encouraging him to utter conciliatory statements to Israel that led to American agreement to open a "dialogue" with Arafat's Palestine Liberation Organization.

HEILBRON, ROSE

BORN IN 1914 IN LIVERPOOL, ENGLAND.

ENGLISH LAWYER AND JUDGE.

"Rosie," as she is known affectionately, was admitted to the bar in 1939 and rapidly established a reputation as a criminal advocate of exceptional ability. In 1949, Heilbron was made a king's counsel and in 1956 became a recorder (chief criminal judge) of Burnley, making her the first woman to be appointed a recorder in Britain. At the age of sixty, in July 1974, she was appointed a judge of the family division of the High Court, only the second woman in Great Britain to win such an appointment. In October of that same year, she was made a Dame Commander of the British Empire. Heilbron began a three-year stint as the presiding judge of the northern circuit in 1979. Then, in 1981, she had the dubious distinction of presiding over Britain's most expensive trial to date, one that cost the commonwealth about two million pounds, when international drug dealer Alexander Sinclair was convicted of the murder of an associate. Heilbron sentenced Sinclair to twenty years in jail. In her capacity as vice-president of the British Federation of Business and Professional Women, Heilbron was frequently cited as an example of the professional advancement of women in a man's world. In 1987, she became the first woman barrister to argue a case in the House of Lords. She is also one of the first two women barristers to be made a Queen's Counsel. One English writer, Fenton Bresler, writing in the *Evening Standard,* said that Heilbron "was a younger, much prettier Rumpole with a disarmingly softspoken voice." "Rosie" retired from the bench in late 1988.

HEILBRUN, CAROLYN

BORN JANUARY 13, 1926 IN EAST ORANGE, NEW JERSEY.
FEMINIST SCHOLAR AND MYSTERY-NOVEL WRITER.

Carolyn Heilbrun is widely respected by feminist scholars as the author of *Toward a Recognition of Androgyny* (1973), *Reinventing Womanhood* (1979), and *Writing a Woman's Life* (1988). She is a pioneer in the field of women's biography and autobiography. Heilbrun has developed an alternate career for herself as Amanda Cross, the pseudonymous author of the Kate Fansler series of mystery novels. Graduating Phi Beta Kappa in English and philosophy from Wellesley College in 1947, she received her doctorate from Columbia University in 1959. Carolyn foreshadowed feminist scholarship with her 1957 article in the *Shakespeare Quarterly* called "The Character of Hamlet's Mother," by suggesting that Hamlet's mother was lucid and sensuous rather than weak and shallow. In 1972, Heilbrun became a full tenured professor at Columbia University. In 1986, she became the first director of Columbia's Institute for Research on Women and Gender. She wrote her first mystery novel, *In the Last Analysis,* in 1964. The heroine of her mystery books, Kate Fansler, was, like herself, an English professor at a New York City university, and a feminist. Thinking mystery writing too frivolous a concern for a serious scholar, Heilbrun adopted the pseudonym Amanda Cross for her fiction out of concern that her colleagues at Columbia might deny her tenure. Her mystery series has sold some one million copies, making her a popular writer as well as a respected academic. Recently, she has been working on a biography of the well-known feminist Gloria Steinem. Carolyn has been married for forty-eight years to James Heilbrun, an urban economist at Fordham University. They have two daughters and a son.

HOLLIDAY, JUDY

BORN JUNE 21, 1922 IN NEW YORK, NEW YORK; DIED JUNE 7, 1965.
AMERICAN ACTRESS.

Judy Holliday was best known for playing Billie Dawn in the stage and screen versions of *Born Yesterday.* In 1950, she was given an Academy Award for Best Actress for the movie version of that play. Prior to that, Judy appeared in one other Broadway stage production, *Kiss Them for Me,* and in four other movies, including *Adam's Rib,* which were also well-received. Born Judith Tuvim, Holliday used the short form of her first name, Judy, and adopted Holliday for her surname (Yom Tovim in Hebrew are holidays.) Holliday's parents separated when she was six years old. She was blessed with an exceptionally high I.Q. (172) and did well in school. She was editor of the school newspaper at the Julia Richman High School in Manhattan. After graduation, she became a backstage switchboard operator at the Mercury Theater, run by Orson Welles, hoping to get into acting through the back door. In the fall of 1938, she formed a comedy group called the Revuers (along with Adolph Green and Betty Comden) which did sketches and satirical revues. In 1944, by now relocated to Hollywood, Holliday signed a seven-picture deal with Twentieth Century-Fox. She returned to New York, eventually starring in the

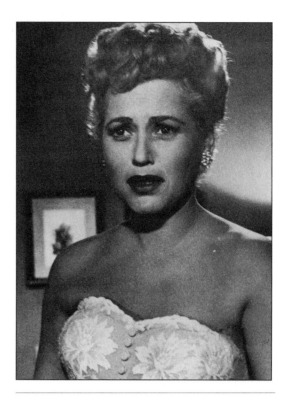

Broadway version of *Born Yesterday,* and was an instant hit. She played the role for four years (1,643 performances) until 1949. To capture the movie role in 1950, however, she had to audition against thirty-eight other actresses, who were also tested for the coveted part. Bosley Crowther, *The New York Times* critic, wrote: "This marvelously-clever young actress so richly conveys the attitudes and vocal intonations of a native of the sidewalks of New York that it is art." Unfortunately for the public, Judy Holliday's life was short. She died of cancer in New York City just two weeks before her forty-fourth birthday.

HOLTZMAN, ELIZABETH

BORN AUGUST 11, 1941 IN BROOKLYN, NEW YORK.
AMERICAN POLITICIAN.

Elizabeth Holtzman graduated from Radcliffe College, where she majored in American history and American literature. In 1965, she graduated from Harvard Law School, one of fifteen women in a class of five-hundred men. Holtzman worked for two years in New York as an attorney specializing in litigation. In 1968, Holtzman was named liaison to the Department of Parks, Recreation and Cultural Affairs during the administration of New York City Mayor John V. Lindsay. She then resumed her private law practice in 1970. In the 1972 Congressional elections, newcomer Elizabeth Holtzman defeated a veteran Democratic politician, octogenarian Emanuel Cellar, who had represented the 16th Congressional District for fifty years. At age 31 Holtzman thus became the youngest woman ever elected to Congress. In her eight years in Congress, Holtzman was an outspoken champion of the rights of minorities, women, the elderly, and the poor. Her incisive interrogation during the 1973 and 1974 Congressional Watergate hearings brought her national attention. In 1980, she ran for the U.S. Senate seat from New York State and won a hotly contested primary race, but was narrowly defeated in November by Alphonse D'Amato. In 1981, Holtzman became the first woman elected district attorney of Brooklyn, making her New York City's first female district attorney. Her political career grew even stronger when she was elected city comptroller in 1989. In 1992, however, she ran again for the U.S. Senate, but was defeated. Holtzman is unmarried and fiercely protects her privacy. *The New York Times* described her in March 1993 as "an unlikely politician...a petite, ramrod-straight woman with stiff mannerisms, a roughened, squeaky voice and a taste in clothes that inclines to bright colors....Her manner is brusque at times, and she seldom cracks a joke in public. But for all that, she has also managed to project the image of a tough, honest, principled liberal."

HURST, FANNIE

BORN IN 1889 IN HAMILTON, OHIO; DIED IN 1968.
AMERICAN WRITER.

Fannie Hurst grew up in St. Louis in an assimilated, middle-class family. After graduating from Washington University in 1909, Hurst did graduate work at Columbia University. Struggling through the early part of her life as she tried to become a published writer, Fannie Hurst peddled her stories to publishers only to be met by a string of rejections: "I wrote all day from loneliness," she said, "and all evening for the same reason." To become more worldly wise, Hurst got jobs as a waitress, nursemaid, salesgirl, and sweatshop worker. Once she even crossed the Atlantic, riding steerage for the experience. Finally in 1914, a collection of her stories entitled *Just Around the Corner* was published. Her first novel, *Star Dust*, appeared in 1921. Two years later, Hurst established her reputation as a novelist with her second novel, *Lummox*. After visiting Russia in 1924, her third novel, *Appasionata,* was published a year later. Other novels followed: *A President is Born* (1928), *Back Street* (1937), *Imitation of Life* (1933), and *Great Laughter* (1936). She became more and more conscious of her Judaism. Hurst's books focused on the aspirations, disappointments, dreams, triumphs, defeats, and struggles of the common people.

KAYE, JUDITH

BORN AUGUST 4, 1938 IN MONTICELLO, NEW YORK.
AMERICAN JUDGE.

Chief Judge of New York's highest court, the New York State Court of Appeals, since March 1993, Judith Kaye could have become Attorney General or Associate Justice of the Supreme Court. She turned down both positions, clearing the way for Janet Reno and

Ruth Bader Ginsburg respectively to accept the two most coveted posts in the American legal system. Kaye's parents were farmers. When she was five, Judith attended a one-room schoolhouse in Maplewood, New York. Her family then moved to Monticello where her father owned a women's clothing store. Graduating from high school at age fifteen, Judith went to Barnard College, where she worked on the school newspaper. When she graduated in 1968, she was eager to become a professional journalist. But she had to settle for "a woman's job" as the society reporter at *The Hudson Dispatch,* then in Union City, New Jersey. To be taken more seriously as a reporter, Kaye began studying law at night at the New York University School of Law. She changed jobs and during the day she edited copy at the General Features Syndicate. Fascinated with the study of law, Kaye abandoned her thoughts of remaining in the journalism field, and decided to become an attorney. She graduated from law school in 1962, sixth in her class (out of 290). However, she found it almost impossible to break into New York's male-dominated legal profession. She sent resumes to 75 law firms but was told that the firms' "woman quotas" had been filled. Finally, the law firm of Sullivan and Cromwell hired her; she was the firm's first female associate. In 1965, Kaye left the firm to join IBM's legal staff. That same year she married attorney Stephen R. Kaye. They have three children. Kaye was one of the first women to practice at another of New York City's most prestigious law firms. In 1969, Kaye was the first female lawyer to join Olwine, Connelly, Chase, O'Donnell & Weyher. She eventually became the first and only female partner in the twenty-two-partner firm. She specialized in commercial law. In September 1983 Kaye was confirmed as the first woman to serve on New York's highest court, the State Court of Appeals, for a term of fourteen years. Judith Kaye minimized the significance of a woman reaching the high court, however. "Quite frankly, I'm going to be judged as a judge and not as the first woman judge," she contended.

KLEIN, MELANIE

BORN IN 1882 IN VIENNA; DIED IN 1960.
AUSTRIAN PSYCHOANALYST.

At age fourteen, Melanie Klein become a physician, like her father. Three years later, however, she chose to study art and history at the University of Vienna instead. She didn't graduate but moved to Budapest where she was drawn to the works of Sigmund Freud and the study of psychoanalysis. Klein married and later took her three children to Berlin (without her husband, whom she had divorced). By 1926, she had settled in London and began practicing psychoanalysis though she had no previous academic training. While Sigmund Freud had never worked with children, Klein did, at times with ones who were under the age of three. Klein's great contribution to her field was to show that children's play was not without meaning, but was in fact the product of a rich fantasy life. Much of what Freud hypothesized as happening in a child's Oedipal stage—from ages three to five—Melanie Klein argued actually occurred during the first year of life. In her 1937 monograph, *Love, Guilt and Reparation* (in *Love, Hate and Reparation,* co-authored with Joan Riviere), Klein emphasized that the instinctual urges of a child are experienced through unconscious fantasy. Her study of these processes contributed greatly to the understanding of child development.

KOHUT, REBEKKAH BEITELHEIM

BORN IN 1864 IN KASCHAU (KOSICE, SLOVAKIA), HUNGARY; DIED IN 1951.
AMERICAN EDUCATOR AND COMMUNITY WORKER.

Rebekkah Kohut was the daughter of a rabbi who brought his family to the United States from Hungary in 1867. At the age of twenty, she married Rabbi Alexander Kohut, a Hungarian rabbi and scholar, twenty years her elder. He had eight children from a previous marriage. Seven years later, he died, and Rebekkah was to care for the children by herself. To support the family, Kohut lectured about Jewish subjects. In 1897, she was elected the first president of the New York section of the Council of Jewish Women and served in that post until 1901. In 1899, she established the Kohut School for Girls, a boarding and day school that offered both secular and religious training. Not only was she interested in better education for girls, but she also crusaded for improved working conditions for women. In 1914 she organized and led the Young Women's Hebrew Association Employment Bureau. Her work seeking solutions for employment problems continued into the 1930s. In 1933, she became executive director of the Columbia Grammar School, an independent school in New York City, serving as its head for the next several years. In 1942, she was named president of the World Congress of Jewish Women.

KUNIN, MADELEINE M.

BORN SEPTEMBER 28, 1933 IN ZURICH, SWITZERLAND.
AMERICAN POLITICIAN.

Courtesy of *The Jewish Week*, New York

Madeleine Kunin is a U.S. Deputy Secretary of Education. In June 1940, as France was falling to Hitler, Kunin's mother, who was widowed when Madeleine was three years old, fled to Italy along with 3,000 other Jews. Taking Madeleine and her brother Edgar with her, the three crowded aboard a liner with only nine-hundred berths, the last ship permitted to leave Genoa with Jews aboard. The family settled in western Massachusetts, and Madeleine graduated from high school in Pittsfield, Massachusetts. In 1957, Kunin earned a Bachelor's degree in history at the University of Massachusetts. She went on to earn Master's degrees in journalism (Columbia University School of Journalism) and English literature (University of Vermont). She then worked for a year as a reporter for *The Burlington Free Press* in Burlington, Vermont. In 1959, Madeleine married a Vermont physician, Arthur Kunin, and spent the next decade raising their four children. In 1970, while on a year's sabbatical with her family in Switzerland, Kunin grew interested in the struggle of Swiss women to win the right to vote. "... I realized that we'd had the right to vote since 1920 and that we really hadn't done much—we hadn't elected any women to public office." When she returned to America, Kunin became involved in politics and was elected to the Vermont House of Representatives in 1972, serving three, two-year terms. In 1978, she was elected lieutenant governor, and was re-elected two years later. She ran for governor unsuccessfully in 1982. In the spring of 1983 Kunin taught a criminal justice seminar at the Kennedy School of Government at Harvard University. In November 1984, she was elected Vermont's seventy-fourth governor, the first Jew, the first woman, and only the third Democrat to be elected governor in this traditionally Republican state. Re-elected twice more, Kunin announced in 1990 that she would not seek a fourth term. Credited with appointing a record number of women to state offices, Kunin was also hailed for developing an open style of government that relied upon consensus. During her administration, priority was given to legislation that improved the environment, education and human services. As for her Jewishness, Kunin said in 1990 that "The whole proximity to the Holocaust...strongly influenced my values and my thinking. I think it has made me even more appreciate the democratic system and the openness of it."

LEWIS, FLORA
BORN IN 1923 IN LOS ANGELES, CALIFORNIA.
AMERICAN JOURNALIST.

Flora Lewis reported hard news for *The New York Times* during an era when women journalists usually worked on the women's pages or the society columns. Among her assignments were the Vietnam War and the 1967 Six-Day War in Israel. Lewis's first newspaper job came during her senior year at UCLA when she was campus reporter for *The Los Angeles Times*. For the next four years, Lewis worked for the Associated Press in New York, Washington, D.C., and London. Free-lancing from 1946 to 1954, Flora Lewis became the first female foreign correspondent to work for *The Washington Post* in 1956. She was based in Warsaw, Prague, and Bonn. From 1967 to 1972, she wrote a syndicated column for *Newsday*. She joined *The New York Times* in 1972 as its Paris bureau chief and became European diplomatic correspondent in 1976. In March 1980, Flora Lewis became the *Times'* foreign affairs correspondent, writing a twice-weekly column. Considered one of the sharpest media analysts of the international scene, Lewis has written four books on foreign affairs, including *Europe: A Tapestry of Nations,* a country-by-country study of twenty-seven European countries. "She's at home anywhere in the world—in London, Paris, Bonn, Rome, Warsaw, and Prague," wrote John Larabedian of the *The New York Post.* "She's aggressive. She has more courage than many men, but is very much the woman—slender, feminine, a sculptured face, blue eyes, chic." In 1945, Flora Lewis married Sydney Gruson, a *New York Times* foreign correspondent. They have three children, and were divorced in 1973. Lewis has received many awards, including four Overseas Press Club prizes. She has made her home in Paris for many years. At the end of 1990, Lewis retired as the foreign affairs columnist and became the *Times'* senior columnist.

LICHTENSTEIN, TEHILLA
BORN IN 1893 IN JERUSALEM; DIED IN 1973.
AMERICAN RELIGIOUS LEADER.

In 1938, Tehilla Lichtenstein became the director of the Society of Jewish Science, thus becoming the first Jewish woman to assume formally a position of religious leadership in the United States. In her sermons and addresses, Lichtenstein sought to put a stop to the drifting of American Jews away from Jewish religious life. Her hope was to re-instill a belief in God as the source of happiness, goodness, and healing—to convince her listeners that Judaism could help them become aware of God. Born to Chava (Cohen) and Rabbi

Chaim Hirschensohn, Tehilla traveled with her family to the United States in 1904. She grew up in Hoboken, New Jersey where her father was the spiritual leader of a small Orthodox congregation. Tehilla did her undergraduate work in classics at Hunter College and received a Master's degree in literature from Columbia University. While studying for her doctorate in English literature, she dropped out of school to marry a Reform rabbi, Morris Lichtenstein. From her reading Lichtenstein had become convinced that only through religion was it possible to become pious. To discover God, she thought, one needed only to be optimistic, hopeful and "in love with humanity," and not necessarily observe all the spiritual rituals of organized religion. In 1922, with Tehilla's aid, Morris Lichtenstein founded the Society of Jewish Science. Upon his death, Tehilla became spiritual leader of the movement and served in that post until her death in 1973. Hundreds of Jews joined the society and thousands of other American Jews listened to her regular radio broadcasts during the 1940s and read her sermons, many of which appeared in the *Jewish Interpreter*.

MICHELSON, GERTRUDE G.

BORN ON JUNE 3, 1925 IN JAMESTOWN, NEW YORK.
AMERICAN BUSINESSWOMAN.

Gertrude Michelson is one of the first American women to serve on a board of directors of a major American corporation. She was the first woman to serve on the boards of both Macy's and General Electric. Michelson still serves on both boards. She was the first woman to be a member of the board of directors at the Federal Reserve Bank in New York in the 1970s. She was also the first woman to chair the Board of Trustees at an Ivy League school when she served in that position at Columbia University from 1989 to 1992. Known as "G.G." to her acquaintances, Gertrude Michelson graduated from Penn State in 1945, then received her law degree from Columbia Law School in 1947. In 1972, Michelson became Senior Vice-President for Personnel, Labor and Consumer Relations at the R.H. Macy Company in New York. In February 1979, she was named Senior Vice-President for External Affairs and in November 1980, she moved to the position of Senior Vice-President for External Affairs. Michelson retired from R.H. Macy in September 1992 and serves now as a Senior Advisor for the firm. Her husband Horace has retired from the law firm of Moses & Singer. She is still on the Macy's Board of Directors. The couple has one daughter.

MIRIAM

BORN AND DIED DURING THE THIRTEENTH CENTURY B.C.E.
BIBLICAL HEROINE.

The eldest sister of Moses and Aaron, Miriam was one of the triumvirate who served as leaders during the Egyptian exile of the Jews and of the later exodus from Egypt. She was also the symbolic leader of the women of Israel and a prophet. According to the Bible, Miriam watched over the infant Moses when he lay exposed to the elements on the River Nile. Evidence of Miriam's being a leader in her own right is the fact that, after the crossing of the Red Sea and in celebration of the Jews' escape from Egypt, she directed the singing and dancing of praise. Israeli custom called for women to welcome the men with timbrels and dancing upon their return from the battlefield and as a ritual at other celebrations. The title of prophetess was given to Miriam for that one act of appearing at the head of the singing and dancing women. Miriam is also associated with a mysterious and powerful water well that, according to the *Aggadah,* moves from place to place. According to legend, the well served as a fountain of healing and redemption. She died in Kadesh and was buried there.

MOISE, PENINA

BORN APRIL 23, 1797 IN CHARLESTON, SOUTH CAROLINA; DIED IN 1880.
AMERICAN POET, HUMANIST AND TEACHER.

Penina Moise left school at the age of twelve—when her father died—to take up needle-work in order to support her large, poverty-stricken family. An avid reader during her youth, Penina displayed incredible literary talent. She became a prolific writer of verse. She often contributed poems that were about current events to the *Charleston Courier.* She also wrote for the leading periodicals of the day. In 1833, Moise published a small volume of her poems called *Fancy's Sketch Book.* A devout Jew, Penina was the superintendent of Beth Elohim Congregation's Sunday school. She was the author of the first American Jewish hymnal. When the first organ to be installed in an American synagogue was put in at her Congregation in 1841, Penina composed the hymns for the installation service. In 1856, Congregation Beth Elohim published a book of Moise's hymns called *Hymns Written for the Use of Hebrew Congregations,* eventually used by many other Reform temples. Many of these hymns, noted for a spirit of submission to the will of God, still appear in the *Union Hymnal of the Union of American Hebrew Congregations,* which was published in 1893. This Hymnal contains more of Moise's hymns than any other Jewish author's. Though blind in her sixties, Moise still wrote and composed music by dictating to her niece, making Penina famous as Charleston's "blind poetess." Moise never married. Along with her sister and niece, she ran a small private girls' school. In 1911, Moise's hymns and poetry were published in a book entitled *Secular and Religious Works.* In all, she composed over 190 hymns.

OLSEN, TILLIE LERNER

BORN JANUARY 14, 1913 IN OMAHA, NEBRASKA.
AMERICAN AUTHOR.

Tillie Olsen was almost fifty years old before her first book was published in 1962. Self-taught, with no formal higher education, Tillie focused her writing on the struggles of working people, particularly women who had to cope with the various roles they were expected to perform. As a young girl, Tillie read *Life in the Iron Mills,* a nineteenth-century account of factory workers, written by Rebecca Harding Davis. Tillie was eager to become a writer like Davis. She quit high school before graduating, and was jailed briefly in Kansas City after she tried to organize packing-house workers. Tillie worked full-time as a union organizer. In 1945, she married Jack Olsen, an artist and fervent unionist. While raising the couple's four daughters, Olsen tried to write a novel. It took her forty years to complete it. Her first published book, which came out in 1962, was called *Tell Me a Riddle* and was a collection of four short stories exploring the breakdown of personal relationships. The title story won Tillie Olsen the O. Henry Award. It had been published separately in 1961 and told the tale of an elderly, terminally ill woman who spent her last months visiting her grown children searching for clues that will help her resolve conflicts between her and her husband. Olsen finally completed her novel and it was published in 1974. *Yonnondio: From the Thirties* was the story of the plight of a Midwestern family struggling to cope with the Depression. One critic called the book "the best novel to come out of the so-called proletarian movement of the thirties." In 1985, Olsen edited a book called *Mother to Daugher, Daughter to Mother: Mothers on Mothering*. During the 1980s, Olsen taught at the University of Minnesota, Kenyon College, and UCLA.

OZICK, CYNTHIA

BORN APRIL 17, 1928 IN NEW YORK, NEW YORK.
AMERICAN WRITER.

Cynthia Ozick's first novel *Trust* was published in 1966. Since then she has written numerous novels, novellas, and short stories that are usually set in New York's middle- and lower-upper-class Jewish milieu. Ozick delves into the conflicts of the American Jewish generation that grew up after the Holocaust. In 1976, Ozick's *Bloodshed and Three Novellas* was published; in 1982, *Levitation: Five Fictions;* and in 1989, *The Shawl: A Story and a Novella*. Ozick's themes dabble in ancient Jewish myth and lore, including the use of the esoteric Kabbala. For instance, in the title short story in her 1971 collection *The Pagan Rabbi*, Ozick writes about a rabbi who adopts the pagan manner of Spinoza, the Dutch philosopher. "As soon as I was conscious of being alive," Ozick said in 1983, "...I knew I was a writer." Cynthia Ozick received her bachelor of arts in English cum laude from New York University, where she was also elected to Phi Beta Kappa, in 1949. A year later she earned a master of arts degree in literature from Ohio State University. After writing her Master's thesis on parable in the fiction of American writer Henry James, Ozick spent seven years writing a novel modeled after James' works, but it was never published.

POGREBIN, LETTY COTTIN

BORN JUNE 9, 1939 IN NEW YORK, NEW YORK.
AMERICAN FEMINIST LEADER AND MAGAZINE EDITOR.

Letty Pogrebin was a founding editor of *Ms.* magazine in 1971. She is the author of a number of books relating to women in business and non-sexist child rearing, and is considered one of America's leading feminist journalists. Pogrebin graduated cum laude from Brandeis University in 1959 with a B.A. degree in English and American literature. She worked for a year as an editorial assistant in the publishing firm of Coward-McCann; then as an advertising copywriter. During the next ten years she worked at Bernard Geis Associates as director of publicity, advertising, and subsidiary rights; she became a vice-president of the firm in 1970. Pogrebin published her first book that year, *How to Make it in a Man's World*, a humorous, practical guide to making it in the male-centered world of business. One chapter was entitled: "If You Can't Stand the Heat, Get Back to the Kitchen." Pogrebin wrote a monthly column, "The Working Women," for *Ladies' Home Journal*. Her other books include: *Getting Yours: How to Make the System Work for the Working Woman* (1975) and *Growing Up Free: Raising Your Child in the 80s,* (1980) in which she argues the case for non-sexist child rearing. In 1971, Pogrebin was a founder of the National Women's Political Caucus. Her most recently-published book, *Deborah, Golda and Me: Being Female and Jewish in America,* was published in 1991. She summarized the book "as a deeply personal account of one woman's efforts to merge the feminist ideology of equality and autonomy with the particularity of Judaism and Jewish ethics."

POLLARD, EVE
BORN IN 1947 IN LONDON.
BRITISH EDITOR.

One of the most successful journalists in England, Eve Pollard has moved from one editorship to the next with great success. "My father didn't believe in university for girls," she said. "He believed women should look after their husbands, their children and their fathers. In that order." After a year at art college, Eve decided to switch her specialty. "I was potty about journalism and I thought I had better get on and do something about it," she stated. Pollard got her first real journalism job in 1967 at the thriving *Honey* magazine, working on the lowest rung of the fashion department. "I was the one who packed suitcases for photo sessions," she recalled. She rose to the position of fashion editor at *Honey* before moving in 1968 to the *Daily Mirror* magazine, which eventually folded, but Pollard was women's editor there before it shut down. Fifteen months later, in 1970, she became the first women's editor at the *Observer* magazine. She was married in 1968 to Barry Winkleman. Pollard became pregnant with her first child, Claudia, born in 1972. Eight years later her son was born. She was women's editor of the *Sunday Mirror* from 1971 to 1981. She then worked for the next two years as assistant editor for *Sunday People;* and two years after that she worked as features editor at TVam. In 1985, Pollard moved to New York, when her second husband, Nicholas Lloyd, a journalist, was sent to America. At first she wrote a column for the *Sunday Times* of London. She then was asked to launch Rupert Murdoch's magazine *Elle* and with that accomplishment won a rise in social status and the acclaim of her peers "When *Elle* came along, I suddenly found myself with Andy Warhol on my left (at dinner parties) and Esteé Lauder on my right." In January 1988, Pollard was appointed editor of Robert Maxwell's *Sunday Mirror* (circulation 2.6 million), which made her the second female editor of a British national newspaper and only the second Jewish one. (Wendy Henry, editor of the *News of the World,* was the first Jewish editor.) Pollard was voted National Newspaper Editor of the Year at the Focus 1991 newspaper awards. She was credited with boosting the *Sunday Mirror's* circulation to 2.8 million. In May 1991 she took over as editor of the *Sunday Express* (circulation: 1.6 million). Pollard's husband Nicholas Lloyd is editor of the *Daily Express.*

RACHEL
BORN IN 1821 IN SWITZERLAND; DIED IN 1858.
FRENCH DRAMATIC ACTRESS.

Known simply as Rachel, Eliza Rachel Felix thrilled audiences by reviving the French classical tragedies. The daughter of a peddler, at age ten, Rachel began singing for coins on the streets of Paris to help feed her family. A singing master, Etienne Choron, discovered her and provided the talented future star with free singing and acting instruction. Rachel was slender and dark, but not beautiful. She debuted at the Theatre du Gymnase, performing the plays of Racine and Corneille before European nobility and aristocrats. Rachel was an overnight sensation. Because of her performances, these classical dramatists, out of fashion at the time, had comebacks and remained popular into contemporary times. She portrayed Jewish heroines such as Esther and Judith on the stage. She never married, but became the mistress of a number of men, including Prince Jerome, the nephew of Napoleon. Rachel proved a great source of gossip throughout Europe. She had two sons through her entanglements. Illness befell her at an early age. Still, though frail, she went to America on tour in 1855, and although audiences had little enthusiasm for her style of French classical tragedy, Americans treated her like a queen offstage. She was forced to cancel some performances due to her illness and in 1856 she returned to France. Rachel died at the age of thirty-six from consumption. At her funeral, the chief rabbi of Paris gave the eulogy in Hebrew.

RADNER, GILDA

BORN JUNE 28, 1946 IN DETROIT, MICHIGAN; DIED MAY 20, 1989.
AMERICAN COMEDIENNE AND ACTRESS.

Columbia Pictures Industries, Inc.

Gilda Radner will forever be identified with the irreverent, highly popular comedy-variety television program, *Saturday Night Live*. Gilda was born into a prosperous Detroit family. Her father died when she was fourteen. He had loved show business; enjoying singing and making others laugh. Gilda was fat as a child and that, she claimed, led to her career. "If you can decide to be funny, I decided it at age ten," she said. "When I was ten, I said to myself, 'You're not going to make it on looks.'" Radner went to an all-girls high school, then to the University of Michigan, but left there without earning a degree. She joined an improvisational comedy troupe based in Toronto, Canada, where she performed with her future *Saturday Night Live* colleagues Dan Aykroyd and Bill Murray. Lorne Michaels, later the mastermind of *Saturday Night Live,* was often in the audience. Gilda returned to the U.S. and helped *"Live"* get started on October 18, 1975, joining Chevy Chase, John Belushi, Bill Murray, Dan Aykroyd, Laraine Newman, and Jane Curtin. Radner won an Emmy for her performances in 1978. During her three years on the show, she created a series of eccentric characters including a Jewish "princess," a sniffling, hyperactive child, and a scatterbrained newscaster with a speech impediment. One popular Radner character was a dowdy schoolteacher who gave editorial replies replete with such malapropisms as concern over "Soviet jewelry" and "endangered feces." In the mid-1970s Gilda Radner wrote for and performed in the syndicated *National Lampoon Radio Show* and the off-Broadway revue *National Lampoon Show*. On Broadway she starred in *Gilda Radner—Live from New York* in 1979 and *Lunch Hour* in 1980. She also starred in several films including *The Woman in Red* in 1984, which also featured her future husband Gene Wilder, who was the film's writer and director as well as co-star. Radner wrote *It's Always Something* in 1989, a book that discussed her struggle against the ovarian cancer that eventually took her life. She was called "a gawky...live wire whose stock in trade is the artful klutz."

RAN, SHULAMIT

BORN OCTOBER 21, 1949 IN TEL AVIV.
ISRAELI COMPOSER.

Shulamit Ran has been composing music since she was eight years old. Sometimes Shulamit would come home from school to tell her mother a story she had learned that day, and would sing part of it. She wrote the "Sonatina for Two Flutes" when she was just twelve. "I see composition almost as something physical like a sculpture," she has said. "Music is a raw material that the human imagination takes and sculpts into a work of art." Without informing her, Shulamit's piano teacher sent some of her first piano works to Israel Radio, which played them on the air. In 1968, Shulamit graduated from the Mannes College of Music in New York City at age nineteen. Subsequently she composed, among other pieces, "Hatzvi Israel- Eulogy," a work for female voices and a chamber ensemble based on David's lament for Saul and Jonathan. She also wrote "Oh, the Chimney," a song cycle based on poems by Nelly Sachs. In 1971, Ran performed her own "Concert Piece for Piano and Orchestra" with Zubin Mehta and the Israel Philharmonic. Two years later she became professor of composition at the University of Chicago. Since September 1990, she has been composer-in-residence of the Chicago Symphony. Ran holds dual Israeli and American citizenship and became the first woman to be appointed composer-in-residence of a major American orchestra when she accepted the two-year post with the Chicago Symphony. Successful female composers are rare in the field of orchestral music, making it all the more significant when she was awarded the 1991 Pulitzer prize in the music category. Ran won the prize for her "Symphony," a work commissioned by the Philadelphia Orchestra in 1987 that was first performed in October 1990. She is also the winner of the 1992 Friedheim Award for "Symphony." Ran was the first woman to earn top honors in this competition.

RESNIK, REGINA

BORN AUGUST 30, 1923 IN NEW YORK, NEW YORK.
AMERICAN MEZZO-SOPRANO.

The daughter of Russian immigrants, Regina Resnik graduated from Hunter College in 1942. While there, she sang in Gilbert and Sullivan operettas. Studying singing as a soprano with Rosalie Miller, Resnik was introduced to Fritz Busch, the conductor with whom she sang the part of Lady Macbeth in the Verdi opera based on Shakespeare's play. In 1943, Regina Resnik reached the finals of the Metropolitan Opera Company's Auditions of the Air. Rather than complete the competition, she chose to sing the leading soprano parts in *Fidelio* and *Der Fliegende Hollaender* in Mexico City. As the only woman finalist in the same Metropolitan Opera Company competition in 1944, Regina won a contract for the 1944-45 Met season. During that time she debuted as Leonora in *Il Trovatore*. "I was nurtured by people who taught me style," she recalled in 1992. "During the first three years—for eighty-six dollars to a hundred and fifty dollars a week—I sang a dozen roles in every repertory." For the next decade Resnik sang numerous soprano parts at the Metropolitan Opera, including Ellen Oxford in the New York premier of Benjamin Britten's *Peter Grimes*. Between 1953 and 1955, she performed several mezzo-soprano parts. In 1957, she appeared for the first time at Covent Gardens in London as Carmen; critics praised her for giving one of the greatest performances in that role. Since then she has sung in nearly every major operatic capital in the world. Her theatricality as well as the warmth of her voice have won her countless fans. In later years, Resnik turned to producing operas, such as *Electra* at the Teatro la Fenice in Venice in 1971. She also became a stage director, with her husband Arbit Blatas serving as scenic and costume designer. She directed *Carmen* in Hamburg, Germany in 1971. She and her husband have made homes in Venice and in New York. Still going strong in her seventies, Resnik played and sang Madame Armfeldt in the 1992 New York City Opera production of Stephen Sondheim's *A Little Night Music.*

RIVERS, JOAN

BORN JUNE 8, 1933 IN BROOKLYN, NEW YORK.
AMERICAN COMEDIENNE.

Richard Grant & Associates

Counted among the funniest of American comediennes, Joan Rivers broke new ground by being one of the first comediennes to shatter taboos while lacing her humor with insults. Born Joan Alexandra Molinsky, Rivers was the daughter of Russian-Jewish refugees. Her father, a physician, did comic impersonations of his patients. Emulating her father, Joan loved to tell jokes. After graduating from prestigious private schools, Joan pursued a performing career and landed a small role in the 1941 movie, *Mr. Universe.* She had attended Connecticut College for Women and later Barnard College, and in the late 1950s had a brief marriage to Jimmy Sanger, the son of the Bond stores' merchandiser. In 1958, she set out to become an actress. Her best-selling autobiography *Enter Talking* (1986), captured the essence of those next seven years of struggle. Her big break came on February 15, 1965 when she appeared on Johnny Carson's late-night talk show. That led to Rivers's engagements as a stand-up comic in the most important night clubs. "Can we talk?" became Joan Rivers's signature phrase. She has been popular as a comedienne in various forums—nightclubs, television, and through her best-selling books and records. In 1986, Rivers signed a ten-million-dollar contract with the burgeoning Fox Broadcasting Company network to host *The Late Show Starring Joan Rivers,* going up against "Mr. Late Night," Johnny Carson and his *Tonight Show.* Ironically, she got her first break on that show twenty years earlier and she had even been Carson's *Tonight Show* permanent substitute host. Referring to Carson's divorces and alimony problems, Rivers liked to joke that she was "the only woman in the history of the world who left Johnny Carson and didn't ask him for money." In August 1987, her husband, Edgar Rosenberg, committed suicide. Rivers went through a period of desolation and a troubled relationship with college-aged daughter, Melissa. Eventually, mother and daughter reconciled. Joan was able to resume an even more successful career.

Early in 1994, Rivers began producing *Can We Shop*, a daily home-shopping show on syndicated television.

ROTH, ESTHER

BORN APRIL 16, 1952 IN TEL AVIV.
ISRAELI TRACK AND FIELD STAR.

Israel Government Press Office

Esther Roth's parents emigrated from Moscow to Palestine in 1940. Born Esther Shachamorov, by the age of eighteen, she held the world record of 7.1 seconds for the 60-meter indoor hurdles for one day. She broke Israeli records in the 100- and 200-meter races, long jump, pentathlon, and other events. In 1972, Esther had reached the 100-meter semifinal in the Munich summer Olympic Games when Palestinian Arab terrorists attacked the Olympic village, killing eleven of her Israeli team members. Roth escaped, but because her coach, Amitzur Shapira, was killed, she considered quitting track. In 1973, she married Peter Roth, and that year she also returned to competition, winning the 100-meter, 200-meter and long jump at the Maccabiah Games. Though three months pregnant at the time of the event, she was not aware of her condition. Her son, Yaron, was born in 1974. Esther dominated the 1974 Asian Games, winning three gold medals in the 200-meter dash, the 100-meter hurdles, and the 100-meter sprint. At the 1976 Olympics in Montreal, Esther reached the finals of the 100-meter hurdles, coming in sixth. The first Israeli to reach an Olympic final, she set a new Israeli record of 13.04 seconds for the event. Roth was named Sportsman of the Year in Israel three times by the Israeli newspaper *Ma'ariv*. Esther retired in September 1979. She teaches physical education at a junior high school in Ra'anana, near Tel Aviv. Besides her son Yaron, Esther and Peter have a nine year-old daughter, Michal.

ROTHENBERG, SUSAN

BORN JANUARY 20, 1945 IN BUFFALO, NEW YORK.
AMERICAN PAINTER.

Using the horse as her most important motif in a series of paintings in the 1970s, Susan Rothenberg developed into one of the new wave of figurative artists who reacted against the harsh visual simplicities of minimalist abstraction. Susan's father was co-owner of a chain of supermarkets. But it was Dr. Joseph Rosenberg, family physician and neighbor, who sparked Susan's interest in art; he let her paint in his studio on Sundays. Rothenberg enrolled in the Department of Fine Arts at Cornell University in 1963. She chose to study sculpture because "painting had always come easy to me and I wanted something I couldn't do." She completed her Bachelor's degree in 1966. She moved to New York City in

1969 and started to draw and make collages. In 1974, she completed her first horse paintings. Since then, her paintings have been shown at the Venice Biennale, the Museum of Modern Art in New York City, and the Tate Gallery in London. Paul Richard, writing in the *Washington Post* in 1993, noted that "...dwelling in her pictures are strange totemic presences, bones and boneless beings and horses without eyes...." After her horse phase, Rothenberg's paintings were, in a *Time* magazine art critic's words, "about dismemberment, blockage, and fright." Beginning in 1979, glimpses of the human face and body began appearing in Rothenberg's work. In the late 1980s, she became preoccupied with paintings of dancers. Rothenberg lives in New Mexico.

RUTH

BORN AND DIED TWELFTH CENTURY B.C.E; PLACE OF BIRTH UNKNOWN.
BIBLICAL HEROINE.

The great-grandmother of King David, Ruth is one of the two women in the Bible (the other is Esther) for whom an entire book is named. A unique heroine, she is the only woman in the Bible who is without human fault. It is told in the book of Ruth that Elimelech of Bethlehem, his wife Naomi, and their two sons, Mahlon and Chilion, moved to Moav, escaping from famine. There Mahlon and Chilion married Moabite brides, Orpah and Ruth. Two years later, with her husband Elimelech and their two sons dead, Naomi decided to return to Bethlehem. The two daughters-in-law wanted to join Naomi, but she tried to talk them out of going with her. Orpah agreed to stay behind, but Ruth would not take no for an answer, offering one of the Bible's most oft-quoted passages: "Ask me not to leave you or return from following you; for where you go, I will go and where you lodge, I will lodge; your people shall be my people and your God, my God; where you die, I will die and there also shall I be buried." Because of those words, Ruth has become a symbol in Judaism of the righteous convert. Many converts to Judaism honor her by taking her name. Naomi sent Ruth to Elimelech's relative Boaz to seek protection. He agreed to marry Ruth. Their son, Obed, became the father of Jesse, among whose children was David.

SHOCHAT, MANIA WILBUSHEWITCH

BORN IN 1880 NEAR GRODNO, BYELORUSSIA; DIED IN 1961.
EARLY JEWISH LEADER IN PALESTINE.

To become acquainted with the conditions of workers and to help them, Mania Shochat left her father's home as a child and went to work in her brother's factory in Minsk. Joining revolutionary circles there, she was arrested in the summer of 1899. While in prison she met Zubatov, the chief of the secret police of Moscow. He urged the establishment of a workers' movement that would retain loyalty to the czar. Such a Jewish workers' party, devoid of politics, seeking only to improve the welfare of the Jews, might be tolerated, he suggested. Influenced by Zubatov's ideas, in the summer of 1901 Mania formed the Jewish Independent Labor Party. Mania was a key figure in the party, but it was dissolved in 1903 after the Kishinev pogrom. Early in 1904, Mania's brother Nahum Wilbushewitch urged her to visit Palestine and for a year she traveled around the area. She concluded that only by developing collective farm settlements could a large class of Jewish workers emerge, a prerequisite for Jewish statehood. In 1907, Mania traveled to Europe and the United States to study different communist settlements. Returning to Palestine, she joined with members of the Bar-Giora group, led by Israel Shochat, hoping to implement her beliefs about collective settlement. She and other Bar-Giora members settled on a farm near Sejera in 1907, beginning the first experiment of collective settlement in the Yishuv, the Jewish community in Palestine. The following year, Mania married Shochat, In 1909 they founded Ha-Shomer, an armed organization of Jewish settlers who were the forerunners of the modern-day Israeli Army. With the start of World War I, Mania Shochat and her husband were banished to Bursa, Anatolia. They returned to Palestine in 1919. In 1921, Mania was a member of the first Histadrut delegation to visit the U.S. She helped found the League for Jewish-Arab Friendship in 1930. In 1948, the year the state of Israel was founded, she joined the left-wing Mapam Party and settled in Tel Aviv. There she engaged in the practice of social work until her death in 1961.

STEEL, DAWN

BORN IN 1946 IN THE BRONX, NEW YORK.
AMERICAN FILM PRODUCER.

Dawn grew up in Great Neck, Long Island. Her father Nat Spielberg changed his surname to Steel, became a weight lifter, and called himself "The Man of Steel." When Dawn was nine years old, he suffered a business reversal, leading to an emotional breakdown. After studying marketing at the New York University School of Commerce, Dawn quit in 1968 to become a receptionist for a firm in the city's garment district. She then moved to a job as an editor at *Penthouse* magazine. Next, she and Ronnie Rothstein, a friend, started a mail-order business selling toilet paper printed with a designer-like logo. In 1975, Steel married Rothstein, but the marriage lasted less than a year. In 1978, Steel became director of merchandising at Paramount Pictures, moving to production three years later. Her first major success as a producer came in 1983 with *Flashdance,* a sleeper that became a ninety-million-dollar hit. In 1985, Dawn Steel was appointed Paramount's president of production, one of the few women in Hollywood to achieve such a high position in the film industry. She supervised such films as *The Accused, Fatal Attraction,* and *The Untouchables.* In 1985, Steel married film producer Charles Roven. In March 1987, she was essentially dismissed from her post at Paramount while she lay in the hospital after giving birth to her daughter Rebecca. The following October, Steel was selected to run Columbia Studios, a post she held until January 1991. Since then she has been an independent film producer.

A

Aaron, 335
Aaronson, Sarah, 7-9
Abraham, 242, 243
Abzug, Bella, viii, 10-13, 95
Adelson, Merv, 301
Adler, Luther, 14
Adler, Stella, 14-16
Agnew, Spiro, 12
Agnon, S.Y., 238, 240
Aguilar, Grace, 17-19
Ahaseurus (Xerxes), 75, 76
Akiva, Rabbi, 53
Albert, Eddie, 14
Alcott, Amy, viii, 20-22
Alexandra, Queen Salome, 321
Alioto, Joseph, 79
Allen, Woody, 157
Aloni, Shulamit, 23-25
American, Sadie, 258
Anderson, Sherwood, 265
Antin, Mary, 26-28
Arad, Yael, viii, 29-31
Arafat, Yasser, 327
Arbus, Allan, 32, 33
Arbus, Diane, 32-34
Arden, Elizabeth, 235
Arendt, Hannah, 2, 35-37, 260
Arnold, Roseanne Barr, 321-22
Arnstein, Nicky, 64, 65
Asch, Sholem, 196
Astaire, Fred, 300
Athaliah, 322
Austen, Jane, 124
Avedon, Richard, 33
Aykroyd, Dan, 338

B

Baal Shem Tov, Israel, 219
Bacall, Lauren, 38-40
Bach, Johann Sebastian, 142
Bankhead, Tallulah, 119
Bar Kochba, Simon, 54
Bara, Theda, 41-43
Barak, 70, 71
Barna, Victor, 231
Barrymore, Ethel, 82
Baryshnikov, Mikhail, 40
Beatty, Warren, 14
Beckett, Samuel, 263
Begin, Menachem, 301
Belushi, John, 157, 338
Ben-Gurion, David, 23, 166, 196, 206

Ben-Porat, Miriam, 44-46
Berg, Gertrude, 4, 47-49
Bergman, Ingrid, 116
Berkman, Alexander, 104, 105
Berlin, Irving, 250
Bernhardt, Sarah, 4, 50-52, 234, 322
Bernstein, Carl, 324
Bernstein, Leonard, 120
Berson, Dr. Solomon A., 313
Beruriah, 53-55
Bierce, Ambrose, 325
Bing, Rudolf, 207, 208
Blues Brothers, 157
Blume, Judi, 322-23
Blunt, Anthony, 67
Bluwstein, Rahel, 56-59
Bogart, Humphrey, 38-39
Bohr, Niels, 173
Botha, P.W., 108, 276
Boxer, Barbara, viii, 4, 60-62, 78
Brando, Marlon, 14
Braque, Georges, 265
Brecht, Bertold, 127, 128
Breslin, Jimmy, 11
Breuer, Josef, 198
Brice, Fanny, 63-65, 271, 288
Briks, Karen, 30
Britt, Harvey, 79
Bronte, Charlotte, 68
Brookner, Anita, 3, 66-68
Burgess, Guy, 67
Bush, George, 62
Buxton, Angela, 323

C

Campbell, Naomi, 111
Cantor, Eddie, 288
Capasso, Carl A., 185
Capote, Truman, 300
Carson, Johnny, 340
Carter, Jimmy, 12, 140, 301
Caveye, Gella Van de, 31
Celeste, Richard, 224
Cellar, Emmanuel, 329
Charles, Prince of Wales, 147
Chase, Chevy, 338
Chisholm , Shirley, 95
Christie, Agatha, 40
Clapton, Eric, 158
Clay, Henry, 112
Cleese, John, 158
Cleopatra, 42, 43
Clinton, Bill, 4, 96, 158
Clurman, Harold, 16
Colby, Anita, 300